# BANNED BOOKS

## Literature Suppressed on
# SOCIAL GROUNDS

Ken Wachsberger, General Editor

# BANNED BOOKS

## Literature Suppressed on

# SOCIAL GROUNDS

### Dawn B. Sova

Introduction by
### Ken Wachsberger

Foreword by
### Joan Bertin

Facts On File, Inc.

**Banned Books: Literature Suppressed on Social Grounds**

Facts On File, Inc.
11 Penn Plaza
New York NY 10001

**Library of Congress Cataloguing-in-Publication Data**

Sova, Dawn B.
Banned books : literature suppressed on social grounds / Dawn B. Sova ; foreword by Joan Bertin.
p.   cm.—(Banned books)
Includes bibliographical references (p. 269) and index.
ISBN 0-8160-3303-X (acid-free paper)
1. Censorship—United States—History. 2. Prohibited books—United States—History. 3. Censorship—History. 4. Prohibited books—History. 5. Social problems—United States—History. 6. Social problems—History. 7. Social problems in literature.
I. Title. II. Series.
Z658.U5S69  1998
363.3′1′09—dc21              97-45158

Facts On File books are available at special discounts when purchased in bulk quantities for businesses, associations, institutions or sales promotions. Please call our Special Sales Department in New York at 212/967-8800 or 800/322-8755.

You can find Facts On File on the World Wide Web at http://www.factsonfile.com

Text design by Cathy Rincon
Cover design by Whizbang! Studios

Printed in the United States of America

MP HERM 10 9 8 7 6 5 4 3 2

This book is printed on acid-free paper.

*To my son, Robert Gregor,
and to all young people who will
try to make the world they
have inherited a better place.*

# CONTENTS

Acknowledgments

XI

Introduction by Ken Wachsberger

XIII

Foreword by Joan Bertin

XV

Preface

XIX

Works Discussed in This Volume

XXI

**LITERATURE SUPPRESSED ON SOCIAL GROUNDS**

1

Biographical Profiles

245

Bibliography

269

Works Discussed in the Other Volumes of This Series

286

Index

305

*There is no freedom either in civil or ecclesiastical [affairs], but where the liberty of the press is maintained.*

—Matthew Tindal

*If all mankind minus one were of one opinion, and only one person were of the contrary opinion, mankind would be no more justified in silencing that one person, than he, if he had the power, would be justified in silencing mankind.*

—John Stuart Mill

*Dare to think for yourself.*

—Voltaire

# ACKNOWLEDGMENTS

The long history of censorship has created many heroes, both famous and obscure, who have dared to defy the restrictions of their times to write and publish the truth as they understood it. Some are discussed in this volume, but many others have been silenced, their works destroyed. To all, however, this book owes both life and purpose. Had they acquiesced to those who suppress, censor and ban ideas or language that displease powerful authorities, smug majorities or vocal minorities, our intellectual universe would be significantly smaller.

I am grateful for my association with Bert Holtje of James Peter Associates, Inc., whose support and advice as both literary agent and friend helped me to maintain perspective throughout this lengthy project. His insight and literate commentary helped to resolve seemingly insurmountable problems.

My sincere gratitude also belongs to former Facts On File editors Gary M. Krebs, who saw potential in the idea and courageously proposed a censorship series, and Drew Silver, who provided substance and direction to the work. Gary gave the project life, and Drew worked with me to form its personality as he guided the work to completion. I also appreciate my collaboration with general editor Ken Wachsberger, who had the often thankless task of structuring the project and keeping the writers focused on their task.

Some of the works discussed in this volume have been difficult to locate. I would have been unable to consult this literature without the efforts of I. Macarthur Nickles, director of the Garfield (New Jersey) Library, a man whose professional expertise and insight have been invaluable. He has made certain that my sometimes obscure research requests have been satisfied and continues to introduce innovations in my hometown library. I am also grateful to reference experts Kathleen Zalenski and Karen Calandriello, who have tracked down unusual books, odd quotations, dates and notes, always persevering long after I had given up the chase.

In my personal life, no one has meant more to me than my son, Rob Gregor, who helped me to organize my thoughts, contributed insights on various works and kept me human. I appreciate greatly the continued support of my parents, Emil and Violet Sova, whose pride in my accomplishments and unwavering confidence in my abilities have always sustained me.

Finally, although I can never meet them, I appreciate the efforts of the many authors over centuries who risked their lives and livelihoods to stand against those who would oppress and silence them.

# INTRODUCTION

We Americans are proud of our Constitution, especially its Bill of Rights. The First Amendment right to freedom of speech and religion has inspired dissenters and nonconformists everywhere. Censored writers such as Salman Rushdie, Pramoedya Ananta Toer and Aleksandr Solzhenitsyn have looked to our country's example for strength as they battled for their right to express their own thoughts, and that of others to read them, even at the risk of their lives.

Yet censorship has been a major part of American history, from the time of Roger Williams and other early colonial freethinkers. Many of our richest literary works—*The Adventures of Huckleberry Finn, The Color Purple, Grapes of Wrath, The Jungle, Uncle Tom's Cabin, Tropic of Cancer*—have been censored at one time or another. Even today school boards, local governments, religious fanatics and moral crusaders attempt to restrict our freedom to read. Advancing technology has provided more diverse targets—the record, film and television industries, and the Internet—for the censors and would-be censors to aim for, as they work their strategies to restrict free expression and the freedom to read, watch and listen, dumbing us all down in order to shield their children, and you, from original or disturbing thoughts.

Fortunately, our country has a strong tradition of fighting censorship as well. Groups such as the National Coalition Against Censorship, the American Library Association's Office for Intellectual Freedom, People for the American Way, the American Civil Liberties Union and the PEN American Center exist to defend the First Amendment, through legal action and by raising public awareness. They deserve our moral, political and financial support.

The four volumes in this collection add to that rich tradition by spotlighting more than 400 works that have been censored for their political, social, religious or erotic content, in the United States and around the world, from biblical times to the present day. While many of these have been legally "banned"—or prohibited "as by official order"—all indeed have been banned or censored in a broader sense: targeted for removal from school curricula or library shelves, condemned in churches and forbidden to the faithful, rejected or expurgated by publishers, challenged in court, even voluntarily rewritten by their authors. Censored authors have been verbally abused, physically attacked, shunned by their families and communities, excommunicated from their religious congregations and shot, hanged or burned at the stake by their enemies, who thus made them heroes and often enough secured their memory for posterity. Their works include novels, histories, biographies, children's books, religious and philosophical treatises, dictionaries, poems, polemics and every other form of written expression.

It is illuminating to discover in these histories that such cultural landmarks as the Bible, the Koran, the Talmud and the greatest classics of world literature have often been suppressed or censored from the same motives, and by similar forces, as those we see today seeking to censor such books as *Daddy's Roommate* and *Heather Has Two Mommies*. Every American reading these volumes will find in their pages books he or she loves, and will be thankful that their authors' freedom of expression and their own freedom to read, are constitutionally protected. But at the same time, how many will be gratified by the cruel fate of books we detest? Reader-citizens capable of acknowledging their own contradictions will be grateful for the existence of the First Amendment and will thank its guardians, including the authors of this series, for protecting us against our own worst impulses.

✦ ✦ ✦

To prevent redundancy, works banned for multiple reasons appear in only one volume apiece, based on the judgment of the editor and the volume authors. The alphabetical arrangement provides easy access to titles. Works whose titles appear in SMALL CAPITAL LETTERS within an entry have entries of their own elsewhere in the same volume. Those whose titles appear in *ITALICIZED SMALL CAPITAL LETTERS* have entries in one of the other volumes. In addition, each volume carries complete lists of the works discussed in the other volumes.

—Ken Wachsberger

# FOREWORD

*. . . learning has brought disobedience and heresy, and sects into*
*the world; and printing has divulged them. . . .*

—Sir William Berkeley, 1671[1]

*Without Freedom of Thought, there can be no such thing as Wisdom;*
*and no such thing as Publick Liberty, without Freedom of Speech. . . .*

—Ben Franklin, 1772[2]

This volume, describing books censored for their social content, reveals the wide gulf between official belief and actual practice. Americans officially subscribe to an expansive definition of the right to free expression—our First Amendment rights—that encompasses expression in all forms, written, oral or visual, in all genres, on all subjects. But this official and universal profession of "the first freedom" is only part of the story. Equally important is that, as documented here, the principle is often ignored. In real life, censorship occurs, and succeeds, with regularity.[3]

The instances detailed here are particularly telling because the First Amendment provides no apparent justification for suppressing material because of socially objectionable content. Unlike obscenity, "fighting words," libel, fraud, commercial speech, profanity on the airwaves and other forms of expression that the courts have ruled may be regulated under the First Amendment, there is no recognized exception that would permit the suppression of material because someone doesn't like it or finds it offensive or disagreeable.

"Objectionable to whom?" one naturally asks. As the history of censorship has revealed time and again, possible definitions of "objectionable" or "offensive" more or less equal the number of people asked. The subjectivity of this enterprise has been conceded on all sides of the ideological spectrum. As Catherine MacKinnon observed about the rule that restrictions on speech must be "viewpoint neutral": "When do you see a viewpoint as a viewpoint? When you don't agree with it. When is a viewpoint not a viewpoint? When it's yours."[4] Ellen Willis expressed much the same sentiment in more colorful language: "What turns me on is erotic; what turns you on is pornographic."[5]

The enormous range and diversity of material that has been censored or challenged because it contains "socially unacceptable" ideas is its own most powerful argument against censorship. For this reason, this volume, while remaining agnostic on the merits of the objections it describes, provides powerful ammunition to those who oppose censorship. Included among the books banned for their social content are Anne Frank's *Diary of a Young Girl*, William Faulkner's *As I Lay Dying*, and Lewis Carroll's *Alice's Adventures in Wonderland*, to name but three classic books. One wonders what else would be at risk if First Amendment protections were not at least theoretically available to defend these works and our access to them.

Those who believe that works like these should not be suppressed because of someone else's objections to them must at the same time be prepared to tolerate messages and material that they find objectionable. This has become an increasingly controversial proposition, as assaults on free expression from all ideological perspectives have increased in the recent past. It will not do, of course, to deny that words and ideas can hurt, or that they can make both positive and negative contributions to social outcomes. But it is precisely because of this power that freedom of expression must be carefully guarded.

There is no sharp demarcation between "good" ideas and "bad" ideas. History is replete with misguided efforts to draw such a line. Nor should we assume that suppression of "bad" ideas, even if we could all agree what those might be, would result in the disappearance of those ideas or of acts premised on them. As some advocates of censorship have learned to their dismay, censorship of the "bad" establishes a principle that can also justify censorship of its critics. Discomforting as this may be, because it denies us the option of apathy, we are left with Brandeis's famous observation that the best remedy for bad speech is "more speech, not enforced silence."[6]

This volume is shocking because it contains evidence of frank and widespread disregard for free speech rights and principles. It should serve as a reminder that the First Amendment is not self-enforcing. The right to speak, read and think freely exists only if we claim it. As the saying goes, use it or lose it!

—Joan Bertin, Executive Director
National Coalition Against Censorship

## NOTES

[1] Quoted in Louis Edward Ingelhart, *Press and Speech Freedoms in America, 1619–1995* (Westport, Conn.: Greenwood Press, 1997), p. 9.

[2] Ingelhart, p. 15.

3 In the 1995–1996 school year, People for the American Way identified 475 challenges to curricular materials, and 300 censorship attempts, of which 41% succeeded. People for the American Way, *Attacks on the Freedom to Learn: 1996 Report* (Washington, D.C.: PAW, 1996), p. 11.

4 Quoted in Marjorie Heins, *Viewpoint Discrimination*, 24 Hastings Const. L.Q. 99, 136 (1996).

5 Ellen Willis, "Feminism, Moralism and Pornography," in Adele M. Stan, ed. *Debating Sexual Correctness* (New York: Delta/Bantam Doubleday Dell, 1995), p. 44.

6 *Whitney v. California*, 274 U.S. 357, 377 (1927) (concurring opinion).

# PREFACE

The broad nature of obscenity laws has made possible a wide interpretation of what constitutes an essentially "obscene" literary work. The language of American law stresses work that "depicts or describes sexual conduct in a patently offensive manner." The law also specifies that the "average person, taking contemporary community standards, would find that a work, taken as a whole, appeals to the prurient interest." Often what this has meant in reality is that works containing words deemed "vulgar" by specific members of a community or presenting interracial or homosexual relationships that are unacceptable to the standards of a given community acquire the label "obscene." These are social factors, the topic of this volume, and they are distinctly different from erotic, religious and political content.

Censors have so frequently applied such general guidelines to published writing that a wide range of literature has been declared "obscene." This volume avoids such generalization. Instead, the books discussed in this volume are literary works that have been banned, censored or challenged because of language, racial characterization or depiction of the drug use, social class or sexual orientation of characters, or other social differences, that their challengers have viewed as harmful to readers. Thus Mark Twain's *The Adventures of Huckleberry Finn* is included, while D. H. Lawrence's *Lady Chatterley's Lover* is not, even though both have been banned in the past for being "obscene"; the first has attracted the label because of its language and depiction of race, while the second contains graphic sexual description and has been banned for its erotic content. The books discussed here have been censored because their subject matter and characters do not conform to the social, racial or sexual standards of their censors.

There are currently no books in print that systematically examine and describe the content and controversy surrounding books that have been banned, censored or challenged because they contain socially unacceptable ideas or speech. A survey of the literature on censorship reveals that many texts of the past that were condemned for "vulgar" and "offensive" language, or portrayals of lesbian or homosexual relationships, racially volatile incidents or themes, or socially offensive behavior such as drug use were condemned under the broad laws governing obscenity. Thus, while their subject matter, intention and presentation might differ substantially, such works as Ray Bradbury's *Fahrenheit 451* and D. H. Lawrence's *Lady Chatterley's Lover* were both condemned as obscene. This study separates the two.

To a great extent, existing books emphasize defining what is obscene and describing the litigation and court decisions, rather than examining the censored writings from a particular vantage point. Much commentary was published during or soon after the issuance in 1973 of the Report of the 1970 United States President's Commission on Obscenity or soon after the 1986 U.S. Attorney General's Commission on Pornography released its findings. Thus, books on the subject of pornography are plentiful. However, little attention has been paid to nonerotic books that have been censored as "obscene" and condemned under the same laws, for social factors characterized as "offensive" by individuals or communities.

The goal of this volume is to identify and discuss books that have been censored as obscene, in centuries past as well as in the 20th century, either because the authors or the works did not conform to the social expectations of their censors or because they contain socially unacceptable ideas or speech. Several works, despite limited censorship histories, are included to exhibit the lengths to which censors' fears will take them, as in the case of *Alice's Adventures in Wonderland* and *The Adventures of Sherlock Holmes*. Other works have extensive histories of censorship, exhibiting the multiplicity of reasons that motivate censors. Taken as a whole, the entries provide a fascinating view of socially motivated censorship.

—Dawn B. Sova, Ph.D.

# Works Discussed in This Volume

*THE ADVENTURES OF HUCKLEBERRY FINN*
Mark Twain

*THE ADVENTURES OF SHERLOCK HOLMES*
Sir Arthur Conan Doyle

*THE ADVENTURES OF TOM SAWYER*
Mark Twain

*ALICE'S ADVENTURES IN WONDERLAND*
Lewis Carroll

*THE AMBOY DUKES*
Irving Shulman

*THE AMERICAN HERITAGE DICTIONARY OF THE ENGLISH LANGUAGE*

*AND STILL I RISE*
Maya Angelou

*ANNE FRANK: THE DIARY OF A YOUNG GIRL*
Anne Frank

*ANNIE ON MY MIND*
Nancy Garden

*ANOTHER COUNTRY*
James Baldwin

*APHRODITE*
Pierre Louÿs

*APPOINTMENT IN SAMARRA*
John O'Hara

*AS I LAY DYING*
William Faulkner

*THE AUTOBIOGRAPHY OF BENJAMIN FRANKLIN*
Benjamin Franklin

*THE AUTOBIOGRAPHY OF MALCOLM X*
Malcolm X, with Alex Haley

*THE AUTOBIOGRAPHY OF MISS JANE PITTMAN*
Ernest J. Gaines

*BEING THERE*
Jerzy Kosinski

*THE BELL JAR*
Sylvia Plath

*THE BEST SHORT STORIES BY NEGRO WRITERS*
Langston Hughes, Editor

*BLACK LIKE ME*
John Howard Griffin

*BLESS THE BEASTS AND CHILDREN*
Glendon Swarthout

*BLUBBER*
Judy Blume

*BRAVE NEW WORLD*
Aldous Huxley

*BRIDGE TO TERABITHIA*
Katherine Paterson

*CAIN'S BOOK*
Alexander Trocchi

*CAMILLE*
Alexander Dumas Jr.

*THE CANTERBURY TALES*
Geoffrey Chaucer

*CATCH-22*
Joseph Heller

*THE CATCHER IN THE RYE*
J. D. Salinger

*THE CHOCOLATE WAR*
Robert Cormier

*A CLOCKWORK ORANGE*
Anthony Burgess

*THE COLOR PURPLE*
Alice Walker

*CUJO*
Stephen King

*DADDY'S ROOMMATE*
Michael Willhoite

*A DAY NO PIGS WOULD DIE*
Robert Newton Peck

*DELIVERANCE*
James Dickey

*A DICTIONARY OF AMERICAN SLANG*
Harold Wentworth

*DICTIONARY OF SLANG AND UNCONVENTIONAL ENGLISH*
Eric Partridge

*DOCTOR DOLITTLE* (Series)
Hugh John Lofting

*DOG DAY AFTERNOON*
Patrick Mann

*DOWN THESE MEAN STREETS*
Piri Thomas

*DRACULA*
Bram Stoker

*EAST OF EDEN*
John Steinbeck

*ELMER GANTRY*
Sinclair Lewis

*END AS A MAN*
Calder Willingham

*ESTHER WATERS*
George Moore

*FAHRENHEIT 451*
Ray Bradbury

*A FAREWELL TO ARMS*
Ernest Hemingway

*THE FIXER*
Bernard Malamud

*FRUITS OF PHILOSOPHY: THE PRIVATE COMPANION OF MARRIED COUPLES*
Charles Knowlton

*GARGANTUA AND PANTAGRUEL*
François Rabelais

*GO ASK ALICE*
Anonymous

*GONE WITH THE WIND*
Margaret Mitchell

*GORILLAS IN THE MIST*
Dian Fossey

*GO TELL IT ON THE MOUNTAIN*
James Baldwin

*GRENDEL*
John Gardner

*HEATHER HAS TWO MOMMIES*
Leslea Newman

*A HERO AIN'T NOTHIN' BUT A SANDWICH*
Alice Childress

*HOWL AND OTHER POEMS*
Allen Ginsberg

*I KNOW WHY THE CAGED BIRD SINGS*
Maya Angelou

*IN THE NIGHT KITCHEN*
Maurice Sendak

*INVISIBLE MAN*
Ralph Ellison

*JAMES AND THE GIANT PEACH*
Roald Dahl

*JAWS*
Peter Benchley

*JUNKY*
William S. Burroughs

*KINGSBLOOD ROYAL*
Sinclair Lewis

*LAST EXIT TO BROOKLYN*
Hubert Selby Jr.

*LEAVES OF GRASS*
Walt Whitman

*LITTLE BLACK SAMBO*
Helen Bannerman

*LITTLE HOUSE ON THE PRAIRIE*
Laura Ingalls Wilder

*LITTLE RED RIDING HOOD*
Charles Perrault

*LORD OF THE FLIES*
William Golding

*MANCHILD IN THE PROMISED LAND*
Claude Brown

*MARRIED LOVE*
Marie Stopes

*MY HOUSE*
Nikki Giovanni

*THE NAKED APE*
Desmond Morris

*NAKED LUNCH*
William S. Burroughs

*NANA*
Émile Zola

*NEVER LOVE A STRANGER*
Harold Robbins

*NEW DICTIONARY OF AMERICAN SLANG*
Robert Chapman
(discussed with *A DICTIONARY OF AMERICAN SLANG*)

*OF MICE AND MEN*
John Steinbeck

*OF TIME AND THE RIVER*
Thomas Wolfe

*ONE FLEW OVER THE CUCKOO'S NEST*
Ken Kesey

*ORDINARY PEOPLE*
Judith Guest

*THE OX-BOW INCIDENT*
Walter Van Tilburg Clark

*THE RED PONY*
John Steinbeck

*THE SCARLET LETTER*
Nathaniel Hawthorne

*A SEPARATE PEACE*
John Knowles

*SISTER CARRIE*
Theodore Dreiser

*SOUL ON ICE*
Eldridge Cleaver

*STEPPENWOLF*
Hermann Hesse

*STRANGE FRUIT*
Lillian Smith

*STRANGER IN A STRANGE LAND*
Robert A. Heinlein

*THE SUN ALSO RISES*
Ernest Hemingway

*TO HAVE AND HAVE NOT*
Ernest Hemingway

*TO KILL A MOCKINGBIRD*
Harper Lee

*WELCOME TO THE MONKEY HOUSE*
Kurt Vonnegut Jr.

*THE WELL OF LONELINESS*
Radclyffe Hall

*WOMAN IN THE MISTS*
Farley Mowat
(discussed with *GORILLAS IN THE MIST*)

*WORKING: PEOPLE TALK ABOUT WHAT THEY DO ALL DAY AND
HOW THEY FEEL ABOUT WHAT THEY DO*
Studs Terkel

*A WORLD I NEVER MADE*
James T. Farrell

# LITERATURE
# SUPPRESSED ON
# SOCIAL GROUNDS

## THE ADVENTURES OF HUCKLEBERRY FINN

**Author:**  Mark Twain (Samuel Langhorne Clemens)
**Original date and place of publication:**  1884, London
**Original publisher:**  Self-published
**Literary type:**  Novel

### SUMMARY

This novel relates the adventures and struggles of a rambunctious young southern boy in the early 19th century. Told from the first-person point of view, *The Adventures of Huckleberry Finn* portrays river life in a developing America, and young Huckleberry Finn's adventures while on the journey from boyhood to manhood. The story begins with Huck's escape from his brutal father, and follows him up the Mississippi River as he and his slave friend Jim run from authorities and various other scoundrels.

As the novel opens, Huck reminds readers that many of his adventures have already been detailed in Mark Twain's THE ADVENTURES OF TOM SAWYER. He states that the $12,000 that he and Tom had found in the previous novel was invested for them and was earning interest. As the novel opens, Huck, who now lives with the Widow Douglas and Miss Watson, expresses annoyance with the amount of concern placed on making him conform to society. Huck sees no point in this lifestyle and yearns to be a rambunctious youth, as is his nature.

As the narrative progresses, Huck's father, the town drunk and a general burden on society, learns of Huck's recent wealth. He kidnaps Huck and holds him hostage in a shack in a remote area outside the town. While Huck waits to be either freed or rescued, his father repeatedly beats him, leaving Huck convinced that escape is the only feasible solution. To accomplish this, he conjures up a plan to make it appear that he has been murdered. Succeeding in his plan, Huck flees to safety on Jackson's Island, where he is reunited with Miss Watson's runaway slave, Jim. Jim is also hiding, fearful that he will be caught and punished for leaving his mistress. Huck agrees not to speak of Jim to anyone, and the two become partners. Aware that men are looking for Jim, the two decide to leave the island in search of adventure and the free states.

They board a raft that they found on the island and begin their journey. By day they hide on land, and by night they travel on the river. All goes well until one night when, during a violent storm, the raft is torn apart by an oncoming steamship. This experience not only almost ends Huck's young life, but it also separates him from Jim.

Huck swims to shore and finds himself in the midst of a feud between two families, the Grangerfords and the Shepherdsons, and he is immediately attacked by members of the Grangerford family. He states his name as

George Jackson and explains quickly that he fell off a riverboat and was washed ashore. He stays with the family for a short time, enjoying their lifestyle and making new friends along the way, and he even manages to be reunited with Jim. When the family feud escalates and Huck and Jim watch numerous members of both families die, they decide to resume their adventure on the river, where they meet two men known as the duke and the king. The unscrupulous men specialize in robbery and deceit, and they do not hesitate to pose as a dead man's next of kin in order to receive a rather large inheritance. The innately moral Huck refuses to cooperate, and he reveals the duke and the king's deceit. The scoundrels flee, but they first sell Jim to Silas Phelps.

Seeking to obtain Jim's freedom, Huck visits the Phelps farm where he is mistaken for Tom Sawyer, who is expected to arrive the same day. Huck allows the deception to continue, then meets with the real Tom, who agrees that Huck will continue to pose as Tom, and Tom will pose as his brother Sid. The two also agree to free Jim as soon as possible. After many attempts, Jim finally escapes, but Tom is accidentally shot in the leg during the effort. Although Jim has been portrayed as ignorant throughout the novel, he is a morally decent man who temporarily puts aside his dreams of freedom to nurse Tom back to health.

The novel closes as Jim and the boys learn that Jim is already a free man, as decreed by the last will and testament of Miss Watson, his former owner. This puts an end to all escape plans, and allows Jim to be the one thing that he has always wanted to be, free. Huck also decides to leave and wander on his own, convinced that the civilized world is no place for him.

## CENSORSHIP HISTORY

The novel excited controversy from the outset, when Concord (Massachusetts) Public Library banned the book in 1885, charging that the novel was "trash suitable only for the slums." Conventional morality was offended by the street vernacular spoken by Jim and Huck, as well as by their coarse behavior. Denver (Colorado) Public Library banned the novel in 1902, and Brooklyn Public Library removed it from the children's room on the charge that "Huck not only itched but he scratched, and that he said sweat when he should have said perspiration." In 1930, guards at the USSR border confiscated the novel, along with THE ADVENTURES OF TOM SAWYER.

In the United States, the furor quieted down for five decades, as the novel became an American classic and a mainstay of school reading lists. A new challenge emerged in 1957 when the National Association for the Advancement of Colored People protested the racist aspects of the book and demanded that it be removed from high schools in New York City. African-American author Ralph Ellison noted that Huck's friendship with Jim demeaned the stature of black males, because the adolescent Huck is portrayed as equal or superior to the adult Jim in decision-making capability. In 1969 Miami Dade (Florida) Junior College removed the novel from the required reading list, charging that the book inhibited learning in black students by creating an emotional block.

In 1973 the Scott, Foresman publishing company yielded to the demands of school officials in Tennessee and prepared a version of the novel that omitted material to which officials objected. The version omits the passage in Chapter 18 in which the young men of the Grangerford family toast their parents each morning with alcohol. It appears in *The United States in Literature*, a textbook distributed and used nationally.

The most frequent objection to the novel has been its language in reference to African Americans. Yielding to pressures from school districts across the nation, textbook publishers up to 1975 met challenges by substituting euphemisms for the term "nigger." Scott, Foresman rewrote passages to eliminate the word, Singer replaced the term with "slave" and McGraw-Hill replaced the term with "servant." In a 1975 dissertation, Dorothy Weathersby found that Ginn and Company was the only textbook publisher to retain the word, but their textbook included an essay by Lionel Trilling to explain the need to include the word in the novel.

The novel has been frequently banned or challenged by school districts for its language, particularly its racial references and the use of the slur "nigger." A significant number of such challenges have come from well-educated, middle-class, African-American parents who wish to prevent their children from exposure to such insulting references. The Winnetka (Illinois) school district challenged the novel as being racist in 1976, as did school districts in Warrington, Pennsylvania in 1981; Davenport, Iowa in 1981; Fairfax County, Virginia in 1982; Houston, Texas in 1982; State College, Pennsylvania in 1983; Springfield, Illinois in 1984; and Waukegan, Illinois in 1984.

In 1988 Rockford (Illinois) public schools removed the book from their required reading list because it contained the word "nigger." Berrien Springs (Michigan) High School challenged the novel that same year, while Caddo Parish (Louisiana) removed the novel from both its school libraries and required reading lists, charging that it contained racially offensive passages. The following year, the novel was challenged at Sevierville County (Tennessee) High School due to perceived racial slurs and the use of ungrammatical dialect.

The 1990s brought new challenges and continued antagonism to the novel. Citing derogatory references to African Americans, parents challenged its inclusion on the supplemental English reading list in Erie (Pennsylvania) High School in 1990. That same year, the novel was challenged as being racist in Plano (Texas) Independent School District.

In 1991 citing the repeated use of the word "nigger," parents in Mesa (Arizona) Unified School District challenged inclusion of the novel in the curriculum and claimed that such language damaged the self-esteem of young African

Americans. For the same reason that year, the novel was removed from the required reading list in the Terrebone Parish public schools in Houma, Louisiana. Also in 1991 it was temporarily removed from the Portage (Michigan) curriculum after African-American parents charged that the portrayal of Jim and other African Americans made their children "uncomfortable."

In 1992, the school superintendent of Kinston (North Carolina) School District removed the book from the middle school in the belief that the students were too young to read a work containing the word "nigger." Concern with the same word, as well as additional "offensive and racist language," motivated a 1992 challenge to including the novel on the required reading list in Modesto (California) High School. In 1993, challengers charged in the Carlisle (Pennsylvania) school system that the racial slurs in the novel were offensive to both African-American and Caucasian students. In contrast to other areas, the Lewisville (Texas) school board retained the novel on school reading lists in 1994, despite challenges of its racism. The most comprehensive objection to the novel regarded its use in English classes at Taylor County (Butler, Georgia) High School in 1994, when challengers not only claimed that it contained racial slurs and improper grammar, but it also did not reject slavery.

## FURTHER READINGS

Bradley, Julia T. "Censoring the School Library: Do Students Have the Right to Read?" *Connecticut Law Review* 10 (Spring 1978): 747–771.

Cloonan, Michele. "The Censorship of the Adventures of Huckleberry Finn." *Top of the News* (Winter 1984): 191–194.

Geller, Evelyn. *Forbidden Books in American Public Libraries, 1876–1939: A Study in Cultural Change.* Westport, Conn.: Greenwood Press, 1984.

Nelson, Randy F. "Banned in Boston and Elsewhere." *The Almanac of American Letters.* Los Altos, Calif.: William Kaufman, 1981.

*Newsletter on Intellectual Freedom.* (May 1969): 52; (July 1976): 87; (September 1976): 116; (November 1981): 162; (January 1982): 11, 18; (May 1982): 101; (July 1982): 126; (September 1982): 171; (January 1984): 11; (May 1984): 72; (July 1984): 121–122; (November 1984): 187; (January 1985): 38; (September 1988): 152–153; (November 1988): 201; (January 1989): 11; (March 1989): 43; (May 1989): 94; (January 1991): 17–18; (March 1991): 44–45; (May 1991): 90–92; (March 1991): 43, 64; (July 1992): 126; (September 1992): 140; (May 1993): 73; (May 1994): 99–100; (March 1995): 42.

People for the American Way. *Attacks on the Freedom to Learn, 1990–91.* Washington, D.C.: People for the American Way, 1991.

Reichman, Henry. *Censorship and Selection: Issues and Answers for Schools.* Chicago: American Library Association; Arlington, V.A.: American Association of School Administrators, 1993. A joint publication.

Weathersby, Dorothy T. *Censorship of Literature Textbooks in Tennessee: A Study of the Commission, Publishers, Teachers, and Textbooks.* Ed.D. dissertation, University of Tennessee, 1975.

# THE ADVENTURES OF SHERLOCK HOLMES

**Author:**   Sir Arthur Conan Doyle
**Original date and place of publication:**   1892, United States
**Original publisher:**   Harper & Row, Publishers
**Literary type:**   Short story collection

## SUMMARY

The 12 short stories contained in the collection first appeared in *The Strand Magazine* during the 1880s: "A Scandal in Bohemia," "The Red-Headed League," "A Case of Identity," "The Boscombe Valley Mystery," "The Five Orange Pips," "The Man with the Twisted Lip," "The Blue Carbuncle," "The Adventure of the Speckled Band," "The Adventure of the Engineer's Thumb," "The Adventure of the Noble Bachelor," "The Adventure of the Beryl Coronet" and "The Adventure of the Copper Beeches." Narrated by John Watson, M.D., they relate the activities of Sherlock Holmes, who functions as a scientist of crime, approaching his adventures with the objectivity and caution of a man of science.

His creator, a physician like Watson, made Holmes the perfect Victorian hero who remains unmoved by emotion and invulnerable to passion. Single-minded in his devotion to the detection of crime, Holmes examines even the most minute piece of evidence, leaving nothing to chance. Thus he can tell by examining ashes the type of tobacco a man smoked, which leads to the place where such tobacco might be sold. Dust and soil particles at a crime site yield information about a region the criminal has recently visited. Holmes the man is condescending toward ordinary mortals, yet he often assumes disguises that allow him to appear among common men, as a tramp, opium addict, minister or other figure of daily life. A more damaging vice than condescension is Holmes's cocaine addiction, which he works hard to eliminate.

The main concern of many of the stories is to prevent scandal, an important preoccupation of Victorian England. All begin similarly, with Watson reminiscing about cases to date. Holmes may be performing chemical experiments or sitting in his study and smoking his pipe as he waits for the next client to appear. Once a client is shown to the rooms at 221B Baker Street, Holmes dazzles his visitor by using careful observations of the individual's clothing, speech, appearance and mannerisms to reveal aspects of the client's profession and personal background. The client then tells his story and Holmes gets to work.

The stories are influenced by the interests of their creator, and Doyle's early dabbling in spiritualism and interest in the occult enters several of the stories. These interests do not dominate the stories, but they become points of reference against which Holmes exhibits his own seemingly mysterious skills.

## CENSORSHIP HISTORY

The censorship history of *The Adventures of Sherlock Holmes* is brief, and it is not based upon the main character's cocaine addiction, as might be the case in a more recent attempt at suppression. Rather, in 1929, the USSR banned the short story collection because references to the occult and spiritualism are made in several of the stories.

## FURTHER READINGS

Cox, Don Richard. *Arthur Conan Doyle*. New York: Frederick Ungar Publishing, 1985.
Lamond, John. *Arthur Conan Doyle: A Memoir*. Port Washington, N.Y.: Kennikat Press, 1972.
Orel, Harold, ed. *Critical Essays on Sir Arthur Conan Doyle*. New York: G.K. Hall, 1992.
Weil-Norden, P. *Sir Arthur Conan Doyle*. Centenary edition. Garden City, N.Y.: Doubleday & Company, 1959.

# THE ADVENTURES OF TOM SAWYER

**Author:**   Mark Twain (Samuel Langhorne Clemens)
**Original date and place of publication:**   1876, United States
**Original publisher:**   Self-published
**Literary type:**   Novel

## SUMMARY

The novel is a first-person account of the life of young Tom Sawyer along the banks of the Mississippi before the Civil War.

When the novel begins, Tom is missing, and his Aunt Polly is worriedly searching for him. She is furious when she learns that he has been swimming all day instead of attending school. As punishment, Tom must whitewash a fence on Saturday, instead of playing as usual, but he fools his friends into doing the job.

After Tom shows off "his" work on the fence, Aunt Polly agrees to let him play for the remainder of the day. Tom later spots Becky Thatcher and attracts her attention with flamboyant antics, earning a flower as his reward.

In catechism class the next morning, Tom receives a Bible for having enough tickets to indicate that he memorized 2,000 passages in the Bible. But Tom cheated and traded various items with friends in order to amass the correct number of tickets. The Sunday School teacher asks him to answer a Scripture question, and he is unable to do so. Later that morning, Tom creates chaos in church when his pinch bug attacks a wandering dog.

On Monday, Tom once again attempts to avoid school, but he is forced to go. On the way, Tom meets Huckleberry Finn, and the two plan to take the corpse of a cat to the cemetery at midnight in order to cure warts. Once Tom reaches school, he is automatically punished for his tardiness. He must sit in the female section of the schoolroom. Tom sits next to Becky, but she acts repelled by Tom's presence. Instead of staying, Tom and Joe Harper leave and take the rest of the day off.

That night Huck and Tom go to the cemetery with the cat. While there, the two boys see Dr. Robinson, Injun Joe and Muff Potter unearthing a recently interred body. The three men argue and struggle, leaving Muff Potter unconscious, after which Injun Joe stabs Dr. Robinson to death and leaves. The frightened boys swear never to tell anyone about the murder. The next day, Injun Joe names Muff Potter as Dr. Robinson's slayer.

Tom, Huck and Joe Harper decide to become pirates for a short while, so they run away to Jackson's Island. Days go by, and the boys continue to enjoy their carefree, adventurous life, while the townspeople frantically search for them. After their efforts prove fruitless, the townspeople legally declare the boys dead and plan a memorial service. On a brief return to his house to leave his Aunt Polly a note, Tom hears that there will be church services the following Sunday for the repose of the three boys' souls. The three guests of honor interrupt the services and casually stroll down the main aisle of the church.

The boys retire from piracy and return home. Back in school, Tom continues his courtship of Becky, finally winning her admiration by taking the blame and the punishment for something that she did. Tom and the others are able to have their revenge when, on the last day of school, Tom humiliates the schoolmaster by exposing his bald head to the entire school.

When Muff Potter is placed on trial for the murder of Dr. Robinson, Tom is called as a surprise witness. He tells the court that it was not Muff Potter but Injun Joe who ruthlessly murdered Dr. Robinson. Injun Joe escapes the court and imprisonment by jumping through a window and fleeing.

Tom and Huck are exploring an abandoned house when two men enter, one of whom is Injun Joe disguised as a Spaniard. The men take gold and silver coins to use at a tavern, and Injun Joe states that he isn't going to leave the area until he can take revenge upon the boys.

At a picnic a few days later, Tom and Becky become lost in McDougal's cave. Later that night, Huck overhears Injun Joe plot to attack the Widow Douglas in retaliation for a whipping that he received from her late husband. Huck informs Mr. Jones of the plot, and Injun Joe and his companion are quickly driven off. Huck then becomes ill, but tke Widow Dauglas takes care of him.

The townspeople discover that Tom and Becky are missing and search for the two children. In the cave, Tom sees Injun Joe, who is in hiding. The two children finally find a back opening to the cave and return to town. After hearing about Tom and Becky's ordeal, Judge Thatcher orders the cave sealed and unintentionally imprisons Injun Joe. When Tom learns that the cave has been sealed, he tells Judge Thatcher that Injun Joe is inside. Injun Joe's body is later found near the cave entrance.

Tom and Huck return to the cave and recover $12,000 of treasure, which is divided between the boys and invested for them. Huck is taken into the Douglas home, to be educated in the moral lifestyle by the Widow Douglas. He agrees to this ordeal and seems placated as long as he can join Tom's newly established robber gang.

## CENSORSHIP HISTORY

The novel was censored from its first publication, although it has not provoked as much controversy as Twain's later novel, THE ADVENTURES OF HUCKLEBERRY FINN. In 1876, Brooklyn (New York) Public Library banned the book from the children's room; that same year, Denver (Colorado) Public Library removed it from the library shelves. Five decades later, in 1930, guards at the USSR border confiscated the novel, along with *The Adventures of Huckleberry Finn*.

The novel proceeded to earn a reputation as an American literary classic and remained unchallenged until 1985, when education officials in London (United Kingdom) removed the novel from all school libraries after determining that the book was "racist" and "sexist." In 1990, the novel was challenged, along with *The Adventures of Huckleberry Finn*, as being racist in the Plano (Texas) Independent School District. In the O'Fallon (Illinois) schools in 1992, parents challenged the inclusion of the book on the required reading list and charged that the use of the word "nigger" was degrading and offensive to black students. They won the right to request that an alternative reading choice be offered. In 1994, parents of seventh-grade students in the West Chester (Pennsylvania) schools claimed that the book contained an abundance of racially charged language, and it was removed from the curriculum.

## FURTHER READINGS

Burress, Lee. *Battle of the Books: Literary Censorship in the Public Schools, 1950–1985.* Metuchen, N.J.: Scarecrow Press, 1989.

Geller, Evelyn. *Forbidden Books in American Public Libraries, 1876–1939: A Study in Cultural Change.* Westport, Conn.: Greenwood Press, 1984.

*Newsletter on Intellectual Freedom.* (September 1985): 156; (January 1991): 18; (March 1991): 45–46; (May 1991): 92; (May 1992): 97; (September 1994): 152.

# ALICE'S ADVENTURES IN WONDERLAND

**Author:** Lewis Carroll (Reverend Charles Dodgson)
**Original date and place of publication:** 1865, England
**Original publisher:** The Macmillan Company
**Literary type:** Novel

## SUMMARY

Lewis Carroll's *Alice's Adventures in Wonderland* began as an amusing story created especially for Alice Liddell, the young daughter of the author's Oxford colleague, Henry Liddell; it first appeared as a handwritten manuscript entitled *Alice's Adventures Under Ground*. Although the work is filled with numerous parodies of his age, puns, mathematical puzzles and turns of phrase, contemporary interpretation has concerned psychoanalytic and allegorical meaning. In addition, much attention has been paid to the author's numerous and intense friendships with young girls. The sequel, *Through the Looking Glass and What Alice Found There*, was published in 1871.

Set in Victorian England, the story relates the dream of a curious young girl named Alice who dozes off and, in her dream, catches sight of a white rabbit, whom she follows into the strange and exciting world of Wonderland. In this world, ordinary logic fails to apply, and Alice can find little pattern or order in the events that befall her. She finds a key to open a necessary door, but she is too large to fit through the doorway. A magic elixir in a bottle marked "Drink Me" shrinks her to the correct size, but she becomes too small to reach the key. Alice consumes a cake marked "Eat Me," hoping that it will make her grow a little. Instead, her neck grows until her head reaches the ceiling, as she cries large teardrops. As she attempts to come to terms with the chaotic environment, Alice converses with numerous animals. The White Rabbit reappears and drops his fan and gloves in fear. Alice sits in a pool of her own tears and meets a parrot-like creature named a Lory, with whom she discusses the proper way to dry off. A mouse attempts to dry everyone off by interpreting a "dry" history of the Archduke of Canterbury, and the Dodo suggests that they have a Caucus-Race in which the contestants run for however long and far they wish, stop whenever they like and all win.

The White Rabbit reappears and orders Alice to retrieve a fan and pair of gloves from his home, where Alice drinks from a bottle marked "Drink Me" and immediately grows to an enormous size. The White Rabbit scolds Alice and attempts to evict her from the house by ordering a serpent gardener to forcefully move her. The serpent and a lizard, the rabbit's servant, hit Alice with pebbles, but the stones become cakes as they hit the ground. Alice eats one and shrinks, then runs off in fear and finds herself under a mushroom on which a caterpillar reclines. The caterpillar tells her the secret of the mushroom before she leaves, which is that one side will make her taller and the other, smaller. She nibbles the magic mushrooms for a while and learns to control their enlarging and reducing effects.

Alice next meets the Duchess, who is nursing an infant, and the famous Cheshire Cat. Alice makes a snide comment, which offends the Duchess, who sentences Alice to be beheaded. The Duchess tosses the baby to Alice, and the baby immediately is transformed into a pig, which runs off squealing. Alice focuses on the Cheshire Cat, but he appears to speak in riddles.

Alice wanders to the home of the March Hare, who is having a tea party with the Dormouse and Mad Hatter. The tea party is dominated by horrible puns and insane behavior, and Alice leaves, only to find herself in the original hallway with the glass table. She eats more of the mushrooms and shrinks to a size that allows her to enter a garden where she meets the King and Queen of Hearts, who look like oversized playing cards, playing croquet. Alice offends the Queen and is sentenced to death, along with many of the other cards. The Queen then orders all of the croquet players except Alice to be taken away and executed, thus leaving the King, herself, and Alice to play for the remainder of the afternoon.

The Knave of Hearts is brought before the Queen, accused of stealing tarts. After emphatically denying this heinous crime, he is proved guilty by "solid" evidence and executed. This upsets Alice, who pleads with the Queen, then suddenly finds herself back in her world where she awakens and contemplates the dream of Wonderland.

## CENSORSHIP HISTORY

Despite the concerns raised in the author's own time regarding his apparent lack of maturity and the questions of possible sexual impropriety, the novel has not been challenged for either of these reasons. The sole ban occurred in 1931, when the governor of Hunan Province in China ruled that the book was unacceptable because it portrayed animals using human language. The censors asserted that "it was disastrous to put animals and human beings on the same level."

## FURTHER READINGS

Bjork, Christina. *The Other Alice: The Story of Alice Liddell and Alice in Wonderland*. New York: R&S Books, 1993.

Cohen, Morton N. *Lewis Carroll: A Biography*. New York: A.A. Knopf, 1995.

Lennon, Florence Becker. *The Life of Lewis Carroll*. New York: Dover Publications, 1972.

Wullschlager, Jackie. *Inventing Wonderland: The Lives and Fantasies of Lewis Carroll, Edward Lear, J. M. Barrie, Kenneth Grahame and A. A. Milne*. New York. Free Press, 1995.

# THE AMBOY DUKES

**Author:**  Irving Shulman
**Original date and place of publication:**   1947, United States
**Original publisher:**  Bantam Books
**Literary type:**  Novel

## SUMMARY

The novel, which gained a large following among high school students when it was first published, offers a sordid and realistic look at the sad and aimless lives of young men growing up in the slums of a big American city during World War II. Left largely to fend for themselves and to create their own moral code, as they see little of their parents who work in the large defense plants, the boys develop a herd instinct that leads them to form a gang, the Amboy Dukes. Although the novel was written in the mid-1940s, the bleak portrait of slum life and the pervading sense of hopelessness transcend the time period and apply as well to the 1990s as to the book's age. The actions of the members of the Dukes, and the reactions of others around them, make them the precursors of the highly popularized "juvenile delinquent" of books and movies of the 1950s.

The author explains the elements of gang life through each of his characters, and he portrays these unsupervised young misfits as being as much the victims of their environment and of society in general as they are of callous families and indifferent social institutions. To portray the gang members realistically, Shulman peppered their speech heavily with vulgarities. They use crude terminology in referring to relations with women. Their appearance and attitude are provocative, but the author also includes incidents in which individual adolescent gang members suffer harassment from the police as well as from school officials, with little hope of recourse. The lives of teenagers are presented in a sympathetic manner, with an attempt at gritty reality, and the author offers a strong indictment of the conditions that lead these boys to crime and brutality.

Despite his empathy with members of the Dukes, the author graphically portrays the toll of their abandonment by established society, and the subsequent formation of their own gang society, on both the boys and those with whom they come into contact. Robberies, fighting, muggings and other crimes pervade the novel. In one episode, the gang members pay a girl to have sex with all of them, then forcibly try to take their money back from her. The novel ends with no solutions to the problems it exposes. There are no happy endings for members of the Amboy Dukes.

## CENSORSHIP HISTORY

The novel was severely criticized from the outset and blamed for promoting delinquency among poor young slum dwellers. In 1949, the book was challenged as obscene in Brantford, Ontario (Canada), but Judge D. J. Cowan cleared the bookseller and the book of obscenity charges when the case came to trial. That same year, local authorities in Milwaukee, Detroit and Newark, New Jersey, challenged sales of the book, claiming that it was obscene, but no formal charges were lodged.

In 1952, the Gathings Committee Report criticized the book for contributing to delinquency, a conclusion that made the novel a favorite target of attempted but unsuccessful censorship in the 1950s. In a statement to the Gathings Committee, Judge James V. Mulholland of the New York Domestic Relations Court supported restriction of the novel and stated that two recent cases involving juveniles, one a boy who viciously attacked several other children and the other a 14-year-old girl who had committed incest, could be directly linked to the influence of the book. In 1954, the novel was placed on the disapproved list of the National Organization of Decent Literature.

## FURTHER READINGS

Burress, Lee. *Battle of the Books: Literary Censorship in the Public Schools, 1950–1985.* Metuchen, N.J.: Scarecrow Press, 1989.
Loth, David. *The Erotic in Literature.* New York: Dorset Press, 1961.
Select Committee on Pornographic Materials, House of Representatives, 82nd Congress. *Report of the Committee on Pornographic Materials.* House Report No. 2510. 1952. (Known as the Gathings Committee Report because E. C. Gathings was chairman.)

# THE AMERICAN HERITAGE DICTIONARY OF THE ENGLISH LANGUAGE

**Author:**   American Heritage Publishing Company
**Original date and place of publication:**   1969, United States
**Original publisher:** American Heritage Publishing Company and Houghton Mifflin Company
**Literary type:**   Dictionary

## SUMMARY

*The American Heritage Dictionary of the English Language* is a comprehensive lexicon containing over 170,000 entries. The words defined range from the common and conventional to slang and technical jargon. Many of the entries give word origins, as well as meanings, along with sample phrases to show the different meanings in context. Entries seek to explain all connotations of the word.

## CENSORSHIP HISTORY

In June 1976 a group of parents who were members of People for Better Education complained that *The American Heritage Dictionary* was obscene and demanded that all copies be removed from classrooms in Anchorage, Alaska.

They cited offensive entries for such words as "bed," defined as a noun meaning "a place for lovemaking" and "a marital relationship with its rights and intimacies" and as a verb meaning "to have sexual intercourse with." They also objected to "knocker," "balls" and "nuts" defined with their slang meanings. The assistant superintendent headed a review committee that examined the dictionary and approved it unanimously. In reporting the committee findings, the assistant superintendent stated that the dictionary provided children with the opportunity to look up the designated words, which "helped diffuse excitement and curiosity about them." The committee further defended *The American Heritage Dictionary* as being "an excellent reference for advanced students, especially for scientific terms." The school board ignored the defense and, citing their list of definitions taken from the dictionary, voted to remove it from the schools.

In September 1976, parents in Cedar Lake, Indiana, complained that 70 or 80 words in the dictionary were obscene or otherwise inappropriate for high school students to see, and they demanded that *The American Heritage Dictionary* be removed from the schools. The word "bed" was again the most frequently criticized entry. The school board voted to remove the dictionary from the high school, and the board president refused to listen to the protests of teachers, whom he characterized as "unqualified to select learning materials." In mid-November 1976, the school board reversed its decision, by a 3-2 vote, and allowed the dictionary to be used in the senior English classrooms. This action was taken after counsel advised the board that the dictionary could not be considered obscene. In April 1977, 24 parents of junior high school students in Eldon, Missouri, signed a complaint in which they listed 39 words in *The American Heritage Dictionary* that were objectionable. One parent was quoted on page 1 of the *St. Louis Post-Dispatch* for April 18, 1977, as stating, "If people learn words like that it ought to be where you and I learned it—in the street and in the gutter." The school board agreed with the parents and voted to remove the dictionary from the junior high school. In later cases, the school library in Folsom, California, removed the dictionary from its shelves after parents issued complaints, and the dictionary was challenged but retained in the Churchill County, Nevada, school libraries in 1993. That same year, the Washoe County, Nevada, school district removed the dictionary from classrooms, then reinstated it a short time later.

A more extensive case of dictionary censorship occurred in Texas in 1976. *The American Heritage Dictionary* was one of five dictionaries recommended by the State Textbook Committee that the Texas State Textbook Commission banned because they contained definitions that the commission viewed as obscene. The other four were *The Doubleday Dictionary, The Random House College Dictionary*, revised edition; *Webster's New World Dictionary of the English Language*, college edition; and *Webster's Seventh New Collegiate Dictionary*. The move was spearheaded by Mel and Norma Gabler, who operated Educational Research Analysts, a tax-exempt organization that initiated local censorship efforts and sent out textbook reviews that pointed out what they viewed as questionable material. They had numerous supporters, among them the Texas Society of the Daughters of the American Revolution, whose textbook chairperson stated in a Bill of Particulars to the Texas commissioner of education, "Reviewer is shocked that a supposedly reputable publisher would offer for adoption a book which is debasing the English language. Students need the basics rather than sub-standard language." Her remarks were in reference to *Webster's New World Dictionary of the American Language*. In addition to citing the obvious words, such as "cunnilingus," "fart," "fuck," "piss," "screw" and "shit," the report also noted that the following words in the five dictionaries were objectionable; the reason cited for the objection appears in parentheses: "across-the-board" (betting on horse racing in Texas was illegal); "Arab" (incomplete definition); "ass" (unnecessary); "attempt" (ties word into subject of murder); "banana republic" (insulting to Latins); "bawdy house" (unnecessary); "bed" (Why is sexual intercourse mentioned?); "the big house" (slang, unnecessary); "block busting" (inaccurate and unnecessary); "boob" (a female breast); "brain" (denotes violence); "bucket" (slang for the buttocks); butt (slang for the buttocks); "cherry" (the hymen; virginity); "clap" (slang for a brothel and gonorrhea); "coke" (slang for cocaine); "crocked" (slang for intoxicated); "deflower" (to cause loss of virginity); "dyke" (a female homosexual); "fag"/"faggot" (slang for male homosexual); "fairy" (slang for male homosexual); "gay" (slang for male homosexual); "G-string" (slang, unnecessary); "head" (slang for one who uses or is addicted to a drug); "hooker" (slang for prostitute); "horny" (slang for sexually excited); "hot" (slang for sexually excited); "john" (slang for a customer of a prostitute); "john" (slang for toilet); "keister"/"keaster" (slang for buttocks or rump); "kinky" (slang for sexually abnormal); "knock" (slang for to make pregnant); "queer" (homosexual; a contemptuous term); "rubber" (slang for a condom); "shack"/"shack up with" (slang for to share living quarters with one's lover); "slut" (a dirty, untidy woman; slattern; a sexually immoral woman); "tail" (slang for the buttocks); "tit" (a breast). In efforts to sell their books, the publishers of the dictionaries wrote to the Texas commissioner of education to defend the inclusion of these words, citing their appearance in classic literature and the Bible, as well as highly reputable contemporary books and publications. Despite their efforts, the dictionaries were placed on the "no-purchase" list.

## FURTHER READINGS

Hung, Pham Thien. "Parents Protest Textbooks." In *Censorship and Education*. Ed. by Eli M. Oboler, 135–139. New York: H.W. Wilson Company, 1981.

Massie, Dorothy C. "Censorship in the Schools: Something Old and Something New." *Today's Education* (November 1980): 56–60.

*Newsletter on Intellectual Freedom.* (September 1976): 115–116; (November 1976): 145; (January 1977): 7; (July 1977): 101; (March 1983): 39; (March 1991): 71.

# AND STILL I RISE

**Author:** Maya Angelou
**Original date and place of publication:** 1978, United States
**Original publisher:** Random House
**Type:** Poetry collection

## SUMMARY

*And Still I Rise* is a collection of 31 autobiographical poems that celebrate life and the survival of the human spirit. The subject matter ranges from the author's proud examination of her powers to attract men, through references to the range of roles that women, especially African-American women, have been forced to assume throughout time. Angelou speaks in rhyme and rhythm as they suit the specific subject of a poem, and the diction ranges from the lofty speech of a sermon to the vernacular of a welfare mother challenging the system. She challenges readers in her references to rape as well as in her frank statements regarding exuberant sexuality.

In "Remembrance," the poet states that "mystery rapes my reason," and she speaks of feeling melancholy after a lover leaves her bed, "when only the smell of your love lingers between my breasts." The harshly analytical "Men" speaks of the "breasts of a young girl" and the betrayal of the young persona, "Fifteen years old and starving for them [men]," who learns that the soft romanticism of the initial encounter will result in her body being "slammed shut. Forever." The soft caresses give way to the unpleasant physical reality that "it is your juice that runs down their legs." In "Lady Luncheon Club," a male speaker at a woman's club attempts to relate to his bored audience as "he sighs for youthful death and rape at ten," while the mother in "Momma Welfare Roll" is "too fat to whore."

On a more positive note, Angelou celebrates her sexuality and that of all African-American women in "Through the Inner City to the Suburbs" as she speaks of "the juicy secrets of black thighs." This celebration of the self reaches its peak in "Still I Rise," in which the author challenges readers, "Does my sexiness upset you? / Does it come as a surprise / That I dance like I've got diamonds / At the meeting of my thighs?"

## CENSORSHIP HISTORY

*And Still I Rise* has been challenged both for its language and for the "suggestive sexuality" contained in many of the poems. In 1982 parents at Northside High School in Lafayette, Louisiana, demanded that the book be withdrawn from the high school library because of its references to rape and sexual activity, but the book was retained. In 1987 a Wake County High School parent group approached the school board in Raleigh, North Carolina, and protested that the work was unsuitable to be required reading for junior-level English classes. Among their concerns were the mentions of rape and the references to the breasts of young girls and to their sexual awareness. Critics also protested that several of the poems exhibited a "bitterness and hatred toward whites." The board sided with parents and removed the work from the required list. Protests by parents in Longview (Washington) School District in 1987 resulted in the temporary removal of the collection from high school reading lists until the school board could consider claims that "some students could be harmed by its graphic language." The book was retained on the reading list, but students were provided numerous alternative reading choices.

## FURTHER READINGS

Kallen, Stuart A. *Maya Angelou: Woman of Words, Deeds, and Dreams.* Minneapolis: Abdo and Daughters, 1993.
*Newsletter on Intellectual Freedom* (May 1982): 83; (May 1987): 91; (September 1987): 195.
Pettit, Jayne. *Maya Angelou: Journey of the Heart.* New York: Lodester Books, 1996.
Spain, Valerie. *Meet Maya Angelou.* New York: Random House, 1995.

## ANNE FRANK: THE DIARY OF A YOUNG GIRL

**Author:**  Anne Frank
**Original date and place of publication:**  1947, The Netherlands
**Original publisher: Contact Publishers**
**Type:**  Diary

## SUMMARY

*Anne Frank: The Diary of a Young Girl* is a compilation of the notebooks and papers left behind by a 15-year-old Jewish girl, Anne Frank, when she and her family were taken from their hiding place in Amsterdam by German soldiers during the Nazi occupation of the Netherlands in World War II. The hiding place was a "secret annex," a group of rooms at the top and back of a building that served as a warehouse and office for a Dutch-owned business. Those hiding remained quiet by day, while business was conducted in the lower part of the building, but they moved freely at night when the building was deserted. After the Frank family was taken, members of the Dutch family that had sheltered them gathered the papers and hid them in a desk without reading them. When Otto Frank, Anne's father and the only one of the family to survive the war, returned from the death camps, he took the papers and sought to publish them. He would thus fulfill his late daughter's dream for her work, and make her live again through her writing.

The final published diary is the combination of Anne's original text with the later edited version that she began, modifying her earlier, more childish phrasing. She also used pseudonyms for the other occupants of the annex, as well as for their protectors, to prevent hurt feelings in instances in which she is critical of them. She writes at several points in the diary that she wants it to live on long after her death and would like it published as *Het Achterhuis* (The House Behind), the title under which the work first appeared.

The small red-checkered diary, which Anne named "Kitty," was a birthday present from her father on her 13th birthday, June 12, 1942, less than a month before they would enter the annex. She began the diary on her birthday, writing in it and in notebooks for the family's 25 months in hiding, from July 5, 1942 through August 1, 1944, three days before Gestapo Sergeant Silverbauer and four soldiers broke in and took them away. In the diary Anne followed the course of the war and recorded her hopes, dreams, fears and desires, as well as her observations of daily life. The increasingly bad news brought by their protectors, as well as what they heard on the English radio, also prompted Anne's reflections.

Anne's observations about her family as well as the dentist, Mr. Dussel, and the Van Daan family (a father, mother and 16-year-old son), who share the annex with the Franks, are followed in the diary. She irritably records Mrs. Van Daan's attempts to flirt with Otto Frank, noting that "she strokes his face and hair, pulls her skirt right up, and makes so-called witty remarks," and registers her relief that her father "doesn't play ball." She also records the idiosyncrasies of the other inhabitants, as well as her coldness toward her mother. The reader also learns that the three young people managed to read a lot during their stay and even completed a correspondence shorthand course. Anne also manages to maintain her sense of humor as conditions worsen, remarking at one point when food becomes scarce, "Whoever wants to follow a slimming course should stay in the 'Secret Annexe'!"

## CENSORSHIP HISTORY

Censorship of *Anne Frank: The Diary of a Young Girl* began with its initial publication in the Netherlands. Anxious to spare the feelings of their protectors and the memory of the other occupants, Otto Frank excised details of the squabbling among the occupants of the annex, and sections in which Anne complained about the selfishness or insensitivity of others. Because she viewed the diary as her private writing, Anne frequently expressed unadorned thoughts and concerns, and used the diary as a means of venting her frustrations with the situation. Her father removed such passages without changing significantly the overall representations of the others or their relationships.

Once Otto Frank sought a publisher, additional censorship was required. The Dutch publisher, Contact, required that certain passages that the editors viewed as "tasteless" or "unseemly" be removed. These included Anne's references to her and her sister's menstruation. Anne's growing sexual curiosity was also deemed unacceptable, despite the naturalness of such curiosity in an adolescent. Therefore, a passage in which she recalls a friend's developing breasts and muses about wanting to touch them was removed. The publisher also asked that Otto Frank delete all "offensive" remarks made by Anne about her mother.

In 1950 the German publishing firm of Lambert Schneider commissioned a German translation, and additional censorship occurred. The *Critical Edition* notes that material that would have been especially offensive to German readers was removed. One such passage written by Anne related the rule in the annex that everyone was required "to speak softly at all times, in any civilized language, therefore not in German," which Lambert Schneider changed to "All civilized languages . . . but softly."

The 1952 publication of the diary in England restored most of the excised material. More recent challenges have focused on Anne's growing sexual awareness. In a January 5, 1944, entry Anne recollects sleeping with a girlfriend and having "a strong desire to kiss her," which she did. She states further that she was terribly curious about the other girl's body, "for she had always kept it hidden from me. I asked her whether, as proof of our friendship, we should feel one another's breasts, but she refused. I go into ecstasies every time I see the naked figure of a woman, such as Venus, for example. . . . If only I had a girl friend!" At the same time, she develops a crush on Peter Van Daan, who shows her "the male organs" of a cat, and with whom she experiences her first ardent kiss on the mouth, questioning if she "should have yielded so soon." She also observes increased flirting between the dentist and Mrs. Van Daan and notes that "Dussel is beginning to get longings for women."

In 1982, parents in Wise County, Virginia, challenged the use of the book in school and asserted that Anne's discussion of sexual matters was "inappropriate" and "offensive" and that the criticism of her mother and of the other adults "undermines adult authority." Others have objected to the discussion of "the mistreatment of the Jewish people" and one parent of Arab ancestry objected to the portrayal of a Jewish girl. In 1983, four members of the Alabama Textbook Commission wanted to reject the title for use in the schools because it was "a real downer."

## FURTHER READINGS

Frank, Otto. "Introduction." In *Anne Frank. The Diary of a Young Girl: The Definitive Edition.* Ed. by Otto Frank and Mirjam Pressler. New York: Doubleday & Company, 1995.

*Newsletter on Intellectual Freedom* (March 1983): 39.

Wisse, Ruth. "A Romance of the Secret Annex." *New York Times Book Review* (July 2, 1989): 2.

# ANNIE ON MY MIND

**Author:**  Nancy Garden
**Original date and place of publication:**  1982, United States
**Original publisher:**  Farrar, Straus & Giroux
**Type:**  Young adult novel

## SUMMARY

*Annie on My Mind* details what happens to two teenage girls who recognize that they love each other. Students at different schools who start out as friends, Annie and Liza meet at a museum and share a common interest in art and the Middle Ages. Annie is the daughter of minimally educated Italian immigrant parents and attends an inner-city school. In contrast, Liza is from an affluent family. Her parents are professionals and she attends Foster Academy, a private school where she is student council president.

The main setting of the book is Foster Academy, run by a headmistress who demands that even minor infractions of rules be disciplined. The academy is in financial trouble, and a fund drive is in progress, a complication that requires that all hint of scandal be eliminated or the academy will suffer.

The love between Annie and Liza develops gradually. They have difficulty admitting their feelings because of the stigma attached to their love, and there is no place for them to become physically intimate. When two of the academy's best-liked teachers, Ms. Widmer and Ms. Stephenson, who share a house, go on vacation, Liza offers to care for their cats, then realizes that she and Annie can be alone there. Liza also discovers that the two teachers are lovers when she explores the empty house, sees books about lesbians in the master bedroom and notices the bedroom furnishings. During that spring vacation, Liza and Annie meet at the house and explore their sexual relationship. They are discovered by another student and a nosy school secretary who tells the headmistress and exposes the two teachers as well.

Liza is suspended from school and required to attend a disciplinary meeting of the school's board of trustees, who will decide if the incident should be placed on her permanent record and if the board should inform the Massachusetts Institute of Technology, which has accepted Liza as an architectural student. Annie attends another school, so she is spared the humiliation and her parents never learn about the incident. The academy board takes no disciplinary action, but Liza must bear nasty remarks and whispering when she returns to school. The two teachers, however, lose their jobs because the school mistakenly believes that they influenced the girls.

Annie attends the University of California at Berkeley on the West Coast, while Liza remains on the East Coast and attends MIT in the fall. Annie writes Liza a letter, but Liza does not answer it. Finally, after realizing that she does love Annie, Liza telephones her and they decide to get together during Christmas vacation.

## CENSORSHIP HISTORY

The novel has frequently been attacked on the grounds that it promotes, idealizes or encourages homosexuality. Challengers who have not read the book mistakenly charge that it contains explicit sex. Other critics cannot accept the positive portrayal of the gay characters, who are not psychological misfits, nor are they condemned. Yet the book makes a compelling point that homosexual behavior risks harsh consequences and may often result in pain and suffering for individuals who dare to challenge the majority.

In 1988, patrons of Cedar Mill Community Library in Portland, Oregon, challenged the book because it portrays lesbian love and sex as being normal. The book was temporarily removed from shelves, then returned. In 1990, a parent in Sedgwick, Maine, became upset when she learned that the novel was included in the seventh- and eighth-grade library. She objected to the lesbian relationship portrayed. The matter was referred to the school board because the school district did not have a complaint policy in place. The board created a review committee consisting of board members, educators and parents, who voted to retain the book in the library.

In 1991 *Annie on My Mind* disappeared mysteriously from two high school libraries in San Ramon, California. The librarians later discovered that the vice principals of the two high schools had taken the book from the libraries, claiming to want to examine them. The copies had been donated by a community member, who publicly accused the vice principals of censorship and stated, "They might as well burn the books; clearly the intent is to deny students books having a gay or lesbian theme." Although the vice principals denied censoring the books, a representative of the American Civil Liberties Union determined that this had been the intent and stated that "a school district cannot exclude the topic of homosexuality from a school library."

In 1992 librarians at Colony (Texas) Public Library received numerous requests to remove the novel because "it promotes and encourages the gay lifestyle." After receiving the first complaint, the library board members voted unanimously to retain the book in the library and issued a statement that it was not the job of the library to tell children what they could read, "it is the parents' job." The board maintained that position when other complaints followed and encouraged parents to evaluate themselves the materials to which their children were exposed.

In 1993 parents of students at Bend (Oregon) High School challenged the book in their school library because it "encourages and condones" homosexuality. The school board considered the complaints and voted to retain the book. That same year the book was also challenged but retained in the Lapeer (Michigan) West High School library. Several Kansas school districts also experienced challenges in 1993 after the schools received a donation of library copies of the novel from a national group that sought to give young adults "fair, accurate, and inclusive images of lesbians and gay men." The book was first removed, then returned to general circulation in the library in Shawnee Mission School District. Copies of the book were doused with gasoline and burned by a minister and his followers in the Kansas City School District, but a copy of the novel was retained in the high school library, and the school district donated the novel to the city's public library.

In 1994 the novel was banned from the libraries of five junior high and three senior high schools in Olathe, Kansas, by the superintendent of schools with the backing of the school board. When the district refused to return the book to the school libraries, six students and their families contacted the American Civil Liberties Union and filed a lawsuit against the school. The case was decided in December 1995, when a U.S. district judge ruled that the school board and superintendent had violated the First Amendment of the United States Constitution by removing the novel from the school libraries. The judge ordered the district to return copies of the novel to the school libraries and to pay legal fees and expenses for the plaintiffs.

The novel was also removed from the Chanute (Kansas) High School library in 1994, after parents challenged the work. Librarians returned the book to a limited-access shelf and made it available only to those who had written parental permission.

## FURTHER READINGS

"Annie Goes Back to School." *School Library Journal* 42 (January 1996): 13.
Cart, Michael. "Carte Blanche: Winning One for the First Amendment." *Booklist* 92 (April 15, 1996): 1,431.
*Newsletter on Intellectual Freedom* (January 1990): 4–5; (January 1992): 5–6; (July 1992): 125–126; (September 1993): 158-159; (November 1993): 191–192; (January 1994): 13; (March 1994): 51–52; (May 1994): 84; (July 1994): 129; (September 1994): 140–141; (March 1995): 40.
Olson, Renee. "Battles over Books Usher in New School Year." *School Library Journal* 41 (October 1995): 10–11.

## ANOTHER COUNTRY

**Author:**   James Baldwin
**Original date and place of publication:**   1962, United States
**Original publisher:**   The Dial Press
**Literary type:**   Novel

### SUMMARY

The novel is set in New York City and moves freely from Greenwich Village to Harlem, as it recounts a year in the lives of the seven major characters.

*Another Country* spotlights the interrelationships and artistic careers of African-American jazz drummer Rufus and his sister Ida, a singer, with those of five white characters: Vivaldo, Ida's lover and a would-be writer; Yves, a young Frenchman, and his lover, Eric, an actor; Richard, a pulp novelist, and his wife, Cass. Through the often complex interaction of the characters of both races set in the period of the mid-1950s, the author investigates the deep racial wounds suffered by both groups. He experiments with the concept of equality by placing his characters on roughly similar levels, then examines the reasons for their failure to remain at these levels. Baldwin seeks to shatter prevailing social concepts as he erases established color and sex lines, and spends social expectations of the period by the freedom with which he writes of interracial sex and homosexuality.

Written in social-realist style, the novel examines the lives of its characters at a specific moment in time; in so doing, it successfully recreates the people, streets, stores, apartments and sounds of the city, its glory as well as its more sordid aspects. In keeping with the stress on reality, the characters speak as their real-life counterparts speak, expressing their fears, frustrations, desires and emotions in street vernacular and sprinkling their conversations with obscenities. White characters are sexually attracted to African-American characters, men are drawn to men and the surrounding city casts a squalid gloom on all their lives.

From the outset, despite their efforts, the characters are doomed to succumb to a fate beyond their control. Rufus Scott, a talented and successful musician, internalizes the low opinion of African-American men held by the society of his time. When his white lover, Leona, professes her love and seeks his approval, his lack of self-esteem and inability to overcome the pain of former rejections prevent him from returning her love. Instead, he labels her "white trash" for loving a black man, physically abuses her and accuses her of sneaking out with his male friends. Unable to deal with the hopelessness of his fate, Rufus, the most fully developed character in the novel, commits suicide by jumping off the George Washington Bridge in the first fifth of the novel. In the remaining four-fifths, the rest of the characters cope with their loss, recalling from their unique perspectives their relationships with Rufus and their own frustrations in life.

Although reviewers criticized his unconventional sexual pairings in the novel, the public made it a success and *Another Country* became the second-best-selling novel of the year when it came out in paperback in 1963.

## CENSORSHIP HISTORY

Upon publication in 1962, the novel caught the attention of the Federal Bureau of Investigation, which viewed it as being similar in many ways to Henry Miller's *TROPIC OF CANCER* and *TROPIC OF CAPRICORN*. The novel was considered of sufficient importance by the Bureau that it warranted a separate file, *FBI HO 145-2625*, apart from their main file on Baldwin. On September 19, 1962, FBI Director J. Edgar Hoover sent the novel to the FBI laboratory to be "examined," expressing particular concern regarding its interracial and homosexual sex scenes. The General Crimes Section returned an unexpected decision, declaring that the novel "contains literary merit and may be of value to students of psychology and social behavior."

In 1963 a New Orleans bookseller was arrested for stocking copies of the novel in violation of city ordinances related to the sale of obscene literature, but the Louisiana district attorney dropped the case. That same year, the New Orleans (Louisiana) Public Library asserted that the novel was obscene and banned it. The case went to court and, after a year of litigation, the book was restored.

In 1965, the FBI received a letter from a Fort Worth (Texas) citizen, claiming that the novel contained "sex perversion at its vilest" and demanding action to curtail the sale of the novel, which was available at stores throughout the city. Hoover replied to the writer, assuring him that the FBI appreciated his concern but stated that the author had not yet broken any federal laws. The air of tolerance is subverted by an entry made in the 1969 FBI summary on the author, which included the suggestion of an informant that Ku Klux Klansmen obtain copies of the novel "to determine whether it is suitable reading for college students."

## FURTHER READINGS

Campbell, James. *Talking at the Gates: A Life of James Baldwin*. New York: Penguin Books USA, 1991.

Nelson, Emmanuel. "Critical Deviance: Homophobia and the Reception of James Baldwin's Fiction." *Journal of American Culture* 14 (Fall 1991): 91–96.

Robins, Natalie. *Alien Ink: The FBI's War on Freedom of Expression*. New York: William Morrow & Company, 1992.

Rowden, Terry. "A Play of Abstractions: Race, Sexuality, and Community in James Baldwin's *Another Country*." *Southern Review* 29 (Winter 1993): 41–50.

## APHRODITE

**Author:**   Pierre Louÿs
**Original date and place of publication:**   1896, France
**Original publisher:**   Privately published
**Type:**   Novel

## SUMMARY

*Aphrodite*, a novel set in Alexandria, Egypt, in 57 B.C., recounts the adventures of a courtesan in the pagan, decadent society that preceded the reign of

Cleopatra. Chrysis, one of 1,400 courtesans in the city, relentlessly pursues sensual pleasures that include orgies, lesbian encounters and "all dangerous feats of passion before which the living recoil." The novel also includes instances of extreme cruelty, including a crucifixion.

Chrysis attracts the attention of Demetrios, a sculptor who is also the lover of Queen Berenice. Before she will promise to spend the night with him, Chrysis demands that he exact revenge for her by stealing three treasures: a rare silver mirror from a courtesan named Bacchis who recently took away an admirer, a precious comb from the wife of the high priest and a necklace made of seven strands of pearls from the statue of the goddess Aphrodite. Demetrios carries out her wishes, and his acts help to reveal the inhumane and unfeeling nature of Chrysis, as well as his obsession with her. When a young and beautiful slave who is supposed to be freed is accused of stealing the mirror, Chrysis fails to correct the error and allows the girl to be crucified for the crime. The comb can only be obtained by cutting off the hair of the high priest's wife, and Chrysis knows that Demetrios must first stab the woman to death to accomplish this. Obtaining the necklace requires that Demetrios desecrate the temple of Aphrodite.

The novel includes several types of exotic sexual behavior. Hermaphrodites guard the temple, Scythian courtesans who couple "only in the attitude of the beasts" are discussed and gay and lesbian relationships are identified. While he is obtaining the articles, Demetrios visits a 10-year-old courtesan who professes to know all of the arts of love, and Chrysis romps in bed with two adolescent lesbian companions. When the philosopher Naucrates visits Chrysis to invite her to Bacchis's feast, he finds her naked and in bed with the two young girls and protests that too many women have been taking girl lovers. He notes, "Already a great many women achieve perfect pleasure only with their own sex. Soon you will refuse to receive us entirely, even as a makeshift." Chrysis informs him, "Only a woman knows how to love. Only a woman knows how to be loved. Therefore, an amorous couple made up of two women is perfect; if there is only one woman, it is only half as good; and if there is no woman it is perfectly idiotic."

After meeting Chrysis's demands, Demetrios realizes the gravity of what he has done and grows to hate Chrysis. As he coldly rejects her, Chrysis protests wildly that she really loves him and wants him to stay with her forever. To prove her love, she dresses herself in the stolen items and appears to the throng of people gathered at the temple of Aphrodite. Chrysis is charged with the crimes and sentenced to die. In her jail cell awaiting her death by poison, the courtesan begins to chant half-remembered prayers from her childhood in Galilee, verses from the Old Testament. Demetrios visits her and watches her drink the cup of hemlock, then later poses her body and makes a clay model of it. At the end, Chrysis's two young lesbian lovers claim the body and bury it.

## CENSORSHIP HISTORY

*Aphrodite* was banned in 1929 by the United States Customs Bureau, along with Louÿs's *The Songs of Bilitis* and *The Twilights of the Nymphs* for being lewd, lascivious, corrupting and obscene. Although none of the three books contains explicit sexual content, all three portray lesbian relationships and advocate an unrestricted sensuality among women and, to a lesser degree, between women and men. In the preface to the original work, Louÿs asserts that "it is, then, by conscious and willful fraud that modern educators from the time of the Renaissance to the present day have presented ancient ethics as the inspiration of their narrow virtues." He declares, instead, that "there is nothing under the sun more sacred than physical love, nor more beautiful than the human body." In this spirit, Louÿs aims to return with his reader in *Aphrodite* to "a time when the most sensual love, the divine love of which we are born, was without blemish, without shame, and without sin."

The first English translation was made in 1925 and published in an edition limited to 1,000 copies in the United States and 500 copies in Great Britain. In 1930, John S. Sumner, secretary of the New York Society for the Suppression of Vice, seized 54 copies of the book from New York book dealer Earl Marks and filed a complaint against Marks and his distribution company, the Mutual Circulation Company. The New York City magistrate who bound Marks over for trial claimed to have read *Aphrodite* and declared it to be "filthy" and too obscene for his daughter to ever read. The case was heard before three Special Sessions judges who refused to concur with Marks's defense that the book was a recognized classic and, as such, could not be viewed as obscene. Marks lost the case and paid a fine of $250 for violating state laws against objectionable literature, but he was spared the 60-day jail sentence.

Two years later, the Liveright Publishing Corporation included the 1925 translation in its *Collected Works of Pierre Louÿs* without challenge. In 1933, the Modern Library edition translated by Lewis Galantiere appeared and also remained unchallenged, but U.S. Customs prevented attempts to import a deluxe edition in 1935. At the time of the ban, however, the novel was freely advertised in *The New York Times Book Review* for 49 cents per copy, with mail delivery anywhere in the United States for only an additional 10 cents. As recently as 1954, the novel was condemned by the National Organization for Decent Literature and placed on its blacklist, where it remains.

## FURTHER READINGS

"*Aphrodite* Brings Fine." *New York Times* (June 24, 1930): 8.
"Book Scored, Seller Held." *New York Times* (March 5, 1930): 25.
"Class *Aphrodite* as Indecent Book." *New York Times* (June 14, 1930): 12.
Louÿs, Pierre. "Preface." *Aphrodite*. Trans. by Lewis Galantiere. New York: Modern Library, 1933.

# APPOINTMENT IN SAMARRA

**Author:** John O'Hara
**Original date and place of publication:** 1934, United States
**Original publisher:** Harcourt, Brace Publishing
**Type:** Novel

## SUMMARY

*Appointment in Samarra*, O'Hara's first novel after the successful publication of short stories, covers three days during the Prohibition era in the lives of the country club set in the fictional town of Gibbsville, Pennsylvania. The characters are driven by money, status and sex, and they worry continuously about which clubs, prep schools, colleges and other associations bring high social status.

The main plot concerns the social and moral disintegration of Julian English, son of a woman of means and a respected physician who heads the staff of the Gibbsville Hospital. Wealthy from childhood and well liked by women, Julian is married to Caroline Walker, to all appearances the ideal wife, but their marriage is strained by Julian's drinking and womanizing. The seemingly prosperous head of a Cadillac automobile dealership, Julian has mismanaged funds and must borrow $20,000 from a newly rich member of the country club, Harry Reilly. Resentful of the obligation and drinking heavily one evening, Julian throws a drink in Harry's face, blackening his eye with an ice cube. Rebuffed when he tries to apologize the next day, Julian then drinks even more heavily and commits suicide by sitting in his car in a closed garage with the motor running. Survivors are mystified, because they cannot see that Julian was any more unhappy than they.

Although no graphic sex scenes occur, sexual references are made and offensive ethnic comments appear throughout the novel. A character kids his wife that the newspaper reports that straitlaced Mervyn Schwartz has been "shot in a whorehouse last night." He then teases her that he plans to take his six-and-a-half-year-old son "out and get him laid tonight" and brags "when I was Teddy's age I had four girls knocked up." When a young woman rejects Julian's sexual advances, he has the desire "to call her all kinds of bitches." Throughout the novel, characters drink liquor heavily and there are numerous instances in which they are drunk. The mobsters in the town are of Italian background, and they are also the grade-school dropouts with long arrest records.

Anti-Semitism is even more pronounced. A character awakens on Christmas morning, thinks disparagingly about Mrs. Bromberg across the street, feels momentarily guilty, then reminds herself that "Jews do not observe Christmas, except to make more money out of Christians, so you do not have to treat Jews any different on Christmas than on any other day." She considers that having the Bromberg family on their street has "hurt real estate values" and expresses concern that others will move into the neighborhood. "Pretty soon there would be a whole colony of Jews in the neighborhood, and the Flieglers and all the other nice children in the neighborhood would grow up with Jewish accents." At the hearing when Julian's death is ruled a suicide by the coroner, Dr. Moskowitz, Julian's father sees the verdict as revenge for having excluded Moskowitz from a dinner at the country club for the County Medical Society and thinks, "let the little kike quack Moskowitz have his revenge."

## CENSORSHIP HISTORY

*Appointment in Samarra* aroused criticism when it was first published from those who believed that it contained "thoroughgoing vulgarity . . . an insufferable vulgarity, which has crept into many of our supposedly advanced novels that someone not squeamish, nor unread in earlier literatures, must protest against. . . ." Aside from sporadic and weakly enforced pressure placed by the Watch and Ward Society on Boston booksellers to curtail sales of the novel because of its risqué language and situations, *Appointment in Samarra* was openly sold for nearly seven years without major protest.

In 1941, the novel was declared not mailable because of "obscene language," after the solicitor to the United States Department of the Post Office reviewed a copy of the novel. He then advised O'Hara's publisher of the ban, the impetus for which was a complaint brought by the New York Society for the Suppression of Vice that charged the book with being "of an obscene character" because of its sexual references and slurs on various ethnic groups. The post office department would not permit the work to be mailed, and the publisher was told that copies of the book would be confiscated. The novel remained on the United States Post Office's index of banned books through the mid-1950s.

The novel also attracted the attention of the National Organization for Decent Literature, a Roman Catholic organization that identified "objectionable" literature and advised members against reading "offensive" and "obscene" novels. In 1953, NODL found the novel to be "objectionable" and placed it with O'Hara's *Ten North Frederick* on their list of blacklisted books. The list was then sent to cooperating book dealers who agreed to remove the book from their racks. Such NODL blacklists resulted in elaborate collegial pressure among booksellers, although not legal enforcement against the work. Instead, the organization supplied cooperating booksellers with a certificate to display, containing the following notice: "This store has satisfactorily complied with the request of the Committee [the local committee of the NODL] to remove all publications listed as 'OBJECTIONABLE' by the National Organization for Decent Literature from its racks during the above month." As a result of NODL action, the work was banned from sale in St. Cloud, Minnesota; Port Huron, St. Clair County, Michigan; and Detroit.

Sales were limited in numerous other cities, through the efforts of local chapters, until the demise of the organization in the late 1950s.

## FURTHER READINGS

Bruccoli, Matthew Joseph. *The O'Hara Concern: A Biography of John O'Hara*. New York: Random House, 1975.

Paul, James C. N., and Murray L. Schwartz. *Federal Censorship: Obscenity in the Mail*. New York: Free Press of Glencoe, 1961.

Podhoretz, Norman. "Gibbsville and New Leeds: The America of John O'Hara and Mary McCarthy." *Commentary* (March 1956): 493–499.

Trilling, Lionel. "John O'Hara Observes Our Mores." *New York Times Book Review* (March 18, 1945): 1, 9. Reprinted as the introduction to *Selected Short Stories of John O'Hara*. New York: Random House, 1956.

# AS I LAY DYING

**Author:**   William Faulkner
**Original date and place of publication:**   1930, United States
**Original publisher:**   Jonathan Cape & Harrison Smith, Inc.
**Literary form:**   Novel

## SUMMARY

The novel tells the story of a poor white Mississippi farm family. Mother Addie Bundren is dying. Using multiple points of view and short, quick-paced chapters, the author chronicles and examines the feelings and reactions of each character to her dying as well as to the death itself. The feelings portrayed are raw and often selfish, as Faulkner uses regional dialect, stream-of-consciousness and interior monologue to provide a realistic view of a family in crisis. As the novel progresses, ensuing sections reveal the basic selfishness of the family members, including the dying woman, and of others who make up this microcosm.

Surviving family members consist of Addie's husband, Anse, her four sons and one daughter who must all deal with the struggle between their self-centeredness and fulfilling their late mother's final wish to be buried in the family cemetery in Jefferson. The cemetery is a day's ride from their farm, and several seasonal obstacles must be overcome. Heavy rains and an overflowing river upset their wagon and drown their mules. In the process, the coffin containing Addie falls off the wagon and nearly washes down the river. After substantial frustration and significant effort on the part of all family members, Addie's final wish is granted, and she is buried in the family cemetery. By the time the process is complete, Addie has been dead for 10 days, and the odorous nature of the decaying body in the Mississippi heat is noted frequently.

Throughout the story, each character reflects upon his or her past, using occasional epithets in realistically portrayed inner monologues. Addie is revealed to be a former schoolteacher, whose married life and drudgery made her an embittered and controlling woman even to the end. Her son Cash builds the coffin outside his dying mother's window, because she wants to make certain of the quality of the finished product. That same son appears to be more interested in crafting a perfect coffin than in grieving for his mother. Addie's daughter eagerly supports the trip to Jefferson to bury her mother, despite the effort and sacrifice, because she is secretly pregnant and the town of Jefferson will offer the opportunity for an abortion. Anse, Addie's husband, professes great love and devotion to his late wife, but he is more interested in going to Jefferson to be fitted for false teeth. Addie's other children recall their own fears, doubts and anxieties, at times questioning the mercy of God for allowing suffering, both their mother's and theirs. At the end of the novel, only a short while after the decomposed body has finally been buried, Anse marches toward his children, with newly bought false teeth in his mouth and the next Mrs. Bundren following close behind.

## CENSORSHIP HISTORY

In 1986, Graves County School District, in Mayfield, Kentucky, banned the novel from the school classrooms and libraries, charging that it used "offensive and obscene passages referring to abortion and used God's name in vain." The ban was heartily supported by the Graves County Baptist Association, an organization that represented the 41 Baptist churches in the county. Two weeks later, after the story had been in numerous newspapers and the American Civil Liberties Union had intervened, the school board reversed the decision and the novel returned to the curriculum.

The following year, parents challenged the inclusion of the novel as required reading in the advanced English class at Pulaski County High School in Somerset, Kentucky. They claimed that the book was inappropriate because of its profanity and the contemplation of masturbation by one character. The book was retained. It was also challenged and then retained in the Carroll County, Maryland, school district, where in 1991 two school board members expressed concern regarding the use of coarse language and uneducated Southern dialect.

In 1994, the novel was banned for a few months by officials at Central High School, in Louisville, Kentucky, due to its profanity and the questions that various characters express regarding the existence of God.

## FURTHER READINGS

Blaine, Diana York. "The Abjection of Addie and Other Myths of the Maternal in *As I Lay Dying*." *Mississippi Quarterly* 47 (Summer 1994): 418–419.

Hale, Dorothy J. "*As I Lay Dying*'s Heterogeneous Discourse." *Novel: A Forum on Fiction* 23 (Fall 1989): 5–23.

Hayes, Elizabeth. "Tension Between Darl and Jewel." *Southern Literary Journal* 24 (Spring 1992): 49–61.

Kincaid, Nanci. "As Me and Addie Lay Dying." *Southern Review* 30 (Summer 1994): 582–595.

*Newsletter on Intellectual Freedom* (November 1986): 208; (May 1987): 90; (March 1992): 64; (November 1994): 189.

Noble, William. *Bookbanning in America: Who Bans Books?—And Why?* Middlebury, Vt.: Paul S. Eriksson, Publisher, 1990.

Reichman, Henry. *Censorship and Selection: Issues and Answers for Schools*. Chicago: American Library Association; Arlington, Va.: American Association of School Administrators, 1993.

# THE AUTOBIOGRAPHY OF BENJAMIN FRANKLIN

**Author:**  Benjamin Franklin
**Original date and place of publication:**  1791, France
**Original publisher:**  Buisson
**Literary type:**  Memoir

## SUMMARY

*The Autobiography of Benjamin Franklin* is an honest and sometimes lusty chronicle of a man who lived life fully. Franklin originally began to write his memoirs for his son, William Franklin, from whom he later became estranged. The *Autobiography* relates the author's rise from poverty as the youngest of 17 children of a soap and candle maker through his apprenticeship as a printer and to his role as Pennsylvania's agent in England in 1757. He provides details regarding his constant struggle to improve himself in education and in business and explains his passion for improvement, of both self and the public. The *Autobiography* ends when Franklin's activities reach an international scope, and he becomes a truly public figure.

Despite the emphasis upon moral improvement in much of the *Autobiography*, Franklin also admits to human failings. He acknowledges that the "hard-to-be-governed passion of youth had hurried me frequently into intrigues with low women that fell in my way, which were attended with some expense and great inconvenience, besides a continual risk to my health by a distemper." He also admits that he has been the victim of passionate bouts of indulgence, and that he has not always stood by his beliefs. Instead, he changed "opinions which I had thought right but found otherwise."

In one episode, Franklin speaks of his hasty departure from Boston in 1723 and writes that he left people to speculate that he left because he "got a naughty Girl with Child." In a later episode, Franklin recounts the incident that caused a breach with a friend named James Ralph, who left behind a wife and child when he traveled to England with Franklin to find work. Ralph began an affair with a young Englishwoman, Mrs. T., and they had a child. Unable to find work teaching in London, Ralph left to teach in a country school and asked Franklin to look after Mrs. T. Franklin lent her money and responded to her frequent calls for assistance. On one of those visits, he "attempted familiarities, which she repulsed with proper resentment," and later told Ralph.

The *Autobiography* presents a very human view of a well-known historical figure.

## CENSORSHIP HISTORY

Franklin's *Autobiography* is one of the most frequently expurgated books ever published in America, and it was censored from its first publication. In 1789, Franklin sent copies of the manuscript to friends Benjamin Vaughn and Guillaume Le Veillard, the mayor of Passy, France, asking for their advice. After Franklin died in 1790, a pirated edition of the book appeared in France. With the goal of publishing a more "acceptable" version, Franklin's grandson, William Temple Franklin, edited the French version, which he published in 1818 as part of the comprehensive *Works*. This edition made 1,200 changes in the phrasing of the original *Autobiography* with the expressed aim of modernizing the language for the 19th century. Instead, the changes altered Benjamin Franklin's sometimes salty tone and word choice, providing a vastly different view.

In 1886, Houghton Mifflin published an edition of the *Autobiography* which included the story of James Ralph's affair with the young woman but removed Franklin's admission of a sexual advance. Instead, the editor inserted this explanation of the strained relationship between the old friends: "In the mean time other circumstances made a breach." In 1888, Ginn & Company removed the entire episode. Houghton Mifflin retained the expurgated account in its 1892 edition, but the editor, Middlebury College professor Julian Abernethy, changed the substituted statement to read, "In the mean time another matter which gave offense made a breach." The publishers justified these and similar changes in nearly a dozen editions on the grounds that they were meant for high school students, who must be protected.

Franklin published more overtly bawdy works that earned the approval of his peers, but which are not frequently found among suggested readings. In his "Advice to a Young Man on the Choice of a Mistress," Franklin suggests that more pleasure can be found with an older woman than with a younger because "regarding what is below the Girdle, it is impossible of two Women to tell an old one from a young one" and "They [old women] are so grateful!" In "Polly Baker's Speech," printed in *Gentleman's Magazine* in 1747, he purports to speak as a New England woman who defends herself for being brought to trial, yet again, for having another illegitimate child. Franklin takes flatulence as his subject in "To the Royal Academy at Brussels," in which he parodies scientific reports in the suggestion that chemical additives to food might make "Wind from bowels" less offensive and puns using the slang term "fart."

As Chief Judge Clarke noted in *Roth v. United States, 345 U.S. 476 (1957)*, the discussed works by Franklin "which a jury could reasonably find 'obscene,' according to the judge's instructions in the case at bar" would also have subjected a person to prosecution if sent through the mails in 1957 and "to punishment under the federal obscenity statute." The judge further noted that Thomas Jefferson wrote approvingly of "Polly Baker's Speech" and that James Madison not only praised Franklin's humor but wrote similarly Rabelaisian anecdotes. That Franklin is popularly known as "the father of the Post Office" (he was designated postmaster general by the First Continental Congress) is ironic, because his own works, with their tongue-in-cheek sexual references, would have been considered too obscene to mail according to federal statutes such as the Comstock Act which applied to such matters until recent years.

## FURTHER READINGS

Haney, Robert W. *Comstockery in America: Patterns of Censorship and Control.* Boston: Beacon Press, 1960.

Larabee, Leonard W., ed. *The Autobiography of Benjamin Franklin.* New Haven, Conn.: Yale University Press, 1964.

Padover, Saul Kussiel. *The Complete Jefferson.* New York: Duell, Sloan & Pearce, 1943.

———. *The Complete Madison.* New York: Harper & Brothers, 1953.

Perrin, Noel. *Dr. Bowdler's Legacy: A History of Expurgated Books in England and America.* Boston: David R. Godine, Publisher, 1992.

Van Doren, Carl. *Ben Franklin.* New York: Bramhall House, 1987.

## THE AUTOBIOGRAPHY OF MALCOLM X

**Author:**   Malcolm X, with Alex Haley
**Original date and place of publication:**   1965, United States
**Original publisher:**   Grove Press
**Literary type:**   Autobiography

## SUMMARY

The autobiography articulates the anger, the struggle and the beliefs not only of Malcolm X but of many African Americans during the 1960s. The work charts the development of the African-American leader from his birth as Malcolm Little in 1925 in Omaha, Nebraska, to his assassination in New York City in 1965. Throughout, he uses fiery rhetoric to preach revolution to African Americans as the only means by which they can achieve full social equality.

As background to his beliefs, he relates the main abuses that occurred in his own life. He recalls his father's adherence to the philosophy of black separatist Marcus Garvey and relates the threats he and his seven siblings endured because of his father's fiery preaching. The work not only chronicles the author's life, but it also presents a sociological examination of the changing roles and growing social and political awareness of African Americans in the United States over four decades.

Particular bitterness is aimed at the welfare system, with its white caseworkers, which strikes a final blow against his family. After their father is murdered, his mother is left a widow with eight children to support, and she works hard at whatever jobs are available to keep the family together. Yet, intrusive caseworkers keep a constant watch on the Little home, finally placing the children in foster care and committing Mrs. Little to the state mental hospital at Kalamazoo, Michigan, where she has a mental breakdown after her children are removed. Such images stayed with the author, despite his early efforts to be a "good Negro" and to play the role that white society expected of him.

The autobiography candidly admits that he "tried to be white," like many other lighter-skinned African Americans of his day. From having his hair "conked" (straightened) to buying a "zoot suit" to conducting a five-year affair with a blonde white woman, he allows himself to be "brainwashed." He becomes involved in substantial illegal activity, from running a numbers racket to pimping, selling drugs and committing robberies. When caught, he claims that he received a much longer jail term than usual because he was involved with a white woman.

At the age of 21, he begins serving seven years in jail. There he learns about the Nation of Islam and becomes a member of the Black Muslim faith. After his conversion and release from prison, the author drops the name Little, his "slave name," and takes "X" to denote an unknown quantity as his last name.

The second half of the autobiography relates the author's efforts to advance the Black Muslim cause, his gradual disillusionment with Black Muslim leader Elijah Muhammad and his eventual expulsion from the Nation of Islam. He describes his experiences in visiting Africa as well as in the United States, speaking frequently at college campuses and influencing new converts. He also relates the betrayal that he experienced when rumors of an assassination plot surfaced from within the Nation of Islam.

The final three chapters of the work detail the reasons why Malcolm X left the Nation of Islam to form his own organization, Muslim Mosque, Inc. Later called the Organization of Afro-American Unity, its tone was one of militant black nationalism. As threats on his life occurred, the author became certain that the Nation of Islam was the source of the various attacks and threats. In the Epilogue, Alex Haley notes that Malcolm X became convinced that he would be murdered and felt that he would be a martyr "in the cause of brotherhood." His final hope for the autobiography was that it would motivate social action.

## CENSORSHIP HISTORY

*The Autobiography of Malcolm X* was deliberately kept out of classrooms and school libraries when it first appeared because the work openly criticized the role of white society in restricting the achievements and accomplishments of African Americans in the United States. Parents complained that the language was "filthy" and "racist," and the work was viewed for years largely as a radical text that had no place in the high school curriculum, although it enjoyed substantial popularity on college campuses during the 1960s and 1970s. Librarians used "selection" as the criterion for excluding the work from public libraries in predominantly white communities. By the 1980s, the work had come to be viewed as a historical work and the language and situations, including those in which Malcolm X uses street vernacular and candidly describes the illegal and immoral activities of his early life, seemed commonplace. The 1992 film, *Malcolm X*, directed by Spike Lee, reawakened interest in the book and high schools added it to their reading lists.

In 1993, parents in the Duval County (Florida) public schools challenged the use of this book in the curriculum, charging that the anti-white racism and the violence espoused by the assassinated Black Muslim leader were disruptive of racial harmony. Citing passages from the book, the parents identified "vulgar" language and "criminal" acts that they felt did not provide decent models for their children to emulate.

The Jacksonville (Florida) school district restricted the availability of the book in the middle school libraries in 1994, after parents complained to the school board that the book was a "how-to" manual for crime and that it represented white people as racist in their views. Only students who had notes from their parents were allowed to take the book out.

## FURTHER READINGS

Carson, Clayborne. *Malcolm X: The FBI File*. New York: Carroll & Graf, Publishers, 1991.

Dyson, Michael Eric. *Making Malcolm: The Myth and Meaning of Malcolm X*. New York: Oxford University Press, 1994.

Early, Gerald. "Their Malcolm, My Problem." *Harper's* 285 (December 1992): 62–74.

*Newsletter for Intellectual Freedom* (September 1993): 147; (May 1994): 83.

Vincent, Ted. "The Garveyite Parents of Malcolm X." *Black Scholar* 20 (March 1989): 10–13.

# THE AUTOBIOGRAPHY OF MISS JANE PITTMAN

**Author:**   Ernest J. Gaines
**Original date and place of publication:**   1971, United States
**Original publisher:**   Bantam Books
**Literary type:**   Novel

## SUMMARY

Written from the point of view of a 110-year-old former slave, *The Autobiography of Miss Jane Pittman* celebrates the life of a woman from her birth into slavery to the beginning of the civil rights movement in the United States. Divided into parts entitled "The War Years," "Reconstruction," "The Plantation" and "The Quarters," the episodic novel is structured as an oral history project undertaken by an African-American history teacher interviewing Miss Jane, whose voice and personality direct the story.

The novel opens with a young Jane, still bearing her slave name Ticey, serving water to a Yankee soldier on a Louisiana plantation near the end of the Civil War. The soldier tells her that she should replace the name Ticey with the more attractive Jane, which she does and for which she later suffers a beating from her mistress, who tries to force Jane to respond to the old slave name. The change of name corresponds to a change of attitude as the formerly mischievous slave girl becomes self-reliant and assumes responsibility for herself as well as for young Ned Douglass, whose mother is beaten to death by racist vigilantes. Hoping for a better life, she flees to the North with the child but finds the promised land to be only an illusion. Jane returns to Louisiana, where she meets and falls in love with horse trainer Joe Pittman, whose name she takes when they live together. The two are happy together for seven years despite Jane's inability to have children, but Joe is killed trying to tame a wild black stallion.

In the years that follow, Jane experiences the dehumanizing effects of institutionalized racism and loses her beloved Ned, who is murdered by white racists after he begins speaking out about racial dignity and assertiveness. A half century passes and the civil rights movement erupts in Louisiana, led by young civil rights worker Jimmy Aaron, who is following the example of Dr. Martin Luther King. Successful in mobilizing African-American citizens in a nearby town, Jimmy becomes a threat and is also murdered by white racists. The novel ends with the 110-year-old Jane Pittman preparing to go into town to lend her support to the civil rights movement by attempting to drink from a "whites-only" water fountain.

The novel contains numerous instances of language unfavorable to African Americans, spoken by both races. As Miss Jane herself says approvingly of Louisiana governor Huey Long at one point, "When he said nigger he said, 'Here a book, nigger. Go read your name.' When the other ones said nigger, they said, 'Here a sack, nigger. Go pick that cotton.'" The offensive term and other words of derision are spoken by white characters who aim insults at African Americans. In addition, characters of both races use a range of slang terms and insults.

## CENSORSHIP HISTORY

The novel has frequently been the source of complaints from both white and African-American parents and students who charge that *The Autobiography of Miss Jane Pittman* contains obscene and inappropriate language as well as incidents that promote immoral behavior. The complaints range from the frequency with which both African-American and white characters use the racial slur "nigger" to charges of stereotyping and improper references in the text. Early in the book, a "slow wit" who has taken the free name of Brown is described as "opening and closing his mouth like a baby after his mama's titty." The behavior of characters has also motivated complaints. Parents have voiced objections to the positive manner in which Gaines portrays the relationship of Miss Jane with Joe Pittman, a seven-year live-in relationship during which they fail to marry even though she takes his name.

Objections have also been raised in regard to the section entitled "Plantation," in which a young mixed-race woman employed on the plantation as a teacher for the workers' children is said to have been "ravished" by the son of the white plantation owner. Although the most frequently voiced concern is the reference to violent sexual activity, a small number of white parents contend that the portrayal of the white man as the ravisher perpetuates unfavorable stereotypes. Beyond these aspects of the book, the use of dialect by the African-American characters has also raised concerns because such use of language makes the characters appear ignorant.

Gaines has been told that his book is unacceptable in many schools for even stranger reasons. The author spoke, in an interview, of "a white teacher in Mississippi at one time who told me that black students didn't want to read the book because of certain terms used." That same teacher told him that white students also did not want to read it "because they felt that the black characters in the book were all angels."

In January 1995, parents in Conroe (Texas) Independent School District complained that the book contained racial slurs and demanded that it be withdrawn from a junior high school course in racial tolerance. A school spokesperson stated that the parents "'expressed concerns that the students were made uncomfortable when passages from this book were read aloud prior to discussion of the passage.'" A school committee determined that the novel was not appropriate for use, and the school board ordered the book withdrawn from the classroom.

## FURTHER READINGS

Babb, Valerie Melissa. *Ernest Gaines*. Boston: Twayne Publishers, 1991.

Gaines, Ernest. *Porch Talk with Ernest Gaines: Conversations on the Writers' Craft*. Baton Rouge: Louisiana State University Press, 1990.

"'Miss Jane Pittman' Is Removed from a Class at Blacks' Behest." *New York Times* (January 22, 1995): A19.

*Newsletter on Intellectual Freedom* (March 1995): 46.

Popkin, Michael. *Modern Black Writers*. New York: Frederick R. Ungar Publishing, 1978.

# BEING THERE

**Author:**   Jerzy Kosinski
**Original date and place of publication:**   1970, United States
**Original publisher:**   Harcourt Brace Jovanovich
**Type:**   Novel

## SUMMARY

*Being There* is a cynical look at the American political and intellectual scene as viewed through the eyes of Chance, a man whose whole life has been spent in tending a garden and passively watching television. He is a man without a past whose identity is formed by circumstances, and his perceptions of the world and of others reflect what he has seen on television. When he is forced to leave his home and to navigate the modern world, his simple answers related to gardening are taken by statesmen, financiers and the news media to be brilliant assessments of the political and economic scene. Within four days of leaving his anonymous existence, he is considered as a candidate for vice president of the United States.

At the outset, Chance maintains the garden and grounds for a wealthy patron called simply Old Man. An orphan, his mother died when he was born and he never learns the identity of his father, Chance cannot read or write and brain damage from birth has limited him to life in his quarters and the garden. He must do exactly as told or risk being sent to a home for the insane where, as the Old Man tells him, he would be locked in a cell. Thus, his only contact with the outside world is through the large color television in his room. In this surreal world, Chance controls life by rapidly turning the television dial to make images flip past each other and raising and lowering the volume at will.

Once the Old Man dies, estate lawyers determine that no record of Chance exists. He has no birth certificate, and he has never paid taxes, served in the army or visited a doctor or dentist. Forced to leave his home, Chance dresses in one of his late employer's expensive suits, packs an expensive leather suitcase and steps into the street, where he is promptly hit by the luxurious limousine of wealthy Elizabeth Eve Rand. Married to the much older, ailing Benjamin Rand, EE, as she is called in the novel, insists that "Chance, the former gardener," whose name she misinterprets to be Chauncey Gardiner, go home with her to receive medical attention and to have a place to recuperate. Her husband is a close adviser to the president of the United States, who visits the day after Chance arrives. When both men invite Chance to air his views regarding the nation's economy, he responds in terms of gardening with what appear to be highly appropriate metaphors to the two powerhouses. The president later quotes Chance in a televised speech, and the media mistakenly assume that he is a major financier, statesman and presidential adviser. Asked to escort EE, head of a major United Nations committee, to a United Nations function, Chance attracts the attention of the Russian ambassador, who mistakenly believes that he not only speaks Russian but is pro-Soviet in his political and economic sympathies. The ambassador also quotes Chance in a televised speech.

As Chance hobnobs with important people, his physical attractiveness draws both male and female admirers. At one official reception, a well-dressed, silver-haired man suggests a sexual encounter, but Chance does not understand what he means because nothing of the sort has ever appeared on television. Thus, he tells the man that he chooses to watch, not participate. As they ride in the elevator, the man "thrust his hand into Chance's groin." Chance remains the spectator, watching as the man "cupped his own flesh in a hand, groaning and jerking and trembling as he did so . . . the erect extended part grew stiffer . . . a white substance coursed forth in short spurts." Chance also tells EE that he wants to watch when she approaches him for sex, and she masturbates as he watches her writhing with pleasure. Afterward, she compliments him for uncoiling her wants, for with him "desires flow within me. . . . You make me free." At one point, Chance examines his body to see how his sexual organ compares with those pictured in the pornography that a maintenance man had once shown him, but finds that "his organ was small and limp; it did not protrude in the slightest. . . . Though Chance prodded and massaged his organ, he felt nothing . . . his organ refused to stiffen out; it gave him no pleasure at all."

As Chance's detached attitude in his sexual encounters passes for experience, his lack of involvement and total obliviousness to the prevailing political and social realities pass for wisdom. At the end of the novel, the president decides to choose Chance as his running mate, because the lack of any past makes him the perfect candidate with no sins to live down.

## CENSORSHIP HISTORY

*Being There* has been challenged in high schools for containing "inappropriate images" and for its depiction of masturbation and the homosexual near-experience of the main character. Critics have charged that the book is "sex-oriented" and that the sexual content and "suggestive language" are unsuitable for high school students.

Parents of students attending Crete (Nebraska) High School in 1989 criticized the inclusion of the book as a reading assignment for the eleventh-grade English class and requested that the requirement be changed. School board officials determined that the book should remain as one of several choices of reading assignment, with suitable alternatives provided to those who preferred not to read it. Also in 1989, parent objections to the homosexual encounter of the main character resulted in the removal of the book from Mifflinberg (Pennsylvania) High School classes. After reconsideration of the text and the removal of the book from the recommended list, the book was reinstated for use as an alternative reading choice.

In 1993, parents of students enrolled in a senior advanced English course in the Davenport, Iowa, high school challenged the inclusion of the work as a required reading, claiming that the description of masturbation was too graphic and unnecessary to the text. After reconsideration, school board officials reversed themselves and the teacher removed it from the required list.

## FURTHER READINGS

*Newsletter on Intellectual Freedom* (May 1989): 79, 93; (July 1993): 105.

Sloan, James Park. *Jerzy Kosinski: A Biography*. New York: E.P. Dutton and Company, 1996.

———. "Kosinski's War." *New Yorker* (October 10, 1994): 46–53.

Straus, Dorothea. "Remembering Jerzy Kosinski." *Partisan Review* 60 (Winter 1993): 138–142.

## THE BELL JAR

**Author:**   Sylvia Plath
**Original date and place of publication:**   1963, United Kingdom
**Original publisher:**   William Heinemann Ltd.
**Type:**   Novel

### SUMMARY

*The Bell Jar*, first published under the pseudonym of Victoria Lucas, is a thinly veiled autobiographical account of the inner conflict, mental breakdown and later recovery of a female college student in the 1950s. The novel covers approximately eight months in the life of Esther Greenwood, the 19-year-old narrator, and the plot is divided into three parts. In the first part, Esther embarks on a one-month residence in New York City as a guest editor for the college issue of a fashion magazine. Once in the city, she recalls key incidents from the past, exhibiting her emotional and mental disintegration as the recollections become more real and meaning-filled to her than incidents in her daily life. Her unsatisfactory relationships with men dominate her thoughts, and the reader learns of her disappointing date with Constantin, who makes no attempt to seduce her, the brutal and woman-hating Marco, who beats her up, and her conventional and ordinary college boyfriend Buddy Willard, who wants marriage and a traditional life. At the end of the first part, her last night in New York, Esther throws all her clothes off the hotel roof in a mock ceremony that reveals her disorientation.

In the second part, covering chapters 10 through 13, Esther's psychological deterioration continues as she returns home to see the "white, shining, identical clap-board houses with their interstices of well-groomed green [that] proceeded past, one bar after another in a large but escape-proof cage." Increasingly depressed, Esther cannot work or sleep, and she refuses to wash her hair or to change her clothes. Shock treatments deepen her depression and increase her obsession with death and suicide. At the end of this part, Esther visits her father's grave, then crawls beneath her house and consumes sleeping pills until she becomes unconscious.

The third section of the novel, chapters 14 through 20, details Esther's slow and painful recovery after the suicide attempt. She resists all efforts to help her when first hospitalized in the psychiatric ward of a public facility, but her move to a private mental hospital produces great progress. During short leaves from the hospital, she goes to Boston and obtains a diaphragm, then experiences her first sexual encounter, a wholly unpleasant experience. Despite this disillusionment, and despite the death of Joan, another mental patient to whom she has become close, Esther looks forward to leaving the mental asylum and returning to college. Yet, she remains unsure if she will have another breakdown: "How did I know that someday—at college, in Europe, somewhere, anywhere—the bell jar, with its stifling distortions, wouldn't descend again?"

## CENSORSHIP HISTORY

*The Bell Jar* has been challenged for its characters' discussions of sexuality and because it advocates an "objectionable" lifestyle. In one instance, the main character observes that her boyfriend's genitals are disappointing because they remind her of "turkey neck and turkey gizzards." The young college women yearn for sexual experience, and the main character purchases a diaphragm and seeks an anonymous sexual encounter. Beyond perceived obscenity, the novel aroused challenges because it openly rejects traditional marriage and motherhood. Characterizing marriage as a prison of dull domestic duties, Plath describes mothers as drudges with dirty, demanding children, while wives are subservient and inferior to their husbands.

In 1977 in Warsaw, Indiana, Teresa Burnau, a first-year English teacher at Warsaw Community High School, was assigned to teach an elective course entitled "Women in Literature" using texts that had previously been approved and ordered for the course. Before school began in September, the principal ordered Burnau to remove the literary anthology *Growing Up Female in America* and the novel *The Stepford Wives* from the reading list. The books were removed because "someone in the community might be offended by their criticism of traditional roles for women." By mid-October, the principal demanded that GO ASK ALICE also be removed from the list, because it contained "dirty" words. In November, the principal directed that Burnau remove *The Bell Jar* from her list, after reviewing the book and determining that it was "inappropriate" because it spoke of a birth control device (the diaphragm) and used "profanity." Burnau's written protest brought the warning that she would be dismissed for insubordination if she included that book. Although Burnau complied with the demand and dropped the book, the principal later wrote in her evaluation that she exhibited "resentment and a poor attitude" when told not to use *The Bell Jar*. The school board did not rehire Burnau, giving only the reason that she failed to meet her responsibilities and displayed "a poor attitude."

A 17-year-old Warsaw Community High School student and her family challenged the decision of the board. In early 1979, Brooke Zykan, her brother Blair and her parents became the plaintiffs in a suit that charged the school district with violating the First and 14th Amendment rights of students and called for the court to reverse the school board decision to remove the books, which also included *The Feminine Plural: Stories by Women About Growing Up* and *The New Women: A Motive Anthology of Women's Liberation*. A group called People Who Care was formed to deal with the controversy and to further the aim of removing "filthy" material from the classroom and to press their agenda. As one member stated, "School decisions should be based on the absolutes of Christian behavior." In *Zykan v. Warsaw (IN) Community School Corporation and Warsaw School Board of Trustees (1980)*, the plaintiffs claimed that the school board had removed the books from classrooms because "words in the books offended social, political, and moral tastes and not because the books, taken as a whole, were lacking in educational value."

The American Civil Liberties Union attorney associated with the case hoped that the state would recognize academic freedom as a First Amendment right. The suit charged that the school officials had violated students' "right to know" and the constitutional guarantee of academic freedom, but on December 3, 1979, the Indiana District Court rejected these claims and dismissed the suit. The plaintiffs appealed the decision, but the Court of Appeals sided with the school board and proclaimed that the school board had not violated anyone's constitutional rights, because the right of "academic freedom" is limited at the secondary school level. On August 22, 1980, Judge Walter J. Cummings of the Seventh Circuit Court determined that "the student's right to and need for such freedom is bounded by the level of his or her intellectual development" and noted that the local school board has many powers to regulate high school classrooms. This case further strengthened the authority of school boards to select and remove books from school libraries and classrooms and provided warning to individuals who sought academic freedom within the school structure.

## FURTHER READINGS

Alexander, Paul. *Rough Magic: A Biography of Sylvia Plath*. New York: Viking Press, 1991.
Butscher, Edward. *Sylvia Plath: Method and Madness*. New York: Seabury Press, 1975.
Hawthorn, Jeremy. *Multiple Personality and the Disintegration of Literary Character: From Oliver Goldsmith to Sylvia Plath*. New York: Ballantine Books, 1983.
MacPherson, Pat. *Reflecting in the Bell Jar*. New York: Routledge Kegan Paul, 1991.
*Newsletter on Intellectual Freedom* (March 1980): 40; (July 1981): 102.

## THE BEST SHORT STORIES BY NEGRO WRITERS

**Editor:**   Langston Hughes
**Original date and place of publication:**   1967, United States
**Original publisher:**   Little, Brown & Company
**Literary type:**   Short story collection

## SUMMARY

The work is a collection of 47 short stories, which form a comprehensive anthology of writings by African Americans, ranging in time from the first well-known writers Charles W. Chestnutt and Paul Laurence Dunbar through such popular writers of the 1960s as Ronald Milner, Robert Boles and Alice Walker. Also included are works by such noted African Americans as Jean Toomer, Richard Wright, Zora Neale Huston, Ralph Ellison, Willard Motley, John A. Williams, Frank Yerby and James Baldwin.

The subject matter of the stories ranges widely, from the fears, violence and lynchings experienced in the Deep South to the glittering interracial parties in the North during the Harlem Renaissance. They contain characters as diverse as the tragically overworked sharecroppers and the well-dressed, glamorous Harlem dancers. Characters in these stories exhibit the range of African-American experience in the United States over seven decades. The settings are equally diverse, including as they do the South, North, East, West, Panama Canal Zone, Chicago Loop and Harlem. The writers use dialect and realistic dialogue to provide a true-to-life portrayal of African Americans whose lives cover time periods from the Reconstruction through the Harlem Renaissance, the Depression, World War II and the 1960s.

In faithful renderings, the writers also reveal society across time without a polite veneer to soften the criticism. White Americans are not spared their criticism but neither are African Americans. People are portrayed both in their ordinary, day-to-day pursuits and in pursuits that are unique to their history. Several of the stories present light-skinned characters who "pass" to avoid discrimination and to gain a toehold in white society, but stories also appear whose characters wear their color proudly.

## CENSORSHIP HISTORY

In 1976, the school board of Island Trees (New York) Union Free District removed the short story collection from the junior and senior high school libraries along with *Black Boy*, THE FIXER, GO ASK ALICE, *Slaughterhouse-Five*, DOWN THESE MEAN STREETS, A HERO AIN'T NOTHIN' BUT A SANDWICH, *Laughing Boy*, THE NAKED APE, SOUL ON ICE and *A Reader for Writers*. The books were charged by complainants with being immoral, anti-American, anti-Christian or "just plain filthy." As entered in the court record, the specific objections to *The Best Short Stories by Negro Writers* concerned the use of street vernacular, as well as such allegedly obscene passages as the following: "You need some pussy. Come on, let's go up to the whore house on the hill." "She first became aware of the warm tense nipples on her breasts. Her hands went up gently to calm them." "In profile, his penis hung like a stout tassel. She could even tell that he was circumcised."

In deference to the protests of parents and students, the school board appointed a committee made up of parents and teachers to review the books and to determine which, if any, of the books had merit. The committee recommended that seven of the books be returned to the library shelves, that two be placed on restricted shelves and that two be removed from the library, but the school board ignored these recommendations and voted to keep all but one of the books off the shelves. One junior high school student and four high school students challenged this censorship, claiming that the school board had violated their constitutional rights under the guise of protecting their social and moral welfare. The case, *Board of Education v. Pico*, 457 U.S. 853, 102 S.Ct. 2799, 73 L.Ed.2s 435 (1982), was heard before a federal district court, which ruled in favor of the school board. The students appealed the decision, and the appellate court remanded the case for trial before the U.S. Supreme Court, which determined that the district court had acted without authority in rendering a summary decision against the students.

The justices were sharply divided and, in a 5-4 decision, upheld the right of the students to challenge the board's actions. The majority decision determined that a school board had the right to use its discretion in deciding issues within its district, but such decisions must be made within the boundaries of the First Amendment. In announcing the decision, Justice William J. Brennan wrote, "Local school boards have broad discretion in the management of school affairs but this discretion must be exercised in a manner that comports with the transcendent imperatives of the First Amendment; the First Amendment rights of students may be directly and sharply implicated by the removal of books from the shelves of a school library; and local school boards may not remove books from school library shelves simply because they dislike the ideas contained in those books."

In their dissenting opinion, Chief Justice Warren Burger and Justices Sandra D. O'Connor, Lewis Powell and William H. Rehnquist issued a warning as to the role of the Supreme Court in making local censorship decisions: "If the plurality's view were to become the law, the court would come perilously close to becoming a 'super censor' of school board library decisions and the Constitution does not dictate that judges, rather than parents, teachers, and local school boards, must determine how the standards of morality and vulgarity are to be treated in the classroom." Thus, in their reluctance to place the Supreme Court in the position of local censor, the conservative justices recommended that the task of setting local community standards remain in local hands.

The U.S. Supreme Court ruled against the school board on June 25, 1982 in *Board of Education, Island Trees Union Free School District No. 26 v. Pico*, and the books were returned to the libraries.

## FURTHER READINGS

Hurwitz, Leon. *Historical Dictionary of Censorship in the United States*. Westport, Conn.: Greenwood Press, 1985.

Jenkinson, Edward B. *Censors in the Classroom: The Mind Benders*. Carbondale: University of Southern Illinois Press, 1979.

*Newsletter on Intellectual Freedom* (May 1978): 57; (November 1982): 197.

Williams, John A. "Blackballing." In *Censored Books: Critical Viewpoints*. Ed. by Nicholas J. Karolides, Lee Burress and John M. Kean: 11–18. Metuchen, N.J.: Scarecrow Press, 1992.

## BLACK LIKE ME

**Author:**   John Howard Griffin
**Original date and place of publication:**   1961, United States
**Original publisher:**   Houghton Mifflin Company
**Literary type:**   Journal

## SUMMARY

Written in journal form, the personal narrative presents an introspective look at racism, examining its consequences in a chronicle of the experiences of a Caucasian social scientist who darkens his skin, shaves his head and assumes the life of an African-American man in the Deep South in 1959. The author acknowledges that as the result of this experiment his life and his views of both races must change forever. Griffin learns that, after having immersed himself in black culture and dealt with the white world as an African American, he can never again live completely as a Caucasian, for his views regarding his own race have changed.

In the opening pages of the work, the author identifies the background of his study and explains his reasons for concern with skin pigmentation. He rationalizes that, even though he is considered to be an expert on racial issues, he has no real idea of what it is like to be an African American and to live in the Deep South. After arranging funding with the magazine *Sepia*, the author travels to New Orleans, where he locates a doctor and begins to undergo the skin-darkening treatments that will change his racial appearance.

Griffin examines his anxiety once the dosage is stabilized and he completes his transformation. Wandering the New Orleans streets, he talks to people with whom he had spoken when he was white and observes a difference in their response now that he approaches them as an African American. He identifies the issues and problems that come with his new, nonwhite identity. First and foremost is the unwritten line between the black and the white races that he violates when he mistakenly allows a white woman to sit near his fellow blacks on a bus. His efforts to deal with the sometimes confusing segregation laws involving rest rooms and restaurants offer a strong indictment against a society that rigidly controlled the access of African Americans to necessities that white Americans could take for granted. In contrast, Griffin enjoys the acceptance of his newly adopted race when the one man in whom he confides his secret eases the transition by teaching him the informal rules of "Negro" behavior.

The author observes that life as an African American is difficult and that security and the respect of others are determined by skin color. As an African American, he is a more frequent target of violence and looked upon as little more than trash by society as a whole. By day he hunts for the jobs available to him as a black man, and for a semblance of humanity from the society in which he lives. By night, he roams the New Orleans pavements, falling deeper and deeper into his blackness. The author finds that other blacks treat him with a great deal of respect and kindness, more so than when he was white. But he also finds that white individuals have lost the humanity and respect they showed when he was white.

Griffin's divergent experiences lead him to postulate that the problem of the "Negro" is twofold. African Americans confront the racism and prejudice of white society, and they must also deal with self-hatred, low self-esteem and loss of pride. He suggests that the two races will be able to live in harmony only when these two ills are eradicated from society.

Griffin reports both blatant and subtle differences in the way that white society in New Orleans treats each race. In one instance, a woman who had conversed with him pleasantly when he was white refuses to cash a traveler's check for him when he is black, even though the transaction involves no financial risk. He observes that instances such as this are common for the black man, and learns that most cafés and bathrooms become off limits to him due to his dark skin color.

In order to widen the significance of the study, Griffin extended the setting to other cities in the South. His reported observations show that the response to his new identity remained relatively consistent. Griffin records that he was addressed by whites as "boy" or "nigger," and that the actions of whites grew increasingly difficult to tolerate as he experienced the persecution and bigotry of segregation and racism. In Mobile, Alabama, white men demanded to know his business in the area and threatened him with death should he cause trouble. Griffin reports that the way in which the threats were expressed strongly suggested that, if he were murdered, nothing would be done to identify his killers because of his race.

Shortly before terminating his one-month odyssey, the author experienced a revealing incident regarding the nature of white liberalism. Griffin visited the Tuskegee Institute for a day and met a visiting white academic who insisted on proving that he was a trustworthy white whom blacks should not fear. Despite good intentions, his ingrained prejudice emerged all too clearly when he suggested that a black man who was legitimately selling turkeys on the street might have stolen them.

The author reports in the final entries of the work that his experiment elicited hostility from people all over the country. He and his family received death threats and were forced to leave their home.

## CENSORSHIP HISTORY

The book has been one of the 30 most frequently attacked books in the United States since its first, partial appearance in 1960 as an article in *Sepia* magazine and its publication as a book in 1961. The principal charge, in most challenges, has been obscenity. Researchers, however, postulate that more likely the truth is that those who challenge the book are opposed to books about African Americans or other minorities. As one teacher stated in a 1982 nationwide survey conducted by Lee Burress, "'In a rural community, people don't care to have their children read about Negroes'." This position is supported by an examination of the 20 most frequently attacked titles between 1965 and 1977. One third depict individuals belonging to a minority group in strong protest against racism.

In 1966, the paperback edition of the novel was widely attacked as being unfit for children to read. In Wisconsin, a man sued the local school board, claiming that the book contained obscene language, that it was integration-centered, vulgar, filthy and unsuitable for any age level. He further charged that his child was damaged by having read the book as an assignment in English class. The court dismissed the case.

In 1967, the parent of an Arizona high school student challenged the use of the book in the classroom because of its obscene and vulgar language and the situations depicted. The school board removed the book from the classroom. Language, particularly "four-letter words," was the charge leveled in 1977 by a Pennsylvania parent and a clergyman, but the challenge was denied. An objection to the subject matter was similarly denied in a 1982 challenge of the book in Illinois. In Missouri in 1982, however, the material was placed on a closed shelf when a parent challenged the book on the grounds that it was obscene and vulgar and "because of black people being in the book."

## FURTHER READINGS

Burress, Lee. *Battle of the Books: Literary Censorship in the Public Schools, 1950–1985.* Metuchen, N.J.: Scarecrow Press, 1989.

Farrell, Walter C., Jr. "*Black Like Me*: In Defense of a Racial Reality." In *Censored Books: Critical Viewpoints.* Ed. by Nicholas Karolides, Lee Burress and John M. Kean: 117–124. Metuchen, N.J.: Scarecrow Press, 1993.

Griffin, John Howard. *Racial Equality: The Myth and the Reality.* ERIC Education Document Reprint Series, No. 26 (March 1971).

Sharpe, Ernest, Jr. "The Man Who Changed His Skin." *American Heritage* 40 (February 1989): 44–55.

# BLESS THE BEASTS AND CHILDREN

**Author:**   Glendon Swarthout
**Original date and place of publication:**   1970, United States
**Original publisher:**   Doubleday & Company
**Literary type:**   Novel

## SUMMARY

Swarthout's *Bless the Beasts and Children* is a novel that identifies the fears of six boys, ages 13 through 17, and examines how they bond to face these fears. The story takes place in the Box Canyon Boys Camp, a dumping ground for the misfit children of wealthy parents who are too busy with their own lives to give their children attention, and describes how six losers become winners on one supreme mission of peace and love.

The novel begins on a warm summer night, as Cotton, the leader of a group called the Bedwetters, is awakened by a bad dream in which he imagines the boys as hunted animals. He learns that one of the boys, Lally 2, is missing, so he awakens Lally 1, the missing boy's brother, and the rest of the Bedwetters.

Cotton informs the others that Lally 2 is missing, and the group leaves camp to find him. When they find Lally 2 near the main road, he refuses to go back with Cotton because of what he and the others had seen earlier that day. The reader is not yet made aware of the incident.

Cotton and the boys discuss breaking camp and completing a life-or-death mission. They vote, and the decision to go on with the mission is unanimous. Cotton gives the boys five minutes to return to the tent and pack for the long trip. They then push one of the trucks out of camp for Teft to hotwire but abandon this scheme when the incline becomes too steep. Instead, they ride horses into town, where Teft hotwires a pickup truck that they steal.

On the road, the six boys, none of whom possesses a driver's license, fear the police and keep a low profile to avoid arousing suspicion. They stop to eat at an all-night diner, where they are harassed by a couple of cowboys who joke about their ages. To avoid trouble, the boys return to the truck and drive off, but the two cowboys follow them. The two men run the pickup truck off the road and taunt the boys until Teft takes out a rifle and shoots the tires of the cowboys' car. This silences the two men and allows the boys to exit the scene with a modicum of pride.

As they near their destination, the pickup truck runs out of gas. Cotton tells them that they have an important decision to make. If they continue by foot and succeed at their mission, they will be found truant from camp and incarcerated. However, if they head back to camp, there is a good chance that they will not get caught. This is when the reader learns the purpose of the mission and the horror the boys had seen on the previous day. While returning from a camping excursion, they had gone to view some buffalo, but, to their utter dismay, it was slaughtering day for the poor beasts. People had been randomly chosen to kill the animals. This sent terror through the boys' hearts and motivated them to rescue the remaining buffalo.

Cotton votes to go back, but the rest of the boys vote to persevere and save the beasts, so Cotton joins them. They reach the buffalo preserve where, after a failed rescue attempt that almost kills five of the boys, Cotton devises a plan that will save the buffalo.

Teft will drive a game preserve truck through the field while several of the boys throw hay to entice the buffalo out of the pen. The buffalo will follow along while eating until they reach the distant fence that separates them from freedom and capture. This plan is automatically implemented, but the fence proves too strong for them to break through.

The boys also hear vehicles in the distance. Cotton orders Teft to fire the rifle at these vehicles in order to buy him some time. As Teft complies, Cotton boards the truck and revs the engine. Then, followed by about 40 buffalo, he crashes the truck into the fence, knocking it down and freeing the buffalo. He does not stop but continues along at full speed until the truck overturns and he is killed. The other vehicles arrive at the scene to find the buffalo free and the five boys crying.

## CENSORSHIP HISTORY

The ingenuity and independence of the boys have motivated parents and school officials to charge that the book is critical of parents and that it encourages critical attitudes toward authority. In addition, parents have charged that the book contains questionable subject matter, regarding the issues of bedwetting and running away, as well as "objectionable" language.

In 1978, parents in Wakesha, Wisconsin, complained that the novel was "psychopathically sick" and should not be required reading for students in the course entitled "Perspectives on Death and Aggression." The issue was heard by the school board, one member of which stated that endorsing the novel would be akin to "putting a rubber stamp" on violence. Although the boys are on a quest to save the buffalo from needless slaughter, the board member cited the descriptions of the slaughter and the boys' plan to rescue the buffalo as being unnecessarily "graphic." The school board voted to allow the course to continue but determined not to buy enough copies of the book for all enrolled students, so the teacher could not assign it to the class as a whole. Thus, while the board agreed that existing copies of the book would remain available for use by students in the course, their decision not to purchase enough books effectively prevented the entire class from discussing it.

In 1987, parents in Dupree, South Dakota, complained to the school board that the novel should not be allowed in the classroom because of its violent descriptions and obscene language. After considering the complaint, the school board banned the novel from all high school English classes, charging that it contained "offensive language and vulgarity."

## FURTHER READINGS

Jenkinson, Edward B. *Censors in the Classroom: The Mind Benders*. Carbondale, Ill.: Southern Illinois University Press, 1979.
*Newsletter on Intellectual Freedom* (January 1988): 12.
"Using Adolescent Novels as Transitions to Literary Classics: *Bless the Beasts and Children*." *English Journal* 78 (March 1989): 83–84.

# BLUBBER

**Author:** Judy Blume
**Original date and place of publication:** 1974, United States
**Original publisher:** Bradbury Press
**Type:** Young adult novel

## SUMMARY

*Blubber* teaches a lesson to all those children who take pleasure in tormenting an easy victim, by showing them that today's tormentor can easily become tomorrow's tormented. The novel opens in a fifth-grade classroom as students take turns giving oral reports on mammals. Students sitting in their seats pass around notes and pictures, look at the clock and yawn openly, while Mrs. Minish, the teacher, tries hard to look interested. Linda Fischer, "the pudgiest girl in our class, but not in our grade," is the last to report, and her study is about whales. She covers the topic methodically, then speaks about the removal and uses of whale blubber and shows the class a picture of blubber.

This gives her classmate Wendy an idea. She writes "Blubber is a good name for her" on a scrap of paper and passes it to Caroline, who then passes it to Jill Brenner. The note soon makes its way halfway around the class, creating a disruption as Linda tries valiantly to finish her report. On the bus after school, Jill and the other students tease Linda, calling her "Blubber," taking her jacket and covering her hair with spit balls.

Halloween is near, and Jill decides to be a "flenser," a person who strips the blubber off whales, a term that she learned from Linda's report. The students wear their costumes to school, and when Jill, Caroline and Wendy encounter Linda in the girls' room they strip off her costume cape and threaten to strip her entirely, because Jill is dressed as a flenser "and the flenser's the one who strips the blubber." They rip open her blouse and pull up her skirt. Then Wendy, dressed as a queen, commands Linda to kiss her sneaker. The frightened and crying girl obeys. That night, the girls wind toilet paper through the trees of the Fischer house, spray plastic string on the house and write "Blubber lives here" in blue chalk on the sidewalk.

At school, the fifth-grade students blame Linda for everything bad that happens to them, from low grades to being punished for talking. The abuse escalates until the class, usually left unmonitored in their room during lunch, decides to place Linda on trial. Wendy declares herself the judge and demands that Linda not have a lawyer. Jill, whose father is a lawyer, protests the "legality" of the trial and, with a sudden feeling of fair play, releases Linda from a locked closet.

The following day, Jill learns that Wendy has retaliated by declaring that she and Linda are now "best friends," and Jill becomes the class scapegoat. Labeled "B.B." for "Baby Brenner," because she refused to participate in the terrorizing, she is ostracized and mocked. Although despondent at first, Jill eventually resumes friendships with some of her less popular classmates.

## CENSORSHIP HISTORY

*Blubber* is one of many books written by Judy Blume that have been challenged in schools and libraries. Some of the challenges, notably those regarding *Forever*, *Deenie* and *Then Again, Maybe I Won't*, have resulted in restrictions and banning because of their sexual content that mirrors the realistic thoughts and actions of teenagers. Other books by Blume, such as *It's Not the End of the World*, *Starring Sally Freedman as Herself*, *Superfudge* and *Tiger Eyes*, have been challenged and banned because they contain what one community or another deems to be "objectionable" or "indecent or inappropriate" language or because the characters do not exhibit model behavior. *Blubber* is in the second category. Challenges to this novel have arisen, in part, because of the determined nastiness of the characters and the unwillingness of adults to stand up to these nasty children. Many people who have challenged the book also admit to having "a problem with the language."

In 1980, *Blubber* was removed from all of the elementary school libraries in Montgomery County, Maryland, and in 1981, the novel was temporarily banned in Sunizona, Arizona. In 1983, parents of students in the Des Moines, Iowa, schools challenged the book because of "objectionable" language, the same year that parents of students at Smith Elementary School in Del Valle, Texas, challenged the book because it contained the words "damn" and "bitch." They further complained that the book sets a bad example because it shows children cruelly teasing a classmate. The book was retained in both districts. Also in 1983, parents of students in the Xenia (Ohio) School District called for the removal of the novel from the school libraries, claiming that it "undermines authority since the word 'bitch' is used in connection with a teacher." It was also challenged in the Akron (Ohio) School District, where parents requested its removal from the school libraries. It was retained in both cases.

The novel was placed in "restricted areas" of the elementary school libraries in Lindenwold, New Jersey in 1984, because of "a problem with language." In the same year, parents of students in the Peoria (Illinois) School District complained that the novel contains "strong sexual content" and "obscene language" and cited its alleged "lack of social or literary value" in requesting its removal from the school libraries. After the book was considered by a specially created review committee, the school board voted to restrict it to students whose parents had given them written permission to take out the book.

In another 1984 incident, the novel was removed from Hanover (Pennsylvania) School District elementary and secondary school libraries, after parents challenged the book as being "indecent and inappropriate." The school board considered the book and decided to authorize its placement on the "restricted shelf." That same year, the book was also challenged but retained in the Casper, Wyoming, school libraries. In 1985, *Blubber* was challenged as "profane, immoral, and offensive" but retained in the Bozeman, Montana, school libraries.

In 1986, parents of students in Muskego (Wisconsin) Elementary School asked to have the book removed from the reading list because "the characters curse and the leader of the taunting [of an overweight girl] is never punished for her cruelty." A similar complaint was voiced in 1991 by parents of students at the Perry Township, Ohio, elementary schools who demanded the removal of the book from the school libraries; they claimed that the book contained no moral message. "Bad is never punished. Good never comes to the fore. Evil is triumphant." In both cases, the school boards decided that the book should remain.

## FURTHER READINGS

Clark, Elyse. "A Slow, Subtle Exercise in Censorship." *School Library Journal* 32 (March 1986): 93–96.
Donelson, Kenneth L., and Alleen Pace Nilsen. *Literature for Today's Young Adults.* Glenview, Ill.: Scott Foresman, 1989.
Klein, Norma. "Some Thoughts on Censorship: An Author Symposium." *Top of the News* 39 (Winter 1983): 137–153.
*Newsletter on Intellectual Freedom* (May 1980): 51; (March 1982): 57; (May 1982): 84; (July 1982): 124, 142; (May 1983): 73, 85–86; (July 1983): 121; (September 1983): 139, 153; (November 1983): 197; (November 1984): 185; (January 1985): 8–9; (March 1958): 3, 42, 58; (July 1985): 112; (January 1987): 31; (March 1992): 41; (July 1992): 124.
Webb, C. Anne. "The Battle Continues." *English Journal* 84 (September 1995): 123–124.

# BRAVE NEW WORLD

**Author:**   Aldous Huxley
**Original date and place of publication:**   England, 1932
**Original publisher:**   Chatto & Windus Collins
**Type:**   Novel

## SUMMARY

*Brave New World* is a satire in which science, sex and drugs have replaced human reason and human emotion in the "perfect" society to which Huxley gives the name "Utopia." The novel depicts an orderly society in which scientifically sophisticated genetics and pharmacology combine to produce a perfectly controlled population whose entire existence is dedicated to maintaining the stability of society. People are genetically engineered to satisfy the regulated needs of the government in regard to specific mental and physical sizes and types. Sexual promiscuity is demanded by the state for the sake of pleasure, not procreation, and women are equipped with contraceptive cartridge belts to avoid pregnancy. The only respectable way to enter the world is through incubation in a bottle—people are decanted rather than born— and learning occurs through preconditioning.

Inhabitants are created and conditioned to fit into specific social slots. Thus, in the Hatchery and Conditioning Center, varying amounts of alcohol are placed into the decanting bottles that contain the embryos to stunt mental growth and create a hierarchy of genetic classes.

Those who will be conditioned to do the monotonous and hard labor of this society receive the highest doses of alcohol to create a low mentality. Labeled in descending order of intelligence as Gammas, Deltas and Epsilons, they are the most numerous and are produced by subjecting the fertilized egg to the Bokanovsky Process, a budding procedure that enables division of the egg into as many as 96 identical beings from one egg and up to 15,000 brothers and sisters from a single ovary. The Alphas and Betas, who carry out the work of the government, remain individualized, yet they, too, are manipulated through early conditioning. The concept of family is unknown, and the terms "mother" and "father" are viewed as smut. In this systematically promiscuous world, men and women are encouraged to experience many sexual partners to avoid the development of intimate emotional relationships that might threaten their obsessive loyalty to the state.

The expected ills of human life have all been eliminated, and inhabitants of this brave new world have been freed of the worries of disease, pain, unhappiness, old age and death. Disease has been eradicated through sterilization and pain or unhappiness are easily banished by liberal doses of *soma*, a drug that provides a high without side effects. Smaller dosages are used to counteract depression, while larger dosages are taken to provide a long-term sense of euphoria, described by one character as a two-week vacation. Blind happiness is necessary for social stability, so all emotions are dulled. Even death takes on a new appearance. People are given treatments that keep them youthful-looking until they near the age of 60, at which time their bodies are allowed to experience a brief, soma-controlled period of aging before they disappear into the prominently placed crematoria that turn human bodies into phosphorus to be used in fertilizer.

Huxley exhibits the undesirable aspects of such a world through the characters of the Alpha-class misfit Bernard Marx and the savage John, who lives on the Savage Reservation, a precivilized region that has been preserved for study. John is the son of the director of Hatcheries and Conditioning (DHC) and a Beta woman who was left on the reservation by the DHC. Taken to England by Marx, John is highly uncomfortable in the emotionless and intellectually vacuous Utopia. He wants love and rejects the promiscuity of Lenina Crowne, a Utopian woman to whom he is sexually attracted but whose morals are repugnant to him. Treated as a curiosity by Utopians who clamor to see him and who gawk at him, John finds only misery in this brave new world and decides that suicide is his only solution.

## CENSORSHIP HISTORY

*Brave New World* has evoked a range of responses from those who are made uncomfortable by Huxley's satire of society. The novel has been charged with being sordid, immoral and obscene, and it has been condemned for vilifying the family, for giving too much attention to sex and for encouraging illegal drug use. Many cite the sexual promiscuity of the Utopians, as did the Board of Censors of Ireland when it banned the novel in 1932, yet the novel contains no graphic scenes of sexual behavior. For the most part, people who seek to ban the novel believe that *Brave New World* is "depressing, fatalistic, and negative, and that it encourages students to adopt a lifestyle of drugs, sex and conformity, reinforcing helpless feelings that they can do nothing to make an impact on their world."

The novel has been frequently challenged in schools throughout the United States. In 1965, a teacher of English in Maryland claimed that the local school board had violated his First Amendment rights by firing him after he assigned *Brave New World* as a required reading in his class. The district court ruled against the teacher in *Parker v. Board of Education, 237 F. Supp. 222 (D.Md)* and refused his request for reinstatement in the teaching position. When the case was later heard by the circuit court, *Parker v. Board of Education, 348 F.2d 464 (4th Cir. 1965)*, the presiding judge affirmed the ruling of the lower court and included in the determination the opinion that the nontenured status of the teacher accounted for the firing and not the assignment of a particular book.

In 1979, a high school principal in Matthews County, Virginia, requested that a history teacher in the high school withdraw an assignment that included *Brave New World*. The teacher assigned it anyway, and the school board terminated the teacher's contract. No further actions were taken by either party.

Use of the novel in the classroom was challenged in 1980 in Miller, Missouri, where it was removed from the curriculum, and in 1988, parents of students at Yukon (Oklahoma) High School demanded the removal of the book as a required reading because of its "language and moral content." In 1993, parents challenged the novel as a required reading in Corona-Norco (California) Unified School District based on charges that it "centered around negative activity." After consideration by the school board, the book was retained on the list, but students who objected to the novel were given alternative choices.

## FURTHER READINGS

"Another Furor over Books." *Ohio State University Monthly* 55 (December 1963): 8–12.

Bedford, Sybille. *Aldous Huxley: A Biography*. London: Chatto & Windus Collins, 1973–74. 2 vols.

Massie, Dorothy C. "Censorship in the Schools: Something Old and Something New." *Today's Education* 69 (November/December 1980): 56–62.

Matter, William W. "The Utopian Tradition and Aldous Huxley." *Science Fiction Studies* 2 (1975): 146–151.

Nahmod, Sheldon H. "Controversy in the Classroom: The High School Teacher and Freedom of Expression." *George Washington University Law Review* 39 (July 1974): 1,031.

*Newsletter on Intellectual Freedom* (May 1980): 52; (September 1981): 127; (July 1988): 140; (January 1994): 14; (March 1994): 70.

# BRIDGE TO TERABITHIA

**Author:**  Katherine Paterson
**Original date and place of publication:**  1977, United States
**Original publisher:**  Thomas Y. Crowell Company
**Type:**  Novel

## SUMMARY

*Bridge to Terabithia* is a Newbery Award–winning novel that relates the adventures and tragedy of a 10-year-old farm boy in contemporary rural Virginia who makes an unexpected new friend, then loses her to a drowning death for which he blames himself. The fastest runner in the fifth grade, Jesse Aarons has a lively imagination and loves to draw. Leslie Burke, the new girl in school, shares his imaginative view of life and challenges his position as the fastest runner in the fifth grade. She and her parents have moved from the city, hoping to find tranquillity in rural life. Despite the taunting of his schoolmates, Jesse becomes friends with the unusual newcomer who prefers to wear sneakers and blue jeans and who has a firm and extensive knowledge of literature. Her parents, whom she calls by their first names, are writers who have moved to the country because they are "reassessing their value structure." For them and for Leslie, that means a simplified life that excludes television but includes an expensive stereo set and a small, expensive Italian sports car. The two friends find a secret hiding place where they create their imaginary world of Terabithia. To inform Jesse of the way a magic kingdom runs and how rulers behave, Leslie lends Jesse her books about Narnia. Later, Leslie tells Jesse stories that she has read in the numerous literary works owned by her parents. When a seventh-grade girl steals Twinkies from Jesse's little sister May Belle, Leslie devises a suitably sneaky revenge to humiliate the older girl.

Terabithia becomes a haven for Leslie and Jesse, and they build a bridge of tree branches to cross the creek into their secret world. On Easter morning, after heavy rains, Jesse heads for Terabithia to meet Leslie, but he turns back after he sees that the creek is nearly overflowing its banks. Later that day, he learns that Leslie has drowned in the creek after the rope on which she was swinging broke. He runs away as guilt and anger overwhelm him, but his father finds him and makes him return. Weeks later, he takes May Belle to the site and she nearly falls into the creek while trying to cross the fragile bridge. Jesse rescues her and later builds a sturdy bridge over the creek with lumber that Leslie's parents buy for him. He also vows to share the magic of Terabithia with May Belle.

## CENSORSHIP HISTORY

*Bridge to Terabithia* was challenged in 1986 as recommended reading for the sixth-grade curriculum in the Lincoln, Nebraska, schools because it contained "profanities" and unsuitable expletives. In 1990, the parent of a Burlington, North Carolina, excelling fifth-grade student demanded that the book be removed from the reading list, alleging that it contained profanities, violence and disrespect for authority. When school officials offered an alternative selection, the parent declined, stating, "We care about not only what our daughter reads, but what other children read as well." Other parents called for the creation of a review committee to systematically review books in the school curriculum to root out "anything that in any way seeks to erode traditional, moral values," but the school denied their request.

The same year, parents of children in Harwinton, Connecticut, challenged the use of *Bridge to Terabithia* and other books in the classroom, claiming that they offered a negative view of life to impressionable students, and their language and subject matter set bad examples for young people. A review committee disagreed and the books were retained. Vulgar language was similarly the basis for a 1991 challenge in Apple Valley (California) Unified School District. A district review committee recommended that the novel be retained, citing its literary value and the strong interest in it by parents and students. The district board of trustees refused to ban the novel and, instead, offered students an alternative selection.

In 1992, parents in the Mechanicsburg (Pennsylvania) Area School District requested that the novel be removed from the school library because it contained offensive language and encouraged a morbid fascination with death. One objector cited four instances in which "damn" is used, two of "hell" and one of "birched," and several objectors demanded that all material in the library should reflect the opinions of parents. The superintendent agreed with an especially formed review committee which decided unanimously that the novel should be retained and defended the language, stating that it was not meant to be disrespectful and that it was integral to the purpose of the story. That same year, parents in the Cleburne (Texas) Independent School District cited the profane language in the book and demanded that it be removed from the school libraries. The novel was retained in the libraries but removed from the required reading list.

Parent concerns in 1993 regarding alleged "obscenities" in the novel led the Oskaloosa (Kansas) school district board of education to enact a new policy regarding the assignment of books in the curriculum. Teachers were made responsible for examining each of the required texts used in their classes to determine the number of profanities included in each. They must now list each profanity and the number of times that it appears in the book, then send the list home for parents to review. Before any given book can be used in the classroom, parents must provide written permission for their children to read it. Parents in Gettysburg, Pennsylvania, also challenged use of the book in 1993, voicing a similar concern for the use of offensive language by characters in this book and in *Jacob Have I Loved*, by the same author.

## FURTHER READINGS

*Newsletter on Intellectual Freedom* (March 1987): 67; (March 1991): 44; (May 1992): 95; (September 1992): 162–163; (November 1992): 198; (March 1993): 45; (July 1993): 105–106; (March 1994): 55.

People for the American Way. *Attacks on the Freedom to Learn: 1990–1991 Report.* Washington, D.C.: People for the American Way, 1992.

## CAIN'S BOOK

**Author:**  Alexander Trocchi
**Original date and place of publication:**  1960, United States
**Original publisher:**  Grove Press
**Type:**  Novel

### SUMMARY

*Cain's Book* recounts in journal form the sordid activities of a heroin addict who lives on a garbage scow on the Hudson River in New York. The preface disclaims any association between the author's life and the narrator's heroin use and illegal adventures, but Trocchi permits his narrator a family that resembles his own. In addition, like the narrator of the novel, Trocchi had also served in the Royal Navy and had a more than passing familiarity with Edinburgh and Paris.

The first chapter opens with the words "Half an hour ago I gave myself a fix" and proceeds in a prose style that seeks to mimic the musings of a man whose mind is unhinged by the effects of hard drugs. In language that is sometimes philosophical but more often anarchical, Cain rants and raves about a system that condemns his heroin use. He states broadly, "I say it is impertinent, insolent and presumptuous of any person or group of persons to impose their unexamined moral prohibitions on me." To those who would deny him or anyone else access to the drug, Cain angrily issues the challenge, "To think that a man should be allowed a gun and not a drug. . . . I demand that these laws be changed."

The narrator relates what led him to his present drug-addicted life, including memories of his adventures as a seaman during World War II. In one particularly bleak passage, Cain describes his first sexual experience with a prostitute, which took place on the stone steps of an air raid shelter during a wartime blackout in Edinburgh. Devoid of any attempt at erotic arousal on the part of the reader, the incident is presented in stark naturalistic detail in which the narrator observes of his sexual companion, "I had never seen such ugly thighs nor ever imagined it like that, exposed for me in matchlight, the flaccid buttocks like pale meat on the stone stairs. . . ." His account and others throughout the book punctuate the journal and his continuing defense of his drug use.

The novel also incorporates the author's defense of art. The narrator muses that art should be free of prohibitions, and he expresses the essential value of drugs in stimulating creativity in the artist. Overall, the narrator is not remorseful about his addiction nor does he speak against the use of heroin. Instead, Cain's journal is a polemic that condemns the prohibitions that society places both on the artist in society and on the individual who makes a conscious choice to use hard drugs and who rejects all efforts to rehabilitate him and to deny him the right of his addiction.

## CENSORSHIP HISTORY

The censorship of *Cain's Book* is significant, because the judge's 1964 decision that the book was obscene marked the first time a judgment of obscenity had been made based not on the vulgar language, depiction of sexual activity or depravity in a work but on the lifestyle it advocated. The novel was published in the United States by Grove Press in 1960, but the little-read author stimulated only minimal interest with it. By 1963, when John Calder issued *Cain's Book* under his imprint, Trocchi had gained a following in the United Kingdom as a poet and a leading figure of the beat movement. At first little known for his fiction, Trocchi became well known after his highly publicized argument with Scottish poet Hugh MacDiarmid at the 1962 Edinburgh Festival Writers' Conference. The younger poet's arguments against Scottish chauvinism brought international attention and resulted in the publication of *Cain's Book* in the United Kingdom.

The publisher limited distribution of the book to established bookstores, in an effort to avoid the crackdown on books that had followed earlier convictions for the sale of FANNY HILL. The novel was kept out of less reputable stores that dealt in sexy photographs, "French" letters and pornography to avoid its being scooped up in police raids, but the effort failed. In February 1964, police in Sheffield, England, raided a number of bookstores and confiscated *Cain's Book* with numerous other novels and magazines. Police defended their seizure of the novel on the grounds that it "seems to advocate the use of drugs in schools so that children should have a clearer conception of art."

In the subsequent trial, which began in April 1964, the publisher defended the literary merit of the novel. Calder stated to the jury that the novel was "one of the most important books written by a British author that has an affinity with the beat movement which is a revolt against conventional values." The prosecution claimed that the book was obscene. Among the witnesses for the prosecution was the Sheffield city librarian, who testified that the library owned 20 copies of *Cain's Book*, "kept in a reserve category available only for adults." After only 45 minutes of deliberation, the jury gave its verdict that the book was obscene and that it was too offensive to remain available to citizens. All copies of *Cain's Book* in Sheffield were ordered confiscated. At the Edinburgh Festival in September 1964, Trocchi and his supporters devised a protest against the verdict, a public burning of copies of *Cain's Book* in a large bonfire to which were added fireworks.

An appeal filed later in 1964 was unsuccessful, and the judge dismissed the case with costs going against the publisher. In rendering his decision in December 1964, Lord Chief Justice Parker determined that the narrator's heroin addiction was the reason for censoring the book. He stated " . . . the book, highlighting as it were the favourable effects of drug taking, so far from condemning it, advocates it and . . . there is a real danger that those into whose hands the book comes might be tempted, at any rate, to experiment with drugs and get the favourable sensations highlighted by the book."

## FURTHER READINGS

O'Higgins, Paul. *Censorship in England.* London: Nelson, 1972.
Robertson, Geoffrey. *Obscenity: An Account of the Censorship Laws and Their Enforcement in England and Wales.* London: Weidenfeld & Nicolson, 1979.
Sutherland, John. *Offensive Literature: Decensorship in Britain, 1960–1982.* London: Junction Books, 1982.

## CAMILLE

**Author:** Alexandre Dumas Jr.
**Original date and place of publication:** 1848, Brussels
**Original publisher:** Meline, Cans
**Literary type:** Novel

## SUMMARY

Known by the title *la Dame aux camélias* when originally published, the novel is a sensitive and sympathetic portrayal of Marguerite Gautier, a French courtesan who dies young of consumption. The work gained early notoriety because it is drawn from life and features a main character who is the thinly veiled fictional version of an actual courtesan named Marie Duplessis. Her lavish lifestyle and many relationships with men are presented in the nonjudgmental narration of her life and death. Dumas purifies the courtesan's image and plays down her true-life desire to accumulate wealth and jewels. As such, it offered for its time a new treatment of social and moral problems.

Marguerite is so sensitive that she cannot even endure the scent of flowers; thus, for her adornment she selects the lush yet delicate camellia, which has no scent. This theme of simple yet lavish beauty characterizes Marguerite, with whom the 25-year-old Armand Duval remains deeply in love, even after her death at the age of 23.

The novel is framed as a story being told to the narrator by Duval, a now-impoverished former lover of the high-living courtesan. Dumas does not glorify her life; rather, he exhibits her effect upon others, especially her negative effect upon Duval. Of all her many lovers, Duval is the only one who places flowers (camellias) on her grave, even after she has ruined him financially. He is also the only person who seeks to move her body from its place in a cemetery plot with only a five-year lease to a large plot having a perpetual lease. When Duval becomes seriously ill with "brain fever," the narrator nurses him and, thus, learns the entire story as Duval narrates it to him.

Mingled with accounts of Marguerite's frivolous life and conspicuous luxury is the poignance of her realization that being a courtesan makes her of interest to others only as long as she can "serve the vanity or the pleasure of . . . lovers." She warns her young admirer Duval at the outset of their acquaintance that her lavish lifestyle is expensive to maintain and that she must continue her liaisons with older rich men in order to survive. Soon after they meet, Duval learns that Marguerite has been coughing up blood, yet she continues to meet and to fascinate her wealthy lovers. He becomes obsessed with her. He learns that she is 40,000 francs in debt and spends hundreds of thousands of francs annually. As his own health deteriorates, Duval is also drawn into debt as he borrows money and gambles to try to pay Marguerite's debts. After enduring months of working to convince the courtesan to give up her wealthy suitors and lavish lifestyle, Duval is successful and they go to live in the country in a home that was purchased for her by a wealthy and elderly duke. Duval and Marguerite live together openly, supported by the profits from the sale of her numerous jewels and possessions.

After four months of remaining faithful to her young lover, Marguerite returns to her old life, more ill with consumption than before yet still able to attract a wealthy count who buys back for her the horses, carriage and jewels that she had pawned. In revenge, Duval takes a new mistress, upon whom he lavishes money and jewels to make Marguerite jealous, thus driving himself even further into debt. When Marguerite dies, Duval is devastated and becomes ill shortly thereafter.

## CENSORSHIP HISTORY

The novel has drawn criticism as much for its sympathetic portrayal of a courtesan as for the wisdom that Dumas expresses through the character of Armand Duval: "To be loved by a pure young girl . . . is the simplest thing in the world. But to be really loved by a courtesan, that is a victory of infinitely greater difficulty." Duval refers casually to Marguerite as "a kept woman," and he has Marguerite solemnly swear to Duval, "I gave myself sooner to you than I ever did to any man."

In 1850, the performance of the opera *La Traviata*, based on the novel, was permitted but the translation of the text as a libretto was forbidden. In

France, from 1849 through 1852, the play *La Dame Aux Camellias*, based on the novel, was forbidden on the Paris stage. Finally, in 1852, an influential government minister in the cabinet of Napoleon III intervened, and the play was produced.

The novel was singled out in 1857 by Lord Campbell, the lord chief justice of England, when he introduced to the House of Lords a bill that was aimed at strengthening the law of obscenity and made books liable to destruction by the magistrates. He assured his peers that the law was aimed at eliminating those works "written for the single purpose of corrupting the morals of youth and of a nature calculated to shock the common feelings of decency in a well-regulated mind." As he presented his arguments, he held a copy of *Camille* in his hands and referred to it with horror as an example of literary works of a polluting character that must be stopped. The bill became the Obscene Publications Act of 1857.

In 1863, all of Dumas's works were placed on the Vatican's list of forbidden books, and he was identified as one of only 11 authors whose total works had been condemned by the Roman Catholic church for emphasizing the treatment of impure love. As recently as 1948, all of Dumas's works were listed in the Vatican's *Index Librorum Prohibitorum* and declared to be forbidden to Catholics throughout the world and in every translation.

## FURTHER READINGS

Burke, Redmond A. *What Is the Index?* Milwaukee, Wis.: Bruce Publishing Company, 1952.

*Index of Prohibited Books*. Revised and published by the order of His Holiness Pope Pius XII. Vatican: Polyglot Press, 1948.

Saunders, Edith. *The Prodigal Father*. New York: Longmans, Green and Company, 1951.

# THE CANTERBURY TALES

**Author:**   Geoffrey Chaucer
**Original date and place of publication:**   1387–1400, England
**Original publisher:**   Unknown
**Type:**   Short story collection

## SUMMARY

*Canterbury Tales* is a group of stories, mostly in verse, written in the closing years of the 14th century. Chaucer establishes the framework for the book in a lengthy prologue in which he describes the 29 individuals who meet with their host at the Tabard Inn in preparation for a pilgrimage to the popular shrine of Thomas à Becket at the Canterbury Cathedral. They agree that, to pass the time on the journey, each pilgrim will tell four stories, two on the way to the shrine and two on the way home. The host will judge the best tale, and the winner will receive a sumptuous feast at the inn. Chaucer originally planned a book of 120 tales but died in 1400 before completing the work. Only 24 of the tales remain. Of these, 20 are complete, two are deliberately left incomplete because the pilgrims demand that the tellers cease and two others were left unfinished by Chaucer's death.

The pilgrims extend across all levels of 14th-century English society, from the nobly born Knight, Squire and Prioress to the low-born Miller, Cook and Yeoman. None are spared Chaucer's critical examination of the human condition as he uses his characters and their tales to expose the absurdities and inadequacies of all levels of society. The travelers quarrel, interrupt and criticize each other, become drunk and provoke commentary. Members of the religious hierarchy are shown to be corrupt, women are lusty and the dark underbelly of society is exposed. The tales reflect the tellers, from the gentle Knight, "modest as a maid," who describes an abstraction of womanhood in his pure Emily, to the bawdy Miller, who describes his Alison as a highly provocative physical object.

Risqué language and sexual innuendo pervade most of the tales. "The Cook's Tale" describes "a wife [who] whored to get her sustenance." In "Introduction to the Lawyer's Prologue," provocative images of incest emerge in "Canace, who loved her own blood brother sinfully" and "wicked king Antiochus [who] bereft his daughter of her maidenhead." "The Reeve's Tale" tells of a miller named Simpkin whose wife "was a dirty bitch" and whose daughter was "with buttocks broad and round breasts full and high." "The Wife of Bath's Tale," one of the two most commonly anthologized of all the tales, offers an extraordinary view of women and sexuality. Described in the prologue as having had five husbands, "not counting other company in her youth," the Wife of Bath questions the concern over virginity and asks "Tell me also to what purpose or end the genitals have been made?" She lustily promises, "In wifehood I will use my instrument as freely as my Maker has sent it."

The second of the two most popularly anthologized stories is "The Miller's Tale," a story about adultery. Alison, an 18-year-old woman married to a middle-aged miller, is courted by Absalom the parish clerk, but she is already having an affair with the boarder, a student named Nicholas. Absalom serenades her outside her window and promises to leave her alone only if she will let him kiss her. She agrees and, when he arrives at her window in the dark, she offers "her naked arse," which he kisses. He soon realizes the trick, for "it seem somehow amiss, for well he knew a woman has no beard; he'd felt a thing all rough and longish-haired." Seeking revenge, Absalom returns to the Miller's house carrying a red-hot poker from the fireplace and calls to Alison for another kiss. This time Nicholas, who "had risen for a piss," decides "to have his arse kissed" to carry on the joke. And, "showing the whole bum," he is shocked when Absalom "was ready with his iron hot and Nicholas right in the arse he got." Later, John, the other student boarder, mistakenly climbs into bed with Alison, who thinks it is Nicholas, and he "pricked her hard and deep, like one gone mad."

## CENSORSHIP HISTORY

*Canterbury Tales* has been expurgated from its first appearance in the United States in 1908 in the Everyman's Library edition. Seventeen of the tales were translated into modern English with extensive expurgation, and seven were left intact but in the original Middle English language. In 1953 the tales were innocent victims of the "Red Scare," when critics approached the Texas State Textbook Commission and demanded that the commission bar the Garden City editions of *Canterbury Tales* and *Moby Dick* from their schools. The two works were illustrated by Rockwell Kent, charged by critics with being a communist.

For the most part, however, the off-color references of the original text and blunt "Anglo-Saxon" terms related to the anatomy or to bodily functions have raised concerns among parents and those who select textbooks. Thus, they are routinely omitted from most editions, as are curses or oaths uttered by characters in the original tales. Editing has led to such absurdities as "He caught her by the queynte" being transformed into "He slipped his hand intimately between her legs." Challenges to the inclusion of "The Miller's Tale," "The Wife of Bath's Tale" and even the "Prologue" have sought to remove the readings from classrooms because of the "unhealthy characters" and the "nasty words" of the text. Risqué language and characters have made the tales a ready target for textbook evaluators and community and school watchdogs.

In 1986, a lengthy case arose over the use of a textbook that included "The Miller's Tale" and Aristophanes' play *Lysistrata* in an elective humanities course for Columbia County High School students in Lake City, Florida. The tale appeared in *The Humanities: Cultural Roots and Continuities Volume I,* a state-approved textbook that had been used for 10 years without incident. In 1985, the daughter of a fundamentalist minister had enrolled in the course and objected to the two selections, even though they were not assigned readings but portions referred to and read aloud by the teacher. In lodging a formal complaint, the minister identified "sexual explicitness," "vulgar language" and "the promotion of women's lib" as his reasons for demanding that the text be withdrawn from use. His specific objections identified concern over the inclusion of the terms "ass" and "fart" in "The Miller's Tale," as well as the jocular way in which adultery appears to be treated. An advisory textbook committee made up of Columbia County High School teachers read and discussed the two selections, then recommended that the textbooks be retained and that the two selections not be assigned. The school board rejected their suggestions and voted to confiscate all copies of the book and to lock them in the book room. Anxious to avoid the charge of censorship, board members also voted to allow a copy to remain in the high school library, but it was placed on "the mature shelf."

In 1988, the American Civil Liberties Union submitted an initial brief against the school board in *Virgil v. School Board of Columbia County*, 677 F. Supp. 1547, 1551–51 (M.D. Fla. 1988) and argued that the actions of the board in removing the textbook from the classroom suppressed the free thought and free speech of students. The ACLU based its arguments on decisions made in *Board of Education, Island Trees Union Free School District No. 26 v. Pico*, 457 U.S. 853, 102 S.Ct. 2799, 73 L.Ed.2d 435 (1982), in which the court decided that school boards violate the First Amendment rights of students when they arbitrarily remove books. (See BEST SHORT STORIES BY NEGRO WRITERS.) The defense attorney for the school board relied on *Hazelwood School District v. Kuhlmeier*, 484 U.S. 260, 108 S.Ct. 562, 98 L.Ed.2d 592 (1988) in presenting the case, although the case applied to the right of school administrators to censor articles in a school newspaper that was produced as part of a high school journalism class.

The case went to court, and in deciding *Virgil v. School Board of Columbia County*, 862 F.2d 1517, 1525 (11th Cir. 1989), the judge determined that the *Hazelwood* case was the relevant precedent. The limited scope of that case in interpreting the First Amendment rights of students influenced the court to decide in favor of the school board. In the *Virgil* decision, the U.S. Court of Appeals for the 11th Circuit concluded that no constitutional violation had occurred and the school board could decide to remove books from the classroom provided that the removal was "reasonably related" to the "legitimate pedagogical concern" of denying students exposure to "potentially sensitive topics." The written contention of the board that the two selections contained "explicit sexuality" and "excessive vulgarity" was judged to be a sufficient basis for the removal of *The Humanities: Cultural Roots and Continuities* from the classroom. The plaintiffs decided to appeal the case to the United States Supreme Court and directed the ACLU attorney to file a Petition for Writ of Certiorari in 1988. After more than a year passed, the plaintiffs learned that the Supreme Court had never received the petition, because a secretary newly hired in April 1989 by the office of the ACLU attorney had never sent it out. The plaintiffs decided not to pursue the matter, because the changed character of the higher court did not promise success even if the motion to argue the case were approved.

## FURTHER READINGS

Johnson, Claudia. *Stifled Laughter: One Woman's Fight Against Censorship*. Golden, Colo.: Fulcrum Publishing, 1994.

Scala, Elizabeth. "Canace and the Chaucer Canon." *Chaucer Review* 30 (1995): 15–39.

# CATCH-22

**Author:** Joseph Heller
**Original date and place of publication:** 1961, United States
**Original publisher:** Simon & Schuster
**Type:** Novel

## SUMMARY

*Catch-22* is a comic novel about World War II that literary critics have described as among the best to have come out of that era. The novel concerns the efforts of Capt. John Yossarian, a bombardier with the 256th U.S. Air Force Squadron, to be removed from combat duty after he witnesses numerous friends being killed in action. He acts insane to achieve his goal, but his efforts are thwarted by military regulation number 22, which states that no insane person would willingly go into combat. Thus, anyone who seeks to avoid combat duty must be considered sane.

Set on the fictional Mediterranean island of Pianosa, from which the squadron makes regular bombing runs to southern France and to Italy, the novel contains graphic descriptions of sex and violence and exhibits strong rebellion against authority. Yossarian lies, sabotages military procedures and exhibits gross irresponsibility. He also walks around naked for a few days, even when he is being awarded a medal. Given light duty censoring letters written by enlisted men, Yossarian plays games and blacks out words randomly, sometimes adding the chaplain's signature to romantic letters home. The unpleasant experience of his tent mate Orr in a brothel is carefully detailed, as the "whore" beats him with her high-heeled shoe. Readers learn that the two are naked and of "her wondrously full breasts soaring all over the place like billowing pennants in a strong wind and her buttocks and strong thighs shim-sham-shimmying this way and that way." Another character visits a brothel in the Eternal City, then kills the prostitute because she might damage his reputation should she tell others about their encounter. Throughout the novel, the men casually refer to and address each other as "son of a bitch," "prick" or "bastard." At one point, Yossarian loses his temper and rants, "That dirty goddam midget-assed, apple-cheeked, goggle-eyed, undersized, buck-toothed, grinning, crazy sonofabitchinbastard!"

The women in the novel are largely stereotypes to whom other characters refer as "whore." The woman whom "he had longed for and idolized for months" is "perfect for Yossarian, a debauched, coarse, vulgar, amoral, appetizing slattern. . . . She was interested in fornication." However, he also hopes that "Nately's whore" will find him a woman who is just as eager for sex as she. At the end of the novel, as Yossarian leaves the base to run off to Sweden, "Nately's whore was hiding out just outside the door." She attempts to kill him, but he escapes.

## CENSORSHIP HISTORY

*Catch-22* is part of the school censorship case that set precedent by supporting the *student's* right to know. In 1972, the Strongsville, Ohio, board of education used its discretionary power over textbook selection to disapprove purchase of *Catch-22* and Kurt Vonnegut's GOD BLESS YOU, MR. ROSEWATER, despite faculty recommendation. The board refused to allow teachers to use the books as part of the English curriculum, charging that they were "completely sick" and "garbage." The board then ordered the two books and *Cat's Cradle*, also by Vonnegut, removed from the high school library and "all copies disposed of in accordance with statutory procedure."

Five high school students and their families brought a class action suit against the school district, the school superintendent and the board of education, claiming that their rights under the First and 14th Amendments had been violated. The families argued that the board had not followed proper procedure and had not given good reason for rejecting the novels. In 1974, the United States District Court for the Northern District of Ohio ruled that the board did not violate First Amendment rights because it had followed the law. Ohio law granted school boards the authority to select textbooks, and the board had held open meetings and consulted enough teachers, administrators and citizens to make a reasonable decision. The judge dismissed the complaint of the families regarding the removal of the books from the school library.

The case was then heard in 1976 by the United States Court of Appeals for the Sixth Circuit, and a different decision emerged. The court upheld the right of the school board to determine the choice of textbooks, but it stood firmly against the right of the school board to remove already purchased books from the school library.

> A public school library is also a valuable adjunct to classroom discussions. If one of the English teachers considered Joseph Heller's Catch-22 to be one of the more important modern American novels (as, indeed, at least one did), we assume that no one would dispute that the First Amendment's protection of academic freedom would protect both his right to say so in class and his students' right to hear him and to find and read the book. Obviously, the students' success in this last endeavor would be greatly hindered by the fact that the book sought had been removed from a school library.

The court also chastised the school board for withdrawing books from the school library. Stating in the decision that "a library is a storehouse of knowledge," the presiding judge warned that libraries are created by the state for the benefit of students in the schools. As such, they are "not subject to being withdrawn by succeeding school boards whose members might desire to 'winnow' the library for books the content of which occasioned their displeasure or disapproval." The judge ordered the Strongsville school board to replace the books in the school library. In response, the school district appealed to the United States Supreme Court, but the court refused to hear the case.

The use of the word "whore" at several places in the novel to refer to women resulted in challenges in the Dallas (Texas) Independent School District in 1974, where parents demanded that the novel be removed from all of the high school libraries. The same objection motivated a challenge in the Snoqualmie Valley (Washington) School District in 1979. Critics observed that the use of "whore" and Heller's failure to name one woman, calling her only "Nately's whore," represented a stereotyping of women that was harmful to students. In attempts to remove the novel from use in the school system as well as from the Mount Si High School library, critics also cited the "overly descriptive passages of violence" and the increasingly bizarre threats by squadron members against each other. The efforts to remove *Catch-22* were unsuccessful.

## FURTHER READINGS

Green, Daniel. "A World Worth Laughing At: *Catch-22* and the Humor of Black Humor." *Studies in the Novel* 27 (Summer 1995): 186–196.

Moore, Michael. "Pathological Communication Patterns in Heller's *Catch-22*." *Et Cetera* 52 (Winter 1995): 431–459.

O'Neil, Robert M. *Classrooms in the Crossfire: The Rights and Interests of Students, Parents, Teachers, Administrators, Librarians, and the Community.* Bloomington, Ind.: Indiana University Press, 1981.

Pinsker, Sanford. *Understanding Joseph Heller.* Columbia, S.C.: University of South Carolina Press, 1991.

*Newsletter for Intellectual Freedom* (January 1975): 6; (July 1979): 85.

Potts, Stephen. *Catch-22: Antiheroic Antinovel.* Boston: Twayne Publishing, 1989.

Potts, Stephen. *From Here to Absurdity: The Moral Battlefields of Joseph Heller.* San Bernardino, Calif.: Borgo Press, 1982.

# THE CATCHER IN THE RYE

**Author:** J. D. Salinger
**Original date and place of publication:** 1951, United States
**Original publisher:** Little, Brown and Company
**Literary type:** Novel

## SUMMARY

*The Catcher in the Rye* tells the story of a middle-class, urban, late-adolescent male in the 1950s who confronts crisis in his own life by escaping into the disordered and chaotic adult world. The story, told from the first-person point of view of a boy named Holden Caulfield, details 48 hours in his life, and describes how he views and feels about society and the world in which he lives. As Holden experiences his misadventures, he muses about sex, society and American values. He seeks to remain idealistic, but he is confronted at every turn by the phoniness of society.

Holden narrates his story while in a rest home in California, and the reader becomes aware that he is relating a story from his recent past. He flashes back to his school days, in particular to Pency Prep, where he was a student until his expulsion. It is just after this expulsion that the action takes place. For most of the novel, Holden appears to search for someone or something in which to believe, but he finds that his generally pessimistic view of human nature and human values is reinforced rather than refuted.

Before Holden makes the decision to leave school, he visits his history teacher for one last time and receives a lecture regarding his lack of motivation and poor scholarship. Mr. Spencer even goes so far as to read Holden the last examination he took. The disappointments accrue, as Holden returns to his room in the dormitory and learns that his roommate, Ward, has a date with a girl whom Holden had wanted to date. To compound the pain, Ward asks Holden to write a composition, which he later criticizes severely. After the ensuing physical fight, Holden packs a bag and leaves the campus.

Holden boards a train bound for New York City and registers at a hotel upon arrival. When loneliness sets in, he makes several telephone calls without success, then visits a crowded nightclub, but he still cannot fill the void he feels inside. When Holden returns to the hotel, he asks the doorman to arrange for a prostitute, but he sends her away unpaid because he is too scared and too depressed to enjoy her. The doorman and prostitute later awaken him and demand the five dollars, and the doorman beats Holden to obtain payment.

After meeting a friend at a bar and indulging in underage drinking, Holden sneaks into his family's apartment to see his younger sister, Phoebe, with whom he discusses his fears that he may "disappear" into himself. He tells her that he has a mission in this world: "I keep picturing all these little kids playing some game in this big field of rye and all. . . . And I'm standing by on the edge of some crazy cliff. What I have to do, I have to catch everybody if they start to go over the cliff." In his further idealism, he becomes upset when he finds "Fuck You" scrawled on the walls of Phoebe's elementary school and on the wall of the museum where Phoebe will meet him.

Holden plans to hitchhike to the West but changes his mind and agrees to return home when Phoebe packs a suitcase and insists on going with him. He later watches Phoebe ride the carousel in Central Park and realizes that he really cannot protect her from all of the world's abuses and that he has to let her take chances without interfering.

By the end of the novel, after fending off the advances of a male former English teacher and reviewing his disappointments with the adult world,

Holden appears resigned in the rest home and predicts that he will soon be returning to school.

## CENSORSHIP HISTORY

The novel has long ignited disapproval, and it was the most frequently banned book in schools between 1966 and 1975. Even before that time, however, the work was a favorite target of censors. In 1957, Australian Customs seized a shipment of the novels that had been presented as a gift to the government by the U.S. ambassador. The books were later released, but Customs had made its point that the book contained obscene language and actions that were not appropriate behavior for an adolescent. In 1960, a teacher in Tulsa, Oklahoma, was fired for assigning the book to an eleventh-grade English class. The teacher appealed and was reinstated by the school board, but the book was removed from use in the school.

The following year in Oklahoma City, the novel became the focus of a legislative hearing in which a locally organized censorship group sought to stop the Mid-Continent News Company, a book wholesaler, from carrying the novel. Members of the group parked a "Smutmobile" outside the capital building during the hearing and displayed the novel with others. As a result of public pressure, the wholesaler dropped the criticized novels from its inventory. In 1963 a delegation of parents of high school students in Columbus, Ohio, asked the school board to ban *Catcher in the Rye*, BRAVE NEW WORLD and TO KILL A MOCKINGBIRD for being "anti-white" and "obscene." The superintendent of schools and the school board refused the request and expressed confidence in the ability of their teachers and librarians to choose reading material for the school system.

After a decade of quiet, objections again arose in 1975 in Selinsgrove, Pennsylvania, and the novel was removed from the suggested reading list for an elective course entitled "Searching for Values and Identity Through Literature." Based on parents' objections to the language and content of the book, the school board voted 5–4 to ban the book. The book was later reinstated in the curriculum when the board learned that the vote was illegal because they needed a two-thirds vote for removal of the text.

In 1977 parents in Pittsgrove Township, New Jersey, challenged the assignment of the novel in an American literature class. They charged that the book included considerable profanity and "filthy and profane" language that promoted premarital sex, homosexuality and perversion, as well as claiming that it was "explicitly pornographic" and "immoral." The board of education had originally approved the novel for study. After months of controversy, the board ruled that the novel could be read in the advanced placement class for its universal message, not for its profanity, but they gave parents the right to decide whether or not their children would read it.

In 1978 parents in Issaquah, Washington, became upset with the rebellious views expressed in the novel by Holden Caulfield and with the profanity he uses. The woman who led the parents' group asserted that she had counted 785 uses of profanity, and she alleged that the philosophy of the book marked it as part of a Communist plot that was gaining a foothold in the schools, "in which a lot of people are used and may not even be aware of it." The school board voted to ban the book, but the decision was later reversed when the three members who had voted against the book were recalled due to illegal deal-making. In 1979, the Middleville, Michigan, school district removed the novel from the required reading list after parents objected to the content.

Objections to the novel have been numerous throughout the 1980s and into the 1990s. In 1980, the Jacksonville-Milton School libraries in North Jackson, Ohio, removed the book, as did two high school libraries in Anniston, Alabama. In 1982, school officials removed the book from all school libraries because it contained "excess vulgar language, sexual scenes, and things concerning moral issues." In 1983, parents in Libby, Montana, challenged the assignment of the book in the high school due to the "book's contents." Deemed "unacceptable" and "obscene," the novel was banned from use in English classes at Freeport High School in De Funiak Springs, Florida, in 1985, and it was removed from the required reading list in 1986 in Medicine Bow, Wyoming, Senior High School because of sexual references and profanity. In 1987, parents and the local Knights of Columbus chapter in Napoleon, North Dakota, complained about profanity and sexual references in the book, which was then banned from a required sophomore English reading list. Parents of students attending Linton-Stockton (Indiana) High School challenged the book in 1988 because it "undermines morality," and profanity was the reason for which the book was banned from classrooms in the Boron, California, high school in 1989.

The challenges to the novel have continued well into the 1990s. In 1991, the novel was challenged at Grayslake (Illinois) Community High School for profanity, and parents of students in Jamaica High School in Sidell, Illinois, cited profanities and the depiction of premarital sex, alcohol abuse and prostitution as the basis for their 1992 challenge. Three other major challenges to the novel occurred in 1992. The novel was challenged and removed from the Waterloo, Iowa, public schools and the Duval County, Florida, public school libraries because of the "lurid passages about sex" and profanity, while a parent in Carlisle, Pennsylvania, objected to the book because it was "immoral" and contained profanity. In 1993, parents in the Corona-Norco (California) School District protested the use of the novel as a required reading, because it was "centered around negative activity." The school board voted to retain the novel but instructed teachers to select alternative readings if students objected to it. The novel was challenged but retained for use in select English classes at New Richmond (Wisconsin) High School in 1994, but it was removed as mandatory reading from the Goffstown, New Hampshire, schools the same year because parents charged that it contained "vulgar words" and presented the main character's "sexual exploits."

## FURTHER READINGS

Alvino, James. "Is It Book Burning Time Again?" *The New York Times* (December 28, 1980): 11:18.

"Another Furor Over Books." *Ohio State University Monthly* 55 (4): 8–12.

Booth, Wayne C. "Censorship and the Values of Fiction." *English Journal* 53 (March 1964): 155–164.

Corbett, Edward P.J. "Raise High the Barriers, Censors." *America* 54 (January 7, 1961): 441–444.

*Newsletter on Intellectual Freedom* (November 1978): 138 ; (January 1980): 6–7; (May 1980): 51; (March 1983): 37–38; (July 1983): 122; (July 1985): 113; (March 1987): 55; (July 1987): 123; (January 1988): 10; (September 1988): 177; (November 1989): 218–219; (July 1991): 129–130; (May 1992): 83; (July 1992): 105, 126; (January 1993): 29; (January 1994): 14; (March 1994): 56, 70; (May 1994): 100; (January 1995): 12.

Oboler, Eli M. "Idaho School Librarians and Salinger's *Catcher in the Rye*: A Candid Report." *Idaho Librarian* 15 (October 1963): 137–139.

# THE CHOCOLATE WAR

**Author:**   Robert Cormier
**Original date and place of publication:**   1974, United States
**Original publisher:**   Pantheon Books
**Type:**   Novel

## SUMMARY

*The Chocolate War* is the story of a young boy's struggle against the conformity imposed on him by the restrictive atmosphere of an all-male Catholic prep school as well as by the demands of the Vigils, a secret group that the school does not officially condone but whose existence and infractions it ignores. Jerry Renault, a freshman, has just lost his mother to cancer when the novel opens, and his father is too deep in grief to offer any solace or guidance. Singled out by the Vigils, a secret society at Trinity that manipulates and intimidates students to follow the group's dictates, Jerry is given the assignment by the group to oppose for 10 days the annual chocolate sale at the school and to make a public demonstration of his opposition. The annual chocolate sale, said to be voluntary even though pressures are exerted to participate, is vital to the financial wellbeing of Trinity, and each boy must sell 50 boxes at two dollars each for the school to achieve the necessary level of profit. Knowing that a successful sale is critical for Brother Leon, the leader of the Vigils decides to turn this to an advantage for the group. Brother Leon has already approached Archie, the Assigner of the Vigils, to gain support for the chocolate sale from the group, which he does not name, and Archie hints that they expect certain favors from Brother Leon in return.

When the 10 days end, Jerry, whose locker contains a poster that reads "Do I Dare Disturb the Universe?" continues his refusal to sell chocolates, despite the insistence by the Vigils that he now participate. He insists on the voluntary nature of the project and tries to gain control over his life by bucking the system, but his refusal influences other students to make little effort in the project. The Vigils place relentless pressure on Jerry, Brother Leon glares at him in a menacing manner and other students give him the silent treatment and fear associating with him, but he continues in his refusal to sell chocolates.

Even as he receives brutal punishment in football practice and deals with threats on the telephone, Jerry stands firm on his decision. At the end of the novel, he must take part in a boxing match staged by the Vigils in the football stadium in front of the entire student body and out of sight of the school faculty. The rules demand that both fighters follow directions for blows that students have written on slips of paper. As Jerry is pummeled to near death, students catch sight of Brother Leon standing on the hillside and watching with approval.

## CENSORSHIP HISTORY

*The Chocolate War* was frequently challenged throughout the 1980s and '90s for reasons ranging from objections to the vocabulary and "pervasive vulgarity" to outcries regarding perceived themes of rape, masturbation, violence and degrading treatment of women. In 1981, officials in two Lapeer, Michigan, high schools challenged the novel and temporarily removed it from the English curriculum, charging that it contained "offensive language and explicit descriptions of sexual situations." In 1982, it was removed from the classroom in Liberty High School in Westminster, Maryland, when critics charged that the novel portrayed violence and the degradation of schools and teachers and that it contained "foul language." The language was also the main complaint in 1983 when parents of students at Richmond (Rhode Island) High School demanded that the book be removed from the classroom because of the "repulsive" and "pornographic" text.

In 1984, the novel was banned from the middle school libraries of the Richland Two School District in Columbia, South Carolina, due to "language problems," but the book was later reinstated for use by students in the eighth grade. That same year, school officials removed the novel from the freshman reading list at Lake Havasu (Arizona) High School. When teachers protested the ban, the school board censured the teachers for failing to set good examples for their students and for fostering disrespect in the classroom by failing to support the board in its decision.

In 1985, the novel was removed from the Stroudsburg (Pennsylvania) High School library after the school board determined that it was "blatantly graphic, pornographic and wholly unacceptable for a high school library." Similar charges were made in 1986 when the book was challenged at Barnstable High School in Hyannis, Massachusetts, for its profanity, as well as for "obscene references to masturbation and sexual fantasies" and "ultimately because of its pessimistic ending." Complainants charged further that the novel painted authority and school systems in an unfavorable light and provided a negative impression of religious schools. "Offensive" language motivated the removal of the novel from the Panama City, Florida, school classrooms and from its libraries in the same year. In 1987, parents cited the "profanity, sexual situations, and themes that allegedly encourage disrespectful behavior" in their demand that the novel be removed from school libraries in the Moreno Valley, California Unified School District. A West Hernando (Florida) Middle School principal recommended in 1988 that the novel be removed from the school library shelves because it was "inappropriate" for middle school readers.

In 1990, Methodist minister R. Lee Smith demanded that the novel be suspended from the required reading list for the ninth-grade class in Woodsville High School in Haverhill, New Hampshire, and the school superintendent withdrew the book from use until a district committee could meet. The novel had been on the required reading list for 13 years at the time of the challenge. At the first school board meeting, the minister identified in a list numerous passages from the novel containing expletives, references to masturbation and sexual fantasies and derogatory characterizations of a teacher. After consideration, the superintendent and the school board removed the novel from the required reading list. Similar charges were cited that same year when the novel was challenged in the Harwinton and Burlington, Connecticut, schools, where parents charged that it contained subject matter that set bad examples and gave students negative views on life.

In 1991, a minister in Paola, Kansas, joined the parent of a child in the school system to protest the use of *The Chocolate War* as part of the ninth-grade curriculum. The challengers charged that the novel contained curse words and depicted sexual desires. A review committee, appointed to study the issue, recommended that the novel be retained, and the school board voted 4-3 to affirm the decision of the review committee. The board also reaffirmed its policy of offering an alternative reading assignment to students who objected. That same year, a seventh-grade language arts teacher in

Augusta, Maine, requested that the novel be removed from the middle school library and placed in the high school, alleging that the novel lacked positive role models and that it had an unhappy ending. The district superintendent followed the recommendation of a district review committee to retain the book in the middle school library.

Parents of eighth-grade students in New Milford, Connecticut, challenged the inclusion of the novel on the required reading list in 1992, citing negativism, as well as vulgar language, sexual references and violence that are harmful to students. The assistant superintendent defended the novel and a language arts coordinator supported inclusion of the book as a means of helping eighth-grade students to deal with peer pressure. A districtwide review committee recommended that the novel be retained, but at a higher grade level. The suggestion was countered by parents who opposed the book ban and who claimed that the book addressed issues that were important to middle school children's lives. After hearing discussion, the school board voted 9–1 to retain *The Chocolate War* on the required reading list.

A 1993 challenge to the novel in the Kyrene, Arizona, elementary schools identified the masturbation scene as the sole basis for requesting removal of the novel. The novel was temporarily removed from the 10th-grade reading list at Hephzibah High School in Augusta, Georgia, after a parent complained, "I don't see anything educational about that book. If they ever send a book like that home with one of my daughters again I will personally burn it and throw the ashes on the principal's desk." In 1994, critics identified recurring themes of rape, masturbation, violence and degrading treatment of women in their challenge to the appearance of the novel on the required reading list in the Hudson Falls, New York, schools.

## FURTHER READINGS

Donelson, Kenneth L., and Alleen Pace Nilson. *Literature for Today's Young Adults.* Glenview, Ill.: Scott, Foresman and Company, 1989.

Lewis-House, Nancy. "Books Worth Teaching Even Though They Have Proven Controversial: *The Chocolate War* by Robert Cormier." *English Journal* (April 1993): 88.

McGee, Tim. "The Adolescent Novel in AP English." *English Journal* (April 1992): 57–58.

Nelms, Elizabeth D. "Reading in the Classroom: The Chocolate War/The Chocolate War." *English Journal* (January 1991): 85.

*Newsletter on Intellectual Freedom* (March 1981): 48; (September 1982): 156; (September 1983): 152; (September 1984): 138; (January 1985): 10; (March 1985): 45; (May 1985): 79; (November 1986): 209; (July 1987): 125–128; (September 1987): 168–169; (March 1988): 45; (May 1990): 87; (March 1991): 44; (May 1991): 90; (May 1992): 96–97; (January 1994): 34; (July 1994): 130; (November 1994): 190; (January 1995): 13; (March 1995): 55.

# A CLOCKWORK ORANGE

**Author:**   Anthony Burgess (John Anthony Burgess Wilson)
**Original date and place of publication:**   1962, United Kingdom
**Original publisher:**   William Heinemann Ltd.
**Type:**   Novel

## SUMMARY

*A Clockwork Orange* is a futuristic warning against both mindless violence and the mechanical reconditioning that is often proposed as society's solution to its ills. It offers a horrifying view of a future England in which gangs of hoodlums, or "droogs," roam the streets freely, robbing, fighting, raping and consuming illegal drugs and alcohol. Society is limp and listless, a socialist world in which no one reads anymore, despite streets named Amis Avenue and Priestley Place. Teenage language, "nadsat," consists largely of English mixed with Russian and half-Russian words, and the current music star is a "Russky" singer named Jonny Zhivago. The rule of society is that everyone "not a child nor with child nor ill" must work, yet the prisons are overcrowded and officials work to rehabilitate criminals to make room for the large number of expected political prisoners. Even with regular elections and opposition, the people continue to re-elect the current government.

Alex, the 15-year-old cocky and self-indulgent main character, is both a product of and a reason for the continued breakdown of social institutions. Deteriorating urban life, ineffective law enforcement, the failure of officials to create order from the chaos and sexual violence characterize this world, in which social ills perpetuate the violent behavior and prevent cohesion. It is a nightmarish place in which the droogs drive over a big, snarling, toothy thing and "odd squealing things" in the road throughout the night, accompanied by screams and squelches. The young hoodlums drink doped milk, and before committing robberies Alex and his fellow droogs put on their "maskies," faces of historical personalities: Disraeli, Elvis Presley, Henry VIII and "Peebee" Shelley. Women exist for the droogs only as objects of rape and other violence, and sex has also taken on a mechanical characteristic that is reinforced by the term to describe the sex act, "the old in-out in-out." Even classical music, usually viewed as a sign of civilized taste, gains a new character in the novel. Symphonic music is Alex's passion, and he retreats frequently to his speaker-filled room to lie naked on his bed and listen to the music of Mozart, Beethoven or Bach. As the music swells, he fantasizes raping and terrorizing young girls and grinding his boot heel into the faces of helpless victims.

The novel is divided into three parts. In the first third, Alex simply does whatever he wants without guilt or concern for others, and he experiences joy in violence of every kind, from destruction or theft of objects to every form of sexual and nonsexual assault. He is free to choose whatever pleasures he desires, however destructive to society they might be. However, because his choices are harmful, society asserts its right to deprive Alex of his freedom. Sentenced to 14 years for the murder of an old woman during a burglary, Alex is placed into prison, where he kills a fellow inmate. This ushers in the second part of the novel. The murder focuses attention on him and makes him the likely choice for an experimental treatment that will leave him "transformed out of all recognition" and make him unable to choose any socially deleterious course of action afterward. In essence, he is injected with a drug, strapped into a chair and forced to watch films of Japanese and Nazi atrocities during World War II, as well as specially made films that combine with the drug to condition him against all thoughts of violence. His progress is measured with electronic devices that are wired to his body. The conditioning works, and the doctors declare Alex cured of his violent desires and now "your true Christian . . . ready to turn the other cheek, ready to be crucified rather than crucify, sick to the very heart at the thought even of killing a fly."

In the third part of the novel, the rehabilitated Alex, now a harmless citizen, returns home to find that his parents have rented out his room to a lodger and that his stereo equipment has been confiscated by the police and sold to provide food for the cats of the woman he murdered. He is attacked by a group of old men whom he had victimized earlier, then rescued by three policemen, two of whom are former gang members who tell him that the government has been cleaning up the streets and hiring former hoodlums as police. Rather than help Alex, they beat him severely, leaving him to crawl to a nearby cottage. There, he is bandaged and fed by a man whom he had once attacked and whose wife he had brutally raped and beaten, but the man does not recognize him at first. Instead, F. Alexander sees in Alex an opportunity for propaganda against the government. Professing that "a man who cannot choose ceases to be a man," he calls together his friends but soon realizes that Alex is his wife's murderer. He tortures Alex by playing symphonic music loudly, and Alex tries to commit suicide by jumping out a window. Days later, he awakens in the hospital, completely swathed in bandages, and realizes that he has regained his violent nature. The doctors and government officials are happy because they are now free of the charges that they had perpetrated a criminal reform scheme and violated Alex's rights. While he was in a coma, they used "deep hypnopaedia or some such slovo" to restore his former depraved nature and his appetites for Beethoven and violence. As the old thoughts of violence fill Alex's head, he declares himself "cured all right."

## CENSORSHIP HISTORY

*A Clockwork Orange* has motivated debate since its publication, and the controversy has centered on the language of the book as well as on the brutality and sexual violence of the first third of the novel. In 1973 a book dealer in Orem, Utah, was arrested for selling three purportedly obscene books: *Last Tango in*

*Paris* by Robert Ailey, *The Idolators* by William Hegner and *A Clockwork Orange*. Using the 1973 Supreme Court "local standards" decision, *Miller v. California* (June 21, 1973), the town passed a very specific obscenity ordinance under which police charged bookstore owner Carole Grant. The charges were later dropped, but Grant was forced to close the store and relocate to another city.

In Aurora, Colorado in 1976, the school board at a regularly scheduled meeting approved 1,275 books for use in the high school, but they disapproved *A Clockwork Orange* and the following nine books: *The Exorcist* by William P. Blatty; *The Reincarnation of Peter Proud* by Max Ehrlich; *New American Poetry 1945–1960* by Donald Allen; *Starting from San Francisco* by Lawrence Ferlinghetti; *The Yage Letters* by William Burroughs and Allen Ginsberg; *Coney Island of the Mind* by Lawrence Ferlinghetti; *Kaddish and Other Poems, 1958–1960* by Allen Ginsberg; *Lunch Poems* by Frank O'Hara and *Rosemary's Baby* by Ira Levin. The books had already been included by teachers in their course reading lists, but on January 13, 1976, the school board issued a statement to teachers directing that the books "will not be purchased, nor used for class assignment, nor will an individual be given credit for reading any of these books." The school board did not rule that the books were legally obscene nor did it remove the books from the school libraries. The teachers challenged the decision of the board and the case went to court, where, in *Bob Cary, et al. v. Board of Education of Adams-Arapahoe School District 28-J, Aurora, Colorado, 427 F. Supp. 945, 952 (D. Colo. 1977),* they argued that the decision had impinged on their academic freedom. In his decision, Judge Matsch observed that the board had committed itself to offering students "an opportunity to engage actively in the free exchange of ideas" by offering the courses as electives. He stated, "It is enough to conclude that having granted both teachers and students the freedom to explore contemporary literature in these high school classes, the school board may not now impose its value judgments on the literature they choose to consider." Despite his stated position, the judge was forced to rule against the teachers because the teachers had bargained away their rights to academic freedom in this matter with a specific clause in their master contract.

In Westport, Connecticut in 1977, parents approached members of the school board to protest the use of the novel in the high school classroom. They cited "objectionable" language in their complaints. The work was removed from the classroom. In Anniston, Alabama, in 1982, protests resulted in the temporary removal of the novel from the school libraries, but the work was later reinstated with the restriction that students would need parental permission to take out the book.

## FURTHER READINGS

Aggeler, Geoffrey. *Anthony Burgess: The Artist as Novelist*. Birmingham: University of Alabama Press, 1979.

Coale, Samuel. *Anthony Burgess*. New York: Frederick Ungar Publishing, 1981.
*Modern Fiction Studies* (special Burgess issue) 27 (Autumn 1981).
*Newsletter on Intellectual Freedom* (May 1976): 70; (January 1977): 8; (March 1983): 37.
Pace, Eric. "Fears of Local Censorship Haunt the Book Trade." *New York Times* (January 8, 1974): 26.

# THE COLOR PURPLE

**Author:**   Alice Walker
**Original date and place of publication:**   1982, United States
**Original publisher:**   Harcourt Brace Jovanovich
**Literary type:**   Novel

## SUMMARY

*The Color Purple*, winner of the 1983 Pulitzer Prize for Fiction and the American Book Award, is composed of personal letters written by the main character, Celie, to God and to her sister Nettie. Written in the vernacular of poor Southern African Americans, the letters allow Celie to tell the story in her own words and permit the author to describe the community of women who support and eventually rescue each other from the restrictions placed on them by society.

The primary setting of the novel is Georgia in the years between World War I and World War II. The novel opens with the first letter written to God by 14-year-old Celie, the victim of continual sexual abuse by her stepfather Alphonso, whom she and her sister call "Pa" and whom they believe to be their natural father. When he first rapes her, he tells her to tell no one but God, and so begin her tragic and painful letters. Poor, uneducated and unattractive as Celie believes herself to be, she finds no means of preventing the abuse to herself but she strives to protect her younger sister Nettie from becoming a victim. Celie's two children born of the sexual abuse by her stepfather are taken from her and adopted by missionaries bound for Africa, a couple who also befriend Nettie and take her with them. Soon after, Celie is forced into a harsh and poverty-stricken marriage with Albert, a much older widower who mistreats her, leaving her letters to God and to Nettie as her only comfort. She never receives Nettie's responses because Albert hides the letters for years.

Victimized by men and by the failure to resist her ill treatment, Celie can conceive of no other life and views herself as ugly, talentless and insignificant until the beautiful, sensual, confident and independent Shug Avery enters her life. Albert's former lover and the mother of three of his children years earlier, Shug is a flamboyant blues singer. She returns as Albert's lover, then becomes Celie's lover, awakening her to experience love for the first time and to truly value her body and her talents. After learning that Albert has hidden her sister's letters for years, Celie leaves Albert to live with Shug and discovers her creative talent as she begins a pants company in Memphis. Years later, having become a confident and valued human being, Celie returns to Georgia to claim her family home. Her sister Nettie returns from Africa with Celie's children and the family celebrates the survival of the human spirit.

## CENSORSHIP HISTORY

The novel has been criticized for including such taboo themes as incest, birth of children outside of marriage, rape, sexual pleasure and lesbian activity. Aggressive Shug Avery has not only given birth to three children outside of marriage, but she later becomes sexually intimate with both her former lover and his present wife, Celie. Critics of her behavior emphasize that she shows no remorse for her moral transgressions and, instead, exhibits daring boldness in her pleasure seeking. Some members of the African-American community find the novel insulting to African-American males with its emphasis on Celie's sexual abuse by her stepfather and her physical abuse at the hands of her husband. Parents have also objected to the lesbian theme within the novel, claiming that the book would not have been acceptable for use in schools had the lesbian characters been white. In only rare instances have critics challenged the book for its language, but those who have cite the several instances in which such terms as "tits" and "pussy" appear as the cause of their objections.

The novel was first challenged in 1984 when parents of students in the Oakland (California) High School honors English class complained that the book was inappropriate reading because of its "sexual and social explicitness," especially its "troubling ideas about race relations . . . and human sexuality." The book was removed from the classroom, pending review by the Oakland board of education. After nine months of discussion, the board reluctantly gave approval for use of the book in the honors curriculum. The following year, school trustees in Hayward, California rejected a purchase order for copies of the novel based on their views that it contained "rough language" and "explicit sex scenes." In 1986, school librarians in Newport News, Virginia, removed the novel from the open shelves because of its "profanity and sexual references." The work was made available only to individuals over age 18 or to students who provided written permission from their parents. In 1989, a challenge was raised at the Saginaw (Michigan) Public Library, on the charge that the book was "too sexually graphic for a 12-year-old," but the challenge failed and the book remained on the open shelves. The novel was also challenged but remained in Chattanooga, Tennessee, in 1989, when it appeared as a summer youth program reading assignment.

Challenges to *The Color Purple* continued into the 1990s. A parent in Ten Sleep, Wyoming, complained in 1990 about the inclusion of the book as an optional reading assignment for a sophomore English class. The superintendent of schools refused to remove the book and, instead, reminded parents that the students had numerous alternative readings from which to choose. That same year, parents in Tyrone, Pennsylvania, objected to the inclusion of the novel on a high school supplementary reading list. They found the language and the sexual activity embarrassing. The school board formed a committee to review guidelines for reading lists and to set standards for material that did not appear on approved curriculum lists. Parents of students in New Bern (North Carolina) High School raised objections to the novel, one of the tenth-grade reading assignments, after they read the passage in which Celie is raped by her stepfather. The high school principal appointed a review committee and allowed parents to select another book for their children. The review committee created restrictions that determined how the novel would be taught to future students. Also in 1992, the novel was banned from the Souderton (Pennsylvania) Area School District 10th-grade reading lists when parents protested that the language and sexual situations of the novel made it more "smut" than literature.

## FURTHER READINGS

American Library Association. *Censorship and Selection: Issues and Answers for Schools.* Chicago: American Library Association, 1993.

Christian, Barbara. *Black Feminist Criticism.* New York: Pergamon Press, 1985.

Gentry, Tony. *Alice Walker: Author.* New York: Chelsea House Publishers, 1993.

Kramer, Barbara. *Alice Walker: Author of "The Color Purple."* Springfield, N.J.: Enslow Publishers, 1995.

People for the American Way. *Attacks on the Freedom to Learn: 1991–1992 Report.* Washington, D.C.: People for the American Way, 1992.

Young Adult Services Division, Intellectual Freedom Committee. *Hit List: Frequently Challenged Young Adult Titles: References to Defend Them.* Chicago: YASD, American Library Association, 1989.

# CUJO

**Author:** Stephen King
**Original date and place of publication:** 1981, United States
**Original publisher:** Viking Press
**Type:** Novel

## SUMMARY

*Cujo* is the story of a 200-pound Saint Bernard, a placid and typical "good dog" who becomes a source of terror to the family that loves him and to the inhabitants of the small town of Castle Rock, Maine. The Camber family pet, Cujo is the best friend of 10-year-old Brett Camber. The dog is bitten by rabid bats when he bolts into a cave while chasing rabbits. As Cujo slowly and painfully succumbs to rabies, King introduces his readers to the inhabitants of Castle Rock, some of whom will be attacked violently by Cujo and die.

Joe Camber, an auto mechanic and an abusive husband, makes a strong effort to indoctrinate his son Brett in his brutal ways, an effort that his wife, Charity, tries to counteract. Vic Trenton, a New York advertising executive who has moved with his wife, Donna, and son, Tad, to enjoy the peaceful Maine surroundings, strives to keep his marriage together even as Donna has an affair with local poet Steve Kemp, who cannot resist writing to Vic, "I enjoyed fucking the shit out of her." After receiving the note, Vic imagines their sexual encounter in detail. Aunt Evie, at 93 the oldest inhabitant, foretells the weather and has been labeled "that old loudmouth bitch" by postman George Meara, who is called "an old fart" by Aunt Evie. Gary Pervier, "meaner than a bull with a jackhandle up its ass," turned his Distinguished Service Cross into an ashtray in 1968. When hippies sought him out to tell him that he was "too fucking much," Gary threatened them with his rifle, for he considered them "a bunch of long-haired muff-diving crab-crawling asshole pinko fucksticks," and "told them he didn't give a shit if he blew their guts from Castle Rock to Fryeburg." The novel also contains "country club cunts" and several characters who routinely tell each other, "Fuck you."

Tad Trenton begins to see a monster in his closet each night soon after Cujo is bitten, and the two events are left for the reader to connect as representative of the evil that pervades ordinary life. The monster, "its eyes amber-glowing pits" that seem to follow him, frightens him and leaves "his scrotum crawling." He hears the monster's "purring growl" and smells "its sweet carrion breath." The monster disappears when Tad's parents enter the room, but reappears after they leave and warns Tad that his name "was Frank Dodd once, and I killed the ladies and maybe I ate them, too." He also warns Tad that someday soon he will pounce on the little boy and eat him.

The narrative continues, lapsing occasionally into Cujo's consciousness as he relates his physical deterioration, notes his muscle aches and festering muzzle and puzzles over his growing desire to kill the humans around him. The suspense builds with each kill, until Cujo traps Donna and Tad in their car, which she has taken to Camber's garage for repairs. For nearly two days, Donna struggles to keep her son safe from Cujo until she is forced into a physical confrontation with the dog and eventually kills him, using a baseball bat as her defense. Donna survives, although her deep bites bleed profusely and she must be treated for rabies, but Tad dies of dehydration despite her efforts to save him. As the novel ends, Vic and Donna reconcile, and Charity and Brett Camber begin a new life, free of Joe's brutality.

## CENSORSHIP HISTORY

Many works written by Stephen King have been challenged or removed from school and community libraries, and they include the following: *Carrie,*

*Christine, The Dark Half, The Dead Zone, Different Seasons, The Drawing of the Three, The Eyes of the Dragon, Firestarter, Four Past Midnight, It, Night Shift, Pet Sematary, Salem's Lot, The Shining, The Skeleton Crew, The Stand, The Talisman, Thinner* and *The Tommyknockers*. The most frequently challenged of King's works is *Cujo*, which has been charged with "age inappropriateness," "unacceptable language" and being "violent."

In 1984, parents of students in the Rankin County (Mississippi) School District challenged the appearance of the novel in the school libraries, claiming that it is "profane and sexually objectionable." The school board voted to retain the book in the libraries. In 1985, the novel was removed from the high school library in Bradford, New York, after parents complained that it is "a bunch of garbage." Also in 1985, the school trustees in Hayward, California, refused to approve a purchase order for the book because of the "rough language" and "explicit sex scenes." That same year, the Washington County, Alabama, board of education made a unanimous decision to remove the novel from all school libraries in the county, based on their perception that the novel contains "unacceptable language" and is "pornographic." In 1987, school officials removed the novel from the high school library after parents in Durand, Wisconsin, objected to it because of "violence" and "inappropriate language." The school board appointed a nine-member panel composed of school personnel and community members to review the book, and the issue was not pursued further.

In 1992, parents complained to the school superintendent in Peru, Indiana, that the novel and two other King novels, *The Dead Zone* and *Christine*, contained "filthy language" and were "not suitable for high school students," and they asked for its removal. The superintendent recommended to the school board that the novels be kept in the school library and made available to students who have parental permission. The school board refused to consider the suggestion and voted 5–1 to ban the books entirely from the high school library. Also in 1992, parents of middle school students in South Portland, Maine, requested that the school board remove the novel from the middle school library because of its "profanity" and sexual references. A review committee appointed by the school board to consider the request recommended its retention in the library collection. That same year, parents of students in Sparta, Illinois, appeared before the board of education and requested the removal of all books by Stephen King from the school libraries, claiming they are "violent" and "contain sex and explicit language." The board honored the parents' request to bar their children from using the book, but refused to ban the books.

In 1994, a local minister and a school board member in Bismarck, North Dakota, claimed that *Cujo* and eight other King novels (*Carrie, Christine, The Dead Zone, The Drawing of the Three, The Eyes of the Dragon, Pet Sematary, The Shining* and *Thinner*) should be removed from the school libraries. They challenged the novel on grounds of "age appropriateness."

## FURTHER READINGS

Egan, James. "Sacral Parody in the Fiction of Stephen King." *Journal of Popular Culture* 23 (Winter 1989): 125–141.

Hohne, Karen A. "The Spoken Word in the Works of Stephen King." *Journal of Popular Culture* 28 (Fall 1994): 93–103.

King, Stephen. "Banned Books and Other Concerns: The Virginia Beach Lecture." In *The Stephen King Companion*. Ed. by George Beahm, 51–61. Kansas City, Mo.: Andrews & McMeel, 1989.

*Newsletter on Intellectual Freedom* (May 1984): 69; (January 1985): 8; (May 1985): 75, 77; (July 1985): 111; (January 1986): 7; (January 1987): 12; (March 1987): 54–55; (May 1987): 86; (July 1987): 125; (November 1987): 225, 226; (September 1988): 152; (January 1989): 11; (March 1989): 4; (May 1989): 75; (January 1990): 4–5; (January 1991): 12; (March 1992): 40; (May 1992): 79, 80; (July 1992): 105; (July 1992): 106; (March 1993): 41, 56; (July 1993): 124; (May 1994): 84–85; (September 1994): 166–167.

# DADDY'S ROOMMATE

**Author:**  Michael Willhoite
**Original date and place of publication:**  1990, United States
**Original publisher:**  Alyson Publications
**Type:**  Children's book

## SUMMARY

*Daddy's Roommate* is one of the first children's books to deal openly with the topic of homosexual male parents. Brightly illustrated with only one brief, straightforward sentence on each page, the book relates the story of a young boy whose parents divorce. The young narrator visits his father and meets his father's roommate. The reader learns that the little boy's father and roommate work, eat, sleep, shave and sometimes even fight together but always make up. Both men act as fathers, and the three enjoy days at the zoo, baseball games and the beach.

Near the end of the book, the narrator states to readers that "Mommy says Daddy and Frank are gay." Because he doesn't know what that means, his mother explains that "Being gay is just one more kind of love." Another illustration shows Frank and the father barefoot and curled up on the couch watching television, accompanied by the line, "Daddy and his roommate are very happy together." The book ends with the narrator stating, "And I'm happy too!" as he stands between Frank and his father in line at the movies.

## CENSORSHIP HISTORY

*Daddy's Roommate* has been challenged repeatedly since its first appearance for reasons that range from a criticism of its language as "age inappropriate" to the charge that it is an indoctrination of children into the lesbian/gay lifestyle.

In 1992, nine incidents involving the book were recorded by the American Library Association. Bay Ridge School Board in Brooklyn, New York, removed this book and HEATHER HAS TWO MOMMIES, a book about lesbian parenting, from the district's grade school curriculum. The books had been included in the optional reading list for first-grade students, but the school board president decided after reviewing the books that certain words in the work were "age inappropriate."

Patrons of Timberland Regional Libraries in Olympia, Washington, challenged the book, claiming that it was "offensive" and "promotes homosexuality," but it was retained. Despite challenges by patrons of Roswell (New Mexico) Public Library and the Dauphin County (Pennsylvania) Library System that the intent of the book was "indoctrination into a gay lifestyle," the book was retained in both library collections. Patrons of public libraries in Goldsboro, North Carolina; Grand Prairie, Texas; and Tillamook, Oregon, asserted in their separate challenges that the book "promotes a dangerous and ungodly lifestyle from which children must be protected," but the named libraries retained the book.

A well-organized and well-orchestrated challenge to the book occurred in Gwinnett County, Georgia, where objectors submitted increasingly numerous complaints to the Lake Lanier Regional Library System. The complaints were followed by two petitions, one with 150 names and another with 200. Despite the pressure to remove the book from the library collection, the library staff chose to retain it. The challengers then requested a review of the book by the library board, which voted to removed it from open shelves and to place it behind the circulation desk, where it would be available to patrons who requested it. In explaining the decision, the board president stated that "it might be damaging to a three- to seven-year-old who might get the wrong idea. . . . Homosexuality is something we have to deal with in our lifetime, and we don't want to be censors, but maybe a little restriction."

Three challenges to *Daddy's Roommate* in 1992 included objections to *Heather Has Two Mommies*. The challenge at Fayetteville (North Carolina) County Library was particularly risky to the future funding of the library. Six members of a Right-to-Life group submitted separate objections to the books and a petition. The library held a public hearing at which protesters, one of whom admitted that she had never seen the books, heatedly denounced the books and stated that "anything that promotes or teaches homosexuality is decaying the minds of children." Despite the vehement objections, the library board voted unanimously to keep the books in the children's section. One trustee observed that a ban of the books may have satisfied the objectors, but it would have "probably infuriated many and violated the rights of all." The decision was announced shortly before the city was to vote on a bond issue to finance the library system. The protesters retaliated by organizing a campaign to defeat the bond issue, claiming in their propaganda that the library system "encourages young children to affirm and endorse conduct or a 'life style' that leads to untimely death and serves no biological utility." Unlike the strong support shown for the library in earlier years, only a small majority passed the bond issue.

When the public library in Springfield, Oregon, received donations of *Daddy's Roommate* and *Heather Has Two Mommies*, the children's librarian was forced to decide if inclusion of the books in the library collection would violate a recently passed city charter amendment that prohibited the city from "promoting, encouraging or facilitating" homosexuality. The Oregon Citizens Alliance (OCA), the group that had spearheaded the amendment, warned the library that if either book were to be placed in the library, they would "do everything they can to get it out of there." A representative from the local chapter of the American Civil Liberties Union warned the library that if it rejected the books solely because they violated the city charter amendment, they would file suit. The librarian applied the standard library selection guidelines to the books, and they were eventually retained over the protests of the OCA.

*Daddy's Roommate* and *Heather Has Two Mommies* were also challenged in Elizabethtown, North Carolina, by members of the Bladen Coalition of Christians who approached the Bladen County Commission to prevent the librarian from placing the newly purchased books in the county library. Labeling the books as "wicked, seditious, and dangerous," the protesters demanded their elimination and the appointment of a committee that would include members of their coalition to create new library book selection guidelines. The books were placed in the adult section of the library.

The book faced an increased number of challenges in 1993, making it the most challenged book of the year. After objections from patrons, the book was moved from the children's section to the adult shelves in Manatee (Florida) Public Library and Mercer County Library System in Lawrence, New Jersey.

In Mesa, Arizona, a patron of the public library challenged the book because it "is vile, sick and goes against every law and constitution," but it was retained. It was challenged but retained at Alachua County Library in High Springs, Florida; Seekonk (Massachusetts) Public Library; North Brunswick (New Jersey) Public Library; Cumberland County (North Carolina) Public Library; Chattanooga-Hamilton County (Tennessee) Bicentennial Library; Wicomico County Free County Library in Salisbury, Maryland; Sussex (Wisconsin) Public Library; Dayton and Montgomery County (Ohio) Public Library; and Juneau, Alaska, school libraries. The book was also challenged but retained as a reading in the curriculum in Rosemount-Apple Valley-Eden (Minnesota) School District.

In 1994, officials of the Lane County Head Start program in Cottage Grove, Oregon, removed *Daddy's Roommate* and *Heather Has Two Mommies* from its anti-bias curriculum after receiving complaints from parents. Challenged as being a "skillful presentation to the young child about lesbianism/homosexuality," the books were, nonetheless, retained by Chandler (Arizona) Public Library. In Fort Worth, Texas, however, the book was removed from the children's section and not relocated within the public library after critics charged that the book "legitimizes gay relationships."

## FURTHER READINGS

"Daddy Is Out of the Closet: *Daddy's Roommate* by Michael Willhoite / *Heather Has Two Mommies* by Leslea Newman." *Newsweek* 117 (January 7, 1991): 60.

Hardigg, Viva. "Censors at Work." *U.S. News & World Report* 117 (September 26, 1994): 29.

Hildebrand, Joan M. "Books for Children: *Daddy's Roommate*." *Childhood Education* 70 (1994): 306.

*Newsletter on Intellectual Freedom* (May 1992): 83, 95; (September 1992): 162; (November 1992): 197–199; (January 1993): 7, 9–10, 28; (May 1993): 143–146; (November 1993): 179; (January 1994): 13, 34–36; (March 1994): 69; (July 1994): 115; (September 1994): 147–148, 166; (November 1994): 187; (January 1995): 4, 6, 8.

St. Lifer, Evan. "*Daddy's Roommate* Challenged in VT." *Library Journal* 120 (July 1995): 14–16.

Symons, Ann K. *Protecting the Right to Read: A How-to-Do Manual for School and Public Librarians*. New York: Neal-Schuman Publishers, 1996.

## A DAY NO PIGS WOULD DIE

**Author:**   Robert Newton Peck
**Original date and place of publication:**   1972, United States
**Original publisher:**   Alfred A. Knopf
**Type:**   Young adult novel

## SUMMARY

*A Day No Pigs Would Die* is an autobiographical novel about a predominantly Shaker community in 1920s rural Vermont, during the year the author, as a young farm boy, is forced to grow from a 12-year-old child into a 13-year-old man. The novel opens with a bloody and graphic description of a cow giving birth. Rob, who has skipped school, sees her agony and goes to her aid. She nearly kills him, but the bull calves live and he is rewarded with a piglet that he names Pinky.

Rob's father, Haven, is the community pig slaughterer, an uneducated farmer who wants more for his son. Although the Peck family doesn't follow the Shaker way, the Shakers respect Haven, who, in turn, inculcates strong values and a respect for all living creatures into Rob. This respect contains a tolerance for human error, for the community members are imperfect but decent people. Widow Bascom is said to be "carrying on" with her young hired man, Ira Long, whom she later marries. Sebring Hillman had a child with Haven's cousin Letty years earlier when she cared for his ill wife, and he is tormented with guilt over her murder of the infant and her suicide. One night, Hillman digs up the baby's grave and takes the small coffin to bury in his family plot, a move that seems just to Haven and Rob. Rob uses "damn" and "hell" occasionally, and his father reprimands him. Even Haven is fallible. When he captures a weasel that had been killing his chickens, he invites Ira Long to test the weasel-killing instincts of his "bitch terrier," Hussy, by placing the two in a barrel with the lid on. Hussy kills the weasel, but she is badly injured and they must kill her. Haven decides never to allow that again, no matter how many chickens are killed.

Rob looks forward to breeding Pinky and marketing her offspring. She is mated several times with the neighbor's prize boar, beginning with one violent confrontation in which she fights but is unable to escape. "He was bigger and stronger and ten times meaner than Pinky. And so he had his way with her. All the time he was breeding into her, she squealed like her throat had been cut. Every breath. She just squealed like crying, and wouldn't stop." Afterward, Pinky's rump is bruised, blood runs down her leg and her body shakes violently. For all their efforts, Pinky is barren and Rob must concede that they cannot afford to keep her and must slaughter her for food.

Haven dies after a winter of ill health, and Rob must run the farm for his mother and great-aunt Carrie. He makes the funeral arrangements, speaks the eulogy and leads the mourners to the orchard to bury his father. He is keenly aware of his new responsibilities as the novel ends.

## CENSORSHIP HISTORY

The novel had been in classrooms and libraries for more than a decade before the first objections to content and language appeared. The objections have ranged from concern about the language to objections to the "violence" and "cruelty" of the weasel killing and hog slaughtering to the "graphic sexuality" of the descriptive passage in which Rob's pet sow is mated with a neighbor's boar.

In 1988 parents of students in the Jefferson County, Colorado, school district challenged the book and asked for its removal from the school libraries. They claimed that it was "bigoted against Baptists and women and depicts violence, hatred, animal cruelty, and murder." The school board reviewed their request and voted to retain the book. In 1990, the book was challenged but retained in the Harwinton and Burlington, Connecticut, schools where parents had raised objections to the use of the book in the school curriculum because of its "inappropriate language and subject matter that set bad examples and give students negative views of life."

In Carbondale, Illinois, in 1991, the parent of a ninth-grade student challenged the use of the book in the classroom and its inclusion in the school library. The concern centered on the use of profanity in the book. The school board convened a review committee to consider the challenge, but the parent who complained did not appear at the hearing, so the board voided the complaint. The following year several parents of students in a Califon, New Jersey, sixth-grade reading class demanded the removal of the book from the curriculum, asserting that it described violence to animals and "graphic depictions of animals mating." A review committee established by the school board recommended retention of the book, and the school board unanimously agreed.

In 1993 parents of students attending Sherwood Elementary School in Melbourne, Florida, challenged use of the book in the classroom, stating that it could give students the "impression that rape and violence are acceptable." Their concerns centered on the scene in which Pinky fights being mated. The book was retained. The novel was also challenged but retained in the school libraries in Waupaca, Wisconsin, in 1994, despite parents' objections to "graphic passages with sexuality in the book." That same year, the novel was removed from the seventh-grade classroom of Payson (Utah) Middle School after parents complained that they "had problems with language, with animal breeding, and with a scene that involves an infant grave exhumation."

## FURTHER READINGS

Hartvigsen, M. Kip. "Haven Peck's Legacy in *A Day No Pigs Would Die.*" *English Journal* 74 (April 1985): 41–45.
*Newsletter on Intellectual Freedom* (May 1988): 85; (July 1988): 119–120, 139; (September 1988): 151, 177; (March 1991): 44; (May 1991): 90; (July 1993): 97–98; (May 1994): 98–99; (July 1994): 117, 129.

# DELIVERANCE

**Author:**  James Dickey
**Original date and place of publication:**  1970, United States
**Original publisher:**  Houghton Mifflin Company
**Type:**  Novel

## SUMMARY

*Deliverance* is a stark novel that follows the adventures of four men from the city who embark on a three-day canoe trip into a wild and savage backwoods area of Georgia. Presented in journal form, the novel documents the self-awareness and reality that confront these men on September 14, 15 and 16 of an unidentified year, their efforts to come to terms with the savage environment and find strengths to cope with the dangers that the environment poses.

The four men are individually introduced to the reader in the first section, "Before." Ed Gentry, part owner of a graphics studio, is the narrator and one of the two characters who prove themselves able to deal effectively with the brutal wilderness. The other survivor is Lewis Medlock, a champion archer who owns rental property in the city. The two weaker members of the party are Bobby Trippe, a mutual funds salesman, and Drew Ballinger, sales supervisor for a soft-drink company. The first third of the novel creates a lulling effect for the reader, who learns the reasons why each man feels the need to test his civilized self against the uncivilized environment. The second part of the novel begins abruptly as survival becomes an immediate concern. Events occur in quick succession, as one member of the group, Drew, is killed in an accident, another, Lewis, breaks his leg, and the two remaining members of the group, Bobby and Ed, are confronted by two brutal backwoodsmen who try to force them to commit homosexual acts. Ed succeeds in his struggle against his attacker, but Bobby is ineffective and is sodomized. The author makes this scene a confrontation between the civilized and the bestial, and shows Bobby as a man so emasculated by society that he can only succumb when attacked.

In the final third of the novel, the reader learns the permanent effect of the trip on the surviving members. Ed has recognized his ability to deal with a hostile environment, so he can now accept his civilized life without further need to test himself. Lewis, whose broken leg had forced him to give up his leadership role to Ed, has learned to put aside his former proud and defiant attitude in favor of becoming more in touch with life. Bobby's new awareness is tragic, for he feels dehumanized and recognizes that he is unable to cope with elements outside the city.

## CENSORSHIP HISTORY

*Deliverance* has been challenged by parents, teachers, school board members and concerned citizens who have determined that it is an unsuitable text for several reasons, most prominently the homosexual rape scene. Complaints have been made against the language, claiming that it contained "unacceptable sexual references," "vulgar language" and "subject matter inappropriate for use in school." Parents have lodged stronger complaints against the rape scene, claiming that this made the book nothing more than "pornography and filth" and that it "promotes homosexuality." In several instances, questions have arisen regarding the brutality of the sodomy scene and the need to relegate use of the book to older high school students.

In 1974, parents in Montgomery County, Maryland, challenged the use of the novel as a required reading in the classroom and called for its immediate removal from both the classroom and the school library. In a presentation to the district board of education, challengers asserted that the novel employed "gutter language" and that it depicted "perverted acts." The decision was to offer an alternative reading to students, and the book was removed from the school library but later returned.

Similar complaints surfaced in 1993 voiced by parents of students at Hughes Junior High School in Bismarck, North Dakota. Basing their challenge on passages that they viewed as "obscene," "pornographic" and "filthy," parents protested that the novel was inappropriate for junior high school students. After consideration, the school board agreed and removed the novel both from classroom use and from the junior high school library. Copies of the book remained in use at the high school level.

The most extensive challenge to the novel occurred in 1973, in Drake, North Dakota, where the school board acted on parent complaints to remove *Deliverance*, Kurt Vonnegut's *Slaughterhouse-Five* and a collection of short stories by Hemingway, Faulkner, Steinbeck, Conrad and other writers. The English teacher, who was later fired, assigned the books "to get the kids to think clearly about current problems." He defended his choices, noting that "a few four-letter words in a book is no big deal. These people have all heard these words before; none learned any new words. I've always thought the purpose of school is to prepare these people for the 'big, bad world', but it evidently isn't so." None of the school board members had read the books, but based on parents' complaints, they decided that the books were "dirty."

The board ordered that the books be confiscated from students and burned, although only copies of *Slaughterhouse-Five* were destroyed. The school officials had planned to burn the other two books in equally public incidents but decided against doing so when their burning of the first book attracted nationwide attention, making people in Drake "sick and tired of all this publicity." The school superintendent defended the action of the board, claiming that he did not regret the action, only all of the publicity that it garnered. The English teacher was fired at the end of the school year, but the American Civil Liberties Union filed a suit on his behalf against the school district. The suit resulted in an out-of-court settlement in which the teacher was awarded $5,000 and the school board was ordered not to denigrate the teacher's performance either orally or in writing. Further, the settlement provided that teachers in the high school may use the three books in their junior- and senior-level classes.

## FURTHER READINGS

Baughman, Ronald. *Understanding James Dickey*. Columbia, S.C.: University of South Carolina Press, 1985.

"Book Burning in North Dakota." *Chicago Sun-Times* (November 14, 1973): 40

Ebersole, Peter. "Dickey's *Deliverance*." *Explicator* 49 (Summer 1991): 249–251.

Moorhead, Michael. "Dickey's *Deliverance*." *Explicator* 51 (Summer 1993): 247–248.

*Newsletter for Intellectual Freedom* (July 1975): 118; (November 1975): 174; (September 1993): 145; (November 1993): 178–179; (January 1994): 38.

# A DICTIONARY OF AMERICAN SLANG

**Editors:**   Harold Wentworth and Stuart Berg Flexner
**Original date and place of publication:**   1960, United States
**Original publisher:**   T.Y. Crowell
**Literary type:**   Reference

# DICTIONARY OF SLANG AND UNCONVENTIONAL ENGLISH

**Editor:**   Eric Partridge
**Original date and place of publication:**   1970, United States
**Original publisher:**   Macmillan and Company
**Literary type:**   Reference

# NEW DICTIONARY OF AMERICAN SLANG

**Editor:**   Robert L. Chapman
**Original date and place of publication:**   1986, United States
**Original publisher:**   Harper and Row, Publishers
**Literary type:**   Reference

## SUMMARY

These works are compilations of words and meanings that illuminate the colloquial underpinnings of the American language; many are not found in standard dictionaries. Included are slang terms created by members of a range of subcultures, such as the underworld, the military, industry, law enforcement, show business, sports, various occupational and age groups, as well as the slang of talk shows, technology and different sexual orientations. Some terms have sexual associations, and others give offense because of the challenge they represent to traditional speech. Included are words that are commonly labeled as "vulgar," "obscene" or "dirty."

## CENSORSHIP HISTORY

In 1963 Max Rafferty, the superintendent of public instruction in California, determined that among the approximately 8,000 entries contained in *A Dictionary of American Slang*, there were 150 "dirty" passages that made the book obscene. He suggested those passages necessitated "a little bit of censorship," removal of the book from libraries, and supporters in many communities agreed. The book was banned in Costa Mesa and Newport Beach and removed from library shelves in other communities throughout the state, but most libraries decided to keep the dictionary on a separate shelf for restricted use by "serious" students.

In 1979 a parent in Stuart (Florida) Middle School complained to school officials that the book was obscene. When other parents joined in the complaint, the school returned the book to the publisher. In 1981 the dictionary was removed from the Westminster County (Colorado) elementary and secondary school libraries after parents, members of the John Birch Society and administrators labeled it obscene.

The *Dictionary of American Slang and Unconventional English* became the target of censors in 1973 when the Citizens Commission on Education challenged the Pinellas County (Florida) school board to explain the inclusion of the reference work in the high school libraries. The chair of the commission claimed that the book was responsible for encouraging students to use profanity and blamed the book for the 696 students suspended on that charge in recent years. School officials rebuffed the complaints and retained the book with the claim that to remove the book would be an infringement of students' right to read.

The *New Dictionary of American Slang*, an updated version of the *A Dictionary of American Slang*, was challenged for use in Walled Lake School District in Commerce Township, Michigan, in 1994. Parents approached the school board and complained that the book contained profanity. School officials decided to restrict use of the reference work and labeled it with the following warning: "This book contains words which might be offensive to the reader."

## FURTHER READINGS

Jenkinson, Edward. *Censors in the Classroom: The Mind Benders*. Carbondale, Ill.: Southern Illinois University Press, 1979.
*Newsletter on Intellectual Freedom*. (March 1974): 32; (July 1979): 75; (March 1982): 42–43; (September 1994): 146–147.

# DOCTOR DOLITTLE

**Author:** Hugh John Lofting
**Original date and place of publication (first volume of series):** 1920, United States
**Original publisher:** J.B. Lippincott Company
**Type:** Children's fiction

## SUMMARY

"Doctor Dolittle" is a series of 12 volumes recounting the adventures of an English village doctor, John Dolittle, M.D., who loves animals so much that he gives up his human medical practice to devote himself to them. He is unique among men because he learns to understand and speak animal languages, and his compassion for animals takes him on adventures from his village of Puddleby-on-the-Marsh to strange continents and secret lakes, even to the moon on the back of a giant moth. His domestic menagerie of talking animals includes Dab-Dab, the duck who is his housekeeper; Jip, his loyal dog; Polynesia, the 182-year-old parrot known for her command of "the most dreadful seafaring swearwords you ever heard"; and Chee-Chee, Cheapside and the pushmipullyu.

Doctor Dolittle shows consistent enthusiasm for discovery, even to the point of staying up all night in order to learn the fish language of the silver fidgit. He shows concern for both animals and humans. In one adventure, he crosses the sea in a borrowed boat in order to save the monkeys of Africa from a mysterious, fatal disease. In another, he manages to persuade a judge in the British court to permit Bob, a dog, to testify at the murder trial of his master and thereby to save his master's life.

Throughout the series, Doctor Dolittle and the same animal characters appear and reappear in the selections and provide a sense of continuity to the works.

## CENSORSHIP HISTORY

"Doctor Dolittle" was first expurgated in the 1960s by J.B. Lippincott Company in the effort to make the books conform to the changing sensibilities of a world that was beginning "to coalesce into one international, multiracial society." The society of the 1920s, when the books were first published, was significantly less concerned with minority issues, and unexamined feelings of racial superiority pervaded not only children's literature but politics, religion, entertainment and social ventures. African prince Bumpo, whom Doctor Dolittle and his animals meet when they sail to Africa on a mission of mercy, wants to be white, which produces a great deal of comedy as he sets about trying to achieve his desire. He appears ridiculous, but Lofting also makes the doctor appear ridiculous in many circumstances. In the 1960s, however, the growing pride in culture and multiculturalism made the desire of an African prince to be white offensive to many readers.

The language of the 182-year-old parrot, Polynesia, also a native of Africa, is similarly offensive when she uses the terms "darky" and "coon" in the first book in the series, *The Story of Doctor Dolittle*, then "nigger" in later books in the series. Lippincott purged the series of these terms in the 1960s, but more extensive changes were called for.

In an article in the bulletin of the Council on Interracial Books for Children in 1968, New York librarian Isabelle Suhl charged that "the 'real' Doctor Dolittle is in essence the personification of The Great White Father Nobly Bearing the White Man's Burden and his creator was a white racist and chauvinist, guilty of almost every prejudice known to modern white Western

Man." The stand taken by the council was that editing the language was not enough, because the books were too racist to save. The recommendations of the council influenced librarians in schools and the public sector, and they simply stopped buying the Doctor Dolittle series after 1968. As a result, the 12 books went out of print in the early 1970s and did not reappear until 1988 in greatly altered form.

The 1988 version of the Dr. Dolittle books, published by Dell Publishing, was the result of radical censoring by two editors at Dell and by Christopher Lofting, the author's son. Prince Bumpo became neither black nor white, but colorless. All illustrations of the prince and of other African figures were omitted, and all of the characters were made racially neutral. The incident of the controversial desire of Prince Bumpo to become white so that Sleeping Beauty, his favorite fairy tale character, would marry him was removed. Changes were also made in the characters' responses to Doctor Dolittle. Representative of this change from the earlier version is a response given after Dr. Dolittle has saved the monkeys of Africa from a dread disease. In the original, they cheer him and shout gratefully, "Let us give him the finest present a White Man ever had!" This was changed to "Let us give him the finest present ever given." As a reviewer for *The New York Times* observed, "the present editors obviously hope to obliterate every emotionally tinted word."

## FURTHER READINGS

French, Sean. "Diary." *New Statesman & Society* (February 4, 1994): 8.
Lanes, Selma G. "Doctor Dolittle, Innocent Again." *The New York Times Book Review* (August 28, 1988): 20.
Perrin, Noel. *Dr. Bowdler's Legacy*. Boston: David R. Godine, Publisher, 1992.

# DOG DAY AFTERNOON

**Author:**   Patrick Mann (pseudonym for Leslie Waller)
**Original date and place of publication:**   1974, United States
**Original publisher:**   Delacorte Press
**Type:**   Novel

## SUMMARY

*Dog Day Afternoon* is based on the true story of a man who attempts to rob a bank to obtain money for his transsexual lover's operation. The first third of the novel describes the strange and tortured life of Joe Nowicki, half-Italian and half-Polish husband of the monstrously overweight Tina, "a religious guinea" with "immense breasts" whose "big soft lips" feel as if he "were biting ass" when he nibbles at them. His father never looks at him, but his mother can read his face so he avoids looking at her. He is sensitive about his slight build and wears four-inch clog heels to make himself appear taller, and he proudly flaunts the fact that he has a reputation in Greenwich Village as a tough guy known as Littlejoe.

Joe runs out on the weekly family dinner to meet his lover Lana, a preoperative transsexual with whom he has gone through a mock wedding ceremony. When he later carries a stoned Lana to one of the several "welfare pads" that he maintains to receive multiple welfare checks, the two make love and he tenderly strokes her face, noting that "she needed a shave again." As Lana comes to, she accuses Joe of not loving her enough because he hasn't come up with the $3,000 or $4,000 necessary for the complete operation. Lana then taunts Joe about the size of his penis, telling him that she has had sex with 13-year-old boys who were better endowed. Joe decides that he will prove his worth by obtaining the money needed.

The second part of the novel begins after Joe completes plans to rob a bank of a huge bakery payroll. The plan is carefully followed, and Joe enters the bank with his cohorts right on schedule, but the payroll delivery schedule has been changed so only a few thousand dollars are at the branch. The robbers decide to wait all night until the Wells Fargo delivery of $50,000 the following morning, and they also keep the hostages.

As the scheme begins to unravel, the police move in across the street, and Detective Sergeant Moretti begins a telephone dialogue with Joe. The two bargain while the television cameras move in. To keep the hostages alive, the police promise to meet Joe's demands, which include a million dollars, safe passage to Kennedy airport, a plane gassed and ready for transatlantic flight and his "wife," Lana, to go with him. As they wait, a media circus forms outside the bank, ice cream, pizza and beer vendors appear and pizza is delivered to the bank for the hostages and the robbers. When the police finally locate Lana and bring her to the police barricades, the people realize that she is a man in drag and begin to chant: "Faggot! Faggot!" Lana faints, and inside the bank Joe becomes defensive. Meanwhile, the police try to convince Lana to help them as they learn the real reason that Joe has tried to rob the bank.

When the ordeal appears about to end, the scene assumes an even more absurd tone. Joe's mother arrives, and in front of all of the onlookers and the police, they begin a disagreement about his wife, Tina, and what drove Joe into Lana's arms. Gay protesters appear with signs stating, "We Love You Joe." The limousine that appears to take the robbers to the airport bears a sign stating, "Total Relaxation Baths—Our Hostesses Make Life Worth Living," identifying it as transportation for an escort service. Before getting into the limousine, Joe mugs for the cameras and blows kisses into the crowd as the gay demonstrators chant, "Say it clear. Say it loud. I'm gay and I'm proud."

The novel ends with the FBI closing in and saving the hostages, but of the robbers only Joe survives.

## CENSORSHIP HISTORY

*Dog Day Afternoon* has been quietly kept out of many school libraries over the two decades since its publication simply by librarians' failure to order the book. The language and the sexual situations have motivated much of this reticence and most of the challenges to the work. Both men and women in the novel respond without attention to social niceties. While flipping channels, Littlejoe's father pauses at a soap opera in which a character moans she will never be able to look her friend in the eyes ever again. Annoyed, he suggests, "Look 'er inna twat." When a news bulletin exposes Littlejoe as the robber in a bank robbery standoff, his mother cries for their son, and his father responds, "*Your* fucking son maybe." Littlejoe refers to his heritage from his father's side as being "Polack" while he is a "wop" on his mother's side of the family. His mother asks if he wants to taste something great, and he responds, "Four pounds of shit in a two-pound paper bag?" Although Littlejoe is married, he cruises Greenwich Village and has Lana, a preoperative transsexual, for his lover; his mother suspects, and she questions him regarding his "faggot" and "queer" friends. When he waits for Lana at the bar where she entertains, he confides to a friend, "Gonna ball Lana tonight, man, and that broad don't ball without I lay a few solid blasts on her." Numerous other phrases have been singled out as "offensive."

Concern has also been raised regarding the descriptions of the gay milieu in which Littlejoe functions and the street hustling in which a younger man named Sam and other teenagers at a safe house engage to obtain money. Scenes of Littlejoe's sexual activities with Lana have also drawn criticism, as has the graphic description of Lana's striptease in a bar in which she exposes her breasts and strokes them to a hooting and yelping crowd, then turns away from the crowd for a moment "and stuck out her ass at the crowd . . . then she turned back and her penis, engorged, arose from between her legs like some primeval sea monster searching for its mate."

In 1978, the school board in Vergennes, Vermont, responded to parents' demands that the novel and *The Wanderers* be removed from the Union High School library. The librarian was also forbidden to buy additional works of fiction without having prior approval from both the district administration and the school board. Upset by the decision, a group of parents and students joined the school librarian, Elizabeth Phillips, to challenge the decision of the board.

When *Bicknell v. Vergennes Union High School Board*, 475 F. Supp. 615 (D. Vt. 1979) was decided, U.S. District Court Judge Albert W. Coffin rejected the students' and parents' claims and decided in favor of the Vergennes school board. Basing his decision on *Presidents Council, District 25 v. Community School Board, No. 25* (New York City) (see DOWN THESE MEAN STREETS), the court determined that the policies and actions of the school board did not directly or sharply infringe upon the basic constitutional rights of the students of Vergennes Union High School. The court acknowledged that other courts may have taken a benign view of library freedoms, but it also determined that "neither the board's failure to purchase a work nor its decision to remove or restrict access to a work in the school library violate the First Amendment rights of the student plaintiffs before this court" because the board removed the books for being vulgar and in bad taste.

Judge Coffin relied heavily on the *Presidents Council* decision in further denying that school librarians had the right to independent control over school library collections, rejecting their argument that denying such control amounted to denying their academic freedom. In 1980, the plaintiffs appealed to the U.S. Court of Appeals for the Second Circuit, but the court decision in *Bicknell v. Vergennes Union High School Board*, 638 F.2d 438 (2d Cir. 1980) affirmed that of the lower court.

## FURTHER READINGS

*Newsletter on Intellectual Freedom* (January 1979): 6.
O'Neill, Robert M. *Classrooms in the Crossfire*. Bloomington, Ind.: Indiana University Press, 1981.

## DOWN THESE MEAN STREETS

**Author:**   Piri Thomas
**Original date and place of publication:**   1967, United States
**Original publisher:**   Alfred A. Knopf
**Type:**   Autobiography

## SUMMARY

*Down These Mean Streets* relates the author's life between the ages of 12 and 20 growing up in Spanish Harlem in the 1940s and 1950s. Born of a light-skinned, Puerto Rico-born mother and a mainland-born, African-American father, Thomas bluntly reveals his difficulties as a dark-skinned, Spanish-speaking male in an atmosphere in which to be "cool" means running with a gang, using drugs, committing robberies, using illegal weapons and having indiscriminate sex. He relates his years on the streets, the temporary escape to suburbia and the six years spent in prison before he turned his life around and began to work as a counselor.

As befits the setting, *Down These Mean Streets* is told in the crude and coarse language of the streets. The young Piri is a survivor and he learns how to deal and to use drugs, how to steal and how to make some quick money with a friend who occasionally acts as a male prostitute to obtain money from homosexuals in the neighborhood. The adult Piri graphically describes these adventures, providing detailed instructions for how to get the maximum high while smoking marijuana, how to prepare and to inject heroin as well as specific aspects of the sexual acts performed. He uses ethnic and homophobic insults in describing those with whom he interacts and himself. Thus, "spics," "guineas," "faggots" and "niggers" are terms that frequently appear in the book, and "motherfucker" and "fuck" appear on almost every page. When Piri is sent to prison, the feeling of violence escalates and so does the daily physical threat. In unadorned language, he describes the threat of rape and the constant tensions of prison life that finally make him realize that he wants more in his life. He leaves prison rehabilitated, ready to begin a life of helping others to leave the streets and to make good lives for themselves.

## CENSORSHIP HISTORY

*Down These Mean Streets* contains the raw street vernacular of life in Spanish Harlem and descriptions of experiences that accurately depict a young man's struggle to survive in that brutal environment. These elements of realism have made the work a target of censors who have complained that the language is immoral, obscene and "just plain filthy." First challenged in 1971, the work was removed from the junior high school library by Community School Board 1250 in Queens, New York. The case that followed, *Presidents Council, District 25 v. Community School Board, No. 25* (New York City), 457 F.2d 289 (2d Cir. 1972), was the first to consider the issue of whether or not a school board had the authority to remove books from a school library. Parents were provoked by the language in the book, which they viewed as obscene, and requested the district board to order the book removed from school libraries. Responding to parent demands, the board held a public meeting where the book was described by 75 speakers, 73 of whom favored retention of the book on scholarly or educational grounds. Piri Thomas appeared at the meeting to speak: "I'm not here to defend the book. I'm here to defend the right of the truth to be said." Despite the support, the district board voted 5-3 to remove all copies of the book from the junior high school libraries in the district. Dissatisfied with this decision, a group of parents, students, teachers and a school librarian joined with the New York Civil Liberties Union to bring suit against the board in the United States District Court, but the court refused to hear the case.

Six weeks after removing the book, the board conducted another public meeting, where the original decision was modified to allow the libraries that had bought the book to retain their copies, but only parents, not students, could take out the book. Nearly a year later, when the case was appealed, the Court of Appeals of the Second Circuit affirmed the dismissal of the suit, noting that a specific group must be authorized to determine the makeup of a library collection, and proclaimed that there was no reason to elevate an "intramural strife to First Amendment constitutional proportions." The court ignored the right of students to freedom of expression and their right to receive information, and stated that "to suggest that the shelving or unshelving of books presents a constitutional issue, particularly where there is no showing of a curtailment of freedom of speech or thought, is a proposition we cannot accept." To do so, stated the decision, "would be a constant intrusion of the judiciary into the internal affairs of the school." Adamant in their fight, the group took the case to the United States Supreme Court, but the Supreme Court refused to review the case. Justice William O. Douglas stated in a dissenting opinion: "What else can the School Board now decide it does not like? How else will its sensibilities be offended? Are we sending children off to school to be educated by the norms of the School Board or are we educating our youth to shed the prejudices of the past, to explore all forms of thought, and to find solutions to our world's problems?"

In 1976 *Down These Mean Streets* was among nine books that school board members in Island Trees Union Free School District No. 26 in New York identified as being "objectionable." After a review committee examined the books, *Down These Mean Streets* was placed on a restricted list because it was judged by the committee to be "pornographic and filthy." Students needed parental permission to take out the book. The book was returned to the library on June 25, 1982, after the United States Supreme Court ruling in *Board of Education, Island Trees Union Free School District No. 26 v. Pico et al.* (See BEST SHORT STORIES BY NEGRO WRITERS for the full case.)

## FURTHER READINGS

*Newsletter on Intellectual Freedom* (July 1973): 115; (November 1982): 197.
O'Neil, Robert M. *Classrooms in the Crossfire: The Rights and Interests of Students, Parents, Teachers, Administrators, Librarians, and the Community*. Bloomington, Ind.: Indiana University Press, 1981.
———. "Libraries, Liberty and the First Amendment." *University of Cincinnati Law Review* 42:2 (1973): 209–252.

# DRACULA

**Author:**   Bram Stoker
**Original date and place of publication:**   1897, England
**Original publisher:**   Constable Publishers
**Type:**   Novel

## SUMMARY

*Dracula* is the story of the fiendish Count Dracula, whose activities are related in diary and journal entries written by principal characters. The novel begins and ends in Transylvania, the traditional site of vampire legends. At the outset, the count lures Jonathan Harker to his castle to explain the purchase of a London estate. Before leaving the inn in Bistritz, the young solicitor is puzzled by the behavior of the innkeeper's wife, who exhibits fear at the mention of the count's name and insists that he wear her crucifix around his neck. People in the crowd outside of the inn make the sign of the cross as Jonathan leaves for Dracula's castle. Once there, Harker becomes a prisoner of the count, who functions as his host, valet, driver, butler and maid. Strange dreams and visions pursue Harker, who seeks to escape the intense danger that he senses in the castle.

Two young and beautiful women, Lucy and Mina, are the objects of Dracula's lust for blood. The count hypnotizes them before biting them, and even Jonathan falls under his spell as he must be awakened from "a stupor such as we know the Vampire can produce" after Mina's exchange of blood with Dracula. Once bitten by Dracula, the women become slaves to unlawful hunger for blood. The sweet and virginal Lucy Westenra is turned into a vampire, and former suitors see her returning to her grave after preying on a child, the blood dripping down her chin. Mina just barely escapes the same fate; her saving grace is that "she has a man's brain" and is more resistant than the ordinary woman. The young men who try to defend them are unable to do so alone. They must call in the assistance of Dr. Abraham Van Helsing, a Dutch professor whom Stoker describes as "a philosopher and a metaphysician, and one of the most advanced scientists of his day," and Dr. John Seward, a man of science and the head of "a large lunatic asylum."

The last third of the novel is rational and deliberately scientific in tone, as it documents the efforts of Van Helsing and Seward to use research and such technology as phonograph rolls and typewriters to locate Dracula and his followers and to destroy them.

## CENSORSHIP HISTORY

Stoker professed to favor the censorship of fiction and wrote that "a close analysis will show that the only emotions which in the long run harm are those arising from sex impulses." He observed that "women are the worst offenders in this form of breach of moral law." This stance appears to exhibit a disparity between his prudery and the erotic and homoerotic undertones that readers have identified in *Dracula*. He ignored his own work when in 1908 he wrote a series of scathing articles for *Nineteenth Century* magazine in which he strongly advocated the censorship of eroticism in fiction.

Readers have long recognized the sexual overtones that pervade *Dracula*, from the first publication of the novel. Victorian readers professed to be scandalized by the intimacy of the count's act and the negative effect on Lucy's moral nature. Critics observed that the novel "is offensive to the sensibilities of the fair sex" and recommended that it be kept out of the hands of women.

Booksellers in England were advised to keep the book out of view, so that the "fair sex will not be polluted" by the "devilish mockery of purity" of the work.

Several passages were identified as having motivated particular moral concerns. When Harker lies on a couch in the castle, pretending to be asleep, he is visited by three beautiful, ghostly ladies. As he waits in "languorous ecstasy," one of the women "went down on her knees and bent over me, . . . licked her lips like an animal. . . . I could feel her hot breath on my neck." After Lucy has become a vampire, she is observed sucking the blood from a child, whose body she then throws to the ground after seeing her fiancée, Arthur Holmwood. Having changed from "purity to voluptuous wantonness," she aggressively calls Arthur to her, provocatively telling him, "My arms are hungry for you." When Dr. Seward pries open Lucy's coffin to drive a stake into her heart, he sees "the bloodstained, voluptuous mouth . . . the whole carnal and unspiritual appearance."

*Dracula* has been largely eclipsed by the numerous film and stage adaptations of the work, and most people today have become familiar with the story of Count Dracula through these sources rather than by reading the original. The novel does not appear frequently on required reading lists in schools; thus school censorship has not been a significant facet of its history. Only one such instance has been reported. In 1994, school officials at Colony High School in Lewisville, Texas, banned the novel from the required reading lists for junior and senior advanced placement English classes. Complaints centered on what critics viewed as "unacceptable descriptions in the introduction." The specific statement cited appears in an introduction written by George Stade: "Dracula is the symptom of a wish, largely sexual, that we wish we did not have."

## FURTHER READINGS

Belford, Barbara. *Bram Stoker: A Biography of the Author of "Dracula"*. New York: Alfred A. Knopf, 1996.

Croley, Laura Sagolla. "The Rhetoric of Reform in Stoker's *Dracula*: Depravity, Decline, and the Fin-de-siècle 'Residium'." *Criticism* 37 (Winter 1995): 85–108.

Fowell, Frank, and Frank Palmer. *Censorship in England*. New York: Burt Franklin, 1913. Reprinted in 1970.

Hendershot, Cyndy. "Vampire and Replicant: The One-Sex Body in a Two-Sex World." *Science-Fiction Studies* 22 (November 1995): 373–398.

Leatherdale, Clive. *Dracula: The Novel and the Legend*. Northamptonshire, England: Aquarian Press, 1985.

Schaffer, Talia. "'A Wilde Desire Took Me': The Homoerotic History of *Dracula*." *ELH* 61 (Summer 1994): 381–425.

Senf, Carol A. "Dracula and the Victorian Male Sexual Imagination." *International Journal of Women's Studies* 3 (1980): 455.

Twitchell, James B. "Women and Vampires: *Dracula* as a Victorian Novel." *Midwest Quarterly* 18 (1977): 392–405.

# EAST OF EDEN

**Author:** John Steinbeck
**Original date and place of publication:** 1952, United States
**Original publisher:** Viking-Penguin Press, Inc.
**Type:** Novel

## SUMMARY

*East of Eden* is the story of the classic epic struggle between two brothers, Charles and Adam Trask, whose rivalry reflects that of the biblical Cain and Abel played out in modern times. In part a historical romance, the work relates the lives of several generations of two families, in Connecticut and California, covering significant incidents from the Civil War to World War I. The author incorporates historical events and actual historical figures into the narrative, and these act to mold lives and determine the destinies of the fictional characters. For the most part, Steinbeck does not permit his characters control over their lives. Instead, while they seem to have free will in their moral choices, external factors constantly place them into situations in which they must make choices to survive.

Cyrus Trask is the hard-nosed patriarch who makes his sons, each fathered by a different wife, live a military-like existence. He tolerates no weakness and determines that the gentle-natured Adam must become tougher, so he plans a military career for the boy. Fact blends with fantasy as Cyrus regales everyone with his purported military feats during the Civil War. Among these adventures is his oft-told story of contracting gonorrhea in 1862 when, as a young soldier, he paid ten cents to have sex with a prostitute whom he later hunted for revenge.

When Cyrus dies, he leaves the extensive land holdings in the Salinas Valley and a large amount of money, the source of which remains a mystery, to both sons to share equally. Charles, the stronger son, who has a propensity for evil, stays and farms, but gentle Adam wanders the world at first and returns uneasily to his home. Their lives are dominated by their sibling rivalry, which extends to women, the land and life. After Adam settles down, his wife leaves him to own "a whorehouse, the most vicious and depraved in this whole end of the country," and he follows her to San Francisco, where she hurts him further by telling him that Charles fathered their twin sons. The novel details the drug use, attempt at self-induced abortion and sadistic practices of the prostitutes, even as it shows Adam rising above the immorality.

As the lives of Charles and Adam near their end, the epic rivalry is exhibited clearly in the behavior of Adam's twin sons, who will continue the conflict between good and evil and the struggle of individuals to make the correct choices. In the end, Steinbeck shows that there is no Garden of Eden in this life.

## CENSORSHIP HISTORY

The novel made readers uncomfortable when it was first published because it is a pessimistic look at man's ability to cope with fate. The language is vulgar in parts and the novel contains explicit sex scenes that convey the sense of the characters' slow development throughout. These aspects motivated no legal challenges, but parents and school boards have been uncomfortable with the book.

In 1978, the novel was one of numerous books removed from supplemental high school reading lists in Anaheim, California, despite their use for many years after complaints by parents, who viewed the book as obscene. Teachers were instructed to simply store the book, along with others such as Richard Wright's *Black Boy*, and cautioned that they were not permitted to provide the books for supplemental reading nor were they to discuss the books with students. The local school board warned teachers that they risked dismissal if they taught any of the banned books. The president of the Anaheim board of education denied that the removal of these books constituted a restriction. Rather, he stated the need of the school district to emphasize the basics of grammar and noted that "'the only effort to restrict comes from the content of basic grammar classes. . . . If they teach grammar properly, they will have no need for further books. Nor will they have time for them.'"

The novel was challenged or banned in other areas of the country. In 1982, school board officials ordered that the novel be removed from two Anniston, Alabama, high school libraries, because it was "obscene." They later reinstated the work on a restrictive basis. That same year, the novel was also removed from the Morris, Manitoba (Canada) school libraries due to its language. In 1991, parents in the Greenville, South Carolina, schools challenged the appropriateness of the book because of its profanity and because it contained "inappropriate sexual references." The school board made the decision to allow the book to be read with parental permission.

### FURTHER READINGS

*Newsletter on Intellectual Freedom* (March 1983): 37; (July 1991): 130.
"Steinbeck Novel Creates Controversy." *The Los Angeles Times* (June 3, 1978): 1.
"Steinbeck's *East of Eden*." *The Asterisk: An Occasional Journal of English Traditions* (October 1978): 2.

# ELMER GANTRY

**Author:** Sinclair Lewis
**Original date and place of publication:** 1927, United States
**Original publisher:** Harcourt Brace & Company
**Type:** Novel

## SUMMARY

*Elmer Gantry* is the story of a quintessential scoundrel, charlatan and womanizer, an extravagant faker who also happens to be a minister. He is an opportunist with few scruples or morals, who knows nothing about theology but everything about greed and seduction. Before he is "saved," Gantry is known to his college classmates as "Hellcat," known to become "eloquently drunk, lovingly and pugnaciously drunk." A typical Gantry suggestion is, "Let's go over to Cato and see the girls and get drunk." After his conversion, he vows not to smoke, "to guzzle, to follow loose women, to blaspheme." Hours later, he decides that just one cigarette won't hurt and eventually returns to all of his vices. Gantry decides to preach even if it means losing his waitress girlfriend Juanita, for he can "find skirts like her any place." At Mizpah Seminary, however, his sexual needs lead him to moan, "If Juanita was just here!"

Ordained a Baptist minister, Gantry is appointed to a small church and meets Lulu Bains, a deacon's daughter. When they first meet, he determines, "God, I've *got* to have her!" Soon, "She was in his arms, on the couch . . . limp, unreasoning, at midnight." Lulu, whose babble soon bores him "and her lovemaking was equally unimaginative," expects marriage. He stalls for months and foists her on another man as soon as he can.

Reassigned, Gantry is sidetracked by one too many drinks. Three days late in reporting to his new post, Gantry calls the deacon, who knows all about his four days of drinking and carousing. He is fired, but remains a Baptist minister and works as a salesman with the Pequot Farm Implement Company. For two years he makes a good living, buying himself fancy jewelry and clothing, but he misses the adulation of preaching. In Sauterville, Nebraska, he meets highly successful evangelist Sharon Falconer and decides at their first meeting "he was going to have Sharon Falconer." He follows her and becomes first her assistant, then her lover. Although he adores her, Gantry desires another woman, "feeling that it was sheer carelessness to let the pretty and anemic and virginal Lily be wasted."

Gantry next becomes the lover of a New Thought evangelist, but she ejects him from her circle for stealing. For a time, he preaches his own school of thought, then decides to "get in with a real big machine like the Methodists . . . with all their spondulix and big churches and big membership and everything to back me up." Assigned a church in Banjo Crossing, a town of 900, he feels that he is a failure at the age of 32 after the big-time evangelism with Sharon Falconer. Despite vows to the contrary, when he is led to his room by the Widow Clark's daughter, Jane, a girl of 14 or 15, his lechery surfaces and he thinks, "here was a girl he was going to pursue." Hours later, he meets Cleo, 27 years old and bosomy, and the daughter of a church trustee who is also the most successful man in town, worth at least $75,000. Gantry is soon married to Cleo, although on their honeymoon in Chicago "he concealed his distaste for her" and later discovers that "Cleo would never be a lively lover." His dislike of Cleo grows, and he finds "his whole body yearning toward" Jane Clark, but the promise of greater prominence in the Methodist hierarchy restrains him.

Six years and two churches later, Gantry is assigned to Sparta, a town of 129,000 people. Cleo and he sleep in separate bedrooms and, despite guilt, he does not refuse "whenever he found a woman parishioner who was willing to comfort him," nor does he desist from being "called on important but never explained affairs to Sparta." He becomes reacquainted with Lulu, now married, and resumes an affair with her until a good-looking woman becomes his secretary and his lover. His new secretary sets him up and tries to blackmail him using love letters that he wrote to her, but the clever intervention of lawyer T. J. Rigg clears him. In church the next Sunday, as the congregation crowds around to pray and to show their support, Gantry vows silently to never again become involved with a woman other than his wife. As he looks around, he sees a new choir singer, "a girl with charming ankles and lively eyes, with whom he would certainly have to become well acquainted."

## CENSORSHIP HISTORY

*Elmer Gantry* has been singled out by censors because of the sexual adventures of its title character and for the language that frequently peppers his personal conversation. Completely oblivious to the standards that he is supposed to uphold, Gantry frequently yields when his libido is aroused, then deals with the ensuing problems later. He is also given to interjecting "damn" and "hell" into discussions with trusted friends.

Despite expectations, major efforts to ban the novel were not spearheaded by Baptist or Methodist groups, who might take offense that Gantry holds posts in both churches. Instead, it became the target of the Watch and Ward Society, an organization made up mostly of Catholics in Boston, still a largely Catholic city in the 1920s. The organization differed from the New York Society for the Suppression of Vice because it prosecuted the booksellers, not the publishers. Its usual method was to warn all booksellers that a particular book violated the Massachusetts obscenity statutes, then leave it to the retailers to withdraw the book from sale or risk being taken to court. This method appeared to be more effective in taking books out of circulation, because individual booksellers were less likely than publishers to have the resources or the energy to defend them.

The year 1927 was critical as Massachusetts State District Attorney William J. Foley placed numerous books on the banned list, and *Elmer Gantry* was among the first whose sale he declared indictable. In his edict against the sale of the novel, the attorney general warned dealers of the severe penalties they would pay if they continued to sell it: "Evidence that this book is sold or offered for sale within the confines of Suffolk County will be followed by prompt action by this office."

Among the many books that appeared on the banned list, *Elmer Gantry* attracted the most attention. After Foley informed the Boston Booksellers' Committee that further sales of the novel would be prosecuted, the committee, which consisted of Richard F. Fuller of the Old Corner Bookstore, Charles E. Lauriat of the Charles E. Lauriat Co. and John Tracy of the New England News Co., brought to his office 57 other books that they believed were in danger if *Elmer Gantry* were suppressed. The booksellers claimed that they were in no position to fight the law.

A further repercussion of the ban was economic. Rather than fight the ban the Old Corner Bookstore returned its unsold copies of the novel to the publisher, Harcourt Brace. When the publisher protested, Richard Fuller suggested that it should force legal action by publicly selling a copy of the book in Boston and, when the case came to court, obtain a decision applicable to Suffolk County that would supersede the threat of the attorney general. Harcourt Brace refused and chose to sue the Old Corner Bookstore for its loss on the returned copies in what they described as a "friendly suit" in civil court.

Sale of the novel was also banned in Camden, New Jersey, and Glasgow, Scotland, in 1927, and in Ireland in 1931, as "offensive to public morals." The ban in Ireland was upheld in 1953.

In another incident, a catalog named *Summer Reading, 1927*, published by R.R. Bowker Company, became the target of censorship by the United States Department of the Post Office because it contained announcements of *Elmer Gantry*, as well as John Gunther's *The Red Pavilion* and May Sinclair's *The Allinghams*, all of which had either been banned in Boston or publicly labeled as "immoral" books. A Fifth Avenue bookstore manager was summoned to the New York City Post Office to discuss the catalog after he had sent out 8,000 copies of it with his shop's imprint on them. A copy was submitted to Horace J. Donnelly, solicitor of the U.S. Post Office Department in Washington, and he advised New York officials that the catalog was unmailable. The first 8,000 were permitted to proceed through the mails, but the bookseller and all others were warned that no additional catalogs could be sent, and no further copies were printed or mailed. In 1931, the Post Office officially banned from the mails any catalog that listed this novel. The ban was lifted three years later.

## FURTHER READINGS

"Boston Bans Sale of 'Elmer Gantry'." *New York Times* (April 13, 1927): 16.
"'Elmer Gantry' Banned in Boston." *Publishers' Weekly* (April 16, 1927): 1,569.
Light, Martin. *The Quixotic Vision of Sinclair Lewis.* West Lafayette, Ind.: Purdue University Press, 1975.

# END AS A MAN

**Author:** Calder Bayard Willingham Jr.
**Original date and place of publication:** 1947, United States
**Original publisher:** Vanguard Press
**Type:** Novel

## SUMMARY

*End as a Man* is a satiric portrait of life in a Southern military academy, an institution that is loosely based on The Citadel. The title of the work is taken from the speech of the commanding officer who claims that those who enter the Academy undergo a training so thorough that they enter as boys but each will "end as a man." The reality conveyed by the characters is that the rigid Academy code sadistically transforms each boy into a brute who learns to respect only what he fears. Thus, rather than become a man, each fully trained Academy cadet must recognize that graduation from the Academy marks his end as a man and his emergence as a fear-inducing brute.

The corruption inherent in the Academy is personified by Robert Marquales, an unattractive character whose self-pitying and self-serving nature leads him to become an informer and henchman for Cadet Sergeant Jocko de Paris. Marquales ferrets out the secrets of vulnerable cadets, such as that of Perrin McKee, the homosexual cadet who, in bitterly sarcastic dialogue, vies with Marquales for the attention of de Paris. Marquales also fails to come to the aid of other cadets who are being treated sadistically, especially his roommate, the overweight Maurice Maynall "Sowbelly" Simmons, who prays all night and wets his bed repeatedly. Rather than help his roommate, Marquales disassociates himself from the pathetic cadet, who is later beaten so severely that blood coagulates on his boxer shorts. Simmons is found a few days after this incident lying on the floor of the latrine, exhausted from another beating and with his face and head smeared with human excrement.

While Marquales represents the corrupt aspects of the Academy, de Paris represents the unrelenting cruelty as he leads the upperclassmen in their merciless behavior toward the cadets. In the opening chapter, de Paris bullies Simmons until he vomits at the dinner table, which establishes the cadet as the scapegoat, the "company crap-catcher," of the new first-year cadets. De Paris cheats in card games with fellow cadets, blackmails them and lies to extricate himself from every situation without concern for what his lies will do to others.

The society of the Academy turns even the first-year men against their own, and the less clever cadets often find themselves tortured by their quicker-witted brothers. Simmons's photograph of his dead 10-year-old sister disappears and is desecrated; when it reappears, "the child in the white dress had two breasts, a navel, and pubic hair from which a great penis emerged." Another unsuspecting first-year man lends his pen, engraved "From Myrtle to Bubber with oodles of love," to another cadet who learns that "Myrtle" is the pen owner's mother. The fact is soon made public, and humiliation follows.

The novel recounts one brutish action after another, slowly escalating until the commandant discovers the existence of a secret drinking and gambling club, after a public drinking brawl instigated by de Paris that results in disciplinary action against 28 cadets and the expulsion of four, including de Paris. Marquales saves himself from expulsion by becoming an informer and exposing the role that de Paris played in the scandal. As the novel ends, Marquales receives three crisp $10 bills and a letter from de Paris which states, "I hope your conscience doesn't torture you about what you did. There are worse things than cowardly selling out the best man you ever knew. I'm enclosing your reward." With a smile, Marquales pockets the money and later uses it to buy a portable radio.

## CENSORSHIP HISTORY

John Sumner, appearing on behalf of the New York Society for the Suppression of Vice, issued a complaint against Vanguard Press in 1947 as soon as the novel was published. The unusually forthright language, which had been taboo before World War II, was cited as the chief cause of concern. In the novel, one cadet refers to a waitress as "table pussy," while another cadet speaks of his father finding "a rubber draped over the steering wheel" after he had borrowed the car. At various times, other cadets use such expressions as "Oh, piss," "Go shit in your hat" and "Kiss my butt." Admitting that he is homosexual, cadet Perrin McKee tells Marquales, "I had experiences at the age of 10 that would rot your prostate." In addition, throughout the novel, cadets speak repeatedly of "whores," and "whorehouses," and there are numerous references to masturbation.

The author and literary critics testified on behalf of *End as a Man* in *People v. Vanguard Press, Inc.*, 192 Misc. 127, 84 N.Y.S. 2d 427 (1947). In testimony, Willingham claimed that his purpose was "to show some of the spiritual and emotional consequences on the youths attending such a school" as well as the spiritual and emotional effects of the severe hazing and strict discipline at the Academy. Magistrate Strong dismissed the case. In his decision, he acknowledged the large number of "so-called four-letter words, for the most part used as adjectives or expletives," but he determined that the most vital question is the effect of the book as a whole. After viewing the work in total, he concluded that "its effect on the reasonably normal reader would not be sexually demoralizing."

The following year *End as a Man* was again in court, this time in the Court of Quarter Sessions in Philadelphia County, Pennsylvania, as one of nine novels identified as obscene. Criminal proceedings were brought against five booksellers who were charged with possessing and intending to sell the following allegedly obscene novels: James Farrell's Studs Lonigan trilogy (*Young Lonigan, The Young Manhood of Studs Lonigan* and *Judgment Day*), Farrell's A WORLD I NEVER MADE, William Faulkner's *Sanctuary* and *Wild Palms,* Erskine Caldwell's *God's Little Acre,* Harold Robbins' NEVER LOVE A STRANGER and Willingham's *End as a Man.* Judge Curtis Bok, who sat as trial judge in *Commonwealth v. Gordon et al.,* 66 D. & C. 101 (1949), read the books "with thoughtful care" and wrote the first really thoughtful judicial opinion about the limitations that the First Amendment's guarantees should be interpreted to exert upon obscenity proceedings. He determined that "obscenity" was an indeterminate term, "that different meanings given to it at different times are not constant, not historically or legally; and that it is not constitutionally indictable unless it takes the form of sexual impurity, i.e., 'dirt for dirt's sake' and can be traced to actual criminal behavior, either actual or demonstrably imminent." Judge Bok based his judgment on the books as a whole and upon their place in the arts. He discussed at length the concern whether in censoring obscenity the courts were contravening the principles of freedom of speech and of the press. Judge Bok concluded, "I hold that the books before me are not sexually impure and pornographic, and are therefore not obscene, lewd, lascivious, filthy, indecent, or disgusting." This judgment was later sustained in the Superior and Supreme Courts of Pennsylvania.

## FURTHER READINGS

De Grazia, Edward. *Girls Lean Back Everywhere: The Law of Obscenity and the Assault on Genius.* New York: Random House, 1992.

Lewis, Felice Flanery. *Literature, Obscenity, and Law.* Carbondale, Ill.: Southern Illinois University Press, 1976.

Parr, J. L. "Calder Willingham: The Forgotten Novelist." *Critique,* 11 (1969): 57–65.

# ESTHER WATERS

**Author:**  George Moore
**Original date and place of publication:**  1894, England
**Original publisher:**  J.M. Dent & Sons, Ltd.
**Type:**  Novel

## SUMMARY

*Esther Waters* relates the story of a servant girl who loses her job, her status and her respectability when she becomes pregnant, then fights against her fate to survive and raise her son to manhood. The struggle is realistically presented, as are the temptations to give up, yet she perseveres in a life of unrelieved and uneventful toil. The theme of gambling and its toll on lives also runs through the novel.

The novel opens with 20-year-old Esther standing on the train platform, about to begin her work as a kitchen maid at the Barfields' elegant estate, Woodview. As she walks from the station, she meets William Latch, whose mother is the cook at Woodview and whose father's life had been ruined by betting on racehorses. She cannot return home because "her [step]father would curse her, and perhaps beat her mother and her too. . . . Her little brothers and sisters would cry if she came back. They had little enough to eat as it was."

The obsession with horse racing at Woodview is alien to Esther, who had "heard of racecourses as shameful places where men were led to their ruin, and betting she had always understood to be sinful." She is religious, but a friendly housemaid warns her to keep her religious views to herself because the others will call her a "Creeping Jesus." Fortunately for Esther, Mrs. Barfield is also a "Plymouth Sister" who senses a spiritual soulmate in Esther and tries to teach her to read.

One evening, after an important horse race is won by the Barfields, the servants celebrate with the rest of the household, and ale flows freely. Even Esther, formerly opposed to drink, has two pints of ale, which lower her defenses. When she walks out into the moonlight with her boyfriend William, "she could not put him away . . . though she knew her fate depended upon her resistance." She becomes pregnant after that one sexual experience, but William runs off with one of the wealthy Barfield daughters, deserting her without knowing that she carries his child.

With little money, Esther returns to her family, which she pays 10 shillings weekly for room and board. She soon leaves because her stepfather extorts increasing amounts of money from her, and she takes a room in a house near the hospital. When she goes into labor, she is treated with cold indifference by the nurses and doctors. Later, her only means of earning a living is to become a wet nurse for the baby of Mrs. Rivers, a fashionable lady. To do so, Esther must place her child into someone else's care, until she learns that the infants of two previous wet nurses have died while in such care. Frantic, Esther gives up the position, takes her child and must again look for work.

In the seven years that follow, Esther works long hours to provide for Jackie, then finds a suitable position with a kindly mistress and meets a devout man who wants to marry her and become a father to Jackie. On an errand for her mistress, Esther meets William, her son's father, who expresses his remorse and the desire to be a father to their son and a husband to Esther. He is now prosperous as the owner of the Kings' Head pub and a successful bookmaker for horse racing. Esther struggles to choose between the devout suitor and William and decides that Jackie would benefit from all that William could provide, so she becomes William's wife. They prosper, so much so that Esther now has servants, even though she worries as she views the numerous lives ruined by betting on the horses. When Jackie is 15, disaster befalls the family as William becomes fatally ill with consumption, the Kings' Head is raided because of the betting, and the license to operate is revoked. Esther struggles to keep Jackie in school and to keep life going as William wastes away in a hospital. When he dies, Jackie must leave school to work, and Esther must, once again, tolerate long, painful workdays and low pay.

At Jackie's urging, Esther contacts Mrs. Barfield, and the older woman welcomes Esther back to Woodview, now an impoverished estate, where the two live in seclusion and in anticipation of word from their sons. Mrs. Barfield worries because her son Arthur makes his living at the racetrack and rarely contacts her, and she helps Esther provide for Jackie, who works hard just to survive in London. Finally, unable to find suitable work, Jackie joins the military. The novel ends as the handsome adult son visits his mother before he must leave with his military unit. To Esther, all that she has gone through in "the long fight for his life" has been worthwhile and she truly feels that "she had accomplished her woman's work—she had brought him up to man's estate."

## CENSORSHIP HISTORY

*Esther Waters* is written in a stark and realistic style that both recounts the struggle of a servant girl to raise her illegitimate child alone and presents a bitter indictment of society. The novel was excluded from British circulating libraries in 1894, as both Mudie's Library and Smith's Library refused to stock it, viewing it as too risqué because the main character suffers as the result of her one sexual indiscretion, but she does not die, and because of the candid manner in which her situation is presented. For instance, when Esther returns to live with her family before her baby's birth, her stepfather tells her, "We wants no bastards 'ere." Her mother, like many poor women of the day, is severely abused and economically dependent, as she must bear child after child and eventually dies in childbirth. In a scene considered by censors of the time to be in poor taste simply due to its mention, the doctors and nurses at the maternity ward where Esther gives birth show little consideration for the needs of the financially destitute young woman. After the birth, the young mother learns that many young women of the lower classes allow their own babies to die and use their milk production to gain well-paid positions as wet nurses to babies of the rich.

By censoring the novel, the influential libraries greatly decreased potential sales because they held the power to set the tone for novels. Representatives of the libraries claimed that they sought to protect their subscribers from "certain blemishes of treatment." In essence, they were displeased by the factual, unsentimental account of the birth of Esther's illegitimate child, as well as by the manner in which a hypocritical and inhumane society shuns her, and by her strength and competence to raise her son and to achieve some degree of happiness regardless of public scorn. Despite the efforts to ban *Esther Waters*, the novel became Moore's first financial and artistic success.

The author had experienced a similar reception from the libraries to two earlier novels, *A Modern Lover* (1883) and *A Mummer's Wife* (1885). These attacks motivated Moore to take an aggressive stance against censorship, and he had responded with a scathing attack on the power of the circulating libraries in *Literature at Nurse, or Circulating Morals* in 1885. He denounced the manner in which the circulating libraries had reduced English fiction to formulaic plots, featuring either "a sentimental misunderstanding which is happily cleared up in the end, or . . . singular escapes over the edges of precipices, and miraculous recoveries of one or more of the senses of which the hero was deprived. . . ." Deploring the negative effects of the libraries, which had deprived modern publishing of the novel of analysis and observation, Moore wrote, "Let us renounce the effort to reconcile these two irreconcilable things—art and young girls." His attack failed to reverse the position of the libraries regarding his novels, and when *Esther Waters* came out in 1894, with its theme of unmarried motherhood and scenes of a maternity ward, both Smith's and Mudie's excluded it from their catalogs. When Moore later proved that the libraries had lost a minimum of £1,200 in profits because of their stance, they recanted and added the work to their catalogs.

## FURTHER READINGS

Cirillo, Nancy R. "A Girl Need Never Go Wrong, or, the Female Servant as Ideological Image in Germinie Lacerteux and Esther Waters." *Comparative Literature Studies* 28 (1991): 68–88.

Morgan, Charles. *Epitaph on George Moore*. New York: Macmillan Company, 1935.

Schwab, A.T. "Irish Author and American Critic." *Nineteenth Century Fiction* 8 (March 1954): 256–277.

## FAHRENHEIT 451

**Author:**  Ray Bradbury
**Original date and place of publication:**  1953, United States
**Original publisher:**  Ballantine Books
**Type:**  Novel

## SUMMARY

*Fahrenheit 451* relates the story of an oppressive society in which books are forbidden objects and firemen are required to burn all books they encounter.

The novel, an expanded version of a 1950 story entitled "The Fireman," takes its title from the temperature at which paper ignites: 451°F. One of a number of dystopic novels published after World War II, the work portrays humans as having lost touch with the natural world, with the world of the intellect and with each other. As the fire captain observes, "the word 'intellectual' became the swear word it deserved to be."

People hurry from their homes to their workplaces and back, never speaking of what they feel or think but only spouting meaningless facts and figures. At home, they surround themselves with interactive picture walls, wall-size television screens on three walls (four walls if one can afford them) containing characters who become accepted as family in an otherwise unconnected life. The streets have become dangerous as *minimum* speed limits of 55 miles per hour must be maintained, and speeds well over 100 miles per hour are more common. Teenagers and daring adults race their cars through the streets without concern for human life. War with an unnamed enemy is imminent.

For one fireman, the realization that there is a better life comes in the form of a 17-year-old girl named Clarisse, whose appreciation of nature, desire to talk about feelings and thoughts and appreciation for simply being alive mark her as an "odd duck." Guy Montag likes his job as a fireman, but he has clandestinely taken books from several sites where he and his fellow firemen have burned books and the houses in which they were hidden. Clarisse's questions as to why Montag became a fireman and her observations that the job does not seem right for him are disconcerting. A call to burn the books and house of a woman who refuses to leave the premises and, instead, ignites herself with the books increases Montag's discontent. He tries to speak with his wife Mildred, but she blocks him out with her Seashell ear thimbles, tiny radios worn in the ear that play continuously, and her involvement with her "family" on the picture walls.

Montag learns that the major reason for the abolition of books was to keep everyone happy. His fire captain explains that without books there is no conflicting theory or thought, and no one learns anything more than anyone else. With books, "Who knows who might be the target of the well-read man?"

After his wife reports that Montag has books in the house and their home is destroyed by the firemen, he seeks the help of former English professor Faber, who is part of a broader movement to preserve the knowledge of the past. Following Faber's directions, Montag goes to the railroad yards where he meets a group of old men, all former university professors who have each memorized specific literary works. They claim to be part of a network of thousands of individuals who will keep literature alive in their heads until the time when the oppression ceases and they can set the literature in type once more. Montag, who has memorized several books of the Old Testament, joins them, and the novel ends on a hopeful note.

## CENSORSHIP HISTORY

*Fahrenheit 451* is an indictment of censorship and expurgation, so the fact that this book was expurgated and marketed by the publisher that way for 13 years before the author became aware of the abuse is particularly ironic. In 1967, Ballantine Books published a special edition of the novel to be sold in high schools. Over 75 passages were modified to eliminate such words as "hell," "damn" and "abortion," and two incidents were eliminated. The original first incident described a drunk man who was changed to a sick man in the expurgated edition. In the second incident, reference is made to cleaning fluff out of the human navel, but the expurgated edition changed the reference to cleaning ears. No one complained about the expurgation, mainly because few people were aware of the changes, and many had not read the original. The copyright page made no mention of the changes, but thousands of people read only this version of *Fahrenheit 451* because the edition ran to 10 printings. At the same time, Ballantine Books continued to publish the "adult" version that was marketed to bookstores. After six years of the simultaneous editions, the publisher ceased publication of the adult version, leaving only the expurgated version for sale from 1973 through 1979, during which neither Bradbury nor anyone else suspected the truth.

In 1979, a friend alerted Bradbury to the expurgation, and he demanded that Ballantine Books withdraw completely the expurgated version and replace it with his original. The publisher agreed, and the complete version has been available since 1980.

This act of censorship had far-reaching effects for authors in regard to the school book clubs. The incident set in motion the American Library Association (ALA) Intellectual Freedom Committee, Young Adult division. In 1981, the committee looked into expurgation by school book clubs, such as Scholastic, and found that all of them expurgated books to some extent. Using its clout, the ALA reminded the book clubs that it awards the Newberry and Caldecott medals for children's books, and the ALA also noted that buyers are attracted to books designated as "ALA Best Books." The organization warned that it would strip the award announcements from expurgated books. The ALA also alerted teacher groups to demand that an expurgated book in a school book club be clearly identified on the copyright page as an "edited school book edition."

In a "Coda" that now appears in editions of *Fahrenheit 451*, Bradbury states, "I will not go gently onto a shelf, degutted, to become a non-book."

The "adult" version still has its critics. In 1992, students at Venado Middle School in Irvine, California, were issued copies of the novel with numerous words blacked out. School officials had ordered teachers to use black markers to obliterate all of the "hells," "damns" and other words deemed "obscene" in the books before giving them to students as required reading. Parents complained to the school and contacted local newspapers, who sent reporters to write stories about the irony of a book that condemns bookburn-ing and censorship being expurgated. Faced with such an outcry, school offi-cials announced that the censored copies would no longer be used.

## FURTHER READINGS

Johnson, Wayne L. *Ray Bradbury*. New York: Frederick Ungar Publishing Company, 1980.

Moore, Everett T. "A Rationale for Bookburners: A Further Word from Ray Brad-bury." *ALA Bulletin* 55 (May 1961): 403–404.

*Newsletter on Intellectual Freedom* (July 1992): 108–109.

Seed, David. "The Flight from the Good Life: 'Fahrenheit 451' in the Context of Postwar American Dystopias." *Journal of American Studies* 28, pt. 2 (August 1994): 225–240.

# A FAREWELL TO ARMS

**Author:**   Ernest Hemingway
**Original date and place of publication:**   1929, United States
**Original publisher:**   Charles Scribner's Sons
**Type:**   Novel

## SUMMARY

*A Farewell to Arms* is both a powerful war novel and a love story. Told from the first-person point of view of American Frederic Henry, who becomes an ambulance driver for the Italian army in 1916, it chronicles fighting against the Austrian army along the Italian-Yugoslavian border. With the other offi-cers, Henry first spends a lot of his time drinking and visiting the officers' brothel. On the battlefield, he is reckless in rescuing wounded soldiers and, after valorous conduct in his 11th battle, he is awarded a decoration. He also becomes involved with an English nurse named Catherine Barkley who serves in an Italian military hospital. He begins the relationship as a way to fill the time, after he learns that Catherine's fiancé was killed in the war and she is vulnerable.

After Henry is wounded and hospitalized, the affair intensifies and he dis-covers that he really loves Catherine. He asks Catherine to marry him, but she refuses, knowing that she would then be sent back to England and away from him. However, the war imposes physical separations on them, when Henry is sent to the front just as Catherine learns that she is pregnant. His disillusion-ment with war escalates as he is involved in the retreat from Caporetto, which begins in an orderly, disciplined manner but eventually turns into a panicking mob as authority breaks down and self-preservation becomes paramount. Henry is captured with other officers and held for execution, but manages to escape, thus completing his disillusionment with the war. He locates Catherine and the two escape together to Switzerland where they await the birth of their baby. They spend idyllic months, despite Catherine's worry that her narrow hips will make the birth difficult. When they seem about to achieve happiness together, their child is stillborn and Catherine dies after suffering internal hemorrhaging, leaving Frederick Henry alone.

## CENSORSHIP HISTORY

*A Farewell to Arms* has been censored both for its language and for sexual innuendo, as well as for the sexual relationship between Henry and Catherine and her unmarried pregnancy, although no graphic sexuality occurs in the novel. The soldiers frequent "bawdy houses" or the officers' "brothel." Henry has had "gonorrhea" and a military officer fears having "contracted syphilis from a prostitute." A dead sergeant who had attempted to desert the army is referred to as a "son of a bitch." Early in the novel, a boisterous officer teases a priest that he is often seen with the girls. When the priest protests, the officer jokingly accuses him of masturbating, saying, "Priest every night five against one." At one point, Catherine teases Henry, who says that he is lost without her and states that he at least had something to do at the front. She says, "Othello with his occupation gone." He replies, "Othello was a nigger."

In the few instances in which Hemingway seemed unable to substitute an innocuous word for what might be viewed as a vulgar term, he used dashes. When speaking about their chances against the Austrians, one of two Italian soldiers says, "They'll shell the —— out of us." When the soldiers pass through a small Italian town, they pick up two girls and place them in a jeep, while they speculate about having sex. As they speak, the soldiers reassure the girls that there will be no sex, "using the vulgar word," but Hemingway places dashes in the four places where the "vulgar word" should appear. Then the soldiers bluntly ask the girls if they are sexually inexperienced: "Virgin? . . . Virgin too?"

An officer visits the wounded Henry in the hospital, and he tells Henry that the priest is making big preparations to visit. He teases Henry, "Sometimes I think you and he are a little that way. You know." Catherine visits Henry when he is moved to an American hospital in Milan, and they make love in his room, but the reader has to pay careful attention to the dialogue to know this has occurred. Their lines alternate between Catherine asking if Henry *really* loves her, and Henry reassuring her that he does. Afterward, as she sits in a chair by the bed, "the wildness was gone" for Henry, and Catherine asks, "Now do you believe I love you?" As the novel progresses, they discuss marrying, and the point is clearly made that Henry wants "to make an honest woman" out of Catherine. They are concerned about legitimizing her pregnancy.

The censorship of *A Farewell to Arms* began before the novel was published, leading to Hemingway's complaints to editor Maxwell Perkins that too many necessary "unsavory" words had been removed from the manuscript. In letters to Perkins, he stated that "if a word can be printed and is needed in the text it is a weakening to omit it." Perkins had warned Hemingway in 1926 in regard to the earlier novel *The Sun Also Rises* that "papers now attack a book, not only on grounds of eroticism which could not hold here, but upon that of 'decency,' which means *words*." He had suggested that in that novel another word be substituted for the bull's "balls," as well as for other terms.

Two years later, Hemingway was faced with eliminating the natural speech of men at war. Thus, in the original manuscript in the section that detailed the retreat from Caporetto, Hemingway wrote the following: "'Tomorrow maybe we'll sleep in *shit*,' Piani said. 'I'll sleep with the queen,' Bonello said. 'You'll sleep with *shit*,' Piani said sleepily." The underlined words appear as blanks or dashes in the final novel. Other passages in that same section of the novel have dashes to substitute for "the *fucking* cavalry" and in "So do you, *cocksucker*," as well as in other instances.

In 1929, *Scribner's Magazine* contracted to serialize the book with certain changes. As the editor Robert Bridges explained to the author in a letter:

> we have in several places put in dashes instead of the realistic phrases which the soldiers of course used. This was not done from any particular squeamishness, but we have long been accepted in many schools as what is known, I believe, as "collateral reading," and have quite a clientage among those who teach mixed classics. Things which are perfectly natural and realistic in a book are not viewed with the same mind in a serial reading.

Bridges excised the following words from the manuscript that could not be used in a magazine: "balls," "cocksucker," "fuck," "Jesus Christ," "shit," "son of a bitch," "whore" and "whorehound." He also deleted a passage in which Henry fantasizes about his weekend in bed with Catherine, a passage that would later be returned to the novel when it was published. The second installment contained increased deletions of passages, including the sanitization of the seduction scene. Despite all of the changes, the June 1929 issue of *Scribner's Magazine* was banned from the bookstands in Boston, by order of the superintendent of police.

When Max Perkins edited the novel for publication, the following words deleted by Bridges were returned: "Jesus Christ," "son of a bitch," "whore" and "whorehound." However, Perkins suggested that Hemingway remove the following question: "Would you like to use a bedpan?" He also asked Hemingway to change "'Miss Van Campen,' I said, 'did you ever know a man who tried to disable himself by kicking himself in the balls?'" to substitute the word "scrotum" for "balls." Hemingway fought to retain use of the word "cocksucker" by the soldiers, and he claimed that eliminating it would completely emasculate the novel. His suggestion to use the term c—s—r was considered still too strong, so only dashes appear for that word.

In spite of the modifications to the text, the novel was considered too risqué. In a strongly negative review entitled "What Is Dirt?" in *Bookman*, Robert Herrick claimed that he was "adamantly opposed to censorship" but found that *A Farewell to Arms* presented one of those times when it was necessary. Other guardians of morality sent scathing letters to *Scribner's Magazine* threatening to cancel subscriptions because of the "vileness" of the novel, calling it "vulgar beyond express" and condemning the magazine for exploiting "such disgusting situations."

The novel was banned in Italy in 1929 because of its painfully accurate account of the Italian retreat from Caporetto during World War I. In 1930, the Watch and Ward Society in Boston, buoyed by the earlier successful outcry against the serialization in *Scribner's Magazine*, placed pressure on booksellers to remove the book from their store windows. In 1933, the novel was one of numerous books burned by the Nazis in Germany, allegedly for its "prurience." In 1938, the National Organization for Decent Literature (NODL) found the novel to be "objectionable" and placed it on their list of blacklisted books that was then sent to cooperating book dealers who agreed to remove the books from their racks. Such NODL blacklists resulted in elaborate collegial pressure among booksellers, although not legal enforcement against a work. The novel was also banned in Ireland in 1939, because of the "fornication" of Henry and Catherine and the pregnancy outside of marriage.

The novel has experienced more recent challenges. In 1974, parents of students in the Dallas (Texas) Independent School District demanded that it be removed from the high school libraries, along with Arthur Miller's *Death of a Salesman*, William Golding's LORD OF THE FLIES and Robert Penn Warren's *All the King's Men*. They complained that the novel contained a depressing view of life and "immoral" situations. After reviewing the work, school officials retained the novel. The book was also challenged in the Vernon-Verona-Sherrill (New York) School District in 1980 for being a "sex novel," along with A SEPARATE PEACE, TO KILL A MOCKINGBIRD, *The Grapes of Wrath*, OF MICE AND MEN and *The Red Pony*.

## FURTHER READINGS

Benson, Jackson J. *Hemingway: The Writer's Art of Self-Defense*. Minneapolis: University of Minnesota Press, 1969.

Cohen, Peter F. "'I Won't Kiss You. . . . I'll Send Your English Girl': Homoerotic Desire in 'A Farewell to Arms'." *Hemingway Review* 15 (Fall 1995): 42–53.

Donaldson, Scott. "Censorship and 'A Farewell to Arms'." *Studies in American Fiction* 19 (Spring 1991): 85–93.

Hemingway, Ernest. *Selected Letters: 1917–1961*. Ed. by Carlos Baker. New York: Charles Scribner's Sons, 1981.

Herrick, Robert. "What Is Dirt?" *Bookman* 70 (November 1929): 258–262.

Mandel, Miriam. "Ferguson and Lesbian Love: Unspoken Subplots in 'A Farewell to Arms'." *Hemingway Review* 14 (Fall 1994): 18–24.

Meriwether, James B. "The Dashes in Hemingway's *A Farewell to Arms.*" *The Papers of the Bibliographical Society of America* 58 (Fourth Quarter, 1964): 449–457.

Oldsey, Bernard. *Hemingway's Hidden Craft: The Writing of 'A Farewell to Arms'.* University Park, Pa.: Pennsylvania State University Press, 1979.

Reynolds, Michael S. *Hemingway's First War: The Making of "A Farewell to Arms".* Princeton, N.J.: Princeton University Press, 1976.

Solotaroff, Robert. "Sexual Identity in 'A Farewell to Arms'." *Hemingway Review* 9 (Fall 1989): 2–17.

## THE FIXER

**Author:**  Bernard Malamud
**Original date and place of publication:**  1966, United States
**Original publisher:**  Farrar, Straus & Giroux
**Type:**  Novel

### SUMMARY

*The Fixer*, winner of both the Pulitzer Prize and the National Book Award, is based on the 1913 trial of Mendel Beiliss, a Jew in Russia who was acquitted after being tried in Kiev. The novel takes place in turn-of-the-century Russia and opens with people hurriedly running away from town and toward a ravine that contains numerous caves. They are shouting excitedly that the dead body of a child has been found covered with stab wounds and the body has been bled white. Anti-Jewish propaganda leaflets are quickly circulated that accuse the Jews of the murder and claim that the boy's blood had been collected "for religious purposes . . . for the making of the Passover matzos." The ridiculous charge frightens many, including 30-year-old Yakov Bok, who passes for a Christian and lives in a sector of Kiev that is forbidden to Jews.

Yakov had only come to Kiev from the provinces five months earlier. He is a man whose life has been marred by tragedy. His mother died 10 minutes after his birth, his father was killed in an anti-Semitic incident a year later and he spent a miserable childhood in an orphanage. When he married, his wife Raisl did not become pregnant after five years, so he shunned her and she ran off with another man. In the shtetl, the Jewish ghetto area of Russia, he was known as a fixer, a man who would fix whatever was broken, but half the time he worked for nothing because inhabitants of the shtetl barely had enough to eat. He goes to Kiev hoping to change his luck and to become a financial success. To avoid the bias suffered by Jews, Yakov plans to pass as a Christian.

Passing as a Christian is difficult for Yakov, even after he is offered steady work by a man whose life he saves one bitter, snowy night. One time, for instance, the man's daughter attempts to seduce Yakov, who reluctantly allows himself to be led to her bedroom, but he nearly gives himself away when she stands naked by a washbowl and blood trickles down her leg. His immediate reaction is, "But you're unclean!" Despite her protests that "this is the safest time," he leaves. Already suspicious of Yakov, the woman identifies his reluctance to have sex with her while she is menstruating as a sign of his adherence to Jewish law. His supervisors have already expressed suspicion, and he is soon exposed.

When the murdered child is found, Yakov is made the scapegoat, possibly as punishment for his audacity in attempting to hide his Jewish heritage, and immediately placed in prison where he is subjected to physical and mental torment and spiritual degradation. Dealing with insects, pails of excrement and beatings becomes secondary to enduring the humiliating body searches during which his body orifices are probed first twice daily then six times daily. After a few months of imprisonment, Yakov is offered a deal by the prosecutors to lessen his sentence if he will admit his guilt and sign a form stating that the Jewish Nation used him as its agent in the murder. He refuses, and they increase the pressure by offering a complete pardon and physical freedom if he will sign the confession, but Yakov insists on going to trial because an admission of guilt might motivate a pogrom.

After nearly two years, Yakov's wife visits him in prison and they recall his "curses and dirty names" directed against her because of her inability to conceive. Raisl tells him that she became pregnant after leaving him and that the boy is almost a year and a half old. She asks if Yakov will remove her stigma and her son's by claiming to be the child's father. Yakov agrees and signs a statement to that effect.

To the end, Yakov remains resolute and his case finally goes to trial, but the reader is denied knowledge of the outcome.

## CENSORSHIP HISTORY

*The Fixer* has been challenged for several reasons, ranging from the "vivid grossness of scenes" to being "pornography and filth." The most surprising reason to Malamud has been the attack on the book for being "anti-Semitic" in its language and depiction of characters. Several instances of language use have been identified as "obscene." When his father-in-law suggests that Yakov blames him for Raisl's running off, Yakov responds, "You're blaming yourself for having brought up such a whore." In response to his father-in-law's caution that the horse that he has traded to Yakov is prone to gas if fed too much grass, Yakov replies, "If he's prone to gas let him fart." When a supervisor is accused by Yakov of dishonesty, "lifting his leg Proshko farted" in response. When

Yakov is cautioned to not forget his God, he says angrily, "What do I get from him but a bang on the head and a stream of piss in my face?" When the fixer stops for lunch while on his journey, the horse "spattered a yellow stream on the road" and "Yakov urinated on some brown ferns."

Parents of students in Aurora (Colorado) High School English classes challenged the use of this book in the classroom because of "inappropriate" language, and the school board banned it from use in 1976. A Pennsylvania school district removed the book from classroom use and provided an alternate selection to students because of the "obscenities" in the novel.

The most extensive challenge to the novel occurred in 1982, in Island Trees Union Free School District No. 26 in New York (see BEST SHORT STORIES BY NEGRO WRITERS), where the school board ordered *The Fixer* and 10 other works removed from the junior and senior high school libraries. Special care was taken with *The Fixer*, one of the few books that was also used in English classes, and the principal removed all copies from the classroom and storage closet. In the court record, specific objectionable passages are cited as "filthy" or "anti-Semitic." As the brickyard overseer, Yakov's job is to watch that the men do not steal; when he challenges the supervisor, the man responds angrily, "What do you think goes on in the wagons at night? Are the drivers on their knees fucking their mothers?" After he is jailed, Yakov is harassed by his Russian cellmates who threaten him: "So you're the bastard Jew who killed the Christian boy. . . . Who else would do anything like that but a motherfucking Zhid?" The investigating magistrate asks Proshko what Yakov did with the rubles he is accused of stealing, and the supervisor responds that he probably took the money to bed and gave "it a fuck once in a while." At another point in the novel, Yakov is threatened, "No more noise out of you or I'll shoot your Jew cock off."

Five students filed a suit against the school board, and the American Jewish Committee (AJC) and other organizations also became involved. In an amicus brief, filed by the AJC with the American Jewish Congress, Anti-Defamation League of B'nai B'rith, the American Orthopsychiatric Association, the Ethical Humanist Society of Long Island, Long Island Council of Churches, the National Council of Teachers of English, the Unitarian Universalist Association and Writers in the Public Interest, submitted in the United States District Court for the Eastern District of New York against Island Trees School District, the groups declared their astonishment that *The Fixer* "was banned because it contained anti-Semitic references. That assertion can lead to one of two conclusions: that its author is either illiterate or dishonest. *The Fixer* clearly condemns anti-Semitism, as it does the authoritarian society which is the seed bed of anti-Semitism." The case was heard by the United States Supreme Court which ruled against the school board on June 25, 1982, in *Board of Education, Island Trees Union Free School District No. 26 v. Pico*, and the books were returned to the libraries.

## FURTHER READINGS

Avery, Evelyn Gross. *Rebels and Victims: The Fiction of Richard Wright and Bernard Malamud*. Port Washington, N.Y.: Kennikat Press, 1979.

Helterman, Jeffrey. *Understanding Bernard Malamud*. Columbia, S.C.: University of South Carolina Press, 1985.

*Newsletter on Intellectual Freedom* (May 1977): 79; (November 1982): 197.

# FRUITS OF PHILOSOPHY: THE PRIVATE COMPANION OF MARRIED COUPLES

**Author:**   Charles Knowlton
**Original date and place of publication:**   1832, United States; 1833, England
**Original publisher:**   Privately printed (U.S.); James Watson (England)
**Type:**   Medical handbook

## SUMMARY

*Fruits of Philosophy: The Private Companion of Married Couples*, the first popularly written English-language medical guide to preventing conception, was initially subtitled "The Private Companion of Married People." The book, written by a physician in simple and clear language so that the poorest members of society could understand and benefit from it, deals with reproductive physiology, coitus and conception control. The book began as a slim pamphlet on the methods of preventing conception that Knowlton gave to patients who requested such knowledge.

The book opens with Knowlton's response to the arguments against birth control, then explains its many advantages, including the control of overpopulation, reduction of poverty and crime, prevention of hereditary diseases, preservation and improvement of the species and reduction of abortions and the ill health suffered by women who are subjected to excessive childbearing. In brief, he first discusses the moral philosophy of contraception. He then provides an anatomical discussion of the reproductive organs and explains the processes of menstruation and conception, both promoting and preventing conception. Some of Knowlton's physiological descriptions are inaccurate and need updating, but his chemical methods of contraception were relatively effective and "the tone and point of view are, on the whole, surprisingly modern."

## CENSORSHIP HISTORY

The work gained little notice in the popular press, and the professional medical press waited 11 years after it appeared to publish a first review in the

*Boston Medical and Surgical Journal*. In contrast, the legal authorities in Massachusetts gave it nearly immediate attention as they rushed to prevent the information from reaching readers. In early 1832, only months after publication of the work, a local lawyer circulated a pamphlet in which he accused Knowlton of making prostitution easy and inexpensive at 50 cents per copy, while removing from it the "inconvenience and dangers." The author was brought to trial in Taunton, Massachusetts, and charged with distributing "obscene material," then fined $50 and court costs. In December 1832, a rival physician signed a complaint in Cambridge, Massachusetts, charging that the book was "immoral" and that it "undermines chastity." Knowlton, who suffered from a heart condition, was found guilty of distributing his book and sentenced to three months of hard labor in the Cambridge House of Correction, from January through March 1833. Late in the following year, a clergyman from Ashfield, Massachusetts, registered a complaint that charged Knowlton with "undermining society" by distributing *Fruits of Philosophy*. From late 1834 through mid-1835, Knowlton appeared in court in Greenfield, Massachusetts, three different times to answer this charge, but the case was finally dismissed because the jury in all three trials could not come to a decision.

The notoriety of the trials made the book a best-seller, which went through nine editions in Knowlton's lifetime. He died in 1850, but the book gained international fame after his death because of the epic 1877 Bradlaugh-Besant trial in England. The book had been published by British publisher James Watson; at his death in 1874, London publisher Charles Watts bought the plates from his widow and placed the book back into print. Two years later, Henry Cook published in Bristol, England, a pirated copy of the book with the addition of allegedly obscene illustrations to enliven the book. Cook was arrested, tried and sentenced to two years at hard labor. At the advice of well-known freethinkers Charles Bradlaugh and Annie Besant, Watts sought an audience with the court to identify himself as the original publisher of the book in its original condition. His aim was to return the book to its original condition, minus illustrations, and original level of acceptance, for it had been published in England for 40 years without prosecution. Watts was arrested, taken to London and arraigned. He pleaded guilty to publishing a book about the physiological details of sex and paid a fine in the amount of 500 pounds.

Bradlaugh and Besant were angered by the cowardliness of Watts in admitting to publishing an "obscene" book, and they were determined to test the court. Late in 1877, they published the book themselves, with a new introduction, through their Free Thought Publishing Society. To be certain that the police would arrest them, Bradlaugh and Besant sent the London police a copy of the book and informed the police exactly where and at what time they would sell the first copy. A few days later, a detective in plain clothes purchased a copy of the book for six pence, then arrested the two. They were tried before Lord Chief Justice, Sir Alexander Cockburn.

During the five days of the trial of *Charles Bradlaugh and Annie Besant v. The Queen*, large crowds gathered outside of Guildhall expressing their sympathy with the defendants. Sir Hardinge Gifford, the prosecutor, condemned the book as being "a dirty, filthy book. . . . The object of it is to enable a person to have sexual intercourse, and not to have that which in the order of providence is the natural result of that sexual intercourse." In contrast, Bradlaugh and Besant spoke of population problems and examined the meaning of the term "obscenity." They and their prominent witnesses, among them the consulting physician to Metropolitan Hospital, spoke of England's poor and the need to limit the population.

The jury returned an ambiguous verdict, stating: "We are unanimously of the opinion that the book in question is calculated to deprave public morals, but at the same time we entirely exonerate the defendants from any corrupt motives in publishing it." Although he interpreted the verdict to mean that the jury thought the defendants guilty, Cockburn let the defendants go without a sentence or a fine, but they were told that they had to surrender the book and vow never to publish it again. When Bradlaugh and Besant declared clearly to the judge that they planned to publish, the judge sentenced them to six months in prison, a fine of £200 each, and recognizances of £500 each for two years. The defendants were released on bail while they appealed the case on the grounds that the specific words upon which the prosecution based its charge of "obscene" had never been expressly identified. Thus, in writing the final opinion on the appeal decision, the judge made it clear that "we express no opinion whether this is a filthy and obscene, or an innocent book. We have not the materials before us for coming to a decision on this point. . . . the indictment simply averred that an offence had been committed, and did not shew how it had been committed." The defendants recovered their stock of books, stamped in red "Recovered from Police," and sold them.

## FURTHER READINGS

Arnstein, Walter L. *The Bradlaugh Case*. Oxford: Clarendon Press, 1965.

Fryer, Peter. *The Birth Controllers*. London: Corgi Books, 1967.

Manvell, Roger. *The Trial of Annie Besant and Charles Bradlaugh*. New York: Horizon Press, 1976.

Nethercot, Arthur H. *The Last Four Lives of Annie Besant*. Chicago: University of Chicago Press, 1963.

Petersen, William. *The Politics of Population*. Garden City, N.Y.: Doubleday & Company, 1964.

Reed, James. *From Private Vice to Public Virtue: The Birth Control Movement and American Society*. New York: Basic Books, 1978.

# GARGANTUA AND PANTAGRUEL

**Author:**  François Rabelais
**Original date and place of publication:**  1567, France; 1708, England; 1927, United States
**Original publisher:**  Privately published (France and England); Boni & Liveright (United States)
**Type:**  Satire

## SUMMARY

*Gargantua and Pantagruel*, originally five separate volumes later combined under the one title, reflects the author's changing experiences, interests and attitudes in Renaissance France. The five books were separately titled *Pantagruel* (1533), *Gargantua* (1535), the *Third Book* (1546), the *Fourth Book* (1548–1552) and the *Fifth Book* (1562–1564). Although Rabelais had Cardinal Jean du Bellay as his longtime patron, and he was under the protection of François I of France for the publication of the *Fourth Book*, his bawdy and often obscene satires joined with his lack of attention to social niceties frequently put him into conflict with the authorities.

Written as a burlesque of the classical epic and chivalric romance, the work is an exuberant mock-heroic effort that purports to relate the lives, heroic deeds and sayings of Gargantua and his son Pantagruel, two members of a pleasant race of giants who love to eat and drink heartily and who enjoy earthy pleasures and humor. The author claimed that the work "demonstrates the theme that the real purpose of life is to expand the soul by exploring the sources of varied experience." The unifying philosophy of the work is expressed by Pantagruel, "Do As Thou Wilt." Using puns, wordplay, synonyms and flexible syntax, Rabelais creates a world in which restrictions on sensual or intellectual experience are not tolerated, and excessive discipline is considered inhuman and evil. Those who would restrict freedom are satirized throughout the five books: the militarists, abusers of justice, pedants and medieval scholastics.

The five books are only loosely connected and the work contains nothing resembling a plot, for to force an order on the events would be too restrictive for the author. Because his concern is freedom of the *mind*, anarchy is not an issue, but he avoids the unimaginative, conforming mind. In presenting the adventures, Rabelais used extremely frank language to carry out his purpose, to force readers to recognize the ludicrous preoccupations of mankind and to make them laugh at the incongruities and absurdities of society.

## CENSORSHIP HISTORY

*Gargantua and Pantagruel* contains a large number of humorous references that have been labeled "obscene" for over four centuries. Rabelais frequently speaks of emetic subjects in an exaggerated manner to draw attention and laughter from readers. In one passage, he tells of Gargantua's horse who "pissed to ease her belly, but it was in such abundance, that it did overflow the country seven leagues, and all the piss of that urinal flood ran glib away towards the ford of Vede, wherewith the water was so swollen, that all the forces the enemy had there were with great horror drowned." In a second passage, he suggests that the city walls of Paris would be better fortified if female organs, "callibristis" or "contrapunctums," were used instead of stones because they are cheaper and can more easily be arranged according to size. He states wryly that "no thunderbolt or lightning would fall upon it. For why? They are all either blest or consecrated." In still another passage, Rabelais relates the story of a miraculous codpiece that sexually arouses anyone near it. When its owner enters a theater in which a passion play is being performed, all on stage and in the audience are so sexually aroused that they immediately begin to copulate randomly with each other.

Although less frequently, deviance appears in some of the stories, as in the episode in which hermaphrodites appear and in another in which boys are maintained for sodomy. In an ode to wine, Rabelais speaks bluntly of oral sex: "If there came such liquor from my ballock, wold you not willingly thereafter suck the udder whence it issued?"

The first two books were published under the pseudonym of Alcofribas Nasier without the author's knowledge in 1533 and were promptly suppressed by censors in the French Parliament in 1534 and placed on the *Index* of the Sorbonne for being obscene and sacrilegious. In 1535, a papal bull was issued to remove censure from the work, and the third book was published in France using the author's name with the endorsement of King François I. In 1552, while the king was out of the country, the Sorbonne censored the fourth book upon publication, but in 1554 Cardinal de Chatillon convinced Henri II to raise the ban on the work. In 1564, Rabelais was banned once again and listed in the *Index Librorum Prohibitorum*, and all of his works were banned.

The extreme frankness of Rabelais's language was preserved in a similarly frank English translation in the late 17th century by Sir Thomas Urquhat and Peter Motteux, in an edition that was not published until 1708 as a part of *The Complete Works of Doctor François Rabelais*. The translators used language that has been called "obscene," including such terms as "codpiece," "bunghole," "ballocks," "teats," "genitories" and "spermatic vessels." In 1894, the New York Society for the Suppression of Vice, under the zealous leadership of Anthony Comstock, brought civil proceedings against the bankrupt Worthington Book Publishing Company that sought the right to sell off assets. Among those assets were the complete works of Rabelais, Queen Margaret of Navarre's *The Heptameron*, Giovanni Boccaccio's *The Decameron*, Henry Fielding's *Tom Jones*, Sir Richard Burton's *The Arabian Nights*, Jean-Jacques Rousseau's *Confessions* and Ovid's *Art of Love*. The receiver for the company asked the court to allow sale of the books, expensive volumes of world-renowned literary classics. Comstock appeared in the court record as opposing the sale. In stating the decision of the court in *In re Worthington Company*, 30 N.Y.S. 361 (1894), Judge Morgan J. O'Brien stated that "a seeker after the sensual and degrading parts of a narrative may find in all these works, as in those of other great authors, something to satisfy his pruriency," but he added that to simply condemn an entire literary work because of a few episodes "would compel the exclusion from circulation of a very large proportion of the works of fiction of the most famous writers of the English language." The court decision characterized the specific editions as being "choice editions, both as to the letter-press and the bindings . . . as to prevent their being generally sold or purchased, except by those who would desire them for their literary merit, or for their worth as specimens of fine book-making." In short, even though the text remained the same as that in cheaper editions, the "very artistic character, the high qualities of style, the absence of those glaring and crude pictures [set these books] entirely apart from such gross and obscene writings as it is the duty of the public authorities to suppress."

The United States Customs Office continued to ban the import of all of Rabelais's works until the 1930 Tariff Act ended the censorship of acknowledged literary works, including the Motteaux translation of *Gargantua and Pantagruel* with Frank C. Pepe's illustrations.

In 1951, city and county law enforcement officers obtained a warrant and raided the Dubuque (Iowa) Public Library, where they seized books charged with being obscene. Among those works were *Gargantua and Pantagruel*, *The Decameron* and *Tom Jones*. The works were later returned to library shelves, as "restricted" material.

## FURTHER READINGS

Broun, Heywood, and Margaret Leech. *Anthony Comstock: Roundsman of the Lord*. New York. Literary Guild of America, 1927.

Kronhausen, Eberhard, and Phyllis Kronhausen. *Pornography and the Law*. New York: Ballantine Books, 1959.

Rigolet, François. "Rabelais, Misogyny, and Christian Charity: Biblical Intertextuality and the Renaissance Crisis of Exemplarity." *PMLA* 109 (March 1994): 225–237.

# GO ASK ALICE

**Author:**  Anonymous
**Original date and place of publication:**  1971, United States
**Original publisher:**  Prentice-Hall
**Type:**  Novel

## SUMMARY

*Go Ask Alice* is a fictionalized account said to be based on the actual diary of a middle-class, 15-year-old drug user, the daughter of a college professor. The publisher only identifies "Anonymous" as the author. At the outset, the author has very low self-esteem and expresses dissatisfaction with her appearance. She dislikes her hair, hates the condition of her skin and feels fat, and she has just broken up with her boyfriend. She learns that her family will soon move because her father has received an appointment as dean of political science at another university, and she is excited at the prospect. When school is out for the summer in her new place of residence, the author returns to her old friends while spending the summer with her grandparents.

Bored with her summer, the author jumps at the chance to attend a party given by one of "top echelon," a girl who ignored her before but who wants to attend the university where the author's father is a dean. The partygoers play a variation on the children's game, "Button, Button, Who's Got the Button?" but the author is not aware that 10 of the 14 colas are spiked with LSD and the "lucky" winners are those who unwittingly select the acid-laced soda. This is her first experience, and she is both fearful and pleased afterward. In her entry a few days later, she writes, "I simply can't wait to try pot." She has also decided that LSD is not so bad, and that "all the things I've heard about LSD were obviously written by uninformed, ignorant people like my parents who obviously don't know what they are talking about." Her drug use experiences escalate to "speed" and to stealing her grandmother's sleeping pills and tranquilizers. During her second acid trip, the author has sex, then worries afterward that she might become pregnant. She vows to stop using drugs, but she keeps her grandmother's sleeping pills.

The author returns home and becomes caught up in a vicious cycle of "Bennies," "Dexies" and hashish. She takes pills to give her bursts of energy during the day and pills to calm her down and let her sleep at night. She and a female friend become involved with two male college students who convince the girls to sell pot, which the girls do gladly, because the boys do not have time to sell and fewer girls than boys are "busted" for selling. Further, the author views herself as "Rich's chick all the way" so she has to do what she can to help him. That includes selling marijuana, LSD and barbiturates to not only high school students but junior high and grade school students as well. Rich only allows her to visit the apartment that he shares with Ted when he restocks her supply of drugs. She finds that she has been used when she and Chris arrive unexpectedly at the apartment and find the two young men having sex. The author berates herself for all that she did for Rich, and she and her friend decide that they will "stay clean," which means running away to San Francisco. Introduced to heroin, she and Chris are sexually and sadistically abused. They return to their parents and high school, but the drug use does not stop. The author is eventually sent to a psychiatrist to deal with the drug use, but she runs away to Denver. She shares a hovel with several others who remain constantly stoned, but the dirt and depressing surroundings convince her to return home again.

Once home, the author decides to finally stop her drug use, but her former friends refuse to allow that. When she has remained drug-free for a time, others begin to threaten her. While babysitting, she unknowingly consumes a batch of homemade candy that has been laced with LSD, which results in a placement in the state mental hospital. Upon her release, the author seems determined to remain free of drugs, and her diary entries are all upbeat. In the final entry, she decides not to keep another diary because she now feels strong enough not to need that crutch. An afterword reveals that only three weeks later she is found dead of a drug overdose that may or may not have been accidental.

## CENSORSHIP HISTORY

*Go Ask Alice* has been the target of numerous challenges and attempts to ban it because of the language, the drug use and the sexual violence and promiscuity contained within. In the 1970s, schools cited the "objectionable" language and explicit sexual scenes as their reasons for removing it from their libraries in Kalamazoo, Michigan (1974); Saginaw, Michigan (1975); Eagle Pass, Texas (1977); and Trenton, New Jersey (1977). Written parental permission was required to take the book out of the library in Marcellus (New York) School District (1975), Ogden (Utah) School District (1979) and Safety Harbor Middle School Library in St. Petersburg, Florida (1982).

The work was one of 11 books banned by the school board in Island Trees Free School District No. 26 in New York (see BEST SHORT STORIES BY NEGRO WRITERS) in 1982. The court record specified the following passage as "objectionable" and representative of the reason for the ban: "shitty, goddamned, pissing, ass, goddamned beJesus, screwing life's, ass, shit. Doris was ten and had humped with who knows how many men in between/but now when I face a girl it's like facing a boy. I get all excited and turned on. I want to screw with the girl." The novel was returned to the library after the U.S. Supreme Court ruled in *Board of Education, Island Trees Union Free School District No. 26 et al. v. Pico et al.*, 457 U.S. 853 (1982) that the First Amendment rights of students had been violated in the banning.

In 1983, the book was removed from the school libraries because a school board member in Osseo School District in Brooklyn Park, Minnesota, found the language in the book to be "personally offensive," and the same occurred in the Pagosa Springs, Colorado, schools when a parent objected to the "graphic language, subject matter, immoral tone, and lack of literary quality found in the book." The book was challenged in 1984 in Rankin County (Mississippi) School District because it was "profane and sexually objectionable" and at the Central Gwinnett (Georgia) High School library in 1986 because "it encourages students to steal and take drugs."

Go Ask Alice was removed from the school library bookshelves in Kalkaska, Michigan, in 1986 because of "objectionable language," and that same year the Gainesville (Georgia) Public Library prohibited young readers from checking out the book by keeping it in a locked room with other books on the topics of drug use, sexual dysfunction, hypnosis and breast-feeding.

In 1993, the superintendent of schools of Wall Township, New Jersey, ordered the book removed from the intermediate school library because of "inappropriate" language and claims that it "borders on pornography." He expressed shock that the book was still available, because he had ordered the book removed from all reading lists and classroom book collections five years previously after receiving an anonymous letter that condemned the work. Also in 1993, the work was removed because of "graphic" language from an English class at Buckhannon-Upshur (West Virginia) High School and challenged as a required reading assignment at Johnstown (New York) High School because of "numerous obscenities." In 1994, Shepherd Hill High School in Dudley, Massachusetts, banned the book from its ninth-grade reading list due to "gross and vulgar language and graphic description of drug use and sexual conduct."

## FURTHER READINGS

Hurwitz, Leon. *Historical Dictionary of Censorship in the United States*. Westport, Coun.: Greenwood Press, 1985.

Massie, Dorothy C. "Censorship in the Schools: Something Old and Something New." *Today's Education* 69 (November/December 1980): 56–60.

*Newsletter on Intellectual Freedom* (January 1975): 6; (March 1975): 41; (May 1975): 76; (July 1977): 100; (May 1977): 73; (May 1979): 49; (March 1980): 32; (July 1982): 142; (March 1983): 52; (March 1984): 53; (May 1984): 69; (July 1986): 117; (September 1986): 151–152; (November 1986): 207; (January 1987): 32; (March 1989): 39; (May 1993): 71; (July 1993): 109–110; (March 1994): 54; (September 1994): 150.

# GONE WITH THE WIND

**Author:** Margaret Mitchell
**Original date and place of publication:** 1936, United States
**Original publisher:** Macmillan Company
**Type:** Novel

## SUMMARY

*Gone with the Wind* was one of the two best-selling novels of the 1930s in the United States, with Hervey Allen's *Anthony Adverse*, a story set in the Napoleonic era. One million copies of the novel were sold in the first six months, and 1.5 million in the first two years. In 1937, Mitchell won the Pulitzer Prize and the American Booksellers' Association award for the novel.

Set in the American South from about 1861 through 1873, *Gone with the Wind* is a historical novel that portrays the struggle for survival by people whose secure lives were changed forever by the death and destruction of the Civil War. The daughter of a cultured French mother and a temperamental, hard-scrabble Irish father, Scarlett O'Hara is the spoiled center of life at the expansive plantation, Tara. Her obsession with the weak-willed Ashley Wilkes dominates her life, but he marries his cousin Melanie, a reticent and caring woman who understands his honorable yet ineffectual nature and accepts it. Scarlett spitefully marries Charles Hamilton, who dies in the war and leaves her with a child. After Atlanta is burned by Sherman's troops, Scarlett returns to Tara, where her mother dies and her father goes mad, leaving the sheltered Scarlett to assume responsibility for Melanie, her sisters, her child, Melanie's child and the remaining faithful servants. Worked to exhaustion and suffering from the lack of food, she struggles to keep Tara and vows that she "will never be hungry again."

After the war ends, the carpetbaggers appear ready to take through taxes what the Union Army did not take in battle, so Scarlett marries her sister's fiancé to obtain the needed money to keep Tara. Her second husband, Frank Kennedy, is a modestly successful businessman, and Scarlett dominates his mill enterprise and store to emerge from the poverty and struggle in which the war has left her. After Kennedy is killed when he and area men stage a midnight raid to avenge a physical attack on Scarlett, she makes a third marriage with Rhett Butler, even as she pines for Ashley Wilkes.

Scarlett and Rhett are similar in their lack of scruples, their tenacity and their fierce passions. He has no illusions about Scarlett and he willingly allows her to enjoy the immense wealth that he acquired as a blockade runner during the war, as he waits for her to forget Ashley and to truly love him. After their daughter, Eugenia Victoria "Bonnie Blue" Butler, is born, Rhett works to attain respectability among the Old Guard of Atlanta society for his daughter's sake. He realizes what Scarlett does not, that money alone will not bring acceptance. As Rhett guarantees their daughter's social future, Scarlett continues her unscrupulous business practices, and she continues to associate with what Rhett and her beloved Mammy refer to as "white trash Northerners" and "scalawags."

The indulged Bonnie Blue dies in a riding accident, placing Rhett and Scarlett at even greater emotional distance. Rhett turns with greater frequency to drink and to spending nights at Belle Watling's brothel. When Melanie Wilkes dies, Scarlett recognizes that Ashley is a weak, unstable character and that she really loves Rhett, who is unmoved by her revelation. Faced with the challenge of rekindling Rhett's love, Scarlett decides to return to Tara, the one constant in her life, where she will think about it tomorrow.

## CENSORSHIP HISTORY

*Gone with the Wind* captured the attention of both the public and the censors before it was even published, but a strong advertising campaign by the Macmillan Company produced 100,000 in advance sales that obscured any threat posed by John Sumner and the New York Society for the Suppression of Vice upon its release in 1936. The society had objections to Scarlett O'Hara's serial marriages and her unscrupulous behavior, as well as to the marital rape of Scarlett, but public opinion was clearly on the side of the novel. In Boston, the Watch and Ward Society hoped to arouse some concern about the prominence that brothel madam Belle Watling holds in one part of the novel, as well as the use of "damn" and "whore," but Boston booksellers were unwilling to forego the huge profits that the massive advertising campaign waged by the Macmillan Company promised. The hint of scandal actually fueled sales of the novel.

Direct challenges to the book did not appear until it entered schools as supplemental reading. In 1963, Lee Burress conducted a survey of high school English department chairpersons and school administrators regarding school censorship in Wisconsin. In an unnamed district in the state, a clergyman and a parent had challenged the appearance of the novel on a recommended reading list. They objected to the "immorality" of Scarlett. The district retained the book on the list. In a 1966 national sample of school librarians and high school English chairpersons, Burress reported that a teacher in an unnamed state challenged the availability of the book in the high school library, claiming that it could be "misunderstood." The novel was placed on a closed shelf and made unavailable to students.

In 1978, school officials in Anaheim (California) Union High School District banned the book from all English classrooms, at the same time that George Eliot's *Silas Marner* was banned, according to the Anaheim Secondary Teachers Association. Parents condemned the "ruthless" and "immoral" behavior of Scarlett O'Hara and expressed concern about the negative depiction of freed slaves.

In 1984, an alderman in Waukegan, Illinois, challenged the appearance of the book on the recommended reading list in the Waukegan School District on grounds of "racism" and "unacceptable language." The main complaint was that the word "nigger" appears repeatedly in the novel. Joseph Conrad's *The Nigger of the "Narcissus"*, Harper Lee's TO KILL A MOCKINGBIRD, Harriet Beecher Stowe's *Uncle Tom's Cabin* and Mark Twain's THE ADVENTURE OF HUCKLEBERRY FINN were named in the same complaint and also removed from the list.

## FURTHER READINGS

Burgess-Jackson, Keith. "Rape and Persuasive Definition." *Canadian Journal of Philosophy* 25 (September 1995): 415–454.

Burress, Lee. *Battle of the Books: Literary Censorship in the Public Schools, 1950–1985.* Metuchen, N.J.: Scarecrow Press, 1989.

Harwell, Richard, ed. *Margaret Mitchell's "Gone with the Wind" Letters, 1936–1949.* New York: Macmillan, 1976.

*Newsletter on Intellectual Freedom* (January 1979): 6; (July 1984): 105.

Taylor, Helen. *Scarlett's Women: "Gone with the Wind" and Its Female Fans.* New Brunswick, N.J.: Rutgers University Press, 1989.

# GORILLAS IN THE MIST

**Author:**  Dian Fossey
**Original date and place of publication:**  1983, United States
**Original publisher:**  Houghton Mifflin Company
**Type:**  Zoological study

## SUMMARY

*Gorillas in the Mist*, written by the world authority on the endangered mountain gorilla, relates Dian Fossey's experiences over the 14 years in which she conducted field studies among four gorilla families in the Virunga Mountains shared by Zaire, Rwanda and Uganda. The scientist became well known to villagers, who signaled her approach by shouting, "*Nyiramachabelli!*" meaning, "The old lady who lives in the forest without a man."

To gain the acceptance of the gorillas, Fossey imitated their feeding and contentment sounds, as well as other behavior such as self-grooming and averting her eyes from their glances. After gaining their trust, she tracked the various groups and identified the adult animals with names, then gave names to the offspring that were born during the course of the study. Fossey viewed the gorillas as individuals, and she relates their unique characteristics in the book. She was eventually fully accepted by one gorilla group and made history when a fully mature male gorilla reached out to touch her.

As she studied the gorillas, Fossey meticulously documented male-female interactions, parent-child interactions, mating behavior, parenting skills and both intragroup and intergroup behavior. Fossey's report of the sexual behavior and mating patterns of the gorillas is equally detailed. In one instance, the scientist reports that a young gorilla named Puck goes off alone and Fossey sees him "actively masturbating."

The author also documents mating behavior in careful detail, as well as other behavior of the young, sexually immature but curious gorillas. The book includes a photograph of a female being mounted by a male in her group. Fossey also tells of three-year-old Pablo who is so obsessively interested in sexual activities that "he often tried to examine the penises of the older males but was usually shoved away." He also engages frequently in sex play with Poppy, a female gorilla 20 months his junior.

In addition to studying the lives of the gorillas, Fossey informs readers of the devastation that poachers have wreaked in the gorilla population and calls for a stop to their actions. She also relates instances in which she stood up to poachers and reported them, thus placing her life in danger.

## CENSORSHIP HISTORY

The work was acclaimed by scientists as a breakthrough study, and Fossey was later thrust into the international spotlight after one of the gorillas was killed by poachers. She spoke to groups to focus attention on the rain forest and the plight of the gorillas, and she was brutally murdered in 1985. The passages regarding masturbation and mating behavior in her book are integral to the study and were accepted as such by scientists, but the same passages raised objections when the books appeared in schools and school libraries.

The book was kept out of many classrooms and just not ordered for school libraries to avoid controversy over the details of the gorillas' sexual behavior. Many school administrators viewed the study as suitable for older students but unsuitable for or of less interest to middle school or younger students.

In 1993, teachers in Westlake Middle School in Erie, Pennsylvania, were instructed by school administrators to use felt-tip pens to black out "objectionable" passages in the book. Parents had challenged the use of the book in the classroom, claiming that the passages about gorilla sexual behavior and mating habits were "filthy," "unnecessary" and "inappropriate." The following passage regarding the masturbating gorilla was one of the "objectionable" passages blacked out:

> His head was flexed backward, his eyes were closed, and he wore a semismile expression while using his right forefinger to manipulate his genital area. For about two minutes, Puck appeared to be obtaining great pleasure from his actions. . . . It was the only time I have ever seen a gorilla in the wild actively masturbate.

The teachers were also required to block out lines detailing the sex play of three-year-old Pablo and one-year-old Poppy which "could result in an erection for Pablo, who with a puzzled smile, lay back and twiddled his penis" while Poppy watched with interest "or, occasionally even sucked his penis."

Farley Mowat's WOMAN IN THE MISTS (Warner Books, 1987), which recounted Dian Fossey's dedication to her cause and her brutal death, was also subject to censorship. In 1991, the work was removed from a required reading list in the Omaha, Nebraska, school district. Parents who objected to the book claimed that it contained racial slurs, as well as "profanity" and passages that degraded women. They also objected to Mowat's long discussion of the aftermath of Fossey's abortion.

## FURTHER READINGS

Montgomery, Sy. *Walking with the Great Apes.* Boston: Houghton Mifflin, 1991.

Morrell, Virginia. "Called 'Trimates,' Three Bold Women Shaped Their Field." *Science* 260 (April 16, 1993): 420–425.

*Newsletter on Intellectual Freedom* (March 1992): 44; (July 1993): 109.

Webb, C. Anne. "The Battle Continues." *English Journal* 48 (September 1995): 123–124.

# GO TELL IT ON THE MOUNTAIN

**Author:**  James Baldwin
**Original date and place of publication:**  1953, United States
**Original publisher:**  Alfred A. Knopf
**Type:**  Novel

## SUMMARY

*Go Tell It on the Mountain* chronicles the struggles of a black evangelist and his family as they fight to live a moral life and to save others in the Harlem ghetto. The opening pages of the novel are highly autobiographical, as they show John Grimes, cruelly called "frog eyes" by his stepfather, living in poverty with his parents, Gabriel and Elizabeth, his brother, Roy, and his sisters Ruth and Sarah. People always said that John would be a preacher when he grew older, just like his stepfather, Gabriel, who has imposed a puritanical lifestyle on the boy. Despite John's obedience to Gabriel, the preacher favors his natural son, Roy, and views John as "a stranger, living unalterable testimony to his mother's days in sin."

The novel, which covers 24 hours in actual time, is divided into three parts. Part I, entitled "The Seventh Day," consists of one unbroken narrative that is set in Harlem. It relates the family's experiences as they move from their home to their storefront church, the Temple of the Fire Baptized. The family is an anomaly in the area; dressed in their Sunday best, on their way to church they pass men and women on the streets who "had spent the night in bars, or in cat houses, or on the streets, or on rooftops, or under the stairs." Sex is a fact of life where they live. John and Roy, the preacher's expected successor who would rather be like the people on the streets, have watched a man and woman in the basement of a condemned house who "did it standing up." Roy also claims to have watched others many times, and "he had done it with some girls down the block." Moreover, the family lives in a tenement above "the harlot's house downstairs."

Part II, entitled "The Prayers of the Saints," is more than twice the length of the other two parts. It takes place in the Temple of the Fire Baptized, as each character's prayer is framed into a separate chapter. Through "Florence's

Prayer," "Gabriel's Prayer," and "Elizabeth's Prayer," each beginning with their Southern roots, the reader learns brief histories of John's mother, stepfather and aunt. Their mistakes, joys and pains are revealed and all are shown to have flawed pasts. Gabriel has fathered a child by a "harlot," while married to his first wife. Elizabeth bore John while unmarried. Florence loved her first husband hopelessly and lost him to war. This part ends in the church, with 14-year-old John lying on the floor before the altar, struggling with salvation.

Part III relates John's long night in church, praying and crying as he eventually becomes "saved."

## CENSORSHIP HISTORY

*Go Tell It on the Mountain* was not known as a mainstream novel for many years after it was first published in the United States. Part of the opposition was to its anti-white rhetoric, expressed most forcefully by Gabriel when Roy is slashed in a fight with a white street gang; other objections were made against the discussions of "bastard" children, extramarital sex and frank sensuality. For the most part, before 1960, Baldwin had "a very touch-and-go relationship with censorship" both in the United States and in England. Libraries might purchase the book, but more often than not, it would be kept on the public library "poison shelves," only available to the patron who asked specifically for the book. As with many such books, the novel was only available in an expensive hardcover for nearly 10 years before it was published in inexpensive paperback by Signet Books in 1963. In England, the novel was published in hardcover in 1954 by Michael Joseph, but it did not emerge in paperback until Corgi published it in 1963.

The novel was challenged for much the same reasons once it entered the school libraries and classrooms, and most of the challenges took place in the 1970s. The lack of extensive challenges should not be taken as a sign of acceptance. Rather, the relatively small number of challenges simply reflects the lack of widespread adoption of the novel by schools, who refrained from adding the book to required or supplemental reading lists. In a 1973 national survey of English department chairpersons, Burress found one challenge in an unnamed school district in the North. A student and his parent objected to the required reading as being "nigger" literature. The school board agreed to allow the student to substitute another book for the novel. In 1975, in a survey of book challenges in Tennessee, Weathersby reported that the book was challenged by a parent in an unidentified school district for providing "a trashy idea of sex" and "filling a child's mind with ideas that cause him to lose confidence in the authorities." The book was removed from the classroom. In a 1977 national survey of English chairpersons, Burress reported that a clergyman in Illinois had challenged the book as "immoral" and demanded its removal from the high school classroom. The book was retained as a required reading.

In 1994, parents of students in the Hudson Falls, New York, school district objected to the inclusion of the book as a required reading in the high school English curriculum. Objectors claimed that the book contained "obscene language" and recurring themes of rape, masturbation, violence and the degrading treatment of women. The book was retained, but students could substitute another book from an approved list.

## FURTHER READINGS

Baldwin, James. *Conversations with James Baldwin*. Ed. by Fred L. Standley and Louis H. Pratt. Jackson, Miss.: University Press of Mississippi, 1989.

Burress, Lee. *Battle of the Books: Literary Censorship in the Public Schools, 1950–1985*. Metuchen, N.J.: Scarecrow Press, 1989.

Harris, Trudier. *Black Women in the Fiction of James Baldwin*. Knoxville, Tenn.: University of Tennessee Press, 1985.

*Newsletter on Intellectual Freedom* (November 1994): 190; (January 1995): 13; (March 1995): 55.

Porter, Horace A. *Stealing the Fire: The Art and Protest of James Baldwin*. Middletown, Conn.: Wesleyan University Press, 1989.

Sutherland, John. *Offensive Literature: Decensorship in Britain, 1960–1982*. London: Junction Books, 1982.

Weathersby, Dorothy T. *Censorship of Literature Textbooks in Tennessee: A Study of the Commission, Publishers, Teachers, and Textbooks*. Ed.D. diss., University of Tennessee. 1975.

## GRENDEL

**Author:** John Champlin Gardner
**Original date and place of publication:** 1971, United States
**Original publisher:** Alfred A. Knopf
**Type:** Novel

## SUMMARY

*Grendel* is a novel derived from the classic Anglo-Saxon epic *Beowulf*, in which the monster Grendel is presented as the embodiment of evil, whose vicious attacks serve to test the hero, Beowulf. Gardner modifies the epic to tell the story from Grendel's point of view, creating a sympathetic creature whose actions in *Beowulf* seem justified when the monster explains them. An unlikely hero, Grendel professes to have a highly idealized view of mankind, but he admits that mankind's actions continually tarnish that image and disappoint him. He exhibits a strong sense of conscience for his rages and ravaging of the Danes, and claims that he was blinded by brute rage when he attacked the Danes' mead hall, Heorot, killed the drunken and celebrating men, and destroyed the hall. He also wonders at the human propensity for war and the often petty excuses for it. As he cries out in one instance, "'Why can't these creatures discover a little dignity?' . . . I make a face, uplift a defiant middle finger, and give an obscene little kick."

Before his final battle, Grendel makes astute observations regarding human affairs, as well as the nature of animals. In viewing a very old ruler, Hrothgar, with the young woman Wealtheow, whose brother had offered her as a sacrifice so that Hrothgar's forces would not attack, Grendel muses that she could have given herself to a man whom she could have loved, a more vigorous man. He relates her unhappiness and her courage in fulfilling the role for which she had been sacrificed. When he warns away a mountain goat that will soon be within his dangerous reach, Grendel watches as the goat continues its mindless and mechanical climb, "because it is the business of goats to climb." Similarly, when he later comes across children playing in the deepening twilight, those who choose to feign deafness when their mothers call them in from play "are gone forever. So it goes."

The end of the novel reflects the ending of the epic, as Beowulf kills Grendel in a bloody, violent battle. The difference is that Grendel maintains that Beowulf wins "by mindless chance. . . . Accident." Skill, right and good are not the basis for Beowulf's victory. He only wins because "'Poor Grendel's had an accident.'"

## CENSORSHIP HISTORY

The novel has been challenged, banned and restricted from use in the classroom because of "obscene" language, as well as the violent and graphic nature of the action. Characters go out to "piss," and the word "shit" is freely used throughout. In contemplating various deaths, the monster ponders roasting first the genital area of one character in front of the multitudes. The physical damage and amount of blood spilled in confrontations are graphically presented.

In 1978, the Frederick County, Maryland, school system declared the novel to be "full of vulgarity" and banned it from use in the classroom. In 1986, after the high school principal objected to the "profane" nature of *Grendel*, the novel became the only work placed on the resricted list at Wasco (California) High School. A "restricted list policy" was developed, and use of the novel was prohibited until every student in the classroom brought in written parental permission. A teacher brought suit against the school district, and a settlement was reached in 1991. Under terms agreed upon, the book could remain in the library and on display in the classroom, but teachers were not permitted to assign reading of the book. Also in 1986, the novel was challenged for use as an assignment in an accelerated English class in the Indianapolis, Indiana, school system.

In 1991, the parent of a student in Viewmont High School in Farmington, Utah, challenged use of the book as a required reading. She complained that her daughter had been asked to read sexist passages and passages having sexual overtones in the book and noted further that it "is obscene and should not be a required reading." The district review committee considered the request and voted to retain the book for use only in the twelfth-grade classroom and only in connection with the study of *Beowulf.* The student was given the option of an alternative assignment.

The book was also challenged as part of the English curriculum at Pinelands Regional High School in Bass River Township, New Jersey, in 1992. Parents complained that the book contained "numerous obscenities," but the school board voted to retain the book. The parents then appealed to the mayor, who criticized the book but supported the right for it to remain in the library or for students to buy it, though he added that "it shouldn't be given to children in the school." Complaints about the "violence" and the "graphic nature" of the book were the basis of a 1993 challenge to the placement of the book on the supplemental reading list for advanced English students in Clayton County School District in Jonesboro, Georgia. The book remained on the list.

## FURTHER READINGS

Baldwin, Deborah. "John Gardner: The Serious Optimist." *Common Cause* 15 (September 1989): 34–38.

Fawcett, Barry. "The Twelve Traps in John Gardner's *Grendel.*" *American Literature* 62 (December 1990): 634–647.

Gardner, John. *On Moral Fiction.* New York: Basic Books, 1978.

Henderson, Jeff. *Thor's Hammer: Essays on John Gardner.* Conway, Ark.: University of Central Arkansas Press, 1985.

Howell, John Michael. *Understanding John Gardner.* Columbia, S.C.: University of South Carolina Press, 1993.

*Newsletter on Intellectual Freedom* (March 1978): 39; (May 1978): 58; (May 1986): 81–82; (July 1986): 119; (January 1987): 32; (May 1989): 87; (May 119): 92; (January 1993): 11; (March 1993): 56; (May 1993): 87.

People for the American Way. *Attacks on the Freedom to Learn: 1991–1992.* Washington, D.C.: People for the American Way, 1992.

# HEATHER HAS TWO MOMMIES

**Author:**   Leslea Newman
**Original date and place of publication:**   1989, United States
**Original publisher:**   Alyson Publications
**Type:**   Children's book

## SUMMARY

*Heather Has Two Mommies* is the story of a three-year-old girl being raised by a lesbian couple. For her, having two mothers feels perfectly normal, until she becomes part of a play group. Heather listens to the other children and realizes for the first time that many of them have one mother and a father, and she becomes upset. The leader of the play group encourages the children to talk about the different types of families that exist. As the children learn more about families, they realize that many children are growing up in nontraditional families. They also realize that the most important part of any type of family is love.

In the first part of the book, the events leading to Heather's conception through artificial insemination and her birth are dealt with in a matter-of-fact manner. The choices being made by the two "mommies" are discussed, as are their reasons for those choices. The second half of the book focuses on the family structure and shows that Heather's family is similar to those of other children, except for the "two mommies."

## CENSORSHIP HISTORY

*Heather Has Two Mommies* has been challenged repeatedly since it was first published. In 1992, this book and DADDY'S ROOMMATE were removed from the first-grade reading list in the Bay Ridge School District in Brooklyn, New York, challenged but retained in Fayetteville (North Carolina) County Library and Springfield (Oregon) Public Library and placed in the adult section of the Bladen County Library in Elizabethtown, North Carolina.

In 1993, *Heather Has Two Mommies* and *Daddy's Roommate* were moved from the children's room to the adult section in Mercer County Library System in Lawrence, New Jersey. They were also challenged but retained in the public library in Mesa, Arizona; North Brunswick (New Jersey) Public Library; Cumberland County (North Carolina) Public Library; Wicomico County Free County Library in Salisbury, Maryland; and Dayton and Montgomery County (Ohio) Public Library. In 1994, the two books were taken out of the Lane County Head Start program in Cottage Grove, Oregon, and challenged but retained by Chandler (Arizona) Public Library.

*Heather Has Two Mommies* was also challenged in 1993 by patrons of Chestatee Regional Library System in Gainesville, Georgia, who believed that the book was "not suitable" to be shelved in the children's section. Librarians moved the book to the young adult section, but three state legislators who became involved in the case wanted it removed. The legislators stated, "We could put together a resolution to amend the Georgia state constitution to say that tax dollars cannot be used to promote homosexuality, pedophilia or sado-masochism." The book remained in the young adult section, and the controversy faded away.

In 1994, parents challenged the inclusion of the book in an Oak Bluffs, Massachusetts, elementary school library. The parent who led the protest spoke out at a public meeting and stated that the subject matter of the book "is obscene and vulgar and the message is that homosexuality is okay." The school board created a review committee to examine the book and voted unanimously to keep the book in the library.

## FURTHER READINGS

Buttenwieser, Susan. "A Child's Garden of . . . Diversity." *Ms.* (January 1993): 61–62.
Hildebrand, Joan M. "Books for Children: *Heather Has Two Mommies.*" *Childhood Education* 70 (1994): 305.

# A HERO AIN'T NOTHIN' BUT A SANDWICH

**Author:**   Alice Childress
**Original date and place of publication:**   1973, United States
**Original publisher:**   Coward, McCann & Geoghegan
**Type:**   Novel

## SUMMARY

*A Hero Ain't Nothin' but a Sandwich* is a young adult novel made up of 23 short chapters, each told from a different character's point of view. The number of chapters related by each character provides an indication of the importance of the character to the novel. Thirteen-year-old Benjie Johnson relates seven chapters, his stepfather Butler Craig relates four and other characters relate only one or two of the remaining chapters.

The story focuses on Benjie, whose drug habit worries his family, his close friend Jimmy and two teachers who care very much for him, but Benjie contends that the others are worrying needlessly for he has no habit. He misses his former closeness with his mother, and blames Butler Craig for moving in with them and taking his mother's affections. Bored at home and at school, he begins to distrust everyone around him, including a black teacher named Nigeria Greene who joins another teacher in convincing the principal to sign necessary papers to hospitalize Benjie in a detoxification facility. After the treatment period ends and Benjie returns home, he decides to try drugs one more time, because he wants to remember what he is giving up forever. He steals Butler's best suit and overcoat; then he is caught stealing a toaster from a neighboring apartment. As Butler chases him to their building rooftop, Benjie slips and nearly dives over the edge to his death, but Butler catches him with one hand. Benjie yells out, "Let me die," but Butler holds on and saves him. This leads them to a new level of trust, and Benjie even calls Butler Dad. Butler's action has made him a hero, as has his tenaciousness in regularly meeting the responsibilities that are thrust upon him, despite the difficulties that must be overcome.

At the end of the novel, Butler, his arm in a sling, waits outside the drug rehabilitation center where Benjie has promised to continue treatment. He insists that Benjie is just late, because he has been looking in store windows or otherwise dawdling, and believes that the boy will appear.

## CENSORSHIP HISTORY

*A Hero Ain't Nothin' but a Sandwich* depicts urban ghetto life and people who are fragmented and alienated because of race and class barriers. The language in the novel is a variety of Black English that violates the rules of standard grammar and pronunciation. Drugs pervade the work, and street terms are used with profanity throughout the novel. The setting is ugly as is the devastation created by drugs, and the language is consistent with this devastation. The novel has been challenged for being "objectionable," and for containing "street language" and "abusive language," as well as because of the sexual descriptions.

The novel was one of 11 books banned by the school board in Island Trees Free School District No. 26 in New York (see BEST SHORT STORIES BY NEGRO WRITERS) in 1982. It was charged with being "immoral" and "just plain filthy," and the following passage is specified in the court record as representative of passages determined to be "objectionable": "Hell, no! Fuck the society. They can have back the spread and curtains, I'm too old for them fuckin' bunnies anyway." The novel was returned to the library after the U.S. Supreme Court ruled in *Board of Education, Island Trees Union Free School District No. 26 et al. v. Pico et al.*, 457 U.S. 853 (1982) that the First Amendment rights of students had been violated in the banning.

In 1978, school officials removed the novel from the high school libraries in San Antonio, Texas, after complaints from parents that the novel contained "objectionable" passages. Teachers filed a grievance to protest the banning, and the book was reinstated. That same year, the school board in Savannah, Georgia, ordered that all copies of the novel be removed from all school libraries in the district because of "objectionable language." Calling the book "garbage," the president of the school board stated, "We don't need people going around and calling other people 'jive-asses' and saying 'Fuck the society'."

Language was also the reason that parents of students attending Lamar Elementary School in Darlington, South Carolina, demanded that the book be removed from the school library in 1994. Citing examples from the book, parents stated in their complaint that "offensive language in the book makes it unsuitable for any children." That same year, the novel was challenged in Aberdeen High School in Bel Air, Maryland, for being "racist and vulgar."

## FURTHER READINGS

Gebhard, Ann O. "The Emerging Self: Young Adult and Classic Novels of the Black Experience." *English Journal* 82 (September 1993): 50–54.

Kirk, Ersye. *The Black Experience in Books for Children and Young Adults*. Ardmore, Okla.: Positive Impact, 1993.

*Newsletter on Intellectual Freedom* (September 1978): 123; (November 1982): 197; (July 1978): 87; (May 1994): 85; (January 1995): 12.

Sullivan, Charles, ed. *Children of Promise: African-American Literature and Art for Young People*. New York: Harry N. Abrams, 1991.

# HOWL AND OTHER POEMS

**Author:**  Allen Ginsberg
**Original date and place of publication:**  1956, United States
**Original publisher:**  City Lights Books
**Type:**  Poetry collection

## SUMMARY

*Howl and Other Poems* contains 11 poems that explore what poet William Carlos Williams called "a howl of defeat." Dedicated to fellow Beat writers Jack Kerouac, William Seward Burroughs and Neal Cassady, of whose works Ginsberg claims "all these books are published in Heaven," the work contains the poet's passionate expressions on numerous taboos of the time. The title poem opens with the following lines: "I saw the best minds of my generation destroyed by madness, starving hysterical naked, / dragging themselves through the negro streets at dawn looking for an angry fix." He continues to speak of similarly unsavory topics, including "angelheaded hipsters . . . hollow-eyed and high sat up smoking in the supernatural darkness of cold-water flats . . . staggering on tenement roofs illuminated . . . publishing obscene odes on the windows of the skull." The veiled, symbolic references in these lines kept the poems relatively safe from prosecution, but his distinct references to homosexuality and to anal and oral sex in such lines as "Who let themselves be fucked in the ass by saintly motorcyclists, / and screamed with joy, / who blew and were blown by those human seraphim, the sailors" have been more easily singled out by censors as obscene. References to drug use abound in the poems, as do Ginsberg's private sexual fantasies and excretory images.

Although the title poem has been most heavily criticized for its obscene imagery and language, other poems in the collection celebrate Ginsberg's loss of virginity ("Transcription of Organ Music"), his disillusionment with America and the declaration that "I smoke marijuana every chance I get" ("America") and reference to the "fairy Sam" ("In the Baggage Room at Greyhound"). Taken in total, *Howl and Other Poems* explores the horrors of the poet's life and, as William Carlos Williams states in the final lines of his introduction to the collection, "Hold back the edges of your gowns, Ladies, we are going through hell."

## CENSORSHIP HISTORY

*Howl and Other Poems* was first printed in England by Villiers and passed through Customs without incident to be published by City Lights Bookstore in the fall of 1956. On March 5, 1957, a second printing was seized in San Francisco by United States Customs officials, who confiscated 520 copies with the excuse that "the words and the sense of the writing is obscene. . . . You wouldn't want your children to come across it." Lawrence Ferlinghetti, owner of the City Lights Bookstore, had the forethought to contact the American Civil Liberties Union before sending the work to England to be printed and had received assurance that the ACLU would defend him if the book were challenged. Thus, when the local U.S. attorney's office requested permission from a federal judge to destroy the book, the ACLU notified the collector of Customs and the U.S. attorney that it would defend the book. The U.S. attorney decided to drop proceedings.

Despite clearance from U.S. Customs, copies of the book were later seized by the San Francisco police who claimed that the material was not suitable for children, even though the City Lights Bookstore did not carry books for children. Ferlinghetti was booked and fingerprinted in the San Francisco Hall of Justice, after being arrested by two juvenile squad police officers.

The case went to trial and nine literary experts were called to defend the "social importance" of Ginsberg's poem: Mark Schorer, Leo Lowenthal, Walter Van Tilburg Clark, Herbert Blau, Arthur Foff, Mark Linenthal, Kenneth Rexroth, Vincent McHugh and Luther Nichols. The experts identified the work as "social criticism . . . a literary work that hurled *ideological* accusation after accusation against American society." Prosecuting attorney Ralph McIntosh repeatedly attempted to coerce the witnesses into translating the poetry into prose, reading aloud passages from *Howl* that contained what he classified as "dirty" words and sexual images. He also baited the experts by asking if the terms that he deemed to be obscene could have been worded differently by Ginsberg, but presiding Judge Horn stopped him, saying "'it is obvious that the author could have used another term'" but that it was "'up to the author'" to decide.

In handing down his decision on *Howl and Other Poems*, the judge cited the decision of Justice William J. Brennan only four months earlier in *Roth v. the United States*, 354 U.S. 476 (1957), stating that "unless the book is entirely lacking in 'social importance' it cannot be held 'obscene.'" He added further that, while the poem contained "unorthodox and controversial ideas" that were expressed at times through "coarse and vulgar" words, including "cock," "fuck," "ass," "cunt," "gyzym" and "asshole," the work was protected by the constitutional freedoms of speech and press. Horn stated, "An author should be real in treating his subject and be allowed to express his thoughts and ideas in his own words."

Although Judge Horn's decision freed *Howl and Other Poems* in 1957, the poem has remained controversial. In 1988, the listener-supported Pacifica Radio Network did not carry a broadcast of the poem that was set to be read on radio stations nationwide on the evening of January 6, 1988, as part of a weeklong series about censorship called "Open Ears/Open Minds." The network made the decision after being threatened with possible obscenity prosecution by the Justice Department a few months before for broadcasting a play about homosexuality. The decision was also made based on an April 1987 ruling by the Federal Communications Commission stating that stations faced possible penalties for broadcasting "material that depicts or describes, in terms patently offensive as measured by contemporary community standards for the broadcast medium, sexual or excretory activities or organs." In response to Pacifica's decision, the author said, "The Government now has set out rules which have had an intimidating and chilling effect on broadcasters. . . . it's the last desperate gasp of the Reagan neo-conservatives."

## FURTHER READINGS

D'Emilio, John, and Estelle B. Freedman. *Intimate Matters: A History of Sexuality in America*. New York: Harper & Row, Publishers, 1988.

Robins, Natalie. *Alien Ink: The FBI's War on Freedom of Expression*. New York: William Morrow and Company, 1992.

Yarrow, Andrew L. "Allen Ginsberg's 'Howl' in a New Controversy." *The New York Times* (January 6, 1988): C2.

# I KNOW WHY THE CAGED BIRD SINGS

**Author:**   Maya Angelou (Marguerite Johnson)
**Original date and place of publication:**   1969, United States
**Original publisher:**   Random House
**Type:**   Autobiography

## SUMMARY

*I Know Why the Caged Bird Sings* is the first of five autobiographical books written by the author. The others are *Gather Together in My Name* (1974), *Singin' and Swingin' and Gettin' Merry Like Christmas* (1976), *The Heart of a Woman* (1981) and *All God's Children Need Traveling Shoes* (1986). The first book chronicles Angelou's life from age three to age 16 and the birth of her only child, Guy, to whom she dedicates this book.

The book describes the divorce of her parents and her own difficulties as she is sent with her brother from Long Beach, California, to live with her grandmother and uncle in Stamps, Arkansas, spends a year in St. Louis with her mother, then returns to Stamps and eventually moves to California to be with her mother. The years in Stamps are largely happy years as her grandmother, "Momma," protects and shields the young girl. There are, however, some social realities from which she cannot be protected. The book recalls the despair often felt by the black cotton pickers as they filed into Momma's general store, returning from the fields on bad days. The rampant racism is evident in incidents such as the one in which her uncle must be hidden after a former sheriff warns the family that "Some of the boys'll be coming over here later" because Willie had "messed with a white lady today." When Maya is in need of a dentist, she overhears her grandmother being told by a white dentist to whom she had lent money during the Depression, "my policy is I'd rather stick my hand in a dog's mouth than in a nigger's."

Maya also suffers personal indignities as a child. When she moves to St. Louis to live with her mother, she is raped by her mother's live-in lover, who is later murdered. When she travels to Los Angeles to spend a summer with her father, the woman with whom he lives stabs Maya with a knife. Maya is nearly six feet tall, flat-chested and unsure of sexuality at 15 when she decides to have sex with a handsome neighborhood boy. He forgets her name the next day, but she becomes pregnant and later gives birth to her only child, her son. The autobiography ends with 16-year-old Maya holding her child protectively and going peacefully to sleep.

## CENSORSHIP HISTORY

The majority of the challenges to *I Know Why the Caged Bird Sings* have resulted from parents' complaints about the rape scene and Maya's pregnancy out of wedlock. In 1983, the Alabama State Textbook Committee rejected the book because they believed that it "preaches bitterness and hatred against whites." The book was challenged at Mount Abram Regional High School in Strong, Maine, in 1988, because parents objected to the rape scene. In 1990, a parent in Bremerton, Washington, objected to the book as a required reading for the gifted ninth-grade class because of the "graphic" description of the molestation. The parent also complained that the book "raised sexual issues without giving them a moral resolution." Despite the teacher's defense that the molestation passages were only a small part of the book and that the main focus was the fulfillment that Angelou reached in spite of adversity, the school board removed the book from the classroom. The board president justified the action by explaining that his constituents expected him to uphold a higher level of moral standard than is evidenced by the book.

In 1991, several parents in Benning, California, complained about the explicit passages involving child molestation and requested that the book be removed from the eighth-grade curriculum. One parent complained that her son did not want to go back to class to read that "gross" book, and another characterized the work as "morally and religiously offensive smut." The book was removed from the curriculum. In 1992, the work was retained after the parent of a student in Amador Valley High School, in Pleasanton, California, complained of the sexually explicit language.

The work was challenged but retained in several 1993 incidents, all of which objected to the passage in which the rape of the seven-year-old Maya is discussed. The book was temporarily banned from Caledonia Middle School, in Columbus, Mississippi, on the grounds that it was too sexually explicit. In Haines City, Florida, parents objected to the same passage and challenged inclusion of the book in both the English curriculum and the high school library. The same challenge occurred in Hooks (Texas) High School, where the book was assigned in a freshman honors history class.

In 1994, the work was challenged but retained as required reading for Dowling High School sophomores in Des Moines, Iowa, and the book became an issue at Ponderosa High School in Castle Rock, Colorado, when parents charged that it was "a lurid tale of sexual perversion." In their 1994 challenge to the book parents at Westwood High School in Austin, Texas, claimed that the book was "pornographic, contains profanity, and encourages premarital sex and homosexuality." The challenge motivated a new policy at the school for the reading of potentially controversial literature. The superintendent decreed that children would have to obtain their parents' permission in writing before they would be taught controversial literature.

## FURTHER READINGS

Elliot, Jeffrey, ed. *Conversations with Maya Angelou*. Jackson, Miss.: University of Mississippi Press, 1989.

Fox-Genovese, Elizabeth. "Myth and History: Discourse of Origins in Zora Neale Hurston and Maya Angelou." *Black American Literature Forum* 42 (Summer 1990): 221–235.

*Newsletter on Intellectual Freedom* (March 1983): 39; (January 1989): 8; (March 1989): 38; (November 1990): 211; (March 1992): 42; (July 1992): 109; (July 1993): 107; (January 1994): 34; (July 1994): 130; (January 1995): 11; (May 1995): 56.

Pettit, Jayne. *Maya Angelou: Journey of the Heart*. New York: Lodestar Books, 1996.

Shuker, Nancy. *Maya Angelou*. Englewood Cliffs, N.J.: Silver Burdett Press, 1990.

# IN THE NIGHT KITCHEN

**Author:**   Maurice Sendak
**Original date and place of publication:**   1970, United States
**Original publisher:**   Harper & Row
**Type:**   Children's picture book

## SUMMARY

In the Night Kitchen, a winner of the Caldecott Medal, is a dream fantasy in which a child named Mickey awakens in bed and believes that he hears talking downstairs in the kitchen. He leaps upward out of bed and falls through the night darkness, and out of his clothes, into the night kitchen that is brightly lighted. Three plump bakers dump him into cake batter, but he emerges, then jumps into the bread dough. Mickey then kneads and shapes the bread dough into an airplane in which he flies to the Milky Way to obtain milk for the bakers. He provides the bakers with milk, then stands proudly, and still nude, while he crows, "Cock-a-doodle-doo!" He then slides straight into his bed and into his clothes and goes to sleep.

## CENSORSHIP HISTORY

The book was removed from many public and school libraries that had bought it because parents complained that showing a fully naked child with some semblance of the genitals sketched in the appropriate place was "pornography." In many other libraries where the book had been purchased, the offending organ was either carefully whited out or equipped with a diaper or a pair of shorts drawn on with marker.

In 1974, a mother in Camden, New York, complained to school authorities that the book should be removed from elementary School libraries because it contained nudity and "children are already exposed to enough profanity in the media." The school superintendent reviewed the book and determined that it did not have "sufficient merit" to keep in the libraries. In announcing his decision to remove the book, the superintendent stated that schools had "a real obligation to represent what is moral, what is honest, what is decent."

In 1977, the book was removed from the elementary school library in Northridge, Illinois, because of parent complaints that it contained "nudity for no purpose." That same year, 40 copies of the book sent to 40 kindergarten classes were expurgated in Springfield, Missouri, by Wanda Gray, the director of elementary education, who drew shorts on the nude boy with a black felt pen. No one had yet complained, but the director said that she thought "it should be covered."

In 1985, parents of students attending Cunningham Elementary School in Beloit, Wisconsin, challenged the book as part of the school library collection, claiming that it "desensitizes children to nudity." One of the parents who issued the challenge insisted on parents' right to dictate book selection and stated, "You don't have to have a degree to know that teaching low morals and disrespect is wrong." The school board voted to retain the book in the library. In 1988, the book was challenged but retained after parents of students at Robeson Elementary School in Champaign, Illinois, complained that the book contained "gratuitous" nudity.

In 1990, parents of students in the Morrisonville, New York, elementary school requested that the book be removed from the school library because "it promotes nudity and child abuse." The school board appointed a review committee to consider the request and later accepted the recommendation of the review committee to retain the book in the elementary school library collection.

In 1991, a parent in Jacksonville, Florida, asked that the book be removed from the elementary school classroom because it contained "illustrations of a boy without his clothes." The parent appeared before the school

**149**

board, calling the nudity "disgraceful and appalling." A review committee appointed by the school board voted to retain the book without restriction, and the board concurred.

That same year, parents in Cornish, Maine, requested that the school board remove the book from the elementary school library because the illustrations of a naked boy "encourage child molestation." In their official complaint, the parents stated that the book would cause the following harm: "Child abuse. Children are taught that their private parts are private. This book is contrary to this teaching.' A review committee appointed by the school board voted to retain the book, calling it "a masterpiece example of the timeless theme of childhood fantasy."

In 1992, parents of students attending the Elk River, Minnesota, schools challenged the use of the book in the classroom because the nudity found within it "could lay the foundation for future use of pornography." The school board failed to agree and retained the book. In El Paso, Texas, in 1994, parents challenged the inclusion of the book in the children's section because "the little boy pictured did not have any clothes on and it pictured his private area." The challenge was considered by the library board, but the book was retained.

## FURTHER READINGS

Cech, John. *Angels and Wild Things*. University Park, Pa.: Pennsylvania State University Press, 1993.

Huck, Charlotte S., Susan Hepler and Janet Hickman. *Children's Literature in Elementary School*. New York: Holt, Rinehart & Winston, 1987.

*Newsletter on Intellectual Freedom* (May 1977): 71; (September 1977): 134; (July 1985): 134; (March 1989): 43; (November 1989): 217; (March 1993): 41; (September 1994): 148.

People for the American Way. *Attacks on the Freedom to Learn, 1991–1992 Report*. Washington, D.C.: People for the American Way, 1992.

Sutherland, Zena, and May Hill Arbuthnot. *Children's Books*. New York: HarperCollins Publishers, 1991.

## INVISIBLE MAN

**Author:**   Ralph Ellison
**Original date and place of publication:**   1952, United States
**Original publisher:**   Random House
**Type:**   Novel

## SUMMARY

*Invisible Man* is related by an unnamed narrator who reveals that he is an African-American man who is invisible because of an impersonal and indifferent world. While portions of the narration are realistic, a surreal quality pervades much of the novel as events occur chaotically and in rapid succession. The narrator lives in an underground cellar; after introducing his current situation, he explains his experiences moving from the South to the North that led to his present state.

"Battle Royal," the first chapter, tells of the narrator's experience when he is invited by the town's leading white citizens to give his high school graduation speech at a local hotel. He is made part of a "battle royal" with other blindfolded African-American students, who fight each other as entertainment for the white businessmen. Their reward is the money that they obtain by crawling on an electrified carpet to pick up coins. A well-endowed, blonde-haired stripper with an American flag tattooed between her thighs appears, but she is only for the whites to ogle. During the evening, the narrator makes his speech and receives as his reward a leather briefcase and a scholarship to a state college for blacks.

At college, the narrator is a good student who is entrusted with driving white visitors around campus. In his junior year, he drives a trustee named Mr. Norton out into the country, accidentally meeting the "fieldnigger" family, the Truebloods, who relate their family incest scandal. Norton becomes nauseous and unsteady on his feet because the story reawakens his own desires for his recently deceased daughter. Unsure of where they might find medical help, the narrator decides that a drink of strong liquor might revive Norton, so they stop at a nearby bar and brothel. A brawl breaks out, during which Norton passes out and must be carried upstairs into the prostitutes' quarters where he is revived.

After the narrator returns the trustee to the college, he is expelled. Dr. Bedsoe, the college president, gives him what appear to be letters of recommendation to potential employers in New York, but the letters are actually warnings not to trust the narrator or to help him. He takes a job at the Liberty Paint Company, then is knocked out in an explosion when he fails to follow instructions. After a period of hospitalization, he walks back to Harlem and inadvertently becomes part of a protest against the eviction of an old black couple. This brings him to the attention of The Brotherhood, who ask him to be their speaker in Harlem and to organize black residents. He also becomes the object of the lust of a married white woman who views him as a sexual "stud" and insists on being "taken" by him.

In rapid succession, the narrator is held responsible for the disappearance of another activist, tried by The Brotherhood for conspiracy and mistaken for Bliss Proteus Rinehart, a numbers runner, prolific lover, clergyman and politician. Harlem erupts into violence and, as he strives to head for the safety of his home, he runs into a pillaging crowd that pushes him to the ground and into a coal cellar, where he decides to stay in order to understand what has happened in his life. At the end of the novel, the narrator has burned all of the false promises of his past, including his high school diploma, the recommendation letters and the slip of paper with his Brotherhood name. He has made himself visible by lighting his cellar with 1,369 lightbulbs that run illegally on electricity from the "Monopolated Light & Power" company. The "Epilogue" explains that the narrator's story has also been that of the African-American community and ends by asking: "Who knows but that, on the lower frequencies, I speak for you?"

## CENSORSHIP HISTORY

The novel was well received when it was first published in 1952. Ellison won the National Book Award in 1953, the same year that he won the Russwurm Award and the National Newspaper Publishers' Award. Critics viewed it as signaling a black literary renaissance by its decided difference from the earlier "Negro protest fiction" of Richard Wright, Ann Petry and Chester Himes. Protests against its content did not occur until the work entered the school curriculum. In a 1973 national sample of English department chairpersons, Lee Burress reported that a parent and a student in an unnamed Midwestern city had objected to the assignment of the novel as a required reading for a high school English class. The challenge was based upon three aspects of the novel: 1) the fight staged by the black youths for the white businessmen, 2) the story of the black sharecropper raping his daughter and 3) "vulgarity" of language. The school board retained the book but offered students the right to substitute another book for their assignment.

In 1975, several parents of students in the Butler, Pennsylvania, school district raised objections to *Contemporary American Short Stories*, the reading anthology being used in a high school English class, because it contained the selection "The Battle Royal," the first chapter of *Invisible Man*. They protested against the "vulgar language" of several sentences in the work and reguested that the entire anthology be banned from use. The school board complied with their request and removed the anthology from the classroom.

In 1994, two parents challenged this novel, as well as Carlos Fuentes's *The Death of Artemio Cruz*, Nadine Gordimer's *July's People* and Richard Wright's *Native Son*, as required readings for advanced English classes in the Yakima, Washington, high school. They charged that the books contained "profanity," "images of violence" and "unacceptable" sexuality and requested that the books be removed from the required reading list. A school review committee was convened and voted to retain the books, a move with which the school board concurred.

## FURTHER READINGS

Burress, Lee. *Battle of the Books: Literary Censorship in the Public Schools, 1950–1985*. Metuchen, N.J.: Scarecrow Press, 1989.

Kostelanetz, Richard. *Politics in the African-American Novel: James Weldon Johnson, W.E.B. DuBois, Richard Wright, and Ralph Ellison.* New York: Greenwood Press, 1991.

Lisack, Thomas. "Books Worth Teaching Even Though They Have Proven Controversial: *Invisible Man* by Ralph Ellison." *English Journal* 82 (April 1993): 88.

*Newsletter on Intellectual Freedom* (July 1975): 105; (November 1994): 202–203.

Overmyer, Janet. "The Invisible Man and White Women." *Notes on Contemporary Literature* 6 (May 1976): 13–15.

## JAMES AND THE GIANT PEACH

**Author:** Roald Dahl
**Original date and place of publication:** 1961, United States
**Original publisher:** Penguin Books
**Type:** Children's novel

### SUMMARY

*James and the Giant Peach* is the story of a four-year-old boy whose happy and secure life changes when his parents go shopping in London and are eaten by "an enormous angry rhinoceros which had escaped from the London Zoo." He must live with his cruel and lazy Aunts Sponge and Spiker, who mistreat him, and he becomes a sad and lonely young boy with no friends. He endures this life for three years, then meets an old man who gives him magic crystals that, if ingested, will make "*marvelous* things" start happening to James, "*fabulous, unbelievable* things—and you will never be miserable again in your life." James runs back to the house but trips and falls. The bag bursts open, and the magic crystals scatter and immediately sink into the ground.

The aunts see him lying on the ground and shout at him, then notice a peach growing to giant size high on their tree. Greedily hoping to make money with the peach, they hire carpenters to build a fence around it and charge people to view the peach. A hungry James climbs into the giant peach and nibbles bits of it as he walks through to the stone. There, he finds large and talkative insects who want to leave the tree and James's horrible aunts, so the centipede with his "pair of jaws as sharp as razors" gnaws at the stem that binds the peach to the tree. The peach rolls, crushes the aunts to death and carries its passengers to various adventures. They first roll into the sea, where they encounter sharks that thrash around them. James saves them by convincing the silkworm to produce threads by which sea gulls lift them away from danger. In the air, they become victims of the Cloud Men, who pelt the peach with buckets of paint, frying pans and bottles of hair oil, but they escape.

The peach hovers over New York City, as the centipede bites the strings attaching the peach to the seagulls, so it falls on the Empire State Building. Their appearance first creates pandemonium in the city; then the group is given a ticker tape parade. City workers place the peach on a large truck in the procession, where thousands of children take bites from it.

James and his insect friends decide to stay in America, where "Everyone of them became rich and successful" and where James makes many new friends. The huge peach stone is placed in Central Park and becomes a famous monument as well as James's home, where "hundreds and hundreds of children from far and near" visit the once lonely boy.

## CENSORSHIP HISTORY

*James and the Giant Peach* is only one of several Dahl books that have evoked challenges because of "unsavory activities" or because adult readers believe that the works are "unhealthy for children." Despite challenges in schools, the novel has done well commercially and continues to appear in the children's section of most bookstores and libraries, and it is frequently referred to as a "classic in children's literature."

The novel was challenged in 1991 by the parent of a fourth-grade student in Deep Creek Elementary School in Charlotte Harbor, Florida, who claimed that the book is "not appropriate reading material for young children." When the student took the book home for a reading assignment, the parent, after examining the text, wrote a letter to the local newspaper. Noting that "The whole book is strange if you ask me," the mother urged other parents to complain to the school. The child told her teacher that she was not allowed to read the book, so an alternative assignment was given. The school principal and the director of special projects in the district identified the work as a classic and retained the book.

That same year, the mother of a nine-year-old boy at Pederson Elementary School in Altoona, Wisconsin, demanded that the book be removed from the school library because the word "ass" appears in it. The parent expressed further concern that the book promotes an "unhealthy" lifestyle, because wine, tobacco and snuff appear in it. She requested that the book be removed from the school library to spare other children. The district reconsideration committee reviewed the parent's request and voted unanimously to retain the book, a decision that the school board upheld. In reporting the decision, the school superintendent stated, "According to board policy no parent has the right to exclude material from other students in the district and I think that's a very fair standard."

In 1992, parents of students at Morton Elementary School in Brooksville, Florida, demanded that the book be removed from the school library because it contained "a foul word" and "promotes drugs and whiskey." Two review committees considered the book and both voted unanimously to retain it, a decision with which the county school board concurred. In reporting the decision, the county school superintendent stated that the book was "merely a fantasy about good triumphing over evil."

## FURTHER READINGS

Hitchens, Christopher. "The Grimmest Tales." *Vanity Fair* (January 1994): 26–30.

Meeks, Christopher. *Roald Dahl: Kids Love His Stories*. Vero Beach, Fla.: Rourke Publishing, 1993.

*Newsletter on Intellectual Freedom* (July 1991): 108; (March 1992): 65; (January 1993): 27.

Powling, Chris. *Roald Dahl*. London: Evans Bros., 1993.

Treglown, Jeremy. *Roald Dahl: A Biography*. New York: Farrar, Straus & Giroux, 1994.

## JAWS

**Author:**   Peter Benchley
**Original date and place of publication:**   1974, United States
**Original publisher:**   Doubleday & Company
**Type:**   Novel

## SUMMARY

*Jaws* relates the story of an ocean resort community terrified by the appearance of a great white shark. The year-round residents of Amity, Long Island, depend upon summer crowds for their living, and the biggest holiday is the fourth of July. The shark appears shortly before that date, violently chopping a woman in two and leaving pieces of her body at the water's edge. The businessmen seek to cover up the death, placing Police Chief Martin Brody in a moral dilemma. Leaving the beaches open will expose swimmers to danger, but closing the beaches will ruin summer business. As the town leaders forbid Brody to close the beaches, the shark strikes again, killing a six-year-old boy and a 65-year-old man and leading one witness to describe it as "the biggest fuckin' fish I ever saw in my whole life, big as a fuckin' station wagon." Unwilling to risk more lives, Brody closes the beaches, angering property and business owners.

The appearance of the shark initiates a private crisis on shore for Brody. The town calls upon the services of ichthyologist Matt Hooper, whose older brother once dated Brody's wife Ellen. Learning this makes the police chief's insecurities surface. He recalls his wife's early life, as part of the "country club set" that summered at Southampton and Amity, playing tennis and generally remaining idle. He and the other year-round residents were largely working class. Hooper's appearance also evokes memories for Ellen, who aches for the old days. She examines her naked body in a mirror, assessing her breasts, belly, hips and legs to determine if the "goods were good enough." In an effort to "resuscitate" herself, she calls Hooper, 10 years her junior, to meet her for lunch during which they drink too much and discuss sexual fantasies, penis size and "threesies." At a motel afterward, their intense sexual encounter, with Hooper's "obvious violent climax" when he "continued to pump madly," disturbs Ellen.

Brody and Hooper go out into the ocean with Quint, a charter boat captain, to kill the shark. The men tempt it to come near to the boat with buckets of chum, and Quint stands ready with a harpoon. Hooper asks to be lowered into the water in a cage so that he can take pictures, but the shark butts the cage repeatedly, separating the bars until the huge jaws reach in to grasp Hooper and devour him. When Brody and Quint go out the next day, the shark chases the boat, leading Quint to refer to it repeatedly as a "cocksucker," "an uppity fuck" and a "prick" as he thrusts harpoons into the shark's underbelly. The men believe that the shark is dead, but it rears up in the water, landing its jaw on the deck as the boat sinks. Quint is pulled into the water, leaving only Brody to survive as the shark finally dies.

## CENSORSHIP HISTORY

The novel has been removed from school classrooms and school libraries for complaints ranging from "objectionable" language to explicit sex. In 1977, a parent with the support of a minister in Montgomery, Alabama, challenged the book for containing explicit details about sex and requested the book be removed from the recommended reading list. The school board granted the request. The following year in Gardner-Edgerton-Antioch School District in Gardner, Kansas, several parents of students complained that the book contained an "explicit sex act" and requested its removal from the school library. The school board voted unanimously to take the book out of circulation, and all copies of *Jaws* were removed from all of the school libraries in the district. In 1979, parents challenged the availability of the book in the Ogden (Utah) High School library. The school board voted to place the book in a "restricted circulation" category, requiring students to have written parental permission to take the book out.

In 1980, parents of elementary and middle school students in Clinton, North Carolina, challenged the book for its "objectionable language" and asked for its removal from the school libraries. The school board voted to remove all copies of the book from the elementary and middle school libraries. In 1986, "obscene language" was the basis for a challenge by parents of students in the Gwinnett County, Georgia, public schools. The book was removed from the recommended reading list.

## FURTHER READINGS

*Newsletter on Intellectual Freedom* (May 1978): 56; (May 1979): 49; (September 1980): 99; (March 1987): 65.

# JUNKY (ORIGINALLY, JUNKY: CONFESSIONS OF AN UNREDEEMED DRUG ADDICT)

**Author:**   William Lee (pseudonym for William S. Burroughs)
**Original date and place of publication:**   1953, United States
**Original publisher:**   Ace Books
**Type:**   Novel

## SUMMARY

*Junky* is a graphic rendering of heroin addiction that chronicles the addict's life in full detail. Contained within are the hallucinations, the ghostly nocturnal wanderings, the strange and changing sexuality and the continuous hunger for the needle. The "hero" of the novel, a barely disguised persona of the author, is a young Midwesterner whose quest for the continuous high takes him to New York City, New Orleans and Mexico City, as he experiences on his journey any substance that promises an escape. In often graphic, sometimes surreal, detail, the book identifies and discusses frankly the use and the effects of heroin, marijuana ("tea" or "weed"), "goof balls," "bennies," morphine, codeine and peyote. The author also expresses his "junk equation": "Junk is not, like alcohol or weed, a means to increased enjoyment of life. Junk is not a kick. It is a way of life."

Burroughs also writes of the unscrupulous doctors who give numerous prescriptions ("scripts") for narcotics to addicts and of his efforts to have these prescriptions filled as he travels from one pharmacy to another. Along the way, he reveals the drug laws of the 1930s, providing details about the Narcotics Bureau inspectors who close down both doctors who write too many prescriptions and the pharmacies that fill too many. Burroughs deals bluntly with the fears of the addicts, who give fake names to obtain numerous prescriptions, and he identifies the tricks used to obtain these prescriptions—complaining of kidney stones, gallstones or migraine headaches to obtain prescriptions for morphine or codeine.

Burroughs also discusses his homosexual cruising paired with his addiction, and the nature of his relationships while addicted. Such relationships are rendered in a surreal manner, with violent, nightmare-like details. As the novel draws to a close, the author speaks of his and others' efforts to kick the habit and of the false hope provided by the incarceration of friends on Riker's Island, for what they and law enforcement officials refer to as the "thirty-day cure," after which they return to drugs as soon as they are again on the streets. The work ends with a glossary of terms used in the book, to enlighten the reader regarding the "junk lingo."

## CENSORSHIP HISTORY

Burroughs first published the novel under a pseudonym because of what Allen Ginsberg called his "police state paranoia cultivated by Narcotics Bureaus . . . that if you talked about 'tea' (much less Junk) on the bus or subway, you might be arrested—even if you were only discussing a change in the law."

His first publisher, Ace Books, was even more nervous "lest the publisher be implicated criminally with the author." As protection, the publisher required that the pseudonymous Burroughs write a preface that explained his "distinguished family background" and to exhibit the social significance of the work by giving "some hint how some supposedly normal citizen could arrive at being a dope fiend, to soften the blow for readers, censors, reviewers, police, critical eyes in walls & publishers' rows, god [sic] knows who." Carl Solomon, the editor at Ace Books, who handled *Junky*, also wrote an introduction that emphasized the serious nature of the book and its social importance. As further protection, the publisher excised a description of "Texas agricultural society" that might have opened the company to a lawsuit and included disclaimers throughout the text at "crucial medico-political statements of fact or opinion by Wm. Lee." As a final attempt to avoid prosecution, the publisher justified the existence of the book by binding it back to back with the title *Narcotic Agent*, written by Maurice Helbront. The first printing of 100,000 copies sold out the first year, and more than a million copies were sold over the next decade.

The first complete and unexpurgated edition was not published until 1977, when Penguin Books, in New York, issued the work alone, with an introduction by Allen Ginsberg. The book has remained out of schools because the title is sufficiently blunt to convey the content of the book, and many public libraries have avoided challenges by simply not ordering it.

## FURTHER READINGS

Burroughs, William S. *Letters to Allen Ginsberg, 1953–1957.* Introd. by Allen Ginsberg. New York: Full Court Press, 1982.

Ginsberg, Allen. "Introduction." In *Junky*, v–ix. Written by William S. Burroughs. New York: Penguin Books, 1977.

Morgan, Ted. *Literary Outlaw: The Life and Times of William S. Burroughs.* New York: Henry Holt & Company, 1988.

# KINGSBLOOD ROYAL

**Author:**   Sinclair Lewis
**Original date and place of publication:**   1947, United States
**Original publisher:**   Random House
**Type:**   Novel

## SUMMARY

*Kingsblood Royal* examines the consequences of a previously racist white man discovering that his maternal great-great-great-grandfather was black. Set in the town of Grand Republic, Minnesota, the novel is the story of Neil Kingsblood, an unassuming bank assistant who learns the truth when tracing his family lines. Given the prejudice of the times during which most Southern states and a few Northern ones determined that by law "a 'Negro' is defined by having even 'one drop of Negro blood,'" Neil is understandably upset by what he learns.

Thirty-one-year-old Neil, who served as an army captain during World War II, is married to Vestal and has a golden-haired daughter named Biddy. He has a promising future at the bank where he is developing a new account system. He has also established a Veterans' Advisory Center and hopes to lure new business to the bank in the form of mortgages and new accounts.

Before making his discovery, Neil is a well-liked success, and he is also racist in ways that he does not recognize. He and his wife own a black cocker spaniel named "Nigger," and they fail to understand why their black maid feels insulted. He has also internalized the negative beliefs regarding the intellect, industry and sexuality of blacks.

Neil's self-confidence is shattered after he reads a letter written by his great-great-great-grandfather, which states, "I am to all intent a full-blooded negro born in Martinique. . . . please [do] not say anything about my color and how black it is." Neil is fearful of having to live under the limitations placed on blacks by society, and he begins to feel that he will now have to "live in a decaying shanty," "work in kitchens," "have unpleasant manners," "be an animal physically" and be unable "to grasp any science beyond addition and plain cooking and driving of a car."

His maternal grandmother and grandfather vehemently deny the ancestry, to the point that his grandfather rages, "Are you trying to make me out to be the father of part-nigger kids—make your Uncle Emery and your own mother into niggers?"

Plagued with guilt that he is "passing," Neil tries to find a way to actually "be Negro," but the more that he tries to experience the "Negro culture" and find "special Negro things to be," the more he becomes aware of the similarities rather than the differences between the two races. When white neighbors, coworkers and other townspeople learn his secret, Neil loses his job and his family is shunned. The novel ends as he and Vestal are taken to jail, charged with violence after they defend their home against an angry white mob that attacks them and tries to force them out of the neighborhood.

## CENSORSHIP HISTORY

The novel was a daring effort to explore the issue of racial prejudice in 1940s America, and it won Sinclair Lewis an award from *Ebony* magazine for his attempts to promote racial understanding. In contrast, when the novel was first published in 1947, this effort also cost him and his publisher Random House sales in many small and moderately sized cities in the South, where the company's salesmen were forewarned to not even attempt to market the book. Several objections to the book were raised. One objection was to the intelligence and educational levels of many of the blacks portrayed in the novel. One man holds a Ph.D. in chemistry, another holds a doctorate from Columbia University and all seem to converse about issues of importance. Another objection to the book centered on the negative way in which white characters were portrayed in their reactions to a man who, when thought to be white, was accepted and liked.

Lewis noted in one of his letters that he may have struck a chord with many white Southerners, who had doubts about their own ancestry being revealed. In several large cities, notably Atlanta and New Orleans, booksellers kept copies of the novel on closed shelves, only selling them if someone specifically asked to buy the book. Random House received numerous letters denouncing Lewis and threatening to stop buying any of his books.

In New York City, the Society for the Suppression of Vice sought to prevent sales of the book after complaints arose about the suggested sexual content of the novel. When Neil first learns of his ancestry and seeks out black friends, he meets an attractive black nurse to whose one-room tenement apartment he goes one evening. There, he rests his cheek "on the smoothness of her [clothed] breast" and kisses her "with quietness and propriety." The efforts by the Society to bring charges against the book were fruitless, and only a few booksellers agreed to remove the novel from their stock.

In 1953, the novel was removed from an Illinois library after a mother complained that her daughter had borrowed the book and that it was offensive. The novel was also banned in Ireland in 1953 for the use of the term "nigger" and the "suggestive sexuality."

The novel also aroused interest by the Federal Bureau of Investigation after, in 1947, "the FBI was flooded with letters denouncing Lewis's *Kingsblood Royal*." The FBI report in Lewis's file states that the book was of concern for it seemed "to be propaganda for the white man's acceptance of the negro as a social equal."

## FURTHER READINGS

Conroy, Stephen S. "Sinclair Lewis's Sociological Imagination." *American Literature* 42 (November 1970): 348–362.

Light, Martin. *The Quixotic Vision of Sinclair Lewis.* West Lafayette, Ind.: Purdue University Press, 1975.

Manfred, Frederick. "Sinclair Lewis: A Portrait." *American Scholar* 23 (Spring 1954): 162–184.

Robins, Natalie. *Alien Ink: The FBI's War on Freedom of Expression.* New York: William Morrow and Company, 1992.

# LAST EXIT TO BROOKLYN

**Author:**   Hubert Selby Jr.
**Original date and place of publication:**   1964, United States
**Original publisher:**   Grove Press
**Type:**   Novel

## SUMMARY

*Last Exit to Brooklyn* consists of six linked episodes, each preceded by a quote from the Old Testament, that form a novel detailing the brutal and violent lives of a group of lower economic class Brooklyn youths in the late 1940s through the 1950s. The squalor of the environment and the hopelessness of their drug- and violence-dominated lives leave them devoid of human compassion and lacking in conventional morality. Married and single, gay and straight, the men are portrayed as relentlessly brutal, opportunistic and cruel to other men, to women and to the children whom they conceive. Women, powerless for the most part, accept their limited roles, exacting revenge on those weaker than them whenever possible. Children are conditioned to live life as a daily struggle and to accept abusive behavior as normal. For everyone in this novel, crime is an everyday fact of existence.

The novel takes its title from the sign "Last Exit to Brooklyn" that appears on the Gowanus (New York) Expressway, just before the entrance to the Battery tunnel. That expressway exit is an entrance into a hell composed of waterfront docks, dirty factory buildings, slum housing, cheap bars and subsidized city apartment projects for the poor, with empty, bottle-strewn lots and concrete playgrounds. The language throughout the work is in the vernacular, and the author omits the use of apostrophes in contractions or to indicate the possessive form of nouns and he often runs words together to reflect the characters' states of mind. Four young criminals, each of whom boasts of his prison record, spend their lives "hanging out" at "the Greeks" diner, mocking the prostitutes such as Tralala and boasting of recent "scores," having "lushed a drunk" or "pulled a job." Opportunistic, they claim to be completely heterosexual but become involved with a crowd of male transvestites whom they pretend to view as women in order to take advantage of the free gin, abundant benzedrine tablets and cheap thrills. The young hoodlums pretend to care about the transvestites but their resulting cruelty leads one to overdose on benzedrine tablets. The friends move in different directions, and each later faces his or her own disaster.

Tralala descends into a nightmare of alcoholism and drug addiction, trading her body for drinks and even giving it away for free just to feel wanted. She dies after being taken to a vacant lot filled with broken bottles and rusty cans and raped by 50 or more men from several area barrooms. Afterwards, as Selby writes in a stream-of-consciousness tone,

> . . . the kids who were watching and waiting to take a turn took out their disappointment on Tralala and tore her clothes to small scraps put out a few cigarettes on her nipples pissed on her jerkedoff on her jammed a broomstick up her snatch then bored they left her lying amongst the broken bottles rusty cans and rubble of the lot and Jack and Fred and Ruthy and Annie stumbled into a cab still laughing and they leaned toward the window as they passed the lot and got a good look at Tralala lying naked covered with blood urine and semen and a small blot forming on the seat between her legs as blood seeped from her crotch and Ruth and Annie happy and completely relaxed now that they were on their way downtown. . . .

Later sections explore the brutality of Harry Black, now a union organizer, who repeatedly blames and physically abuses his wife to compensate for his disgust with all women. A braggart and bully who drinks heavily, he has frequent violent dreams in which he sees himself torn to shreds. The dreams end and he achieves temporary happiness and even softens toward all but his wife once he begins a passionate affair with a male transvestite upon whom he lavishes money taken from his union strike expense account. Black believes that he has found true love, but his lover leaves when the strike account closes and the flow of money stops. In a confused state, Black attempts to perform oral sex on a 10-year-old boy in his neighborhood, and his former friends brutally beat him as punishment.

The two sections that deal with marriage, "And Baby Makes Three" and "Landsend," continue the pervasive theme of despair. None of the marriages are happy, because all of the husbands and some of the wives appear to remain eager for extramarital sex. Husbands who work are physically abusive and grudgingly give their stay-at-home wives money to buy food for their children; husbands who do not work but who depend on their wives' paychecks are also abusive and refuse to assume any household or child-care responsibilities. Capital letters dominate the conversations as Selby indicates the continued arguments that pass for marital communication. Children are neglected and subjected to the constant fighting of their parents. The novel portrays a hellish existence that appears to continue as the characters age.

## CENSORSHIP HISTORY

*Last Exit to Brooklyn* has been censored on both sides of the Atlantic. Several of the chapters had appeared separately in *Black Mountain Review, New Directions #17, Provincetown Review* and *Swank*. The section entitled "Tralala" first appeared as a play that was banned from off-Broadway production in 1957. In 1965, in Boston, Massachusetts, a local city attorney sought an injunction against the book, but the complaint was dismissed. The following year, a circuit court in Connecticut issued a temporary injunction against sale of the book, now published by both Grove Press and Dell Publishing, charging that it was "obscene and pornographic." The injunction was overturned and sales were again permitted. The novel has also been banned in Italy and Ireland, and placed on a restricted list in Russia.

The most extensive censorship case occurred in England, where the novel was published by Calder and Boyars. In late 1966, Conservative Member of Parliament Sir Charles Taylor received a copy of the novel, sent to him by Sir Basil Blackwell, member of an Oxford bookselling family and a man in his seventies who claimed that his few remaining years had been "defiled" by reading *Last Exit*. Disgusted by the book, Taylor alerted the attorney general in June 1967 to register a complaint with the Office of the Director of Public Prosecutions (DPP). That office replied that Taylor was too late to make an effective complaint because over 11,000 copies of the book had already been sold, and sales were slowing. Attorney General Sir Elwyn Jones stated further that "Literary Criticism was almost unanimous that it had literary merit." The publisher taunted Taylor by including his name in their advertisement in *The Sunday Times*, stating: "Sir Charles Taylor, MP has described *Last Exit* as filthy, disgusting, degrading. It is one of the most important novels to come out of America. . . ."

The audacity of the publisher angered another member of parliament, Sir Cyril Black (Conservative), who used the private prosecutions feature of Section 3 of the *Obscene Publications Act of 1959* to challenge the publishers. He brought a formal complaint against the book in July 1966, calling upon the publisher to prove that the book had value and to establish why it should not be banned. The magistrate who granted the application was Sir Robert Blundell, a chief opponent of *Fanny Hill*, who issued a search warrant for members of law enforcement to seize all copies from area bookshops. The trial was held at Marlborough Street Magistrates Court in November 1966, and the numerous prosecution witnesses were consistent in expressing their disgust with the scenes depicted in the novel, especially with the brutal rape and humiliation of Tralala. This section has drawn the greatest objection in proceedings against the book because of the horrifying picture that Selby creates of the humiliation and death of Tralala and the cold indifference of onlookers. The presiding magistrate rejected the book, observing that "this book in its descriptions goes beyond any book of a merely pornographic kind that we have seen in this court [and] . . . is more likely to deprave and corrupt than any of those cyclostyled horrors."

Buoyed by the published opinion of several critics that Britain "had made herself the laughing stock of the civilized world," Calder and Boyars announced that they would continue publication. In response, the DPP announced that it would prosecute, using section 2 of the 1959 act that prohibited "possessing an obscene article for gain." The trial was set for November 1967, and an all-male jury was selected to spare women the embarrassment of reading the material. The trial lasted nine days and brought together numerous prominent witnesses. The prosecution spotlighted David Shepherd, a former cricket star who had taken religious orders and would later become a bishop, who claimed that he had emerged "not unscathed" by reading the novel, although as a social worker in the East End of London he could identify many of the character types among his clients. To counter this testimony, Calder and Boyars assembled a list of nearly 30 writers, critics, professors and members of the media who praised Selby's work and his expression of theme. The effort was fruitless for, after deliberating five and a half hours, the jury declared the book guilty of being obscene and that "the effect of reading the book was to horrify, shock, disgust, and nauseate." Although the judge determined that the book had been published in good faith by a respectable publishing house, he fined Calder and Boyars £100 and ordered them to pay £500 in court costs.

The publishers once again appealed the decision, represented this time by John Mortimer, who convinced the appeal judges that the judge in the earlier trial had not sufficiently explained the complexities of the 1959 act to the jury and had left too much to "commonsense" and not enough to law. As a result, the conviction was overturned and *Last Exit* was free to appear in a complete and unexpurgated edition. To avoid further embarrassing litigation based on private prosecution, Section 3 of the *Obscene Publications Act of 1959* was changed. *Last Exit* holds the distinction of being the last serious novel, poem or play prosecuted under the 1959 act.

## FURTHER READINGS

Kermode, Frank. "'Obscenity' and the 'Public Interest'." *New American Review* 3 (April 1968): 229–244.

Lane, James B. "Violence and Sex in the Post-War Popular Urban Novel: With a Consideration of Harold Robbins's *A Stone for Danny Fisher* and Hubert Selby, Jr.'s, *Last Exit to Brooklyn*." *Journal of Popular Culture* 8 (Fall 1974): 295–308.

Sutherland, John. *Offensive Literature: Decensorship in Britain, 1960–1982*. Totowa, N.J.: Barnes & Noble Books, 1983.

Wertime, Richard A. "Psychic Vengeance in *Last Exit to Brooklyn*." *Literature and Psychology* 24 (November 1974): 153–166.

# LEAVES OF GRASS

**Author:** Walt Whitman
**Original date and place of publication:** 1855, United States
**Original publisher:** Self-published
**Type:** Poetry collection

## SUMMARY

*Leaves of Grass* appeared in 1855 as a quarto of 95 pages that had been typeset by Whitman in the Brooklyn print shop of Andrew and James Rome. Whitman's name did not appear on the title page, nor did the name of a publisher or printer appear. He did not hide his authorship, however, for the copyright notice was credited to "Walter Whitman" and his portrait faced the title page. The 12 poems in the 1855 edition had no titles, but Whitman created titles for them, with which we are now familiar, in later editions: "Song of Myself," "A Song for Occupations," "To Think of Time," "The Sleepers," "I Sing the Body Electric," "Faces," "Song of the Answerer," "Europe the 72d and 73d Years of These States," "A Boston Ballad," "There Was a Child Went Forth," "Who Learns My Lesson Complete" and "Great Are the Myths." The collection went through five more editions in Whitman's lifetime. The third edition of the collection, published in 1860, contained more than 100 additional poems, many of them with homosexual overtones that brought more notoriety to the work.

The first edition fulfilled Walt Whitman's goal to write a serious work in a clearly sensuous manner. His subject is the common man, unlike other writers of his time who wrote about and for an educated elite. He chose to draw attention to the ordinary people who made up American society. He also had another purpose to his poetry. Whitman stated in the preface to the 1855 edition of *Leaves of Grass* his purpose of uniting the physical aspect of the human with the spiritual, and this purpose appears in the poetry, as in "Song of Myself," which contains the line "I am the poet of the body, / And I am the poet of the soul."

In developing his theme of accepting everything in life equally, excluding nothing, Whitman included blunt anatomical references that offended many of his readers for whom such references remained taboos for many decades into the future. In accepting all of nature, he wrote of "the litter of the grunting sow as they tug at her teats" and "where the bull advances to do his masculine work, and the stud to the mare, and the cock is treading the hen." He similarly accepted people in all stations and situations of life, as he wrote that "the keptwoman [sic] and sponger and thief are hereby invited—the heavy-lipped slave is invited—the veneralee is invited." He offered friendship and brotherhood "to a drudge of the cottonfields or emptier of privies . . . on his right cheek I place the family kiss."

Throughout the poems, Whitman speaks of the physical actions and realities that his contemporaries strained to keep hidden as not being "nice" or "appropriate" to speak of:

> Copulation is no more rank to me than death is.
> I believe in the flesh and the appetites,
> Seeing hearing and feeling are miracles, and
> each part and tag of me is a miracle.
> . . . .
> The scent of these arm-pits is aroma finer than prayer, . . .
> . . . .
> I turn the bridegroom out of bed and stay
> with the bride myself,
> And tighten her all night to my thighs and lips.
> . . . .
> Darkness you are gentler than my lover—
> his flesh was sweaty and panting,
> I feel the hot moisture yet that he left me.

In numerous lines throughout the collection, Whitman celebrated sensuality and reminded people of their most primitive desires.

## CENSORSHIP HISTORY

*Leaves of Grass* was declared obscene from its first publication. The first bookseller to whom Whitman took his book refused to sell it, claiming that it was "too sensual." Whitman met Lorenzo and Orson Fowler, who agreed to distribute the book, but sales were low and Whitman gave away many copies of the first edition. As cries of "immorality" were raised against the work, the Fowler brothers became frightened and gave existing copies of the second edition of the work to Whitman and resigned the whole edition. Libraries refused to buy the book; the Library Company of Philadelphia is the only one on record in America to have bought a copy when it was first published. Thus, other libraries effectively censored the book by their refusal to buy it.

Critic R. W. Griswold, writing on November 10, 1855, in *The New Criterion*, observed, "Thus, then we leave this gathering of muck to the laws which, certainly, if they fulfill their intent, must have power to suppress such obscenity." A review in the English magazine *Saturday Review* also condemned the collection and stated in March 1856: "After every five or six pages . . . Mr. Whitman suddenly becomes very intelligible, but exceedingly obscene. If the *Leaves of Grass* should come into anybody's possession, our advice is to throw them immediately behind the fire." In 1865, Walt Whitman lost his job with the United States Department of the Interior because Chief Secretary James Harlan found an annotated copy of the poetry collection in Whitman's desk drawer and determined that he was "the author of an indecent book." In 1870, Noah Porter, president of Yale University, wrote in *Books and Reading* that "a generation cannot be entirely pure which tolerates writers who, like Walt Whitman, commit, in writing, an offense like that indictable at common law of walking naked through the streets."

Many people, among them Ralph Waldo Emerson, who had praised the book in a letter that Whitman arranged to have published in the *New York Times*, urged Whitman to permit an expurgated version of the collection. He remained staunchly opposed to expurgation and American copyright law protected him unless he consented to it. From the time that the collection appeared in 1855, his editors suggested that a bowdlerized version for the general public would be good for sales. Whitman violently opposed expurgation, viewing such books as "the dirtiest book in all the world." Not until 1892, not long before his death, did he finally agree to an expurgated version as a gesture of friendship for Arthur Stedman, whose father, Edward Clarence Stedman, had done many favors for Whitman.

*Leaves of Grass* was not expurgated in the United States until 1892, but it was banned entirely, if informally, in New York and Philadelphia bookstores in the 1870s and legally in Boston in the 1880s. As per their usual practice, the Watch and Ward Society in Boston and the New York Society for the Suppression of Vice placed pressure on booksellers to suppress the sale of the book in their shops. Booksellers agreed not to advertise the book nor to suggest its sale to customers.

In 1881, the Society for the Suppression of Vice sought to obtain a legal ban of a proposed new edition of *Leaves of Grass* in Boston. At the urging of the society, the district attorney threatened criminal action against a publisher who had planned a new edition of the work unless it were expurgated. The edition was withdrawn.

In 1883, author, publisher and free-love advocate Ezra Heywood was arrested by Anthony Comstock, the head of the New York Society for the Suppression of Vice, on the charge of sending obscene matter through the mail. The material consisted of *Cupid's Yokes*, a pamphlet that contained "unconventional social and sexual views," and an anthology entitled *The Word Extra* that contained two poems from *Leaves of Grass*, "To a Common Prostitute" and "A Woman Waits for Me." When the case went to trial, the grand jury declared the Whitman poems "too grossly obscene and lewd to be placed on the records of the court." This meant that members of the jury would decide Heywood's fate without being permitted to review copies of the poem nor to hear lines from the poem read before making their decision; they were expected to accept the decision of the prosecution that the works were obscene. Judge T. L. Nelson, presiding in the United States Circuit Court in Boston, threw out the case, "on the grounds that the allegation in the indictment was untrue."

The English bowdlerized the collection from its first appearance in England in 1868. Pre-Raphaelite ex-bohemian William Michael Rossetti, the editor of the expurgated collection, explained in the preface that he had omitted about half the poems of the 1860s edition because he and Whitman lived in "this peculiarly nervous age." He also proudly proclaimed that he was not bowdlerizing the work, because "I have not in a single instance excised *parts* of poems." Perrin observed, "it is the sort of preface a liberal poet might write if he happened to get involved in bowdlerism." Although Rossetti did not excise parts of any poems, he did make numerous changes in Whitman's preface to the original 1855 edition of the collection, excising even the term "prostitute." The expurgated version of *Leaves of Grass* became part of the Everyman Library in 1886 and existed well into the twentieth century. Ernest de Selincourt used that version for Oxford's "World Classics" series in 1920, removing several more poems. Late in life, Whitman considered his work and expressed his dissatisfaction with the English editions, noting that "I now feel somehow as if none of the changes should have been made: that I should have assumed that position: that's the only possible, final, logical position."

## FURTHER READINGS

Blodgett, Harold. *Walt Whitman in England*. Ithaca, N.Y.: Cornell University Press, 1934.

Broun, Heywood, and Margaret Leech. *Anthony Comstock*. New York: Albert & Charles Boni, 1927.

Cavitch, David. *My Soul and I: The Inner Life of Walt Whitman*. Boston: Beacon Press, 1985.

Cowley, Malcolm, ed. *Walt Whitman's Leaves of Grass: The First (1855) Edition*. New York: Viking Press, 1959.

Everson, William. *American Bard: The Original Preface to "Leaves of Grass"*. New York: Viking Press, 1982.

McCoy, Ralph E. *Banned in Boston: The Development of Literary Censorship in Massachusetts*. Urbana, Ill.: University of Illinois, 1956.

Mordell, Albert. *Notorious Literary Attacks*. New York: Boni & Liveright, 1926.

Perrin, Noel. *Dr. Bowdler's Legacy*. Boston: David R. Godine, Publisher, 1969.

# LITTLE BLACK SAMBO

**Author:**   Helen Bannerman
**Original date and place of publication:**   1898, England; 1923, United States
**Original publisher:**   Platt & Munk, Inc. (England); J.B. Lippincott Company (United States)
**Type:**   Children's book

## SUMMARY

*Little Black Sambo*, one of many stories created by the author to amuse her daughters, was made up while on a long railway journey and it "was the favourite." The "Preface" establishes the setting and states: "Once upon a time there was an English lady in India, where black children abound and tigers are everyday affairs, who had two little girls." Bannerman also "drew and coloured the pictures" that became so embroiled in controversy a half-century after publication.

The story is simple. Sambo is "a little black boy," whose father is Black Jumbo and mother is Black Mumbo. His mother makes him "a beautiful Red Coat, and a pair of beautiful little Blue Trousers." His father buys him "a beautiful Green Umbrella, and a lovely little Pair of Purple Shoes with Crimson soles and Crimson Linings" at the bazaar. Feeling very grand, Sambo takes a long walk in the forest and meets four dangerous tigers, one at a time. To prevent them from eating him, Sambo bargains with them, giving each a piece of his finery until he is left with what in the illustrations looks to be a towel around his waist. He walks home, crying, but hears the tigers and believes that they are coming as a group to eat him, so he hides behind a palm tree. As he watches, they remove the clothes and begin to claw each other. Finally, each grabs another's tail as they form a circle around a tree, running around it and "trying to eat each other up," while Sambo retrieves his clothes and goes home. The tigers run so quickly that they melt into a pool of butter, which Black Jumbo finds on his way home from work; he places it into a big brass pot and takes it home for Black Mumbo to use in cooking. The story ends as the family enjoys "a huge big plate of most lovely pancakes" that have been fried "in the melted butter which the Tigers had made."

The book was first published in England nearly a century ago, and it has appeared in nearly 50 different editions and collections over the years, the text or the illustrations varying according to the whims of the publisher. In the first American edition, published in 1923 by the J.B. Lippincott Company in Philadelphia, the title page bears the statement "The Only Authorized American Edition," as do all Lippincott reprintings of the book. In the "Preface," the reader learns that in the Lippincott version, "the pictures [are] copied as exactly as possible" from Bannerman's original illustrations. This point is significant, because the illustrations have frequently been subject to heavier criticism than the text. Also significant is the realization that the Lippincott edition has been "most often in the line of fire and least often on library shelves" in the past three decades.

## CENSORSHIP HISTORY

*Little Black Sambo* first attracted public criticism in the late 1950s, as the momentum of the civil rights' movement in the United States increased. This public criticism intensified in the 1960s as greater attention was paid to the ways in which African Americans were treated and represented in all media. Critics viewed the story as "a dangerous and cruel book" that depicted African Americans in an extremely unfavorable light, dehumanizing them and perpetuating negative stereotypes. The name "Sambo" is itself rooted in controversy. The 1966 edition of *The Oxford Dictionary of English Etymology* defined the word as being "a colloquial term for any Negro," but various popular dictionaries of the time, including the 1964 Webster's *New World Dictionary*, defined "sambo" as a noun of Spanish derivation meaning "Negro, mulatto, monkey." The term does not even appear in the 1991 edition of Webster's *New World Dictionary*.

In 1956, the Toronto Board of Education ordered *Little Black Sambo* removed from classrooms and school library shelves after the board received complaints from several groups that "the popular book was a cause of mental suffering to Negroes in particular and children in general." Canadian librarians protested the move and pointed out that the setting is India, not Africa: "Everything in it pertains to India, even the clothing and the house where Black Sambo lives." A children's librarian asserted that "all the boys and girls who have read *Little Black Sambo* have done so without any suggestion of harboring derogatory feelings."

In 1959, the book was removed from a school library in New York City after a black resident challenged the book as racially derogatory. The school board convened a committee to review the charge. The committee determined that the charge was "unfounded" and voted to restore the book to library shelves.

In 1965, Lincoln (Nebraska) School Superintendent Steven N. Watkins ordered the book removed from the open shelves of the school libraries. The move was made following Watkins' receipt of a letter from the local Human Relations Council, which explained the "inherent racism" of the work. He concluded that the book was "not worth making an issue over . . . There are plenty of good stories left." A few weeks later, Watkins ordered copies of the book taken from storage and placed on the "Reserved" shelves, accompanied by a note stating that even though the book was "not a part of the instructional program, it will be available to those who want to read it as optional material."

A well-publicized banning of the work occurred in Montgomery, Alabama, in 1971. After receiving parent complaints, the county school superintendent in conjunction with a committee of principals, librarians, teachers and a county staff member voted to remove all copies of the book, as well as filmstrips and records featuring the story, from the county school libraries. Committee members labeled the book "inappropriate" and "not in keeping with good human relations." In a memo to principals and librarians announcing the removal, the county director of educational media and technology stated that "the decision is not to be construed as book burning, but rather as book selection."

In January 1972, the Montreal-based Canadian National Black Coalition mobilized efforts to remove the book from school and library shelves. In Hamilton, Ontario, teachers ordered students to tear from school readers the pages that contained the story. The book was banned entirely in New Brunswick.

Later that spring in the United States, a multiethnic committee in Dallas, Texas, lodged a formal complaint against the book and demanded its removal from the city school libraries because it "distorts a child's view of black people." The school district conducted an investigation of the complaint and determined that the book had been informally removed from the school libraries in 1965, but it was later returned because officials questioned if they were depriving children of their literary freedom. The book was formally removed again.

*Little Black Sambo* was also attacked in England in 1972, where a coalition of educators campaigned against retaining the book in libraries and schools because it symbolized "the kind of dangerous and obsolete books that must go." A member of the group noted that the story unfairly "depicts the Negro as an almost unclothed, illiterate and inferior savage from whose antics great humor can be derived."

The banning and removal of *Little Black Sambo* sparked considerable debate regarding the conditions that justify censorship. Howard N. Meyer, an attorney writing in 1980 in the bulletin published by the Council on Interracial Books for Children, took the position of many who demanded the removal of *Little Black Sambo* and other books such as THE ADVENTURES OF HUCKLEBERRY FINN or *Nicodemus and Sally* on the grounds that they were "racist." He stated that "censorship" is an act of "official agencies" and asserted that "citizens who urged that *Little Black Sambo* and *The Adventures of Huckleberry Finn* be removed from school libraries as racial books should not be called censors since they are not state officials." The following year, Michael Farris, president of the Moral Majority in the state of Washington, appeared as a speaker at the American Library Association conference in San Francisco. After claiming that he had searched several libraries and not found a copy of *Little Black Sambo*, Farris labeled as "intellectual hypocrisy" the move to ban presumably "racist" and "sexist" books but to contest the efforts of the Moral Majority to remove what they view as "sexually offensive materials."

## FURTHER READINGS

Baker, Augusta. "The Black Experience in Children's Literature—An Introductory Essay." *New York Public Library Bulletin* 75 (March 1971): 143–145.

Broderick, Dorothy M. *Image of the Black in Children's Fiction.* New York: R.R. Bowker Company, 1973.

Cohen, David. "Selection and Racism." *Library Journal* (October 15, 1969): 3,585.

Davis, Mavis Wormley. "Black Images in Children's Literature: Revised Editions Needed." *Library Journal* (January 15, 1972): 261–263.

Messiano, Lindalee. "Even When It Offends." *Library Journal* (May 15, 1969): 2,031.

Meyer, Howard N. "Neutralism Isn't Neutral." *CIBC Bulletin* 11 (1980): 13.

*Newsletter on Intellectual Freedom* (April 1956): 3–4; (July 1963): 51; (January 1965): 12.

"Sambo Banned by Montgomery County Schools." *Library Journal* (September 15, 1971): 2,813–2,814.

"Sambo Removal Sought by National Black Coalition." *Library Journal* (January 15, 1972): 237–238.

# LITTLE HOUSE ON THE PRAIRIE

**Author:**   Laura Ingalls Wilder
**Original date and place of publication:**   1935, United States
**Original publisher:**   Harper & Row
**Type:**   Young adult novel

## SUMMARY

*Little House on the Prairie* continues the adventures of the Ingalls family, which the author had begun in *Little House in the Big Woods*, published in 1932. The earlier novel told of the hardships suffered by Pa and Ma Ingalls and their daughters, Laura and Mary, and later baby Carrie, who lived on the edge of the Big Woods of Wisconsin and faced the difficulties of pioneer life. *Little House on the Prairie* relates their move to Kansas, an area of the country that was still heavily populated by Native Americans. They travel numerous days until they find a location that is suitable for building a log cabin.

The family soon re-establishes a home and begins to plow and to plant, as well as to hunt wild ducks and turkeys and to raise their livestock. They must also function without close neighbors or family for security and block out the howling of the wolves at night. The Ingalls also live in constant fear of "Indians" without having had any previous contact with them. When Laura yells out to her mother, she is admonished, "you yell like an Indian." Ma Ingalls also cautions her girls that they are "getting to look like Indians."

Numerous tribes gather several miles from the Ingalls' cabin, shouting and yelling in the night and terrifying the girls. Various Native American males visit the cabin, but their presence is upsetting as they frighten Ma Ingalls into preparing food and giving them her husband's tobacco. After several months of worrying about their fate, the Ingalls learn that the tribes have dispersed after the Osage tribe has threatened to fight the other tribes who want to kill all of the white settlers. The settlers also learn that they will have to move, because the government has declared the area to be Indian Territory.

The novel ends as the family accepts its fate, loads the covered wagon and moves on to find another place to settle.

## CENSORSHIP HISTORY

Objections to *Little House on the Prairie* have emerged only in the 1990s. Before this decade, the novel and others in the series were highly praised; in 1954, the Laura Ingalls Wilder Award was established by the American Library Association and was first presented to Wilder for her series. The award is now presented every three years to an author who has produced a body of work that has made a substantial and lasting contribution to children's literature.

In 1993, the novel was challenged by parents of students in the Lafourche Parish elementary schools in Thibodaux, Louisiana, who requested its removal from the school libraries because it was "offensive to Indians." Among their objections, the parents cited the repeated description of the Native Americans as "naked wild men" or "terrible men" with "glittering black eyes." The phrase "The only good Indian is a dead Indian" is repeated several times by the Ingalls' neighbor, Mrs. Scott. Further, the objectors cited the appearance of two Native American males who appear at the house when Charles is out hunting: "Those Indians were dirty and scowling and mean. They acted as if the house belonged to them." The two men look through all of the cupboards and take food and tobacco; then one takes the bundle of furs that are supposed to be traded for a plow and seeds but he is stopped by his companion. The school board denied the request and the book was retained.

In contrast, the novel was banned that same year from elementary school classrooms in Sturgis, South Dakota, because objectors asserted that "it contains statements that are considered derogatory to Native Americans." The objections presented to the Sturgis School Board were mainly those cited in the Lafourche Parish challenge, and Sturgis evidenced significantly greater public support for the ban.

## FURTHER READINGS

McCullough, Debbie. "Idealism and Reality in the Works of Laura Ingalls Wilder." *English in Education* 26 (Spring 1992): 33–37.

Mills, Claudia. "From Obedience to Autonomy: Moral Growth in the 'Little House' Books." *Children's Literature: An International Journal* 24 (1996): 127–140.

Segel, Elizabeth. "Laura Ingalls Wilder's America: An Unflinching Assessment." *Children's Literature in Education* 8 (February 1978): 63–70.

Wolf, Virginia L. "The Symbolic Center: *Little House in the Big Woods*." *Children's Literature in Education* 13 (Fall 1982): 107–114.

# LITTLE RED RIDING HOOD

**Author:** Charles Perrault
**Original date and place of publication:** 1697, Paris; 1729, London (first English translation)
**Original publisher:** Privately printed (Paris and London)
**Type:** Children's story

## SUMMARY

*Little Red Riding Hood* was part of the collection *Histoires ou Contes du temps passé, avec des Moralités*, stories created out of folktales by Charles Perrault, that was intended to be used in the nurseries at Versailles in the court of Louis XIV. Perrault's tales were first translated into English in 1729 by Robert Samber in *Histories or Tales of Past Times*. The story, now often published alone, has undergone numerous transformations. The popular contemporary version found in children's books in the United States is based upon the rewriting of the folktale by Jacob and Wilhelm Grimm that appeared as "Little Red Cap" in their *Nursery and Household Tales*, published in Germany in 1812. The first accurate U.S. translation of this collection appeared in 1944 as *Grimm's Fairy Tales*.

*Little Red Riding Hood* is the story of a sweet young girl who visits her grandmother and takes with her a basket of food and wine. As she travels through the woods on her way to her grandmother's house, she meets a wolf who asks where she is going. After she tells him, the wolf takes a shortcut and arrives at grandmother's house long before Little Red Riding Hood. He eats grandmother, dresses in her clothing and waits for the little girl to arrive. Puzzled by her grandmother's appearance, the little girl states a series of observations regarding the large size of the wolf's eyes, ears and other parts. The final observation is "Oh, Grandmother, what a terribly big mouth you have." The wolf responds by leaping forward and shouting "The better to eat you with, my dear." He then eats Little Red Riding Hood. After the wolf falls asleep, a hunter appears, cuts open the wolf's stomach, and frees the little girl and her grandmother. They gather large rocks and place them in the wolf's stomach. Then the hunter joins them in celebrating by eating the food and drinking the wine.

## CENSORSHIP HISTORY

Perrault's *Little Red Riding Hood* ended with both the little girl and her grandmother dead and no hunter to save them. The fairytales were written for the court of Louis XIV as a means of teaching children about the dangers lurking in the world surrounding them. Perrault's moral is not stated, but his tale may have been intended as a warning against strangers and traveling alone. Contemporary writers, such as Maria Tatar and Jack Zipes, suggest that a specific warning appears to be directed toward women, reminding them of their need for male protectors.

The Grimm brothers softened the ending to suit their intention of entertainment rather than the moralizing of Perrault's tales. They included a fierce woodsman with an axe to rescue and resuscitate the two female characters and retained the violent appearance and behavior of the wolf. Versions published in the United States have maintained the ending, but they have varied in regard to the violence contained within the story, sometimes making the woodsman into a kind hunter who saves Little Red Riding Hood and her grandmother.

Challenges to the story in the United States have involved the 1989 version published by Houghton-Mifflin that won the Caldecott Honor Book Award. In 1990, the Empire, California, school district banned the book from the district because the bottle of wine appeared to "condone the use of alcohol" to district decision makers. The district curriculum director expressed further concern that the descriptions of the hunter's rescue of Little Red Riding Hood and her grandmother were too violent and inappropriate for young students. That same year, the book was also banned from elementary schools in Culver City, California, because the story "gives the wrong impression about alcohol" to children. Assistant Superintendent Vera Jashni expressed specific concern about the final paragraph of the story, which tells that, after the hunter has killed the wolf, the grandmother drinks some of the wine. She then feels strong and healthy enough to clean up that mess left by the wolf.

The presence of the wine bottle in illustrations of *Little Red Riding Hood* motivated challenges by parents of students in the fifth and sixth grades in the Clay County, Florida, elementary schools in 1990. The school board established a review committee to consider the objections and to examine the books, and the books were removed from the classrooms during the three weeks that the committee deliberated. The books were later returned to the classrooms after the review committee voted to retain the books and the school board concurred with their decision.

In 1991, a teacher in Bradford County, Florida, initiated a complaint that the book was violent because of the actions of the wolf. The teacher also questioned the appropriateness of the little girl taking wine to her grandmother and her grandmother later drinking the wine. The book was placed on the "restricted" shelf where it was available only to students who specifically requested the book by title and author while the school sought to locate a "nonalcoholic" version. In the same year, two teachers in Levy County, Florida, challenged the storybook for the same reason, but a review committee of educators and parents voted to retain the book in the schools.

## FURTHER READINGS

Bettelheim, Bruno. *The Uses of Enchantment: The Meaning and Importance of Fairy Tales.* New York: Random House, 1977.

Chase, Richard, Jr. "Little Red Riding Hood: Werewolf and Prostitute." *Journal of History* 57 (Summer 1995): 769–776.

Moore, Robert B. "From Rags to Witches: Stereotypes, Distortions and Anti-Humanism in Fairy Tales." *CIBC Bulletin* 8 (1975): 1.

*Newsletter on Intellectual Freedom* (July 1990): 128.

Tatar, Maria. *The Hard Facts of the Grimm's Fairy Tales*. Princeton, N.J.: Princeton University Press, 1987.

Zipes, Jack. *Fairy Tales and the Art of Subversion: The Classical Genre for Children and the Process of Civilization*. New York: Wildman Press, 1983.

# LORD OF THE FLIES

**Author:** William Golding

**Original date and place of publication:** 1954, England; 1955, United States

**Original publisher:** Faber and Faber (England); Coward-McCann (United States)

**Literary form:** Novel

## SUMMARY

*Lord of the Flies* is an allegorical novel that relates the adventures of a group of English schoolboys whose plane crashes on a deserted island, killing all adults aboard. Using their instincts, early social training and education, the boys attempt to form an organized society. Their efforts result in some of the boys' emerging as leaders or bullies, while others remain destined to follow or to be bullied. Rather than develop a caring and harmonious society free of the corrupting influences of adults, the boys revert to savage behavior and primitive rites.

The novel seems at first to be a simple adventure story of survival, but the growing brutality of the boys toward each other reveals the second level of meaning that questions the nature of civilization and the effect of instinct versus society on behavior. Told from the third-person point of view, the novel opens with a conversation between Ralph and Piggy, who are walking through a tangled jungle on their way back to the beach. The reader learns that they and a large number of other boys, ranging in age from five to 12, were being transported out of a besieged England in the midst of an atomic war when their plane crashed.

The boys emerge in different, seemingly natural roles as the novel progresses. Ralph takes the initiative of calling the boys together and he emerges as leader of the group, much to the disappointment of Jack, one of the older boys who had hoped to become sole leader. The two boys attract followers. Ralph becomes the builder and organizer who takes a careful and rational look at their needs, while Jack hunts with his followers and becomes increasing brutal and primitive in behavior. The two groups take turns at maintaining a signal fire on the beach in the hope of attracting passing ships, but Jack's group irresponsibly allows the fire to go out while they hunt and kill a pig. Aroused by their success, Jack's followers urge the others to join them in hunting, and the boys seem nearly overcome by a blood lust that almost leads to the death of one of the boys.

The island paradise soon becomes filled with fear. The younger boys cry out that they see beasts in the darkness despite the contention of Simon that it is only the beast inside themselves. As Jack fights more strongly for a leadership role, he gathers around him a majority of the boys and they form their own "tribe." They kill a mother pig whom they have surprised while she is nursing her young, and the feast draws all of the boys. As if to worship the dead animal, Jack's followers place the pig's head on a stake as their offering to the beast on the mountain. As flies cover the head, Simon realizes that it represents the potent emergence of the boys' wickedness.

The boys soon begin to direct their brutal behavior at each other. One of the younger boys burns to death when the signal fire rages out of control. Then Simon, the poetic, level-headed member of the group, is beaten to death by the boys in a frenzied ritualistic dance. The last to die is Piggy, one of the remaining boys to continue to act with civilized restraint, killed by the sadistic Roger who crushes him by deliberately rolling a boulder down the mountain. After Piggy's death, Jack hurls a spear at Ralph in a failed attempt to kill him. Forced into hiding, Ralph collapses in exhaustion on the beach and is found by naval officers who have arrived to rescue the boys.

## CENSORSHIP HISTORY

The novel has raised objections regarding its use in the classroom because of its pessimistic view of human society as well as for the scenes of brutality. The novel was challenged in Dallas (Texas) Independent School District high school libraries in 1974 and at Sully Buttes (South Dakota) High School in 1981. Critics at Owen (North Carolina) High School challenged the book in 1981 for being "demoralizing" by implying that man is little more than an animal, and the appropriateness of the novel as a reading assignment was challenged at Marana (Arizona) High School in 1983. The school district in Olney, Texas, challenged the use of the book in the classroom for containing "excessive violence and bad language." The Toronto (Ontario, Canada) board of education ruled on June 23, 1988 that the novel is "racist and recommended that it be removed from all schools," after parents and members of the black community complained that it degraded blacks because the boys paint themselves and savagely hunt and kill both wild boars and later several of their group, while they refer to themselves as a "tribe."

The novel was challenged by parents who demanded that it be removed from the junior high school reading list in Rocklin, California, in 1990. The parents claimed that the book did not provide a good model of "the social standards" and "good citizenship" that are expected of students. The school board rejected the complaint and retained the novel on its lists. The same year, the Gloucester County, New Jersey, school district quietly acquiesced to the protests of parents who claimed that the author's notes to the novel were not appropriate reading for the eighth-grade honors English class. With no formal fanfare, the school simply removed the novel from use until new copies of the novel, minus the author's notes, were obtained.

As recently as 1992, the novel was challenged as indecent by protesters in the Waterloo, Iowa, schools. The challenge was based on perceived profanity, lurid passages and statements viewed as being derogatory to minorities, women and the disabled. The protesters pointed out that Piggy, who suffers from asthma and cannot see without his glasses, is ridiculed by the others and deprived of his glasses. They also identified as offensive a passage in which the boys trap a sow, who is feeding her piglets, pursue her and stab her repeatedly until she falls; then, one boy proudly proclaims that he has stuck a spear "Right up her ass!" In several instances when the boys act in a manner that is out of step with expected masculine behavior, they are criticized as acting "just like a girl." Despite the opposition, only one of the seven school board members voted against purchasing the book for use in the classroom.

## FURTHER READINGS

Barr, Donald. "Should Holden Caulfield Read These Books?" *New York Times Book Review* 91 (May 4, 1986): 1, 50–51.

Egan, John M. "Golding's View of Man." *America* 108 (January 26, 1963): 140–141.

*Newsletter on Intellectual Freedom* (January 1975): 6; (July 1981): 103; (January 1982): 17; (January 1984): 25–26; (July 1984): 122; (September 1988): 152; (July 1992): 126.

Slayton, Paul. "Teaching Rationale for William Golding's *Lord of the Flies*." In *Censored Books: Critical Viewpoints*. Ed. by Nicholas J. Karolides, Lee Burress and John M. Kean, 351–357. Metuchen, N.J.: Scarecrow Press, 1993.

## MANCHILD IN THE PROMISED LAND

**Author:** Claude Brown
**Original date and place of publication:** 1965, United States
**Original publisher:** The Macmillan Company
**Type:** Autobiographical novel

## SUMMARY

*Manchild in the Promised Land* is a fictionalized account of Claude Brown's maturation from drug-dealing gang member to one of America's most powerful writers about the African-American experience. The work bears the following dedication: "To Eleanor Roosevelt, who founded the Wiltwyck School for Boys. And to the Wiltwyck School, which is still finding Claude Browns." Throughout the work, Brown uses the vernacular of the Harlem streets in recounting the drug addiction, prostitution and murders that threatened to destroy the generation of young black boys and girls struggling in the 1940s and 1950s to survive in a hostile environment.

The book is narrated by "Sonny," Claude Brown's persona, who tells his story of growth and endurance in Harlem, where survival depends upon an individual's ability to outfight and outmaneuver everyone and everything. He is unhappy at home, disdainful of his complacent mother and angry with his abusive father, and he makes the streets his home. Just 13 when the book opens, he has been shot while stealing bedsheets from a clothesline and is about to be sent away. Already experienced with heroin use, like many of his friends he is headed for a life of poverty, addiction and early death.

After recovering from his wound, Sonny is sent to the Wiltwyck School for socially maladjusted boys, founded by Eleanor Roosevelt, whom he meets when he sees "this rich old lady hanging around Wiltwyck . . . she used to be married to a cat who was President of the United States." At the school, Sonny is impressed by the school administrator, Mr. Papanek, who commands respect through his knowledge and authoritative personality, and who recognizes Sonny's potential to overcome his environment. For the first time, the young boy realizes that a man does not have to use a gun, a knife or a fist to exert power over others; education and intelligence are far more powerful weapons. That awareness stays with him throughout the years ahead.

Once he is back in Harlem, the abuse at home sends him back onto the street, where he continues to deal drugs and to steal. At 14, he is arrested again and sent to a reformatory. This cycle of crime and arrests lasts through most of his teenage years, but the brief experience at Wiltwyck gives him the power to realize that he is going to be just another Harlem statistic who will die of heroin addiction or a gunshot wound unless he makes some changes. The only course is to get a college education. He begins by leaving Harlem to work and to earn a high school diploma.

Once out of Harlem, Sonny takes any job available to pay for his classes. He explores African-American culture as he becomes involved in the Beat movement in art and literature, and new opportunities to grow and learn appear as he becomes friends with musicians who are proud and passionate in exploring their African heritage. He also learns that drugs become unnecessary when life has purpose as he experiments with spiritual movements. For a time, he is drawn to the Coptic faith, more for its African roots than for the religious aspect; then he becomes deeply involved in the Muslim faith. His belief in formal education also strengthens, and he makes plans to leave New York to attend college. Before making this move, he returns to Harlem, walks the streets and assesses what has happened to the people whom he has known.

One of his best friends has just died of a drug overdose, his younger brother is in jail for armed robbery and many of his acquaintances are heroin addicts. Only one has had the will to rise above the situation, one of his oldest friends, Danny, who survived heroin addiction and now has a stable marriage and family life and religious convictions. Sonny recognizes that his only hope of escaping the human misery of Harlem is to leave New York behind.

## CENSORSHIP HISTORY

*Manchild in the Promised Land* has been the target of criticism as well as of numerous attempts to remove it from school libraries and the school curriculum since its publication in 1965. Criticized upon its first appearance for what one reviewer called its limited vocabulary that was "not a language at all but an impoverished patois," the work has since been condemned for containing a host of other evils.

Lee Burress reported that *Manchild in the Promised Land* was among the ten most frequently challenged books in schools between 1965 and 1975. In a 1973 national survey of English department chairpersons, Burress, who does not identify the cities or states in which the bans occurred, only the geographical region of the United States, found that the book was banned across the nation. In the Northeast, a combined group consisting of a parent, clergyman, student and member of the board of education complained that "Trash like this does not belong in the classroom. . . . That hippie English teacher is perverted." The result was that students would not be required to fulfill any reading assignments if a book was judged "graphically realistic." The book was also placed on a closed shelf in the library to which students had no access.

In a case in the West, a parent complained of the "language and content" and the book was again placed on a closed shelf of the library to which students had no access. In a case in the Midwest, a teacher complained that the book was "obscene" and the book was removed from classroom use. In the Southwest, a group calling itself the Committee of Concerned Parents complained to school officials that the book should be removed from the high school library because of "profanity" and sex scenes that are "too explicit." School officials ordered the book placed on a closed shelf to which students had no access.

In 1974, after one parent of a student in the Waukesha, Wisconsin, school system complained about the language in the work as "filth and obscenity," school administrators removed the work from the high school library. Similar charges were leveled by parents in Plant City, Florida, in 1976 and in North Jackson, Ohio, in 1980; school officials in both these school systems also removed the work from their high school libraries.

A national survey of high school English department chairpersons conducted by Burress in 1977 found that the work had been removed from classroom use in two New York schools because of parents' complaints that the work was "obscene," and it had been removed from the library in a Massachusetts school after the book was brought to the attention of a teacher who found that the book was "not suitable for some grade level students." That same survey reported that a parent's request that the book be removed from classroom use because of objections to the "obscene" language and the masturbation scene was denied in Massachusetts.

In 1977, Concerned Citizens and Taxpayers for Decent Books in Baton Rouge, Louisiana, listed the work with 64 other "offensive" works. Characterizing the book as "pornography and filth," the group called for its removal from the classrooms and the school libraries. The work was removed from classroom use and placed on the restricted shelf in the school library.

In 1987, different complaints were voiced when parents and "concerned citizens" challenged the appearance of the book on reading lists for English classes at Parkrose (Oregon) High School. They protested that the content was "violent, the language offensive, and women are degraded." They further questioned the relevance of the work to the lives of students in Parkrose and claimed that their students "have no need to understand life in a black ghetto."

## FURTHER READINGS

Brown, Claude. "Manchild in Harlem." *New York Times Magazine* (April 14, 1996): 111.

Burress, Lee. *Battle of the Books: Literary Censorship in the Public School, 1950–1985.* Metuchen, N.J.: Scarecrow Press, 1989.

Hartshorne, Thomas L. "Horatio Alger in Harlem: Manchild in the Promised Land." *Journal of American Studies* 24 (August 1990): 243–248.

Miller, Warren. "One Score in Harlem—Review of *Manchild in the Promised Land*, by Claude Brown." *Saturday Review* (August 28, 1965): 49.

*Newsletter on Intellectual Freedom* (September 1974): 111; (May 1980): 51; (September 1987): 176; (November 1987): 240.

# MARRIED LOVE

**Author:**   Marie Carmichael Stopes
**Original date and place of publication:**   1918, England; 1919, United States
**Original publisher:**   Fifield & Co. (England); The Critic and Guide Co. (United States)
**Type:**   Marriage manual

## SUMMARY

*Married Love* was an attempt to explain to married men and women how their mutual sex lives could be made happier, and the chapter titles indicate a blend of the clinical and the romantic: "The Heart's Desire," "The Broken Joy," "Woman's Contrariness," "The Fundamental Pulse," "Marital Adjustment," "Sleep, Modesty and Romance," "Abstinence," "Children," "Society" and "The Glorious Unfolding." Although much of what Stopes says about married sexuality had already been covered in writings by Havelock Ellis, she brought a new perspective by emphasizing "the woman's side of sex questions." Rather than being merely a clinical "how-to," the work includes efforts at counseling couples and pleading with husbands to make greater efforts at understanding the emotional and physical sides of their wives' sexual natures. She also criticizes those men who demand their "conjugal rights" without concern for their spouses' mental and physical comfort.

When it first appeared, *Married Love* was described as a "strange amalgam of purple prose, suffragist philosophy and sage advice on lovemaking." The book became a vital sex guide because it offered frank discussions of the difficulties that may occur for both men and women in sexual intimacy.

## CENSORSHIP HISTORY

In 1919, American feminist activist Margaret Sanger bore "the brunt of insults from publishers because I tried to get 'Married Love' published" before finding an American publisher, but Stopes was completely unhappy with the arrangement. Dr. W. J. Robinson of The Critic and Guide Co. expurgated the manuscript, editing it extensively, toning down the author's enthusiasm and making her specific language more vague. The intent and effect of the book were subverted by the expurgation.

In 1930, the Tariff Act provided the United States Customs Bureau of the Treasury Department with a new procedure for censoring books that permitted officials to judge books before they were permitted to enter American shores and exclude them if they were "below standard." Under the *in rem* ("against the thing") provision, a local Customs official would refuse to deliver the offending book advise in a letter that "this volume will be destroyed unless you claim it and are willing to test the issue in a court." Jail sentences and fines were not meted out to publishers or distributors, but the books were destroyed.

In 1930, *Married Love* was declared "not obscene or immoral" in Philadelphia after Fanny and Ida Teller, two social workers, imported copies of *Married Love* to use in their work. The volumes were seized by Customs and the case went before Judge Kirkpatrick, United States District Judge for the Eastern District of Pennsylvania, who made the ruling. The copies were returned to the Tellers. Despite the judge's decision, the book was again seized later that year and again went to court.

In 1930, before the Philadelphia case had gone to trial, American publisher G.P. Putnam imported *Married Love* and notified Customs officials in advance in an effort to test the new Customs law. Lawyers for the publisher argued in *United States v. One Obscene Book Entitled "Married Love"*, 48 F. 2d 821 (1931), that the law was unconstitutional. Judge John M. Woolsey heard the case of obscenity brought by Customs against the work in New York City and decided that the book was not obscene. Woolsey declared that the Philadelphia decision should have been a bar to another similar proceeding. In a decision handed down on April 6, 1931, he stated: "I hold that Judge Kirkpatrick's decision established the book 'Married Love' as having an admissible status at any point around the Customs' barriers of the United States." To forestall critics who might charge that he was merely concurring with a previous decision, Judge Woolsey stated: "I cannot imagine a normal mind to which this book would seem to be obscene or immoral within the proper definition of the words, or whose sex impulses would be stirred by reading it." Instead of banning the book, the judge asserted that it should "be welcomed within our borders."

In 1931, the work was banned by the Irish Censorship Board for its discussion of contraception, despite the praise of many such as George Bernard Shaw, who called Dr. Marie Stopes "an expert instructress" on technique and claimed that "numbers of unhappy marriages have been set right by her instruction."

## FURTHER READINGS

Beckett, Samuel. "Censorship in the Saorstat." In *Disjecta: Miscellaneous Writings and a Dramatic Fragment by Samuel Beckett*. Ed. by Ruby Cohn, 84–88. London: John Calder (Publishers), 1983.

Rose, June. *Marie Stopes and the Sexual Revolution*. Boston: Faber & Faber, 1992.

Shaw, George Bernard. "The Censorship." *Irish Statesman* 11 (1928): 206–208. Reprinted in *Banned in Ireland: Censorship and the Irish Writer*. Ed. by Julia Carlson, 133–141. Athens, Ga.: The University of Georgia Press, 1990.

# MY HOUSE

**Author:** Nikki Giovanni
**Original date and place of publication:** 1972, United States
**Original publisher:** William Morrow Publishers
**Type:** Poetry collection

## SUMMARY

*My House* is a collection of 36 personal and autobiographical poems that deal with thoughts of home, family and humanness as written from the perspective of a black woman who is trying to verbalize the experience of other black women in balancing the desire to assert oneself and the desire to help others. Grouped into two parts, 23 poems under the heading of "The Rooms Inside" and 13 poems under the heading of "The Rooms Outside," the poems continue the expressions of black pride that characterized her earlier work. The first section contains poems that reflect the warmth, pleasures and comforts of home and family, as well as the intimate relations, personal thoughts and love that are integral to family life. In "The Only Song I'm Singing," she asks "baby please / please somehow show me what i need / to know so i can love you right / now" as the persona struggles to determine her relationship to others.

The second section, "The Rooms Outside," deals with people who are outside of the home environment, and focuses on the struggles that they must face. In "Categories," the persona considers occasions when she has seen "an old white woman" and wants to relate to her as a person, but finds that impossible. She states, "if she weren't such an aggressive bitch she would see / that if you weren't such a Black one / there would be a relationship but anyway— it doesn't matter / much—except that you started out to kill her and now find/ you just don't give a damn. . . ."

The collection is largely a monologue that uses rich, descriptive, rhythmical language to reveal the mood and thoughts of the changing personae of the poems, the African-American woman who is trying "to put her house in order to keep outside atrocities from tearing down her house."

## CENSORSHIP HISTORY

The collection was banned from the public school libraries in Waukesha, Wisconsin, in 1975 for "vulgarity" and for use of the word "nigger." In 1990, parents of students at West Gennessee High School in Syracuse, New York, called for a ban of the book from the classroom, charging that it contained "obscenities." In 1992, school officials in Duval County, Florida, challenged the inclusion of the book in the public school libraries because it contained the word "nigger" and because of numerous identified instances of "vulgarity," racism and sex. That same year, a middle school librarian in Jacksonville, Florida, received complaints that *My House* was vulgar and racist. Questioned by school officials about the book, the librarian asked that it be moved from the middle school library to the high school, or that it be restricted to students who have parental permission to read the book. She concurred with the parental objections that the book contained "explicit sexual connotations" and racial bias. The district review committee voted that the book should remain in the middle school library, but on the restricted-access shelf available only to students with parental permission.

## FURTHER READINGS

Giovanni, Nikki. *Conversations with Nikki Giovanni*. Jackson, Miss.: University Press of Mississippi, 1992.

*Newsletter on Intellectual Freedom* (July 1975): 104; (July 1990): 127; (July 1992): 105.
Webb, C. Anne. "Censorship in the Pennsylvania Schools." *English Journal* 84 (April 1995): 84.

# THE NAKED APE

**Author:**  Desmond Morris
**Original date and place of publication:**  1967, United States
**Original publisher:**  The McGraw-Hill Book Company
**Type:**  Anthropology textbook

## SUMMARY

*The Naked Ape* created a sensation among academics and the public alike when it was first published because zoologist Desmond Morris treated his subject, the human species, as he might an animal and analyzed humans in much the same way. The irreverent tone is evident from the first lines of the introduction, in which Morris notes that there are 193 living species of monkeys and apes, 192 of which are covered with hair. The one exception is the "naked ape," the human who "is proud that he has the biggest brain of all the primates, but attempts to conceal the fact that he also has the biggest penis, preferring to accord this honour falsely to the mighty gorilla." He observes that humans may have acquired "lofty new motives" but they have "lost none of the earthy old ones." It is to these earthy impulses that Morris directs most of his attention in the study.

The study contains chapters that examine humans in much the same terms and contexts that other mammals had been studied by zoologists for many decades. Chapter titles include "Origins," "Sex," "Rearing," "Exploration," "Fighting," "Feeding," "Comfort" and "Animals." The first seven chapters examine the interactions of humans with each other, and the final chapter examines human activities in relation to other animals. The most controversial chapter was Chapter 2, "Sex," which provides detailed discussion of sexual development, sexual practices and sexual aberrations. Using a clinical tone and an analytical approach that has been applied to countless studies of a diverse number of animal species, Morris painstakingly dissects the environmental and nurturing practices that help and hinder human sexual development and details its physical signs. He identifies sexual practices that humans have in common with other animals and the signs of physical arousal and sexual response that appear at each stage of "copulatory behaviour."

In his discussion of sexual "aberrations," Morris explains that he cannot discuss them in "the usual moralistic way." Instead, the zoologist approaches these sexual differences, such as celibacy and homosexuality, as "biological morality in terms of population success and failure." Morris is emphatic in his defense of all sexual practices and asserts that none, "no matter how disgusting and obscene it may appear to the members of a particular culture, can be criticized biologically providing it does not hinder general reproductive success." He makes an exception in regard to the threat of overpopulation and suggests that birth control is sometimes a needed precaution to preserve the human race at its best.

## CENSORSHIP HISTORY

The work was used as a college text for several years after publication without negative repercussions, but challenges arose when it entered high school classrooms and libraries. In 1975, a group in Baton Rouge, Louisiana, called the Concerned Citizens and Taxpayers for Decent Books challenged the inclusion of the book in the local school libraries. They complained that the book was "pornography and filth" and demanded its removal. The school board complied with the demand.

The most extensive challenge to *The Naked Ape* began in 1976, when school board members removed this book with 10 others from the Island Trees (New York) Union Free School District High School library (see BEST SHORT STORIES BY NEGRO WRITERS), claiming that it was "just plain filthy." The court record of the case that was eventually heard before the United States Supreme Court, *Board of Education, Island Trees Union Free School District No. 26 v. Pico et al.*, 457 U.S. 853 (1982), identified the following objectionable passage from the book:

> If either males or females cannot for some reason obtain sexual access to their opposite numbers, they will find sexual outlets in other ways. They may use other members of their own sex, or they may even use member of other species, or they may masturbate.

The book was returned to the school library after the Supreme Court ruled in favor of the book.

In 1989, parents of students in Mifflinburg (Pennsylvania) High School challenged the use of the book as a required reading in the English curriculum. They charged that it contained "explicit, almost manual descriptions of what some would refer to as deviant sexual relations." The book, temporarily removed from the classroom while a review committee considered the complaint, was later reinstated upon the recommendation of the committee.

## FURTHER READINGS

*Newsletter on Intellectual Freedom* (September 1975): 148; (November 1976): 183; (November 1982): 197; (May 1989): 93.

# NAKED LUNCH

**Author:**   William Seward Burroughs
**Original date and place of publication:**   1959, France; 1962, United States
**Original publisher:**   Olympia Press (France); Grove Press (United States)
**Literary type:**   Novel

## SUMMARY

Begun in Tangier in 1955, *Naked Lunch* is a montage of shocking scenes which combine surreal fantasy and hallucination to create a nightmarish blend of drug addiction, pederasty and cannibalism. The unconventional narrative patterns of shifting point of view and stream-of-consciousness rambling make it less a unified novel than it is a series of images that are linked by their theme of the destructive effects of man's addictions. The lack of a consistent narrative and the frequently changing point of view reflect the nightmare world in which William Lee, the main character, fights himself as often as he must fight with others. Burroughs claimed in his "Introduction" to have illuminated his technique through the title that "means exactly what the words say: NAKED Lunch—a frozen moment when everyone sees what is on the end of every fork."

Three sections make up the work: the account of drug withdrawal in the "Introduction," which is subtitled "Deposition: Testimony Concerning a Sickness"; the paranoid-sexual fantasy of the body of the novel with erratically placed subheadings and the scholarly examination of drug addiction in the "Appendix."

The "Introduction" offers Burroughs' explanation of "The Sickness," his 15-year addiction to opium and opium derivatives. The author scrupulously distinguishes between drugs that create physical dependence and hallucinogens, which he claims are wrongly condemned. Using a sometimes jarring word order, he also describes in painstaking detail the economics of drug dealing and the victimization of the addict. The "Introduction" ends with his apocalyptic warning: "Look down LOOK DOWN along that junk road before you travel there and get in with the Wrong Mob. . . . A word to the wise guy."

The body of the novel is the story of William Lee, a junkie who struggles to free himself of the strictures imposed by drugs, sex, language and bureaucracy. He roams from New York to Mexico to Tangier and beyond, searching for escape from "the heat," which at first is slang reference for the police, but which eventually comes to refer to the pressures of life that have driven him to drug addiction. Space and time fluctuate wildly, and Lee lives in a nightmarish world in which time stretches or constricts according to the amount and type of drug consumed. Locations become interchangeable as Lee travels through a world of sadistic sex, extensive drug use and squalid surroundings.

Heterosexual and homosexual acts that emphasize pain and degradation are described in lurid detail, and mutilation imagery abounds in the novel. The names and specific effects of various drugs are detailed, as are the most and least effective means of administering the drugs in order to achieve their maximum effects.

Burroughs juxtaposes seemingly realistic scenes with brutal nightmarish acts that exhibit the degradation of his characters through the violent, bestial acts of others and of themselves. He uses colloquial language to refer to the human body, especially to genitalia, and strives for maximum shock effect in the extended descriptions of drug paraphernalia and use and the forced sexual encounters suffered by men, women and boys.

In the "Appendix," an essay entitled "Letter from a Master Addict to Dangerous Drugs" that was published in *The British Journal of Addiction* (53:2), Burroughs discusses the relative merits and dangers of opiates, *cannabis indica*, peyote, cocaine and synthetic drugs. He interpolates his own experiences with each substance into an examination of sources and precautions, thus providing a guide to the unwary.

## CENSORSHIP HISTORY

The novel has the distinction of being the last literary work to be declared obscene and brought to trial in America. From the 1959 publication of the book until January 1963, Customs agents seized copies of the work entering the United States, justifying their actions under the Tariff Act (1930), which provided for the seizure of allegedly obscene materials. The work was later involved in two legal actions. Although cleared in Los Angeles in 1965 before the case went to trial, it was declared obscene the same year in Boston, where the attorney general argued that the work was "trash." Writers Norman Mailer, Allen Ginsberg and John Ciardi were called as expert witnesses with psychiatrists and academics to testify regarding the literary merit of the work, but Judge Eugene Hudson remained unconvinced. In delivering his verdict, the judge declared the book to be "obscene, indecent and impure . . . and taken as a whole . . . predominantly prurient, hardcore pornography and utterly without redeeming social importance." In response to the claim by the defense that the work held significant social and scientific value, Hudson declared *Naked Lunch* to be trash written by a "mentally sick" individual.

An appeal was made to the Massachusetts Supreme Judicial Court, and *Attorney General v. A Book Named "Naked Lunch,"* 351 Mass. 298, 218 N.E.2d 571 (1966) was heard on October 8, 1965. The Supreme Judicial Court acknowledged that the book was "grossly offensive" and reminded those present that the author had himself described the book as "brutal, obscene and disgusting." They also applied the test of redeeming social value to the work and could find no reason to declare the novel as "not utterly without redeeming social value." Their determination that the work was not lacking in social importance resulted from the many reviews and articles in literary and other publications that discussed seriously the controversial book and showed that a "substantial and intelligent group" within the community believed the book to be of literary significance. On July 7, 1966, the Massachusetts Supreme Judicial Court declared the book not obscene. The four members of the court who delivered the favorable decision and the two dissenting members declared further that the book could be sold in the state, but that people would be subject to prosecution if they "have been or are advertising or distributing this book in this Commonwealth in a manner to exploit it for the sake of its possible prurient appeal."

## FURTHER READINGS

De Grazia, Edward. *Censorship Landmarks*. New York: R.R. Bowker Company, 1969.
Goodman, Michael B. *Contemporary Literary Censorship: The Case History of Burroughs' Naked Lunch*. Metuchen, N.J.: Scarecrow Press, 1981.
Miles, Barry. *William Burroughs: El Hombre Invisible*. New York: Hyperion Publishing, 1983.
Morgan, Ted. *Literary Outlaw: The Life and Times of William S. Burroughs*. New York: Henry Holt & Company, 1988.
Sutherland, John. *Offensive Literature: Decensorship in Britain, 1960–1982*. Totowa, N.J.: Barnes and Noble Books, 1981.

## NANA

**Author:**   Émile Zola
**Original date and place of publication:**   1880, France; 1888, England
**Original publisher:**   Charpentier (France); Henry Vizetelly & Co. (England)
**Type:**   Novel

### SUMMARY

*Nana* is the ninth novel in a 20-novel series entitled *Les Rougon-Macquart*, which traces the fortunes of two families, the Rougons and the Macquarts, their entry into the modern world and into all social classes. Not merely the work of imagination, the novels were based on documented evidence obtained through books, newspaper clippings and first-person investigations to ensure historical, social and political accuracy. *Nana* presents a picture of French life and society from 1852 through 1870, as it follows the career of a vulgar, greedy and cruel courtesan named Nana.

The novel opens at the theater premiere of *The Blonde Venus*, a mediocre play with amateur singer Nana, whose daring appearance in the last act clothed only in her long, golden hair and a transparent gauze veil mesmerizes the audience. The audience is fascinated by Nana's marble-like body, and the former street urchin recognizes the power that her flesh exerts on others.

She is soon a sought-after courtesan, captivating wealthy men who provide the money that she needs for her sickly son, who is living with her aunt, and for her own extravagant nature. With little regard for their feelings, and no delicacy of manner, Nana flaunts her multiple relationships. She is verbally abusive and physically destructive, and demands money from her lovers according to her whims. Her sensuality captivates a coterie of adoring admirers, but the attraction wears thin: Some men return to their more compassionate and accommodating wives and mistresses while others are bankrupted.

Oblivious to anyone's feelings but her own, Nana becomes infatuated with the physically ugly comic actor Fontan and begins to live with him. He soon dominates the relationship, slapping her, bullying her, repeatedly calling her a "whore" and using all of her money while hoarding his own. Once her money is gone, he tells her that they must share costs. Nana loves him, so she plans to support them both, hoping to please him. She returns to streetwalking and meets Satin, a street "slut" who opens her eyes to the world of "perversion." They dine at Laure, "in which faded dresses and tattered hats were to be seen side by side with elegant costumes, in the fraternity of the same perversions." Nana is surprised to find successful courtesans in the restaurant, all flirting with younger women.

Nana becomes jaded, coming to believe that "there was no virtue left in the world. . . . everyone was wallowing in sensuality." She even imagines that if she could look into all of the bedrooms in Paris between nine in the evening and three in the morning, "she could see some funny sights: poor people going at it for all they were worth, and quite a few rich people sticking their noses into filth more deeply than the others." One evening, after running from police rounding up prostitutes, she races home to find the door bolted and Fontan with another woman. He tells Nana that he will kill her if she ever returns. Despondent, she goes to Satin and the two commiserate at a hotel, then go to bed, where they kiss and Nana "began returning Satin's caresses . . . uttering words of love." The romantic interlude is cut short by police raiding the hotel for prostitutes. Nana goes to her aunt's house and she finds her son sickly and anemic.

Nana returns to being a courtesan, recapturing one of her former lovers, Count Muffat, who buys her a mansion and furnishes it elegantly. He looks the other way as she brings home numerous male and female lovers but finally leaves when he catches her in bed with his elderly father-in-law. She visits her son and finds him dying of smallpox, a death that Nana could have prevented by paying for medical care rather than lavish frivolity. Nana becomes ill with smallpox and dies. The final page of the novel emphasizes the destruction that the pustules had wreaked on her beautiful face. "It was as though the virus she had brought from the gutter . . . had risen to her face and rotted it."

## CENSORSHIP HISTORY

*Nana* was censored before it even appeared in book form. In 1879, Zola sold serialization rights to the newspaper *Le Voltaire*, published by Jules Lafitte. Eager to make money on the venture, Lafitte sent sandwich-board men throughout Paris carrying signs stating *"LISEZ NANA! LISEZ NANA!"* ("READ NANA! READ NANA!"), and he inundated the city with large colored posters to announce the forthcoming serialization. Zola felt that the prepublication publicity made his work appear "cheap, nasty and frivolous." Although Lafitte promised not to change a word, he did delete what he considered to be controversial parts to avoid government censorship. Leon Gambetta, the famous Republican leader and opponent of Napoleon III, warned Lafitte that *Nana* was "too strong" and would have to be further sanitized to avoid the risks of a fine, a shutdown of the paper and even jail. Lafitte increased the expurgations with each new installment in the serial, at the end of which Charpentier produced the unexpurgated novel that sold 55,000 copies within a few weeks and required additional printings. People bought eagerly to read what "evil" and "decadence" Lafitte had removed.

In 1885, the United States Customs Department seized the imported French edition of the novel, as well as invoices for an English translation. The department commissioned an official literal translation of the work from the original for the Customs officers to read, after which they ordered all copies of the book burned.

In 1888, Zola's English publisher, Vizetelly, came under attack by the National Vigilance Association (NVA), a group composed mainly of clergymen, founded in 1886, to continue the work of the Society for the Suppression of Vice, which had ceased operation a few years before. All of Zola's works, translated from French into English by the publisher's son, were specifically cited, as were works by Flaubert, Goncourt, Maupassant, Daudet and Bourget. The NVA gained the attention of House of Commons member Samuel Smith, M.P., who spoke in May 1888 against Vizetelly, "the chief culprit in the spread of pernicious literature." Citing Zola's works as an example of "obscene publications," Smith asserted that "nothing more diabolical had ever been written by the pen of man; they are only fit for swine, and those who read them must turn their minds into cesspools." The House passed a motion that "the law against obscene publications and indecent pictures and prints should be vigorously enforced and, if necessary, strengthened." The government would leave the initiation of proceedings to private individuals.

Other politicians and the newspapers joined the campaign against pornography, widening the scope of the battle to include other works, but

Zola remained the focus. The Roman Catholic newspaper *Tablet* attacked him as "a pornographer," the *Globe* charged that Zola "sapped the foundations of manhood and womanhood," and the *Whitehall Review* demanded immediate action against his books. The law firm Collette & Collette, retained by the NVA, obtained a summons on August 10, 1888, against Henry Vizetelly for publishing three "obscene" novels by Zola: *The Soil* (*La Terre*), *Piping Hot* (*Pot-bouille*) and *Nana*. Henry Asquith, prosecutor for the Crown, referred to these novels as "the three most immoral books ever published." The defense argued that Vizetelly had carefully expurgated the books while translating them into English and pointed out that the unexpurgated French versions were being freely circulated and sold in England at the same time. The prosecution declared the fact irrelevant, and the publisher went to trial at the Old Bailey in October 1888. Vizetelly was sentenced to four months in Holloway Prison and ordered not to publish any more of Zola's works. The court further agreed that all of Zola's works must be withdrawn from circulation in England, making Zola the only writer to have his works outlawed in England in the 19th century.

All of Zola's novels were banned at once in 1894 when they were placed on the *Index Librorum Prohibitorum* in Rome, in 1929 when Yugoslavia banned all of his works and in 1953 when Ireland did the same. The major complaints centered on the perception that Zola had made a heroine of a prostitute and had discussed "debased man's nature" by uncovering the often-sordid sexuality of the period.

## FURTHER READINGS

Brooks, Peter. "Storied Bodies, or *Nana* at Last Unveil'd." *Critical Inquiry* 16 (Autumn 1989): 1–32.
Brown, Frederick. "Zola and the Making of *Nana*." *Hudson Review* 45 (Summer 1992): 191–217.
Hemmings, F. W. J. *The Life and Times of Emile Zola*. New York: Charles Scribner's Sons, 1977.
Josephson, Matthew. *Zola and His Time*. Garden City, N.Y.: Garden City Publishing Company, 1928.
Kendrick, Walter. *The Secret Museum*. New York: Viking Press, 1987.
Schom, Alan. *Emile Zola: A Biography*. New York: Henry Holt & Company, 1987.

## NEVER LOVE A STRANGER

**Author:**   Harold Robbins
**Original date and place of publication:**   1948, United States
**Original publisher:**   Alfred A. Knopf
**Type:**   Novel

## SUMMARY

*Never Love a Stranger* is a carefully structured rags-to-riches story of a Depression-era hero who starts life in a Catholic orphanage and later becomes an important figure in the New York City crime world. The early chapters of the novel are largely autobiographical. Francis Kane is the name that Harold Robbins was given by the Paulist fathers in whose New York orphanage he was left as an infant. At the age of 10, he was adopted by a Jewish family and lived the early life of his fictionalized persona in this book.

The novel opens at the home of an Italian midwife who answers her door to find a pregnant young woman in the early stages of labor. After a difficult labor, she gives birth to a male infant, then dies. The midwife gives the baby the mother's name, Francis Kane. It is all that his mother leaves him.

Frankie Kane grows up in St. Therese's Catholic orphanage, eventually working part-time as a numbers runner for a local criminal and, at 15, becoming sexually involved with an older French-Canadian housemaid. Frankie is adopted by his maternal uncle and learns that he is Jewish, but he finds himself unable to attend synagogue after years of daily Mass attendance and instruction in Roman Catholic doctrine. Instead of making a choice, he leaves organized religion entirely.

Happy to have a home, Frankie attends high school, hopes to enter a profession and leaves numbers running far behind. His uncle contracts tuberculosis and the family makes plans to move, but state law requires that Frankie must return to the orphanage. The distraught boy runs away and loses touch with his family. After a tour of duty with the navy, he returns to New York and works his way up to become head of New York City's gambling rackets. His language is coarse and his sexual experiences are frequent, but he leaves this behind when he marries childhood friend Ruth. After she dies in childbirth, he enlists in the army, eventually dying in the war. The novel ends as childhood friends read a letter in which Frankie reveals that his son with Ruth survived and was placed in the Orphanage of St. Therese. He begs his friends to care for his son, "to give him roots in the earth, in society, to teach him the true values in the world."

## CENSORSHIP HISTORY

A trend emerged in the years after World War II among writers toward an increased use of frank language and more detailed description of sexual relationships. In many cases, both tendencies were classified as "obscenity" when litigation occurred. In addition, many novels in this period also depicted a greater social acceptance of extramarital sex. Reviewers criticized the language and the behavior of Frankie Kane, whose tough-spirited attitude and ability to survive read "almost like a handbook on how to be a gangster." Isabelle Mallet observed in a *New York Times* review that Kane's story would have had "more direct appeal" had he been "more introspective." In an article in the *Saturday Review of Literature*, Nathan L. Rothman condemned the use of "obscenities" in the novel and claimed that it "isn't realistic or important."

In 1948, *Never Love a Stranger* was one of nine novels identified as obscene in criminal proceedings in the Court of Quarter sessions in Philadelphia County, Pennsylvania. (See END AS A MAN for complete discussion of the case.) Indictments were brought by the state district attorney, John H. Maurer, against five booksellers who were charged with possessing and intending to sell the books. The other allegedly obscene novels were James Farrell's Studs Lonigan trilogy (*Young Lonigan, The Young Manhood of Studs Lonigan* and *Judgment Day*), Farrell's A WORLD I NEVER MADE, William Faulkner's *Sanctuary* and *Wild Palms*, Erskine Caldwell's *God's Little Acre* and Calder Willingham's *End as a Man*.

In his March 18, 1949, decision in *Commonwealth v. Gordon*, 66 D. & C. 101 (1949) that *Never Love a Stranger* is not obscene, Judge Curtis Bok stated:

> It is a swift story that covers a great deal of ground, its point being to portray a hard and lonely man who could not fully trust or give himself to anyone. Its last and least convincing part is also the least open to attack for obscenity; the rest, particularly the section dealing with New York City during the depression of the early 1930's, is very moving, not because there are sexual incidents but because the lines of the story are deep and authentic.

Bok refused to declare *Never Love a Stranger* "obscene" because the definition in cases that he cited in his decision restricted the meaning of obscenity "to that of sexual impurity, and with those cases that have made erotic allurement the test of its effect." The work also failed to meet Bok's definition of sexual impurity in literature, which he defined "as any writing whose dominant purpose and effect is erotic allurement—that is to say, a calculated and effective incitement to sexual desire." In Robbins's novel, references to sexual activity are brief and general, and Kane's language is important to developing the character.

## FURTHER READINGS

De Grazia, Edward. *Girls Lean Back Everywhere*. New York: Random House, 1992.

Mallet, Isabelle. "Unruly Local Color." *New York Times Book Review* (March 7, 1948): 26.

Parker, Ian. "Making Advances." *The New Yorker* (April 1, 1996): 72–80.

Rothman, Nathan L. "A Slick Toughie." *Saturday Review of Literature* (May 22, 1948): 27.

# OF MICE AND MEN

**Author:**  John Steinbeck
**Original date and place of publication:**  1937, United States
**Original publisher:**  Viking Penguin
**Literary type:**  Novel

## SUMMARY

*Of Mice and Men* is the story of two men, big and simpleminded Lennie and small and cunning George, who drift from one ranchhand job to another as they pursue their dream of owning their own place someday. Despite their mismatched intellectual capabilities, the two men are good friends who share the same dream, the simple desire to have their own farm where Lennie will be able to raise rabbits. As they travel from job to job, George becomes frustrated with Lennie's limitations and often loses patience, but he does not desert the childlike giant. George knows that Lennie will inadvertently become involved in a situation from which he will be unable to extricate himself, so vigilance is necessary.

Although the two men are thrilled to be given a ranch job, George must, as usual, cover for Lennie and make him appear to be more capable and intelligent that he really is. The boss's son Curley bullies the childlike Lennie, who finds himself drawn to the bully's lovely young wife. Curley's wife, however, does not treat Lennie fairly and she teases him playfully, unaware of how seriously he perceives her actions. He sees her as being similar to the soft and cuddly puppy that he once had, and he wants only to stroke her soft hair as he had stroked the puppy's soft fur. When Lennie approaches Curley's wife to stroke her hair, she becomes frightened and struggles and starts to scream. He places his hand on her mouth to quiet her, but he is not capable of judging his strength and breaks her neck. When George finds them, Lennie apologizes and cries that he has hurt her just like he had hurt the puppy. George is aware that the ranchhands led by Curley will not have pity for Lennie, so he tells Lennie to pack up so that they can leave. A short time later, as the two sit on a riverbank, George shoots Lennie to death to save him from the more terrifying tortures of a mob.

## CENSORSHIP HISTORY

*Of Mice and Men* has earned the dubious prestige of being the second most frequently banned book in the public school curriculum of the 1990s, second only to the reading anthology *Impressions*, although challenges were frequent in earlier decades as well. Censors claim that the novel contains crude heroes who speak vulgar language and whose experiences exhibit a sadly deficient social system in the United States.

The novel was placed on the banned list in Ireland in 1953 because of "obscenities" and "vulgar" language. It was banned for similar reasons in Syracuse, Indiana, in 1974; Oil City, Pennsylvania, in 1977; Grand Blanc, Michigan, in 1979; and Continental, Ohio, in 1980. In 1977, in Greenville, North Carolina, the Fourth Province of the Knights of the Ku Klux Klan challenged the use of the book in the local school district, for containing "profanities and using God's name in vain." The same reason was given by parents who challenged the book in Vernon-Verona-Sherill (New York) School District in 1980 and in school districts in St. David, Arizona, in 1981 and Tell City, Indiana, in 1982. The school board of Scottsboro, Alabama, banned the novel from Skyline High School in 1983 because of "profanity," and the chair of the Knoxville, Tennessee, school board vowed to remove all "filthy books" from the local school system, beginning with *Of Mice and Men* because of "its vulgar language."

The novel was challenged as "vulgar" and "offensive" by parents in the Christian County, Kentucky, school district in 1987, but it was later reinstated in the school libraries and English classes. "Profanity" was also the reason for the 1988 challenges in Marion County, West Virginia, schools; Wheaton-Warrenville (Illinois) Middle School; and Berrien Springs (Michigan) High School. In 1989, the school board ordered the novel removed from Northside High School in Tuscaloosa, Alabama, because of "profanity," and it was challenged as a reading assignment at a summer youth program in Chattanooga, Tennessee, because "Steinbeck is known to have had an anti-business attitude." That same year, the novel was also removed from all reading lists and all copies were stored away in White Chapel High School in Pine Bluff, Arkansas, because parents objected to the language. "Offensive language" was the reason that parents in the Shelby County, Tennessee, school system challenged the appropriateness of including the novel on the high school reading list.

The 1990s brought an increase in the number of challenges to *Of Mice and Men*. In 1990, a parent in Salinas, Kansas, challenged the use of the book in a 10th-grade English class because it contained "profanity" and "takes the Lord's name in vain." The school board review committee considered the complaint and recommended that the work be retained as a required reading but cautioned that no excerpts from the book should be read aloud in the classroom. That same year, a parent in Riviera, Texas, complained that the novel contained profanities and requested that it be removed from the 11th-grade English classes. At an open school board meeting to consider the request, 50 teachers and administrators and 10 high school students appeared to support continued use of the book. The only person who spoke against the novel was the parent who raised the original challenge. After the parent went through two more levels of appeal, the school board voted to continue assigning the novel.

In 1991, a Fresno, California, parent demanded that the book be removed from the 10th-grade English college preparatory curriculum, citing "profanity" and "racial slurs." The book was retained, and the child of the objecting parent was provided with an alternative reading assignment. In Iowa City, Iowa, a parent complained of the use of *Of Mice and Men* in the seventh-grade literature courses because of the profanity in the book, such as the word "Goddamn." She claimed that her daughter was subjected to "psychological and emotional abuse" when the book was read aloud and expressed the hope that her daughter would "not talk like a migrant worker" when she completed school. The district review committee retained the book. "Profanity," "excessive cursing" and "sexual overtones" were behind challenges to reading of the novel in high schools in Suwanee, Florida; Jacksboro, Tennessee; Buckingham, Virginia; and Branford, Florida.

A large number of challenges arose in 1992. A coalition of community members and clergy in Mobile, Alabama, requested that local school officials form a special textbook screening committee to "weed out objectionable things." Their first target was to be *Of Mice and Men*, which they claimed contained "profanity" and "morbid and depressing themes." No formal complaint was lodged, so school officials rejected the request. Challenges in Waterloo, Iowa, and Duval County, Florida, were made because of "profanity," "lurid passages about sex" and "statements defamatory to minorities." A parent in Modesto, California, challenged the novel on the basis of profanity for the use of the word "nigger," and the NAACP joined in demanding that the novel be removed from the reading list. "Profanity" prompted the challenge at Oak Hill High School in Alexandria, Louisiana, where it was retained.

One of the more detailed complaints emerged in 1992 in Hamilton, Ohio, where the book was temporarily removed from the high school reading list after a parent complained that it contained "vulgarity" and "racial slurs." The parent, vice president of the Parents' Coalition in Hamilton, stated that the novel contained 108 profanities and 12 racial slurs. The school board suggested the use of alternative reading assignments, which the coalition refused, and the novel was temporarily removed from the optional reading list. At the meeting of the board-appointed review committee, 150 parents, students and teachers appeared and enthusiastically supported the book. One student submitted a petition bearing 333 signatures of people who favored retaining the book. A local minister who opposed the book told the board, "Anybody that's got a child shouldn't want them to read this book. It should be burned up, put in a fire." The board of education voted unanimously to retain the book.

Fewer challenges arose in 1993 and 1994. The novel was challenged in 1993 as an appropriate English curriculum assignment by parents of students at Mingus (Arizona) Union High School who were concerned about the "profane language, moral statement, treatment of the retarded, and the violent ending." In 1994, the school superintendent of Putnam County, Tennessee, removed the novel from the classroom "due to the language in it, we just can't have this kind of book being taught." That same year, parents of students at Loganville (Georgia) High School called for a ban of the book because of "its vulgar language throughout."

## FURTHER READINGS

Carrington, Ildiko de Papp. "Talking Dirty: Alice Munro's 'Open Secrets' and John Steinbeck's 'Of Mice and Men.'," *Studies in Short Fiction* 31 (Fall 1994): 595–606.

Johnson, Claudia. *Stifled Laughter: Woman's Story About Fighting Censorship.* Golden, Colo.: Fulcrum Publishing, 1994.

*Newsletter on Intellectual Freedom* (March 1975): 41; (November 1977): 155; (January 1978): 7; (March 1979): 27; (May 1980): 62; (July 1980): 77; (May 1982): 84–85; (July 1983): 198; (July 1984): 104; (May 1988): 90; (July 1988): 140; (September 1988): 154, 179; (November 1988): 201; (January 1989): 28; (November 1989): 162; (January 1990): 10–12; (March 1990): 45; (March 1991): 62; (July 1991): 110; (January 1992): 25; (March 1992): 64; (July 1992): 111–112; (September 1992): 140, 163–164; (January 1993): 29; (March 1994): 53; (March 1995): 46, 53.

Noble, Donald R. *The Steinbeck Question.* Troy, N.Y.: Whitston Publishing, 1993.

## OF TIME AND THE RIVER

**Author:**   Thomas Wolfe
**Original date and place of publication:**   1935, United States
**Original publisher:**   Charles Scribner's Sons
**Type:**   Novel

### SUMMARY

*Of Time and the River* is an autobiographical novel in which Wolfe, in the persona of Eugene Gant, relates his experiences as a Southern man who leaves home to pursue his education in the North. As the book opens, Gant thinks of the distance, in both time and space, between the little town of Altamount in North Carolina that he is leaving and the city of Boston where he attends Harvard. While on the train moving northward, he recalls his unhappy childhood and the hunger for experience that he could never quite satisfy.

At Harvard, Gant takes a drama class, then wanders the streets to gain experience to use in his own plays. He hungrily reads everything that he can. He also becomes closer with another man from his town, Robert Weaver, who has insanity in his family. After graduating, Gant briefly goes home, where Robert and he get drunk and are jailed. Gant eventually decides to return north to live in New York City and work as an English instructor. Weaver reappears and takes a room at the apartment hotel where Gant lives. Weaver drinks heavily, destroys property, takes a mistress and makes Gant's life miserable. Through another friend, Joel Pierce, Gant is introduced to the wealthy people of New York in their palatial homes. He is at first entranced by the opulence but eventually realizes that the wealth and luxury that he craves result from the misery of others.

On vacation in England, Gant meets old friend Francis Starwick, touring Europe with two women who are paying all of his bills. Gant becomes disgusted with them and travels alone to France. He visits Chartres, Orleans and Tours, which remind him of Altamount, and he thinks of America and of his family and childhood. The thoughts make him homesick, and he makes reservations to return home. While on the ocean liner, Gant sees a woman whose face glows with great excitement. A woman companion calls her Esther and Gant feels that she will be his destiny. The novel ends at that point.

## CENSORSHIP HISTORY

*Of Time and the River* was a lumbering collection of half a million words when famed editor Max Perkins of Charles Scribner's Sons began the task of giving it form in 1933. After reading it, Perkins told Wolfe that the pile of papers contained two complete novels, one which told of "the period of unrest, wandering, search, and hunger in a man's youth" and a second that "was dominated by a unity of a single passion," the fictional account of Wolfe's affair with Aline Bernstein. The publishing house convinced Wolfe that the first part was the superior literary product and that his inability to be fully objective about the affair interfered with the quality of his writing in the second part. The real reason was that Scribner's "could not overlook the grave possibility that Aline Bernstein, or some member of her family, might well sue for libel if Wolfe's account of their love affair was published." Aline had already made Wolfe promise not to write anything about her or her family without approval, and he had given his word. Yet, none of what Perkins read in the lumbering manuscript had been approved and it was not likely to gain her approval. Thus, Perkins and Scribner's censored the author's original work before publication by removing the second half of the work because they "had every reason to think that Aline Bernstein might explode if Charles Scribner's Sons published a major book, half of which was devoted to her love life."

Once published, the novel became the object of criticism and of a call for its suppression by groups who perceived it as being both racist and anti-Semitic. Critics objected to his treatment of African Americans, pointing out that these minor characters are treated more like "frantic children." The growing activism of the New Deal era and the increasing awareness of individual human rights led critics to feel that Wolfe was contemptuous of blacks and that black characters in his books "hardly qualify as human beings." More troubling to Wolfe was the charge of anti-Semitism. He saw nothing wrong in writing in *Of Time and the River* that the main character, Eugene Gant, feels when he begins teaching in New York City that he is in a world "overrun by Jews," and that his students with their "Yiddish" faces are "beak-nosed" and engage in "Kike" laughter. Cognizant of the growing threats to Jews in Germany, a Jewish leader wrote to Scribner's from Philadelphia objecting to Wolfe's "hymn of hate directed against an oppressed minority," while another critic wrote that the novel "fairly reeks of the narrow-mindedness engendered in anti-Semitism." Such criticism angered Wolfe, who had taken pains to create a view that "was so much more flattering than his own personal assessment of the Jews." Aside from isolated individual refusals to buy the novel, no formal banning occurred.

In 1963, the novel was removed from four high school libraries in the Amarillo, Texas, area after parents of students attending the high schools raised charges of obscenity against the book. They protested the depiction of the relationship of Reverend Pentland with the "widder" as "pornographic" because one character teases him with "a lewd smile" that "she's let him have a little of it." The objectors also cited the "profanities" that were "inappropriate for a school," and identified "damn," "hell," "son of a bitch" and the "lovely bastard of a train" used early in the book. Parents also protested references to sex and noted one character's identification of a woman in a play as a "society whore. . . . you can find plenty of her kind for three dollars a throw," as well as the open references to Weaver's mistress.

In 1983, the Alabama State Textbook Committee removed Wolfe's novel from use in the Alabama public schools. At the same time, the committee also removed Maya Angelou's I KNOW WHY THE CAGED BIRD SINGS and Henrik Ibsen's *A Doll's House*. The committee claimed that they took the action in response to parent complaints about the "obscenities" and "inappropriate situations" in the works.

## FURTHER READINGS

Donald, David Herbert. *Look Homeward: A Life of Thomas Wolfe*. Boston: Little, Brown & Company, 1987.

Holman, C. Hugh. *The Letters of Thomas Wolfe to His Mother*. Chapel Hill, N.C.: University of North Carolina Press, 1968.

*Newsletter on Intellectual Freedom* (March 1983): 39.

Roberts, Terry. "Irreconcilable Talents: Thomas Wolfe's Struggle to Compose *Of Time and the River*." *Mississippi Quarterly* 43 (Winter 1989): 22–32.

Stutman, Suzanne, ed. *My Other Loneliness: Letters of Thomas Wolfe and Aline Bernstein*. Chapel Hill, N.C.: University of North Carolina Press, 1983.

# ONE FLEW OVER THE CUCKOO'S NEST

**Author:** Ken Kesey
**Original date and place of publication:** 1962, United States
**Original publisher:** Viking Press
**Type:** Novel

## SUMMARY

*One Flew Over the Cuckoo's Nest* is told from the point of view of Bromden, a tall and heavyset schizophrenic Native American called the Chief, who is an inmate of a mental hospital ward. He pretends to be mute as a defense against his surroundings, but the arrival of Randle Patrick McMurphy, a fast-talking con artist who has feigned insanity to enter the mental hospital rather than a prison work farm, gives Bromden confidence and helps him to rebel against the sterile, domineering Miss Ratched. Known to the inmates as Big Nurse, she runs a tightly controlled, efficient ward in which the heavily medicated patients mechanically follow her orders without question and even the orderlies stand at attention, "ready to quell even the feeblest insurrection." McMurphy disrupts her efficiency with his irrepressible high spirits and his goal to create havoc on her well-run ward. The chilling authority of Nurse Ratched appalls McMurphy who provides a direct contrast to the other patients. They "long ago gave up the struggle to assert themselves. Cowed, docile, they have surrendered completely to her unbridled authority."

The boisterous, fun-loving, rebellious McMurphy is a lusty and profane fighter, whose brawling and gambling challenge the rigidly structured world over which Nurse Ratched presides. Against all hospital rules, he initiates gambling among the inmates and smuggles women and wine into the ward. As he openly defies Big Nurse, the other men gradually emerge from their fear-induced inactivity and learn to express happiness, anger and other emotions that have long been repressed. Such behavior becomes dangerous for McMurphy, because he has been committed by the state, not voluntarily as have most of the men, and his behavior will determine the length of his stay. The greater his rebellion against the repressive atmosphere created by Big Nurse, the greater the danger that he will be forced to remain in the hospital for a longer period of commitment.

From taking forbidden cigarettes left at the nurses' station to stealing a fishing boat for an inmates' fishing expedition, McMurphy shows a disregard for the rules that have so long dominated the lives of the other inmates, as his vitality and enthusiasm radically change them. His escapades have sometimes tragic consequences that result from the clash of authority with the inmates' newfound freedom. One man drowns in the therapeutic swimming pool when his fingers become stuck in the grate at the bottom of the pool, while young Billy Bibbit takes his own life after Nurse Ratched threatens to tell his mother that he has had sex with a prostitute whom McMurphy sneaked onto the ward. Even McMurphy must eventually yield to the misguided technology of the mental hospital after he attacks Big Nurse, blaming her brutal treatment and threats for young Billy's death. A few weeks after the attack, McMurphy disappears from the ward for a week. When he returns, the other inmates refuse to accept the changed man and claim that he is an imposter who looks "like one of those department store dummies.... a crummy sideshow fake lying there on the Gurney." A lobotomy destroys all that has made McMurphy human and makes him the perfect example of what happens to a man who bucks the system. Unable to bear seeing their friend deprived of his vitality, the remaining inmates decide to provide him with a dignified end. The Chief smothers him with a pillow, then escapes from the hospital to freedom.

## CENSORSHIP HISTORY

The novel has been frequently censored and challenged as being racist, obscene and immoral because of its raw language and for its emphasis upon the defiance of authority. The white inmates repeatedly refer to the black orderlies with such racial slurs as "coons," "boys" and "niggers," while the Japanese nurse from the Disturbed ward is spoken of as the "Jap." Numerous obscenities pepper McMurphy's speech, and he appears to purposely taunt the doctors and nurses, as when he challenges their question regarding his psychopathic tendencies: "'Is it my fightin' tendencies or my fuckin' tendencies? Must be fuckin', mustn't it? All that wham-bam-thank-you-ma'am. . . .'" He further describes Nurse Ratched as having "the too big boobs" and as "a bitch and a buzzard and a ballcutter."

Identified as containing "obscene, filthy language," the novel was challenged in 1971 in Greeley, Colorado, where parents in the public school district demanded that it be removed from the non-required American Culture reading list along with *I Never Promised You a Rose Garden* and *Love Story*. In 1974, five residents of Strongsville, Ohio, sued the board of education to remove *One Flew Over the Cuckoo's Nest* and MANCHILD IN THE PROMISED LAND from the classroom. Labeling both books "pornographic materials," they charged that the works "glorify criminal activity, have a tendency to corrupt juveniles, and contain descriptions of bestiality, bizarre violence, and torture, dismemberment, death, and human elimination." In 1975, the book was removed from public school libraries in Randolph, New York, and Alton, Oklahoma, and school officials in Westport, Massachusetts, removed the novel from the required reading list in 1977.

In 1978, the novel was banned from St. Anthony Freemont (Idaho) High School classrooms, and the contract of the instructor was not renewed after parents complained about the language in the book. The school superintendent did not read the book, but he collected all copies from students without attempting to determine its literary or scholastic value. The teacher claimed to have sent home a list of books to be read with the condition that alternative titles would be provided for students wko chose not to read a specific assigned book, and no one had objected. The teacher worked with the American Civil Liberties Union to file a complaint in the United States District Court for the District of Idaho, claiming that his rights and the rights of his students under the First and 14th Amendments had been violated. *Foga-*

*rty v. Atchley* was filed but not decided. The novel was also challenged in 1982 by parents of students in Merrimack (New Hampshire) High School, where it was removed, but in a 1986 challenge to the novel as part of the honors English curriculum at Aberdeen (Washington) High School, the school board voted to retain the novel.

## FURTHER READINGS

*Newsletter on Intellectual Freedom.* (May 1971): 59; (November 1974): 152; (May 1975): 41; (July 1975): 108; (May 1978): 57; (July 1978): 96, 100; (May 1980): 52; (September 1982): 170; (November 1986): 225.

O'Neil, Robert M. *Classrooms in the Crossfire: The Rights and Interests of Students, Parents, Teachers, Administrators, Librarians, and the Community.* Bloomington, Ind.: Indiana University Press, 1981.

Tebbel, John. *A History of Book Publishing in the United States.* Vol. IV. New York: Bowker and Company, 1981.

## ORDINARY PEOPLE

**Author:**  Judith Guest
**Original date and place of publication:**  1976, United States
**Original publisher:**  The Viking Press
**Type:**  Novel

## SUMMARY

*Ordinary People* is the story of a family attempting to come to terms with the death of one son and the attempted suicide of another son who blames himself for his older brother's drowning death. The novel begins a month after 17-year-old Conrad Jarrett has been released from the mental institution where he had spent eight months after using a razor blade to cut the vein in his wrist. The suicide attempt came one year after Conrad and his brother Buck had capsized while sailing on unexpectedly rough waters. For hours, they had held onto the overturned hull, one on each side for balance, but Buck drowned while Conrad was rescued despite Buck's greater endurance and greater strength as a swimmer. Conrad's inability to forgive himself for living coupled with his mother's innately cold nature that deprives her of the ability to even cry at her son's funeral created a feeling of helplessness for Conrad.

The novel traces the difficulties that Conrad faces in returning to school and family life. He had always been the "perfect child" about whom his parents never had to worry, while Buck had been the daredevil about whom they always worried. Whatever danger signals Conrad sent out before the suicide attempt were missed because no one was watching. After he returns from the hospital, his father watches him constantly for changes in behavior or emotional responses.

Tortured with guilt, Conrad quits the swimming team and isolates himself from his former friends, because they were also Buck's friends and the associations are too painful. Describing himself as "Conrad Jarrett, outcast, quitter, *fuck-up*," he is nearly successful in turning everyone away from him, but his salvation comes when he obeys his father and keeps his promise to meet with a psychiatrist to continue the work begun in the hospital. Dr. Berger manages to lead Conrad to recognize that he is punishing himself because of his brother's death. He encourages Conrad to elude the control of others and to say, "Fuck off. . . . Go to hell," if he feels like doing so. He also listens without judging when Conrad admits, "I jack off a lot." Conrad allows himself to become close to Jeanine, a young woman who has her own guilty secret, and his intense physical response to her makes him feel human.

Meanwhile, there appears to be no solution to the marital problems of Conrad's parents, Cal and Beth Jarrett. Beth accuses Cal of allowing himself to be manipulated by Conrad when he refuses to spend Christmas in London. Cal reminds her that they were in Miami the previous Christmas when Conrad attempted suicide. The closer that Cal attempts to become with his wife, the further she pushes him away, until she finally decides to take an indefinitely long vacation in Europe. As the novel closes, Conrad appears to have overcome his past. He has come to terms with Buck's death and seems ready to resume old friendships.

## CENSORSHIP HISTORY

In 1981, the novel was temporarily banned from junior and senior high school English classrooms in Enon, Ohio, because of the language used by the character Conrad, and because he refers to masturbation at several points in the novel. After consideration by a districtwide committee, the book was reinstated as an optional reading choice but not a required reading. In 1982, a parent in Merrimack, New Hampshire, challenged the use of the novel in the classroom as being "obscene and depressing." The parent objected to the topic of suicide and noted that there "is enough tragedy in the world" to not have to subject students to it in their reading. The objection to the language related to the use of "damn," "Goddamn" and the desperate cry at several points in the novel of " . . . who the fuck needs anybody?" Thomas Tryon's *The Other* and Kenneth Kesey's ONE FLEW OVER THE CUCKOO NEST were challenged in the same incident.

In 1985, several parents challenged the novel as an optional summer reading book for 10th-grade students in North Salem, New York, because they believed that the topic of teenage suicide was "too intense," as well as because of "profanity" and "graphic sex scenes." One scene presented as an example occurs between Conrad's parents:

She reaches up to put her arms around him, all tawny, smooth skin, those gray eyes with thick lashes, silent and insistent. She leads tonight, and he follows, moving swiftly down that dark river, everything floating, melting, perfect, and complete. Afterward, she slides away from him, and her hair, soft and furry against his shoulder, smells sweet and fresh, like wood fern."

A second specified scene is more graphic and occurs between Conrad and Jeanine:

Her tongue in his mouth, exploring. He cannot concentrate any more, gathers her against him tightly as his groin hardens, spreads warmth through his whole body. His face in the hollow of her neck, he rocks her slowly, gently in his arms.

They lie drugged and submerged, facing each other on the bed. Conrad's head is on his arm, one hand curved around her breast, eyes closed, shielding himself from the shining look of her. . . . his skin feels branded everywhere that she has touched him. . .

In 1993, parents of students at Anaheim (California) Union High School District challenged the book because it was "degrading to Christians." Cited in the complaint were Conrad's uses of the words "damn" and "Goddamn" and his admission to Jeanine that he did not believe in God. After consideration by a district-appointed review committee, the book was retained with another book that had been challenged for being "obscene and pornographic," Pat Conroy's *The Great Santini*.

In 1994, the book was removed from the required reading list for students at Delta High School in Delaware, Indiana, after parents and student complained of "profanity" and descriptions of "sexual situations," citing those already identified. That same year, the novel was also removed from use in all classrooms throughout the district in Faulkton, South Dakota, because of "profanity."

## FURTHER READINGS

*Newsletter on Intellectual Freedom* (January 1982): 77; (September 1982): 170; (September 1985): 168; (May 1993): 86–87; (November 1993): 192–193; (January 1994): 14; (September 1994): 150, 152.

# THE OX-BOW INCIDENT

**Author:** Walter Van Tilburg Clark
**Original date and place of publication:** 1940, United States
**Original publisher:** Random House
**Type:** Novel

## SUMMARY

*The Ox-Bow Incident*, a tale of mob justice set in the Old West, warns of the danger that results when people take the law into their own hands. The novel begins much like most western tales with two young cowboys entering a small town in the spring after spending months cooped up in a shack on the winter range with a herd. Art Croft, one of the two, is the first-person narrator.

Gil and Art, who are well known by the bartender Canby, go through a familiar routine of criticizing the bar service, commenting on a large, grimy painting above the bar and becoming used to some semblance of civilization. Gil calls the painting, which depicts a full-fleshed naked woman lying on a couch with a man in the background, "The Bitching Hour," and Clark refers to it as the Bitch in the narrative. As they drink heavily, they play poker and bemoan the lack of unmarried women in Bridger's Wells. The players' tempers flare, one calls another "bastard" and the poker game erupts into a fight shortly before a boy runs into the saloon and announces that a ranch foreman named Kinkaid has been killed and that 50 head of cattle have been stolen. The group of men begin to call for justice, and a mob forms to track down the killers and lynch them.

Twenty men join the vigilante group, but only two enthusiastically call for revenge. The rest are indecisive, and most are simply too morally weak to refuse to participate or to oppose the action. The men ride out blindly in the middle of the night, with no specific suspects in mind, and they come across three men sleeping soundly in a valley that contains a mountain stream with a course that looks like an ox-bow. They find 50 head of cattle bearing the brand of the reportedly stolen cattle and refuse to listen to the protests of one of the men, who claims to have bought the cattle that morning from the rancher Drew. The mob leaders, Tetley and the boisterous and belligerent Ma Grier, taunt those members of the group who seem hesitant. When the decision to lynch is put to a vote, only three vote against the action.

The hanging occurs at sunrise. On the ride back to town, the lynching party meets the sheriff, the judge and a much alive Kinkaid, whose head is bandaged. What caused the head wound is never revealed. The mob also learns that the cattle had been bought and not stolen by the hanged men. The realization that they are murderers affects several of the mob deeply, leading a few men to seek affirmation that they did try to stop the act. Two others commit suicide: Young Gerald Tetley hangs himself when they return home, and his father jumps on his cavalry sword to die. The story ends with no legal punishment for any of the participants.

## CENSORSHIP HISTORY

The novel has been challenged in several incidents by parents of students because of "vulgar" and "objectionable" language. In a 1963 survey of school administrators and high school English department chairpersons on censorship in Wisconsin, Burress reported one incident in which a parent complained about the language in the book and asked that it be removed from classroom use. The words objected to were "bitch," "bastard," "shit" and "nigger." The school board voted to grant the request. In 1966, in a national survey of high school librarians and high school English department chairpersons, Burress reported one incident in an unidentified state in which a local parent group called for a ban of the novel from the high school English curriculum. They based their objection on the presence of "too many obscene descriptions" and "swear words." The school board voted to retain the book in the curriculum.

In a 1967 investigation of censorship in Arizona, Burress reported two challenges to the novel. In one incident, parents complained of the "vulgar" language in the novel, citing the term "bastard" that appears throughout. The school board voted to remove the book from classroom use. In a second incident in the same state, parents challenged the work because of the language, but the school board voted to retain the work.

In 1980, several parents of students in the Johnson City, Illinois, school district requested the removal of the book from the high school English curriculum, citing the same words as in earlier challenges. The school board voted to retain the book.

## FURTHER READINGS

Budd, John M. "Law and Morality in *Billy Budd* and *The Ox-Bow Incident*." *CLA Journal* 35 (December 1991): 185–197.

Burress, Lee. *Battle of the Books: Literary Censorship in the Public Schools, 1950–1985.* Metuchen, N.J.: Scarecrow Press, 1989.

*Newsletter on Intellectual Freedom* (September 1980): 107.

## THE RED PONY

**Author:** John Steinbeck
**Original date and place of publication:** 1933, United States
**Original publisher:** The Viking Press
**Type:** Novel

## SUMMARY

*The Red Pony* relates the story of 10-year-old Jody Triflin, who learns very important truths about life and death on his father's ranch. The brief novel is divided into four chapters: "The Gift," "The Great Mountains," "The Promise" and "The Leader of the People." Jody is thrilled when his father presents him with his first horse, a red pony that he names Gabilan. Ranch hand and horse-taming expert Billy Buck promises to teach Jody to ride the feisty Gabilan as soon as the pony is full grown, but until then he shows Jody how to care for the animal. While Jody is at school, Billy leaves Gabilan in the corral during an unexpected rainstorm and the pony becomes fatally ill.

Still grieving for his pony, Jody meets an old man named Gitano who has come to the Triflin ranch to die. He had lived in an adobe hut on the land years earlier, and he now wants to die at the place that he considers home. Jody's father, Carl Triflin, reluctantly lets Gitano stay the night, but he insists that the old man must go to relatives and not "die with strangers." Early the following morning, Jody sees Gitano riding Carl's old horse toward the mountains, with a rapier glittering in his hand. The reader is left to wonder about Gitano's fate.

In the third chapter, Carl tells Jody that he will get another horse because Billy Buck has praised Jody's hard work in training Gabilan. Carl tells the boy to take their mare to the neighbor's range "and get her bred." The book graphically describes Nellie's struggle to free herself from the rope, her high-pitched scream and that of the stallion whose "eyes glittered feverishly" and whose "stiff, erect nostrils were as red as flame." After the violence in their initial encounter, Nellie's mood changes and she becomes "coquettishly feminine. She nibbled his arched neck with her lips. She edged around and rubbed her shoulder against his shoulder." In the months that follow, Jody learns about the birth process from Billy. The discussion is detailed regarding what constitutes "a good right birth." As Nellie's time to "throw her colt" comes near, Jody becomes increasingly anxious. Nellie has difficulty, and Billy reaches inside her to try to turn the colt, but he can't. He kills Nellie and slits her belly open to save the colt, desperate to recapture Jody's trust and respect that he had lost when Gabilan died.

In the final chapter, Jody's maternal grandfather arrives unexpectedly and tells his wornout stories about leading a wagon train and fighting Indians as a young man. Carl is tired of the stories and says that "nobody wants to hear it over and over," hurting the old man's feelings but drawing Jody closer to him.

## CENSORSHIP HISTORY

In a 1966 survey of a national sample of high school librarians and English department chairpersons concerning school censorship, Lee Burress recorded only one challenge in an unidentified locale. A parent objected to the "profanity" in the book and requested its removal from the high school library. The request was denied. In 1980, parents of students in Vernon-Verona-Sherill (New York) School District objected to the novel as being a "filthy, trashy, sex novel" in a challenge that also called for the removal of A FAREWELL TO ARMS, *The Grapes of Wrath*, OF MICE AND MEN, A SEPARATE PEACE and TO KILL A MOCKINGBIRD from a district recommended reading list. Among their objections is one instance in the book in which 10-year-old Jody "could smell the delicious smell of brandy" on his father's breath, and the boy later speaks of the "damn mice." The parents also condemned Billy Buck's explicit description of the birth process and of his efforts to turn the colt inside Nellie as she struggles to give birth. After reviewing the work, the school board voted to retain the book.

In 1994, parents of students attending schools in Oconee County, Georgia, challenged the inclusion of the novel in the school libraries and charged that it contained profanity. Also challenged at that time "due to the filthiness of the material" were 10 books by V. C. Andrews: *Dark Angel, Darkest Hour, Dawn, Flowers in the Attic, Garden of Shadows, If There Be Thorns, My Sweet Audrina, Petals on the Wind, Seeds of Yesterday* and *Twilight.* The Oconee school board voted to remove *The Red Pony* and the books by Andrews from the school libraries. Those who challenged *The Red Pony* objected to Jody's use of the word "damn" and viewed the breeding scene between the mare and the stallion as "filthy." Parents stated that the details regarding the birth of the colt were unnecessary to the story. A review committee recommended removal of the books from the school district, a move with which the district school board concurred. They further decided to evaluate all 40,000 volumes used in the classrooms and existing in the school libraries and to remove from the district public schools any books and teaching materials that contained "explicit sex and pornography."

## FURTHER READINGS

Burress, Lee. *Battle of the Books: Literary Censorship in the Public Schools, 1950–1985.* Metuchen, N.J.: Scarecrow Press, 1989.
Ferrell, Keith. *John Steinbeck: The Voice of the Land.* New York: M. Evans, 1986.
*Newsletter on Intellectual Freedom* (May 1980): 62; (September 1994): 145.
Steinbeck, Elaine, and Robert Wallsten, eds. *Steinbeck: A Life in Letters.* New York: Viking Press, 1975.
Timmerman, John. *John Steinbeck's Fiction: The Aesthetics of the Road Taken.* Norman, Okla.: University of Oklahoma Press, 1986.

## THE SCARLET LETTER

**Author:**  Nathaniel Hawthorne
**Original place and date of publication:**  1850, United States
**Original publisher:**  Ticknor and Fields
**Type:**  Novel

## SUMMARY

*The Scarlet Letter* opens with a long, detailed preface entitled "The Custom House: Introductory to *The Scarlet Letter*" in which Hawthorne creates the illusion that the novel following is based on fact. He claims that, while working as a custom house agent, he found a manuscript and a faded and worn red letter "A" in one of the upper rooms. The manuscript, written by Jonathan Pue, a predecessor of his in the Custom House in Salem, Massachusetts, detailed the story of a Mistress Hester Prynne who had been found guilty of adultery in Boston two centuries earlier and punished. In addition to creating the premise for the novel, the section also makes reference to Hawthorne's ancestors and provides insight into his daily work as a civil servant.

The story of *The Scarlet Letter* is that of a romantic triangle. Hester Prynne, the beautiful young wife of an old and introverted scholar, is separated from her husband for two years after being taken from her home in England to the wildlands of the New World. Lonely and without friends, she falls in love with Arthur Dimmesdale, an attractive young minister, and bears his child, whom she names Pearl for she "was purchased at great price." Condemned by the townspeople, especially the women, who feel that jailing Hester, forcing her to stand on a scaffold in the middle of town and wearing the scarlet letter "A," for adultery, for life are not severe enough, Hester carries herself with dignity.

True to her strong character, Hester bears the shame and punishment alone and never reveals her child's father, although to do so would alleviate a great part of her punishment. Instead, Hester creates her own world for Pearl and supports herself by her excellent needlework skills. Her husband appears as a physician just returned from the frontier, but they agree to keep his identity a secret as the bitter and physically misshapen man takes the name Roger Chillingworth. He treats the physical ailments of Dimmesdale and eventually uncovers the identity of Pearl's father. The evil Chillingworth, feigning friendship, slowly destroys the minister. As Dimmesdale sinks into physical decay and Chillingworth decays morally, Hester wins the respect of the townspeople, who begin to view the "A" as representing "angel" for the many kind deeds she performs.

At the end of the novel, the dying Dimmesdale confesses publicly that he is Pearl's father as he stands holding hands with Hester and Pearl, on the same scaffold on which Hester alone stood soon after Pearl's birth to display her shame to the townspeople. Dimmesdale dies and Hester takes Pearl to Europe, then returns years later to her small cottage. After she dies, Hester is buried under the same grave marker as Dimmesdale.

## CENSORSHIP HISTORY

The novel was a success when it was first published, selling out a first printing within a few days. Although critics and literary figures praised the novel, religious journals and clergymen denounced it as "a dirty story" that belonged only in "a Brothel Library." A review in *Brownson's Quarterly* declared that neither Dimmesdale nor Hester exhibited "remorse" or "really repents of the criminal deed" and that "it is a story that should not have been told." In

*Church Review*, Reverend Arthur C. Coxe also condemned the two main characters as not being sufficiently repentant and stated that "the nauseous amour" was not appropriate subject matter for fiction. In 1852, Coxe called for the banning of *The Scarlet Letter* as he launched a savage attack, proclaiming that he was against "any toleration to a popular and gifted writer when he perpetrates bad morals—let his brokerage of lust be put down at the very beginning." He stated that he could not tolerate a novel that dealt with an "illicit relationship."

The main complaint of those who wanted to ban the novel at the outset was that Hawthorne sided with Hester and condemned her husband's revenge. Strict morality required that Hester suffer in more painful and obvious ways than Hawthorne provided. The citizens of Salem were so incensed by Hawthorne's novel that he moved his family out of the city to a farmhouse in the Berkshires. In 1852, the novel was banned in Russia by Czar Nicholas I in a "censorship terror," but the ban was lifted four years later when Czar Alexander II came into power.

Little attention was paid to the novel for nearly a century. In 1949, in stating the deciding opinion in *Commonwealth of Massachusetts v. Gordon*, 66 D. & C. 101 (1949), Judge Curtis Bok used the novel as an example of the manner in which public morals change when he noted that when first published, "Hawthorne's *Scarlet Letter* was referred to as 'a brokerage of lust,'" but it has become fully accepted by 1949.

In 1961, parents of students in Michigan objected to the assignment of the novel in high school English classes, claiming that it was "pornographic and obscene." They demanded that the book be taken out of the curriculum, but the request was denied. In a 1966 national sample of school librarians and English department chairpersons conducted by Lee Burress, four challenges were raised in locales unidentified by the investigator. In one, a student challenged the assignment of the book to freshman high school students, but no action was taken on the complaint. In a second challenge, a parent complained that the book was "immoral" because it dealt with a "misbegotten" child. The school board denied the request for removal of the book from the curriculum. In a third request to have the book removed from a reading list because it dealt with adultery, the request was also denied. The only successful challenge reported in the survey occurred when a high school principal declared the book too "frank" and "revealing" and removed it from the recommended reading list. A 1967 survey of high school censorship in Arizona conducted by Kenneth Donelson and Retha K. Foster reported one challenge by a parent who demanded the book be removed as a required reading because it discussed adultery. The request was denied.

In 1977, a parent and a principal in Michigan objected to the inclusion of the novel in the high school English curriculum because it dealt with a clergyman's "involvement in fornication." The book was removed from classroom use and from the recommended reading list. That same year, a parent in Missouri condemned the book for its use of "4-letter words" and "other undesirable content" and demanded its removal from the high school library. The school librarian recognized that the parent had not read the book because no obscenities appeared in the novel, and she convinced the parent of his error. The book was retained.

In a 1982 survey of English department chairpersons in Ohio, James Davis reported one challenge to the novel in which a parent claimed that the book was about "adultery," a "womanizing preacher" and "prostitution" and requested its removal as an assigned reading in a high school English class. The school board denied the request.

## FURTHER READINGS

Burress, Lee. *Battle of the Books: Literary Censorship in the Public Schools, 1950–1985.* Metuchen, N.J.: Scarecrow Press, 1989.

Crowley, J. Donald, ed. *Hawthorne: The Critical Heritage.* New York: Barnes and Noble, 1970.

Davis, James E., ed. *Dealing with Censorship.* Urbana, Ill.: National Council of Teachers of English, 1983.

Donelson, Kenneth, ed. *The Student's Right to Read.* Urbana, Ill.: National Council of Teachers of English, 1972.

McClure, Robert C. "Literature, the Law of Obscenity, and the Constitution." *Minnesota Law Review* 38 (March 1954): 325.

Miller, Edwin Haviland. *Salem Is My Dwelling Place: A Life of Nathaniel Hawthorne.* Iowa City: University of Iowa Press, 1991.

Tebbel, John. *A History of Book Publishing in the United States, 1630–1865.* Vol. 1. New York: R.R. Bowker Company, 1972.

Wood, James Playsted. *The Unpardonable Sin.* New York: Pantheon Books, 1970.

# A SEPARATE PEACE

**Author:**   John Knowles
**Original date and place of publication:**   1960, United States
**Original publisher:**   The Macmillan Company
**Type:**   Novel

## SUMMARY

*A Separate Peace* takes place at a small New England preparatory school named Devon, where the narrator Gene Forrester has returned 15 years after graduation. He visits the tree from which his close friend Finny fell and broke his leg the first time and the First Academy Building, where the second break occurred. These locations stimulate a flashback to the summer of 1942, between his junior and senior years, when the novel really begins.

The main character is Gene's friend Phineas, "Finny," who forms the Super Suicide Society of the Summer Session. Seemingly fearless, his fool-hardy behavior, athletic prowess and quirky sense of humor make him a leader of the boys, whom he repeatedly challenges to jump from a tree on the riverbank into the cold water below. As the summer progresses, all except Finny speak of the threat of enlistment after graduation.

Despite their friendship, a rivalry exists between Gene and Finny. Gene tries to do well academically, but Finny's games interfere with his studies. When Gene fails a math test after Finny convinces him to go to the beach rather than study, he believes that his friend wants him to fail. Finny again distracts Gene on the evening before an important French examination by leading him to a jumping session at the riverbank, and Gene becomes vengeful. As the two boys crawl out onto a tree limb, Gene moves on the branch and causes Finny to fall and break his leg. This incident drastically changes Finny's life because he can no longer participate in sports, so he returns home.

As fall term begins, Gene decides that he might as well enlist in the army, but when Finny returns with his leg in a cast, Gene changes his mind and serves as the injured boy's guide and helper. As the year progresses, the two boys make their peace with each other, and Finny's leg heals imperfectly. Other students who are jealous of Finny's attention to Gene decide to hold a mock trial to determine what really happened. One student testifies that Gene shook the tree limb, a statement that upsets Finny and sends him racing out of the room toward a flight of marble stairs, where his cane slips and he falls, breaking the same leg. Finny dies when the doctor sets the bone a few days later; the official diagnosis is that some of the bone marrow must have escaped into his bloodstream and stopped his heart.

After graduation, Gene and many other Devon graduates enlist, but for Gene the war is of little consequence compared with the enemy he has overcome in trying to achieve a separate peace with Finny's death. He observes at the end of the novel, "my war ended before I ever put on the uniform; I was on active duty all my time at the school; I killed my enemy there."

## CENSORSHIP HISTORY

The novel was challenged in 1980 by parents in Vernon-Verona-Sherrill (New York) School District for being a "filthy, trashy sex novel." In their challenge, the parents claimed that the novel contained homosexuality as an underlying theme which "encourages homosexuality." They also complained of "swear words" to which their children should not be subjected, including "bastard," the barely disguised "f——ing" and "damn." The school board voted to offer students another selection and to remove the book from class-room use. In 1985, parents of students at Fannett-Metal High School in Shippensburg, Pennsylvania, challenged the book because of "offensive language." They claimed that the book was "too adult" for high school students and asked that it be removed from the required reading list. The request was denied, but students whose parents objected to the book were given an alternative assignment. In 1989, the novel was challenged by parents of students in the Shelby County, Tennessee, school system who felt that the "offensive language" in the novel made it inappropriate for the high school reading list. The school board replaced the novel with another book, and the issue ended.

After 22 years of being assigned in the local schools in Champaign, Illinois, without complaints, the novel was challenged by three parents who claimed that "unsuitable language" in the novel made it inappropriate for assignment in high school English classes. The parents specified the use of "damn" and "goddamn" in their complaint. The school board appointed a curriculum review committee to respond to the complaint and agreed with the decision of the committee to retain the novel. In a 1991 challenge to the novel issued by the parent of a high school student in Troy, Illinois, profanity and negative attitudes were cited in the request that the novel be removed from the classroom. The parent identified 45 "profane references" in the book, including "God damn," "Shut up" and "I swear to God." Students were offered alternative assignments while the school board took the matter under advisement, but no further action was taken on the complaint.

A more extensive challenge emerged in 1992, when a parent in Jacksonville, Florida, learned that the high school library contained a copy of *A Separate Peace* and challenged it as being "unsuitable for youth" and "encouraging rebellion against authority." The challenge cited "vulgar language" and characters who skip classes, break school rules and trespass on school property as offering inappropriate models for students. The "objectionable language" identified includes "for God's sake," "damn," "hell," "Christ" and "Oh God." The district review committee considered the challenge and voted to retain the work that it characterized as "truly a well-written piece of art." In the report of the decision to retain the novel in the high school library, the committee wrote: "To ban or restrict this book reflects the paranoia existing in today's society. Reasons conjured for the banning of the book are unjustifiable."

## FURTHER READINGS

Knowles, Sebastian. *British and Irish—A Purgatorial Flame: Seven British Writers in the Second World War*. London: Routledge Paul, 1991.

*Newsletter on Intellectual Freedom* (May 1980): 62; (November 1985): 204; (January 1990): 11–12.

People for the American Way. *Attacks on the Freedom to Learn: 1991–1992 Report*. Washington, D.C.: People for the American Way, 1992.

Rice, Anne M. "Still Good Reading: Adolescent Novels Written Before 1967—*A Separate Peace* by John Knowles." *English Journal* (April 1992): 88.

# SISTER CARRIE

**Author:**   Theodore Dreiser
**Original date and place of publication:**   1900, United States
**Original publisher:**   Doubleday Page
**Literary type:**   Novel

## SUMMARY

*Sister Carrie* relates the story of a young Wisconsin girl who leaves her small-town home and travels to Chicago, where she hopes to make her fortune. Eighteen-year-old Caroline Meeber, the naive "Sister Carrie" of the title, desires the fine clothes and financial success that she sees in the fast-paced city, and she views with scorn the impoverished life of her sister Minnie and laborer brother-in-law Hanson, with whom she lives. When she meets again the flashy and seemingly affluent Charles Drouet, a salesman whom she had first met on her train journey to Chicago, she realizes that her rise in society can only occur through her associations with men.

Life in Chicago depresses Carrie at first, as she attempts to find work but learns that her lack of training and inexperience in business make the sweatshop her only job option. Desperate to escape her misery, Carrie eagerly becomes Drouet's mistress, grateful for the modest apartment and equally modest allowance that accompany her new role. Her comfort and contentment soon turn to dissatisfaction as she views the grand homes that line Chicago's Lake Shore and her desire for material items increases. Introduced by Drouet to George Hurstwood, the polished and well-dressed manager of a fashionable restaurant-bar, Carrie leaves Drouet to become the mistress of the married Hurstwood, who risks his family and reputation for her. With money stolen from his employers, Hurstwood runs off with Carrie, first to Montreal and then to New York, where he invests in a bar. As Carrie's dreams become increasingly expensive, Hurstwood experiences economic reversals that drive Carrie to find her own success. She becomes a member of the chorus line in a dance review and, through clever use of her associations with successful men, achieves a stage career. Carrie leaves the now-impoverished Hurstwood, who survives by eating in soup kitchens and sleeping in flophouses before taking his own life.

As she enjoys her success, Carrie becomes close to yet one more man, an electrical engineer named Robert Ames, who reveals to her the emptiness of her life despite her material success. Immune to her desire to forge a physical relationship, Ames exerts the greatest influence over her life of all her relationships by making her see that she has achieved a hollow success. As the novel ends, the materially successful and calculating Carrie realizes that her life remains as empty and unfulfilled as when she first arrived in Chicago.

## CENSORSHIP HISTORY

The novel became an object of censorship before it was even published. Dreiser first sent it to Harper & Brothers, which praised the work but said that they could not publish *Sister Carrie* because of its subject. The returned manuscript contained praise for the work as a "superior piece of reportorial realism," even as the company rejected it. The reader's report noted that the author's touch was "neither firm enough nor sufficiently delicate to depict without offense to the reader the continued illicit relations of the heroine." In response, the author asked his friend Arthur Henry to excise "offensive" passages; in other words, to cut those that alluded in even an indirect way to sexuality.

Dreiser next sent the manuscript to Doubleday Page, which offered the author a contract because of the enthusiasm shown toward the novel by the publisher's reader, author Frank Norris. Despite having signed a contract with Dreiser, firm owner Frank Doubleday tried to stop publication of the novel and contended that the story should not be published by anybody "because it is immoral." Rumors emerged that Mrs. Frank Doubleday had read the manuscript and "was horrified by its frankness." A social worker and moral reformer, she insisted that her husband withdraw the novel from publication, but the legal contract was binding. The firm published the novel, according to contract, but did not make an effort to distribute the book and no copies were sold by Doubleday Page. In 1901, Heinemann in London published an abridged version of the novel, but the uncut version was not published until 1907, when Dreiser persuaded the newly formed publisher B.W. Dodge Company to take a chance. In 1908, Grosset and Dunlap created public outrage when it published the novel, but no legal restraints emerged and the controversy was good for sales. By the time that Harper & Brothers reissued the novel in 1911, public outrage had turned to other subjects.

## FURTHER READINGS

Dreiser, Theodore. "The Early Adventures of Sister Carrie." Foreword to *Sister Carrie*. New York: The Modern Library, 1927.
Lingeman, Richard. *Theodore Dreiser: At the Gates of the City, 1871–1907*. Vol. 1. New York: G.P. Putnam's Sons, 1986.

# SOUL ON ICE

**Author:** Eldridge Cleaver
**Original date and place of publication:** 1968, United States
**Original publisher:** McGraw Hill
**Type:** Collection of autobiographical essays

## SUMMARY

*Soul on Ice* conveys Cleaver's experience of what it meant to be a black man in the ghetto, in prison and in the society of the 1950s and the 1960s. Written while he was in prison, the book is divided into four parts: "Letters from Prison," "Blood of the Beast," "Prelude to Love—Three Letters" and "White Woman, Black Woman." Contained within each part are essays that focus on Cleaver's specific concerns and experiences, from his days as a street hoodlum in East Los Angeles through his long prison career to the emergence of a man who has shaken off his own feelings of bigotry and writes love letters to a white woman, a San Francisco lawyer who assisted in his appeals and in respect for whom he stopped calling women "bitches."

The essays contain a raw edge that reflects the reality of Cleaver's life. The first essay, "On Becoming," relates his experience in 1954 as an 18-year-old who had just begun to serve a sentence in Folsom Prison for a marijuana charge, one month after the Supreme Court decision outlawing segregation. He becomes aware of the sharp divisions of society and makes the connection between race and the burdens of poverty and powerlessness. Released from prison, Cleaver relates that he became a rapist, for whom "rape was an insurrectionary act." Back in prison, he reads voraciously from the Greek classics, American history, the psychology of Freud and Jung and the works of African-American writers. Cleaver also refines his own views of the Civil Rights movement, Black Muslim teachings and the Black Power movement in a way that exhibits his own mental evolution regarding the black struggle.

The final section deals with Cleaver's perceptions of the relationships that black men establish with black women and with white women. He explores the myth of "the walking phallus symbol" of the "Supermasculine Menial" black male with "the fiery steel of his rod," who "wets the juices" of the "Ultrafeminine Doll," the pure white Southern woman. Cleaver perceives them as the embodiments of a racial caste system as he condemns the "Amazon" black women for viewing the black man as only "half a man." In the final essay, Cleaver rants that he is a "Black Eunuch, divested of my balls," but he makes peace with the African-American woman whom he calls "my Queen" and urges her to join him in building a new civilization "on these ruins."

## CENSORSHIP HISTORY

*Soul on Ice* provoked controversy from its first publication, earning rave views from social critics who hailed Cleaver as a man who "throws light on the dark areas we wish he would leave alone" and calling his work "an exceptional volume both in what it says and how the author came to say it." Reviewers also acknowledged that the book "makes you twist and flinch because he is no damned gentleman." The discomfort that the book caused led some groups, such as Save Our Children, to label it "trash" and to call for its removal.

In 1969, California Superintendent of Instruction Max Rafferty, with the backing of the state board of education, barred Cleaver's book and *Dutchman* by Imamu Amiri Baraka from elective courses in black studies. The board claimed that the works contained "obscene" language and images that made them unsuitable for use in the school curricullum.

In 1975, parents of students at Greenwich (Connecticut) High School asked for the removal of the book from the school library, charging that it was "crime provoking and anti-American as well as obscene and pornographic." That same year, a group called the Concerned Citizens and Taxpayers for Decent Books in Baton Rouge, Louisiana, called for the removal from libraries and schools of 65 books including *Soul on Ice*, which they viewed as being "pornography and filth." The books were retained in both incidents.

In a survey of a national sample of English department chairpersons conducted in 1977, Lee Burress recorded one instance in which parent complaints had resulted in the restriction of the work to only the upper grades. In a similar survey of librarians in 1982, Burress reported that a high school principal of an Ohio school district had ordered the book placed on a closed shelf in the high school library, because of complaints that the "obscene language and criticism of whites stirs up trouble." Parents of students in Omak, Washington, challenged the use of the book in the classroom in 1979 because of "profane language," but it was retained.

The most extensive challenge to *Soul on Ice* began in 1976 when two school board members in Island Trees Free School District No. 26 in New York ordered librarians to remove the title and 10 others from the school library (see BEST SHORT STORIES BY NEGRO WRITERS) in 1982. With the others, *Soul on Ice* was charged with being "immoral" and "just plain filthy," and the following passage was specified in the court record as representative of "objectionable" passages:

> There are white men who will pay you to fuck their wives. They approach you and say, "How would you like to fuck a white woman?" "What is this?" you ask. "On the up-and-up," he assures you. "It's all right. She's my wife. She needs a black rod, is all. She has to have it. It's like a medicine or drug to her. She has to have it. I'll pay you. It's all on the level, no trick involved. Interested?"

The work was returned to the library after the United States Supreme Court ruled in *Board of Education, Island Trees Union Free School District No. 26 et al. v. Pico et al., 457 U.S. 853 (1982)* that the First Amendment rights of students had been violated in the banning.

## FURTHER READINGS

Burress, Lee. *Battle of the Books: Literary Censorship in the Public Schools, 1950–1985.* Metuchen, N.J.: Scarecrow Press, 1989.

Cummins, Eric. *The Rise and Fall of the California Radical Prison Movement*. New York: Oxford University Press, 1995.

Haskins, James. *Profiles in Black Power*. Garden City, N.Y.: Doubleday & Company, 1972.

Lockwood, Lee. *Conversation with Eldridge Cleaver: Algiers*. New York: McGraw-Hill, 1970.

*Newsletter on Intellectual Freedom* (May 1975): 87; (July 1979): 75; (November 1982): 197.

Waldrep, Shelton. "Being Bridges: Cleaver, Baldwin and Lorde and African-American Sexism and Sexuality." *Journal of Homosexuality* 26 (1993): 167–180.

# STEPPENWOLF

**Author:**   Hermann Hesse
**Original date and place of publication:**   1927, Germany; 1929, England; 1929, United States
**Original publisher:**   S. Fischer Verlag (Germany); Secker (England); Holt (United States)
**Type:**   Novel

## SUMMARY

*Steppenwolf* begins with a preface narrated by a young businessman who claims to have edited a sheaf of notes left several years before by a lodger in the attic room of his aunt's home. The notes relate the strange adventures of Harry Haller, the eccentric lodger, who refers to himself as a wolf of the steppes, or the Steppenwolf. The preface recounts the narrator's few meetings with Haller—on the stairs in the house, at a concert, in a tavern or at a lecture. He decides to publish the manuscript, subtitled "For Madmen Only," even though he does not know if Haller's account is fact or fiction.

"For Madmen Only" begins as Haller takes a walk at dusk. He follows a flickering sign to a door in a church wall; the door leads into an imaginary world and a peddler who carries a placard that advertises "Magic Theater—Entrance Not for Everybody." Before vanishing, the peddler hands Harry a pamphlet entitled "Treatise on the Steppenwolf." Back in his room, Harry reads the pamphlet and learns that it contains a psychological portrait of men like him, analyzing them as two selves in conflict—half man and half wolf. The pamphlet explains the role in middle-class society of the Steppenwolves, the artists and intellectuals, as well as the role of the geniuses who break free and become the Immortals, those above ordinary social rules. Harry recognizes that he has hundreds of selves, and the pamphlet assures him that he may one day see himself in the magic mirrors of the Immortals or learn in one of their magic theaters what he needs to free his soul.

After reading the treatise, Harry realizes his loneliness. He begins a nightly search, eventually finding again the peddler who leads him to a seedy tavern where he meets a sensuous bar girl named Hermine, the prostitute Maria and the androgynous jazz musician Pablo. Through Hermine, Harry learns to dance and to enjoy sex and the night life of the city. He also enjoys the pleasures of various drugs, including cocaine and opium, supplied by Pablo who "was a master in mixing and prescribing them." Hermine, who "cast the spell of the hermaphrodite," also hints of sensuous nights spent with Maria and tells Harry of having seduced a woman at the masked ball "with the spell of Lesbos." Pablo invites Harry into the Magic Theater, where he experiences a series of surreal adventures and learns that he is condemned to continue living. As the manuscript ends, Harry resolves to go on confronting his inner self and to work toward becoming one of the Immortals.

## CENSORSHIP HISTORY

*Steppenwolf*, the most autobiographical of all Hesse's novels, was severely criticized by critics and readers for its jazz, drugs and sexual practices and behavior, including lesbianism and androgyny. Mileck writes that German critics called the book "pornographic" upon its first publication and Hesse "a man without morals." No formal attempts to suppress the book occurred at its publication in Germany nor when it first appeared in England and in the United States, although the novel appeared on a list of books condemned by the Boston Watch and Ward Society in 1930. In 1932, an increasingly conservative populace focused attention on Hesse, who was openly accused of "wallowing in filth."

Freedman notes that in 1932 Hesse wrote to a friend, H. Zwissler, that "A young adherent of Hitler from Swabia wrote that [the book] was merely an expression of the lewd lustfulness of an aging man and that he hoped I would soon kick the bucket." In 1943 and 1944, Hitler's dictatorship made all of Hesse's books forbidden reading in Nazi Germany, some, like *Steppenwolf*, for their "lewd lustfulness," and others because he did not take a stand and publish pro-Nazi propaganda nor did he speak out against the Nazis.

The novel was accepted again in Germany after World War II ended and became a counterculture favorite in the late 1950s and the 1960s in the United States. The Beat Generation made it an urban underground classic, "a bible for all." Drug proponent Dr. Timothy Leary wrote that *Steppenwolf* was "a psychedelic journey" and offered a "heightened sensibility" that was a response to "a corrupt and menacing external 'reality.'" No formal efforts to suppress the book in the United States occurred until 1982 when the parents of several students attending Glenwood Springs (Colorado) High School demanded that the novel be removed from the high school library. In their complaint to the school board, the parents cited as the reasons references in the book to "lesbianism," "hermaphroditism," "sexual perversion," "drugs," "murder" and "insanity." A committee created by the school board reviewed the novel and voted to retain it.

## FURTHER READINGS

Freedman, Ralph. *Hermann Hesse: Pilgrim of Crisis*. New York: Pantheon Books, 1978.
Leary, Timothy, and Ralph Metzner. "Hermann Hesse: Poet of the Interior Journey." *Psychedelic Review* 1 (1963): 167–182.
Mileck, Joseph. *Hermann Hesse: Life and Art*. Berkeley: University of California Press, 1978.
*Newsletter on Intellectual Freedom* (September 1982): 169.

## STRANGE FRUIT

**Author:** Lillian Smith
**Original date and place of publication:** 1944, United States
**Original publisher:** Harcourt, Brace & World
**Type:** Novel

## SUMMARY

*Strange Fruit* deals with the topic of miscegenation and details a relationship between a young white college dropout, Tracy Deen, and his college-educated black girlfriend, Nonnie Anderson, who works as a servant and is carrying his child. The setting is Maxwell, Georgia, a town divided into "White Town" and "Colored Town," where marriage between the races is still against the law. The other black citizens of the town look upon the "Anderson niggers" as odd because they are all college educated, but the Andersons are tolerated because they "work hard and know their place." The white women envy Mrs. Brown for having a college-educated servant, and the white men in town desire the physically attractive young woman.

As the novel opens, the reader learns that Nonnie and Tracy have been sexually intimate since she was 14 and he was 20 and had recently dropped out of college. Nonnie's sister Bess had hoped that the doomed relationship would end when Nonnie went to Spelman College and Tracy left Maxwell to serve in the army during the war, but it continued once they were together in Maxwell. Tracy served in France and saw racially mixed couples there, but he realized that the same was impossible in his hometown. Nonnie clings to the hope that she and Tracy will be able to marry, but the weight of family opinion and his mother's dominance of his life are too strong for him. His minister counsels Tracy to give up Nonnie, as many white men before him have given up their "colored women," and tells Tracy that Nonnie, like other "colored women," will manage all right. He states that "most of them sooner or later get a man their color, maybe marry them. Live a fairly decent, respectable life—that is, if a nigger woman can live a decent, respectable life. . . . You have to keep pushing them back across that nigger line." Told that Nonnie is pregnant, the minister urges Tracy to "find some good nigger you can count on to marry her" and suggests that Tracy sweeten the deal with money.

Nonnie's family is not any happier with the situation. Her sister Bess wants her to have an abortion. Her brother Ed, now a government employee in Washington, returns for a vacation week and questions Nonnie's willingness to remain subservient when she has a college education and wonders why she remains in Maxwell.

Despite protestations of love, Tracy takes the minister's advice. He arranges a marriage for Nonnie with Henry McIntosh, a man who had exposed himself to her when she was 11 years old and asked her, "How about fuckin' with me?" Henry works for Tracy's parents, Dr. Tutweiler and Mrs. Alma Deen, and used to be Tracy's playmate. One night, Nonnie's brother flies into a rage and shoots Tracy to death. "White Town" blames Henry, who had flashed money only days before and bragged about a "deal" with Tracy. They lynch and burn Henry, despite the efforts of several white men to save him. The novel ends the day after the tragedy, with everything returning to its old routine, appearing on the surface that nothing had happened. One marked difference is that the black citizens of Maxwell are now more deferential than before.

## CENSORSHIP HISTORY

The novel was strongly criticized soon after publication for its references to sexual intercourse, the sexual assault of a young girl, a murder, a lynching and physical descriptions that were perceived as too frequent and designed to titillate. Moreover, the unconventional behavior of the couple unable to marry because of their racial differences and the sexually related language, including the use of the word "fuck" in two instances, also motivated significant complaint. Words like "bitch" and "whore" are common in the novel, "tail" and "teat" are each used once in reference to a woman and one description of "nice little rumps, hard from chopping cotton" is given. Also identified as obscene were the references to urination, the discussion of a rich white man's penchant for deflowering young schoolteachers because he is afraid of syphilis and the use of "coition" and "orgasm" in discussing the frigidity of white women.

In 1945, the United States Department of the Post Office declared the book unmailable in a contradictory assessment of its value. The post office lawyer who assessed the book acknowledged that it was a plea for social equality, noting that "the book aspires to fill the role of 'Uncle Tom's Cabin' in the life of the modern negro problem." Despite the social intent, the book was labeled "obscene" because "it deals with the sexual relations of a ne'er-do-well son of a respected white southern family with a mestee [sic]. Some incidents are too much detailed but the worst part is the filthy language. . . . It is obscene in that it is disgusting, repulsive, nauseating." In the report, the post office lawyer admitted that, under the standards set by the Supreme Court in the 1933 *Ulysses* case, "this book would not be held to be obscene in that the sexual scenes are merely incidental to the principal theme of the book—the social degradation of the negro in the South." Despite this acknowledgment, he found that the book was simply too strongly obscene by his own standard, so he recommended that it be excluded from the mails, even though it was sold in many states in the United States. The solicitor general of the postal department accepted the recommendation.

*Strange Fruit* was also declared obscene in 1945 in a Supreme Judicial Court of Massachusetts decision rendered by Judges Field, Qua, Ronan and Wilkins. In *Commonwealth of Massachusetts v. Isenstadt*, 318 Mass. 543 (1945), a bookseller named Abraham A. Isenstadt was charged with the possession and sale of a book that was "obscene, indecent, or impure, or manifestly tends to corrupt the morals of youth," under Massachusetts statutes. The case came about because a noted literary critic of the time, Bernard DeVoto, sought to test the statute and the concept of extralegal censorship, after *Strange Fruit* was informally banned in Massachusetts. The critic purchased the book, and the bookseller was arrested and convicted by a Massachusetts Superior Court judge without a jury. In an appeal to the Supreme Judicial Court of Massachusetts, the book was again declared "obscene" by four of the five judges presiding. Judge Qua delivered the majority opinion and accepted the work as possessing literary merit, but he noted that "obscenity may sometimes be made even more alluring and suggestive by the zeal which comes from sincerity and by the added force of artistic presentation." Rather, "a book that adversely affects a substantial proportion of its readers may well be found to lower appreciably the average moral tone of the mass."

Judge Lummus, the dissenting judge in the case, acknowledged that the book "is blemished by coarse words and scenes, none of which appear irrelevant to the plot." He stated that, rather than providing erotic allurement, "their coarseness is repellent." He declared further that the book was a serious study of race relations, "a grim tragedy" in which "virtue is not derided, neither is vice made attractive." Judge Lummus ended the dissent by observing that rather than being titillated by the book, "the reader is depressed, unable to solve a tragic problem."

## FURTHER READINGS

Grant, S. S., and S. E. Angoff. "Massachusetts Censorship." *Boston University Law Review* 10 (1946): 147.

Paul, James C. N., and Murray L. Schwartz. *Federal Censorship: Obscenity in the Mail.* Glencoe, Ill.: Free Press, 1961.

# STRANGER IN A STRANGE LAND

**Author:**  Robert Anson Heinlein
**Original date and place of publication:**  1961, United States
**Original publisher:**  G.P. Putnam's Sons
**Type:**  Science fiction novel

## SUMMARY

*Stranger in a Strange Land* relates the story of Valentine Michael Smith, conceived by adulterous lovers on the first human expedition to Mars, a three-year journey. The novel consists of five parts: His Maculate Origin, His Preposterous Heritage. His Eccentric Education, His Scandalous Career and His Happy Destiny. Orphaned soon after birth, the main character is raised by Martians in their culture and returns 25 years later to his home planet as an alien being who becomes the messiah of a new religion. The novel, which became an underground classic and campus cult favorite in the 1960s, attacks human folly under several guises, especially in the person or persons of the Establishment. The government, the military and organized religion are skewered as the author advances a religion of love aimed at revolutionizing human affairs and bringing about an apocalyptic change for the better.

The original *Envoy* expedition of four married couples makes a successful entry into the orbit of Mars, then is never again heard from. World War III prevents an immediate search of space, and 25 years pass before another manned expedition is sent to Mars. When it arrives, the crew finds that Mars is inhabited and that only one survivor of the *Envoy* remains, Valentine Michael Smith. The government views the survivor as "a treasure trove of information" and hopes to study him, but the young man's body must first become acclimated to the increased pull of gravity and changed air pressure. The doctors soon learn that Smith is able to slow his respiration, heartbeat and blood pressure to the point where he appears in shock. This and other observations lead the captain of the expedition to observe that "Smith is not a *man*. He is an intelligent creature with the genes and ancestry of a man, but he is not a man. He's more a Martian than a man. . . . He thinks like a Martian, he feels like a Martian." The differing influences of his human ancestry and his Martian environment form the basis for social criticism in the novel.

Dubbed "Mike," the reclaimed Earthling receives training in human social life from wealthy eccentric Jubal Harshaw and his brain trust in the Pocono Mountains in Pennsylvania. In contrast to the more usual wise adviser in literature, who guides the mythic hero in learning the good of civilization, Harshaw focuses on revealing what is wrong with the world. Mike comes to understand American culture, but from his Martian viewpoint human religion, fear of death and sexual inhibitions seem absurd.

Conversely, other humans view his Martian heritage as absurd, as he reveals his capabilities of suspended animation, astral projection, telekinesis and the ability to will objects and people out of existence. He also exhibits a capability that is even more frightening, "grokking," the total and immediate understanding of people, situations and love. A central term of the Martian language, "to grok" signifies the ability to know in a holistic way that includes intellect and intuition, a knowledge that is as absolute, unambiguous and instant as a god's or an angel's knowledge. Mike can also read minds and change his body shape, but many are more disturbed by his revelation that Martians practice ritual cannibalism.

As Mike becomes comfortable in his new home, he discovers money as an idea, a symbolic structure. He also gains a following as the leader of a new cult, the Church of All Worlds. Water-sharing rituals and guilt-free sexuality characterize the new religion, as does instruction in the psycholinguistic powers and perceptions of Martians. The importance of water sharing and the concept of the "water brothers," both male and female, emerge from the importance of water on a dry planet where its sharing is an intimate ritual between those who seek to grow so intimate that their "eggs share the same nest."

Sexual promiscuity is the norm, marriage is irrelevant and promiscuous group sex is among the religion's ceremonies. Mike fathers several children among his followers, as does his mentor, Jubal, the man whom he calls "Father." After several years, a mob burns down the cult's temple, but Mike, Jubal and their followers escape, only to be threatened again by another mob. In an effort to calm the mob, Mike strips himself and offers himself up to the crowd, which martyrs him by stoning him to death. In their acceptance of his "discorporation," Jubal and the followers make a broth of Mike's body and "share it and grok together. . . . Slowly they drank the broth, stretching it out, savoring it, praising and cherishing it and grokking their donor." The novel ends as the followers join Jubal in planning ways of profiting from Mike's death, from creating a public shrine where he died to writing a stereoplay about his life.

## CENSORSHIP HISTORY

*Stranger in a Strange Land* has an unusual case history. The novel did not sell well when it was first published, but it collected a Hugo, the award for best science fiction novel of the year, and a short time later became a campus bestseller. When Heinlein delivered the original manuscript to editors in 1960, it contained 220,000 words. Editors at G.P. Putnam's Sons asked him to cut the size of the novel by one-fourth and to remove sexual scenes that they considered offensive to public tastes of the time. The novel was published with these changes and remained in print in that form for 28 years. When Heinlein died in 1988, his widow took advantage of the 1976 Copyright Law that stated all old contracts were canceled when a surviving widow or widower renewed the copyright of a spouse's work. Renewing the copyright for *Stranger in a Strange Land* in 1989, Virginia Heinlein obtained the original typescript that her husband had placed on file at the University of California at Santa Cruz, then negotiated a contract with Putnam's to have all 220,000 original words published in a restored version of the novel.

The novel has long been characterized as appealing to unbalanced minds, and the unrestrained sexual activities of the Church of All Worlds, as well as the emphasis upon commune life, were at first responsible for its exclusion from most school reading lists. Its later infamous association with Charles Manson resulted in its exclusion from both school lists and school libraries during the 1970s and 1980s, an action automatically taken by teachers and administrators to prevent what were viewed as inevitable challenges. Lee Burress recorded only one challenge to the book in which a teacher in an unnamed Pennsylvania school district in 1977 objected to the nudity and the inferences that could be drawn from the word "grok," as well as to the sexual references that appear in the last quarter of the book, when the cult leader Mike begins to take advantage of his positions.

The book achieved unwanted notoriety during the trial of Manson, who with his "family" of followers perpetrated the vicious Tate-La Bianca murders in 1969. Manson claimed that the book, along with the Beatles' song "Helter Skelter," formed the cornerstone of his religion of love and hate. Biographer Ed Sanders wrote in 1971 that Manson borrowed a lot of the book's terminology and ideas and identified with the character of Valentine Michael Smith, so much so that he named the first child born to one of his followers Valentine Michael Manson. Other aspects of the Manson family were borrowed from the novel, including the water-sharing ceremony. The "water brother" rituals, as well as the sexual sharing of followers, attracted the attention of other fringe groups who claimed to use *Stranger in a Strange Land* and other Heinlein books as their sacred texts.

## FURTHER READINGS

Aldiss, Brian W. *Billion Year Spree: The True History of Science Fiction*. Garden City, N.Y.: Doubleday & Company, 1973.

Franklin, Howard Bruce. *Robert A. Heinlein: America as Science Fiction*. New York: Oxford University Press, 1980.

Olander, Joseph D., and Martin Harry Greenberg. *Robert A. Heinlein*. New York: Taplinger Publishing, 1978.

Samuelson, David W. "Stranger in the Mirror: Model or Mirror?" In *Critical Encounters: Writers and Themes in Science Fiction*, 144–175. Ed. by Dick Riley. New York: Frederick Ungar, 1978.

Sanders, Ed. *The Family: The Story of Charles Manson's Dune Buggy Attack Battalion*. New York: Berkeley Books, 1971.

Slusser, George Edgar. *Robert A. Heinlein: Stranger in His Own Land*. San Bernardino, Calif.: Borgo Press, 1976.

# THE SUN ALSO RISES

**Author:** Ernest Hemingway
**Original date and place of publication:** 1926, United States
**Original publisher:** Charles Scribner's Sons
**Type:** Novel

## SUMMARY

*The Sun Also Rises* created a sensation when it first appeared, because it was the first novel to depict the lives of American expatriates in Paris in the 1920s. It was viewed as a statement of the "lost generation," expressing the disillusionment and the hedonistic attitude brought on by World War I. Young Americans imitated its dialogue, and the novel started a fashion trend, as young women cut their hair and adopted the clothing worn by the female protagonist, Lady Brett Ashley.

The novel is divided into three sections, narrated by Jake Barnes, an American correspondent in Paris. Jake had suffered a severe groin wound in the war that left him sexually impotent, and this makes the love between Jake and Brett torturous because they are unable to consummate it. Thus, Brett seeks physical satisfaction with numerous men, while maintaining her emotional bond to Jake. In reality, all of Jake and Brett's friends are suffering from wounds, most of them psychological. Brett seeks happiness through romantic conquest, Princeton graduate Robert Cohn through romantic novels and others through frantic and continuous celebrating. Psychological turmoil dominates Jake's days and nights, making him an insomniac as well as emotionally unstable when "his head starts to work." Brett has her own tragedies: the death of her fiancé from dysentery during the war, a later bad marriage to acquire a title, and present plans to marry the bankrupt Mike Campbell, who drinks heavily, despite her real love for Jake.

In the second section of the novel, the action moves to Spain, where Jake and his friends go for the fiesta and bullfighting. Jake and Bill Gorton spend a few peaceful days fishing and discuss numerous serious subjects before they go to Pamplona for the running of the bulls. During this time, Brett has spent a romantic weekend with Robert Cohn, who becomes possessive of her. When Brett expresses an interest in the young bullfighter Pedro Romero, the competition becomes too much for Cohn, who fights with Jake and Mike and then beats Pedro badly. After heroically fighting the bulls the following day, Pedro runs away with Brett.

With the end of the fiesta, members of the group separate and Jake goes alone to San Sebastian. He receives a telegram from Brett, who has left Pedro and wants Jake to meet her. Pedro is only 19, and she has left him for his own good. As they drive away in a taxi, Brett tells Jake, "You know it makes one feel rather good deciding not to be a bitch." The novel ends as it began, with Jake and Brett together, locked in a hopeless love for each other.

## CENSORSHIP HISTORY

*The Sun Also Rises* was the only novel that Scribner vice president Max Perkins had ever contracted for completely unseen, and he had only the vaguest idea of its content. He was concerned about the opinion of the 72-year-old head of the publishing firm, Charles Scribner, "who was formidable on certain topics like obscenity." As editor John Wheelock reminded Perkins, "Charles Scribner would no sooner allow profanity in one of his books than he would invite friends to use his parlor as a toilet." When the manuscript was completed, the old-fashioned and gentlemanly Perkins told Scribner that three words might give the firm difficulty, but he could not bring himself to speak the words. Scribner then insisted that Perkins write them, and Perkins hesitantly wrote two of the words, "damn" and "bitch." He only wrote the third, "balls," when Scribner insisted that he do so.

In correspondence with Hemingway, Perkins asked the author to modify the language, because "it would be a pretty thing if the very significance of so original a book should be disregarded because of the howls of a lot of cheap, prurient moronic yappers." In addition to the words "damn" and "bitch," Perkins, yet unable to write the offending word, asked the author to consider reworking the statements that referred to the "bulls being without appendages." He also expressed concern about Hemingway's comic passage in which Bill Gorton and Jake speak of a purported accident on a bicycle or tricycle, which left Henry James permanently injured and impotent, as Jake explains his own war wound. Perkins protested because the matter "is peculiarly a personal one" that the publisher would not dare to include had James been alive and that seemed even more tasteless since James was now dead. In the final version, the story remains but just the name "Henry" is used, to which Bill adds he "was a good writer."

Hemingway claimed to have eliminated as many potentially offensive words as possible, but he retained the phrase, "Tell him the bulls have no balls," that Mike Campbell shouts four times in two pages. Although the publisher did not feel comfortable with the work as it stood, the firm hesitated to turn down the novel because "young writers, who were the future of the firm, would avoid them for their conservative position." After the novel was published, reviewers labeled it "a dirty book." Hemingway's mother wrote him and asked him if he was happy now that he had published "one of the filthiest books of the year" and stated that he must know other words besides "damn" and "bitch." In 1927, the Watch and Ward Society of Boston added the novel to its list of "obscene" books and requested that booksellers agree not to advertise or to sell the book. (See ELMER GANTRY.) In 1953, the novel was banned in Ireland for the "dissipated lives" of its characters, as well as for "profanity."

In 1960, parents of students in the San Jose, California, school district asked the school board to remove the novel from the class curriculum. They expressed concern with the "personal nature of the one character's [Jake's] wound," as well as the "profanity." The school board banned the novel from the schools. That same year, the Riverside, California, school board withdrew all of Hemingway's works from the school libraries after receiving repeated parent complaints regarding the "obscenities" and "sexual situations" in the books.

In a 1977 national survey of high school librarians and English department chairpersons, Lee Burress reported one challenge by a parent in Virginia who requested that the novel be removed from the recommended reading list. The parent claimed that the characters were "too flagrant" in behavior and that their language was "too explicit." After a review committee considered the parent's complaint, the book was removed from the recommended reading list. Burress also reported in a 1982 national survey of librarians that a parent in Indiana challenged the assignment of the book in the classroom because of the "obscene" language. The school board reviewed the book and removed the material from the classroom.

## FURTHER READINGS

Baker, Carlos. *Hemingway: A Life Story*. New York: Charles Scribner's Sons, 1969.

Burress, Lee. *Battle of the Books: Literary Censorship in the Public Schools, 1950–1985*. Metuchen, N.J.: Scarecrow Press, 1989.

Djos, Matt. "Alcoholism in Ernest Hemingway's *The Sun Also Rises*: A Wine and Roses Perspective on the Lost Generation." *Hemingway Review* 14 (Spring 1995): 64–78.

Elliott, Ira. "Performance Art: Jake Barnes and 'Masculine' Signification in *The Sun Also Rises*." *American Literature* 67 (March 1995): 77–94.

Meyers, Jeffrey. *Hemingway: A Biography*. New York: Harper & Row, 1985.

Pinsker, Sanford. "Individual Authors: A Rotten Way to Be Wounded." *Journal of Modern Literature* 18 (Spring 1993): 277–278.

Reynolds, Michael. *Hemingway: The American Homecoming*. Cambridge, Mass.: Blackwell Publishers, 1992.

Rudat, Wolfgang. "Sexual Dilemma in *The Sun Also Rises*: Hemingway's Count and the Education of Jacob Barnes." *Hemingway Review* 8 (Spring 1989): 2–13.

Strychacz, Thomas. "Dramatizations of Manhood in Hemingway's *In Our Time* and *The Sun Also Rises*." *American Literature* 61 (May 1989): 245–260.

Wylder, Delbert E. *Hemingway's Heroes*. Albuquerque, N.M.: University of New Mexico Press, 1969.

## TO HAVE AND HAVE NOT

**Author:** Ernest Hemingway
**Original date and place of publication:** 1937, United States
**Original publisher:** Charles Scribner's Son
**Type:** Novel

## SUMMARY

*To Have and Have Not* is Ernest Hemingway's most experimental novel and his least financially successful. The work began as two short stories about former Miami police officer Harry Morgan who runs a charter boat business between Florida and Cuba during the Depression. Hemingway added a third section to create a novel in three parts: "Harry Morgan—Spring," "Harry Morgan—Fall" and "Harry Morgan—Winter." He sought to examine economic and social status and to contrast the "haves" with the "have nots."

Harry Morgan is a tough and resourceful figure who struggles to make a living. Desperate for money, he accepts a dangerous mission to transport Chinese refugees from Cuba to Florida. With alcoholic Eddy Marshall as crew, Harry locks the refugees below deck and kills the smuggling organizer after receiving payment. He then forces the 12 men onto the beach and returns home.

The second part opens with Harry Morgan and a black crew member named Wesley suffering gunshot wounds, Harry in the arm and Wesley in the leg, while illegally transporting rum. Fearing that Customs will spot them, they pull close to shore and dump the liquor bottles. Seen by a government official on another boat, they escape temporarily. Harry loses his boat to Customs, but they cannot identify who was piloting the craft.

In part three, Harry has lost his arm after being wounded, and his boat has been taken from him. He agrees to use a borrowed boat to transport Cuban revolutionaries from Florida to Cuba after they rob a bank. The night before he leaves, he and his wife make love and she later thinks, "I could do that all night if a man was built that way." On the boat, Harry considers the Cubans' ideals and thinks "F—— the revolution" as he plans to take the money, but one shoots him. As he lies dying, he worries that his wife is "too old to peddle her hips now."

Contrasted with Harry's desperate efforts to scratch a living are the problems of other characters—a playboy writer and his adulterous wife, a Hollywood director's frustrated wife who masturbates in the night, a grain broker who cheats on his tax returns and a homosexual couple ending their relationship—tourists in Key West who are financially well off but morally and emotionally empty. Helen, the embittered wife of writer Richard Gordon, conveys their cynicism: "Love is that dirty aborting horror that you took me to. Love is my insides all messed up. It's half catheters and half whirling douches. I know about love. Love hangs up behind the bathroom door. It smells like lysol [sic]. To hell with love." Hemingway contrasts their continued survival with the defeat of the relentless individualist Harry Morgan, who is no match for a hostile social and economic environment.

## CENSORSHIP HISTORY

The first submitted draft of the novel contained material that publisher Charles Scribner's Sons told Hemingway to excise before the work could be published. In an extended section, the author had used character Tommy Bradley, husband of the sexually promiscuous Helene Bradley, as a vehicle for savaging writers that he had known. In that initial version, Hemingway spoke of Hart Crane as "an unfortunate bugger, always propositioning the wrong sailors and getting beaten up." Harry Crosby was "a silly ass," and F. Scott Fitzgerald had "jumped from youth to senility. . . . Might pull out of it yet if he wasn't so sorry for himself." Hemingway said of James Joyce that he "wrote two fine books and a very great book and went blind. You cant [sic] blame a man for going blind." The publisher was uncomfortable with the criticism of other writers and asked Hemingway to eliminate the passages or to heavily disguise the individuals. As a result of the revision, the character of Tommy Bradley does not appear and is only referred to in the novel. Another change involves the masturbation scene of Dorothy Hollis. More straightforward in the initial version, it was changed to include an awkward and convoluted soliloquy that suggests rather than states her actions.

Even with the revisions, the language and the sexual suggestiveness of the novel raised cries for censorship after publication. Labeled "obscene" is the frequent reference among the monied tourists to the promiscuous Helene Bradley as a "bitch" or a "whore." Another term that has drawn criticism is "fuck" or "fucking." Midway through the novel, Hemingway uses dashes when Harry thinks "F— — the revolution," yet in Harry's dying thoughts the word is fully spelled out: "No matter how a man alone ain't got no bloody fucking chance." In 1938, the novel was banned in Detroit, Michigan, by the local prosecutor who first ordered it removed from the Detroit Public Library. Booksellers in Detroit were also prevented from selling the book under the ban, an order that they contested. The Wayne County prosecutor had acted after receiving complaints from Catholic organizations that it was "obscene" and contained "sexual situations" that were "corruptive." Harry Schuman, a rare book dealer, and Alvin C. Hamer, a well-known Detroit bookseller, contested the order, and two years later the book was available for sale in Wayne County. The public libraries, however, placed the book on shelves containing works by "writers of standing," meant for the request of adults alone.

That same year, law enforcement authorities in the Borough of Queens, New York, forbade the sale and distribution of the novel after complaints from local Catholic organizations were received. Concerns raised over the "obscene" language and the sexual promiscuity (mostly implied) of the characters were the basis for the ban. The American Civil Liberties Union reported that *To Have and Have Not* was the only novel suppressed in the United States in 1938.

## FURTHER READINGS

Mellow, James R. *Hemingway: A Life Without Consequences.* New York: Houghton Mifflin Company, 1992.
Meyers, Jeffrey. *Hemingway: A Biography.* New York: Harper & Row, 1985.
Wylder, Delbert E. *Hemingway's Heroes.* Albuquerque, N.M.: University of New Mexico Press, 1969.

# TO KILL A MOCKINGBIRD

**Author:** (Nelle) Harper Lee
**Original date and place of publication:** 1960, New York
**Original publisher:** Lippincott and Company
**Type:** Novel

## SUMMARY

Harper Lee's only novel touched a nerve in American society when it was first published, becoming a best-seller as well as a critical success that won the Pulitzer Prize in 1961. The author claimed that her story of racial bias in the sleepy fictional Alabama town of Maycomb was pure imagination, but reporters who visited her hometown of Monroeville, Alabama, on the 30th anniversary of the book's publication found remarkable similarities to the novel in both setting and character. In essence, the racial ills chronicled in the novel appear to have been realistically drawn from the author's life.

The novel is told from the point of view of the adult Jean Louise Finch, known as Scout to her friends, who relates the events of three years, beginning with her sixth summer. With her brother Jem, four years her senior, and summer visitor Dill, modeled after a real-life summer playmate who grew up to be the writer Truman Capote, Scout devises a series of projects to make their mysterious next-door neighbor, Arthur "Boo" Radley, emerge from his house. The early chapters of the novel detail the comfortable cocoon of childhood that Scout enjoys, as she enters school, engages in fistfights with boys and shares confidences with her father, lawyer Atticus Finch.

Scout's comfortable world is shattered when her father agrees to take the unpopular defense of black laborer Tom Robinson, accused of raping white Mayella Ewell. The townspeople want Tom to die, but Atticus believes that Tom is innocent and establishes that Tom's withered left arm could not have made the bruises on the right side of Mayella's face.

As bitterness engulfs the town, Atticus must defend his client not only in court but also from a lynch mob. Atticus manages to prove that Tom is physically incapable of committing the crime, yet the jury brings in a verdict of guilty despite the revelation that Mayella had made sexual advances to Tom that he had refused out of fear for his life. In addition, townspeople are angered because Tom expresses pity for a white woman.

Atticus plans to appeal the decision, but Tom is fatally shot while trying to escape during a jail exercise period. The final chapters of the novel contain Bob Ewell's attempted revenge against Atticus for having defended Tom and the emergence of Boo Radley from his house to save Jem and Scout from Ewell's knife.

## CENSORSHIP HISTORY

Despite its strong annual sales and appearance on required reading lists in numerous high schools throughout the United States, *To Kill a Mockingbird* has frequently been challenged by parents and groups who object to either the language or the way in which race is represented. The Committee on Intellectual Freedom of the American Library Association lists the novel as being among the 10 most frequently challenged books today. In 1977, Eden Valley (Minnesota) School District temporarily banned the book because the words "damn" and "whore lady" appeared in the text, and parents in Vernon-Verona-Sherill (New York) School District challenged the book in 1980 as being a "filthy, trashy novel." Black parents in Warren Township (Indiana) schools charged in 1981 that passages in the book that portrayed the submissive behavior of Tom Robinson, Calpurnia and other blacks, and the frequent use of the word "nigger" advocated institutionalized racism and were harmful to the integration process. Despite their vehement efforts, the attempt to censor the book was unsuccessful. As a result, three black parents resigned in protest from the town's human relations advisory council.

The novel was also challenged in 1984 in the Waukegan, Illinois, schools for inclusion of the word "nigger," and in 1985 Park Hill (Missouri) Junior High School parents challenged the novel because it contained racial slurs and offensive language. The most recent attempt to ban the novel occurred in 1985 in Casa Grande (Arizona) Elementary School District, where black parents and the National Association for the Advancement of Colored People protested that the book was unfit for use in the junior high school. School officials there changed the status of the book from required reading to retention on a supplemental reading list.

## FURTHER READINGS

"Another Furor over Books." *Ohio State University Monthly* 55 (December 1963): 8–12.

Bruell, Edwin. "Keen Scalpel on Racial Ills." *English Journal* 53 (December 1964): 658–661.

Dave, R. A. "*To Kill a Mockingbird*: Harper Lee's Tragic Vision." In *Indian Studies in American Literature*. Ed. by M. K. Naik, S. K. Desai and S. Mokashi, 311–323. Dharwar, India: Karnatak University, 1974.

May, Jill. "In Defense of *To Kill a Mockingbird*." In *Censored Books: Critical Viewpoints*. Ed. by Nicholas J. Karolides, Lee Burress and John M. Kean, 476–484. Metuchen, N.J.: Scarecrow Press, 1993.

*Newsletter on Intellectual Freedom* (March 1966): 16; (March 1968): 22; (March 1978): 31; (May 1980): 62; (March 1982): 47; (July 1984): 105; (March 1986): 57–58.

Skaggs, Merrill. *The Folk of Southern Fiction*. Athens, Ga.: The University of Georgia Press, 1972.

# WELCOME TO THE MONKEY HOUSE

**Author:**   Kurt Vonnegut Jr.
**Original date and place of publication:**   1968, United States
**Original publisher:**   Delacorte Press
**Type:**   Short story collection

## SUMMARY

*Welcome to the Monkey House* consists of 25 short stories, 11 reprinted from Vonnegut's 1961 short story collection *Canary in a Cat House*. All of the stories originally appeared in such diverse publications as *The Atlantic Monthly*, *Colliers*, *Cosmopolitan*, *Ladies' Home Journal* and *Fantasy and Science Fiction Magazine* from 1950 through 1964, but the title story appeared in *Playboy* magazine the same year that the collection was released.

Many of the 25 stories have as their setting Hyannis Port, Massachusetts, where the Kennedy family has long had its compound, and Vonnegut weaves the Kennedy name throughout many of the stories. The settings vary from the present to hundreds of years into the future, but all offer perceptive criticism of contemporary ills. "Welcome to the Monkey House" is the only story singled out for criticism regarding language and sexual situations, but the entire collection has been removed where such cases have occurred.

The story is set in Cape Cod, Massachusetts, and its environs, in an unspecified future in which anti-aging shots make everyone appear no older than 22 and the earth is overpopulated with 17 billion people. The World Government has launched a two-pronged attack on the problem by encouraging "compulsory ethical birth control" and "ethical suicide." Everyone must take the "ethical birth control pill" three times daily. It is the only legal form of birth control and does not interfere with a person's ability to reproduce, "which would have been unnatural and immoral," but it does "take every bit of pleasure out of the sex act." The pills make people numb from the waist down, and they are so effective that you could "blindfold a man who had taken one, tell him to recite the Gettysburg Address, kick him in the balls while he was doing it, and he wouldn't miss a syllable."

The pills were invented by J. Edgar Nation, a pharmacist from Grand Rapids, Michigan, who created them to "introduce morality into the monkey house at the Grand Rapids Zoo." After he and his 11 children went to the zoo one Easter day and saw a monkey "playing with his private parts," he rushed home "to make a pill that would make monkeys in the springtime fit things for a Christian to see." The World Government adopted his discovery after the United Nations announced a population crisis and scientists stated that people had to stop reproducing while moralists declared that society would collapse if people used sex for nothing but pleasure. The pill was the solution. "Thus did science and morals go hand in hand."

The Federal Ethical Suicide Parlors are run by Ethical Suicide Service (ESS) hostesses, all of whom are six feet tall or more, seductively made up and dressed, "plump and rosy," skilled in judo and karate, and virgins. They prepare their clients for death by providing pleasant conversation and a last meal before administering the fatal shot with a hypodermic needle.

"Nothingheads," rebels who refuse to take the ethical birth control pills, threaten society. They are "bombed out of their skulls with the sex madness that came from taking nothing." The most notorious nothinghead is Billy the Poet, who specializes in deflowering the hostesses of suicide parlors. He usually sends his potential victims "dirty poems" far in advance, then abducts them, forces them to wait the eight hours until their pills wear off and "deflowers them with a clinical skill." Afterward, they are "grateful" and join the growing nothingheads movement. After raping Nancy, a 63-year-old virgin ESS hostess, Billy reads a passage from Elizabeth Barrett Browning's *Sonnets from the Portuguese* to her, tells her that lawmakers throughout history "have been absolutely disgusted and terrified by the natural sexuality of common men and women" and gives her a bottle of pills to be taken monthly to prevent pregnancy. The label on the bottle states: "WELCOME TO THE MONKEY HOUSE."

## CENSORSHIP HISTORY

In 1970, Marilyn Parducci, a teacher in Montgomery, Alabama, was dismissed for assigning the title story of the collection to her 11th-grade English class. Three high school juniors of the teacher's 90 students asked to be excused from reading the story, and their parents complained about "vulgarities" and a reference to rape in the story. Objectors stated that the references to the monkey "playing with his private parts" and the phrase "kick him in the balls" were "vulgar." They also objected to lines in two of Billy's poems: "A-goosing statues in the dark," "And when I peed, I peed turquoise" and "Mourn my pecker, purple daughter." The high school principal and the associate school superintendent called the book "literary garbage" and chastised Parducci for teaching a book that promoted "the killing off of elderly people and free sex." Parducci brought suit against the school district in *Parducci v. Rutland*, 316 F. Supp. 352 (M.D. Ala 1970) asking reinstatement and financial remuneration. In rendering his decision, Judge Frank Johnson observed that, despite the "vulgar terms," the story could be considered an appropriate assignment when judged in the larger literary context. He noted that the words objected to were

> less ribald than those found in many of Shakespeare's plays. The reference in the story to an act of sexual intercourse is no more descriptive than the rape scene in Pope's 'Rape of the Lock.' . . . It appears to the Court, moreover, that the author, rather than advocating the 'killing off of old people,' satirizes the practice to symbolize the increasing depersonalization of man in society.

The presiding judge stated further, "that teachers are entitled to first amendment freedoms is an issue no longer in dispute" and such freedom of expression should only be restricted if evidence exists that school activities would be disrupted. Because only three students had requested to be excused from the assignment, the judge determined that no disruption of the school schedule had occurred and ruled in favor of the teacher, who was reinstated in her teaching position.

In 1977, a parent in Bloomington, Minnesota, perused the books in the junior high school library and discovered three that contained "sexually explicit language." The parent complained to the school board, indicating that he had been concerned for a while about the materials used in the school "but when this came out, I really became uncoiled." The offending books were *Welcome to the Monkey House* and the two-volume science fiction story collection *Again, Dangerous Vision*, edited by Harlan Ellison. The parent raised objections to use of the words "balls," "peed" and "pecker" and noted that the word "fucking" was used in two instances as an adjective. The school superintendent stated his own dissatisfaction over "the fact that the obscene books were purchased and made available to students." He explained that the books were supplementary and had not been ordered through the normal purchase authorization channels, so he had not had the power of veto in advance. Although the superintendent promised that steps would be taken to prevent a reoccurrence, the parent removed his seven children from the Bloomington schools.

## FURTHER READINGS

Allen, William Rodney. *Understanding Kurt Vonnegut*. Columbia, S.C.: University of South Carolina Press, 1990.

Hipkiss, Robert A. *The American Absurd: Pynchon, Vonnegut, and Barth*. Port Washington, N.Y.: Associated Faculty Press, 1984.

*Newsletter on Intellectual Freedom* (January 1970): 28; (March 1977): 37.

O'Neil, Robert M. *Classrooms in the Crossfire*. Bloomington, Ind.: Indiana University Press, 1981.

# THE WELL OF LONELINESS

**Author:** Radclyffe Hall (Marguerite Radclyffe-Hall)
**Original date and place of publication:** 1928, England
**Original publisher:** Jonathan Cape
**Type:** Novel

## SUMMARY

*The Well of Loneliness* was the first novel to openly portray a lesbian relationship and, despite an introduction by Havelock Ellis, who characterized the work as possessing "a notable psychological and sociological significance," it shocked readers. The main character of the novel is Stephen Gordon, a young woman of wealthy parents who strongly desire a son and raise their daughter to become the son that they lack. She mimics her father in every aspect of her life, from mannerisms, abilities and tastes through possessing a boyish figure that fails to develop significantly as she grows older. At the age of eight, she develops an intense crush on the housemaid. As she grows older, Stephen refuses to wear stereotyped feminine clothing or to take part in feminine activities. She also refuses to become romantically involved with male suitors.

When she turns 20, Stephen's infatuation with the American wife of a new neighbor leads to her downfall. Although the other woman, a former chorus girl, flirts, teases and accepts several expensive gifts and passionate letters, she stops short at physical involvement beyond kisses with Stephen who becomes furious that she has been led on. To avoid accusations, the former chorus girl tells her husband about Stephen's infatuation and shows him the letters that he, in turn, hands over to Stephen's mother. The mother's reaction is swift, and Stephen is driven out of her home.

Stephen travels to London and Paris, where she meets other lesbians whose company she avoids because she is eager to be taken for "normal." The start of World War I provides her with the chance to enjoy the excitement of driving for the ambulance unit, and she also finds romance with a female coworker. Their feelings remain sublimated for a long while, during which Stephen dashingly protects her love, Mary Llewellyn, as the two drive their assigned ambulance through the battlefields. The valorous Stephen leaves the war with a scar on her right cheek, where a shell splinter had cut it open.

After the war ends, Stephen and Mary set up a household in Paris, and the two vow to remain together, but neither is comfortable with her existence. They shun the bohemian lifestyle of the homosexual community, and they are in turn shunned by conventional society. More sensitive to social criticism, Mary has difficulty living life as an outsider. When an old suitor of Stephen appears and Mary seems to reciprocate the man's show of love, Stephen decides to release her from all promises. Knowing that Mary will remain true to her earlier vow, Stephen decides to force Mary to leave to give her the chance for a normal life, and she pretends to have an affair with the notorious lesbian party hostess, Valerie Seymour. Disillusioned, Mary leaves with her male love to start a new life and Stephen is left alone and suffering with only her dog David for company.

## CENSORSHIP HISTORY

The novel achieved notoriety soon after publication when James Douglas, the book reviewer for the *London Sunday Express*, condemned strongly the theme of a lesbian emotional relationship. Douglas railed against the "hideous and loathsome vices" that he felt existed in this story of "female inverts" and claimed that he "would rather place a vial of prussic acid into the hands of a healthy boy or girl than to place the vile and hateful book into a child's hand."

The passages that so disturbed the reviewer and others later are those that recount Stephen's physical affection with other women, although none of these passages contains graphic sexual activity. Early in the novel, Stephen greets with a kiss the married woman with whom she has become infatuated and to whom she gives an expensive pearl ring. In a room in which they stand lighted only by the fireplace, Stephen's "strong but unhappy arms went round her . . . and Stephen spoke such words as a lover will speak when his heart is burdened to breaking. . . . she spoke such words as lovers have spoken ever since the divine, sweet madness of God flung the thought of love into Creation." Later in the novel, when Stephen returns from war to begin her life with Mary, several passages describe their passionate kisses and expressions of love, but only one line in the novel suggests sexual activity. After Mary declares that she belongs entirely to Stephen, the reader learns " . . . and that night they were not divided." These passages outraged censors and fueled discussion regarding the immorality of the novel.

Faced with growing controversy, the publishers first printed an expurgated version of the book, then offered to withdraw it entirely at the urging of the home secretary Sir William Joynson-Hicks, despite protests by the author and her supporters. In late 1928, Pegasus Press in Paris prepared an unexpurgated version of the novel, but the first shipment of books was seized by British Customs and, using the Obscene Publications Act of 1857, the home secretary ordered that the books be destroyed.

At the trial held on November 9, 1929, the presiding magistrate, Sir Charles Biron, refused to hear the testimony of numerous expert witnesses who asked to speak on behalf of Hall and her book. In rendering his decision that the book be destroyed, Biron condemned the novel for glorifying "unnatural tendencies" rather than condemning lesbianism. He voiced particular displeasure that the relationship between the women in the novel was marked by "extraordinary rest, contentment and pleasure." Hall's defense counsel, Lord Birkett of Ulverston, claimed that the judge refused to let the author testify in her own defense. In defending the book Birkett stated that he could find little of concern in the novel and "I may add that I had to read that book several times before I could discover the alleged obscenity." Despite support from many doctors, psychiatrists and authors, an appeal heard in Quarter Sessions the following year upheld the decision and copies of the novel were burned. The book was banned in England until 1949.

The novel was originally supposed to be published in 1928 by Knopf in New York at the same time as its English publication. The furor in England convinced Knopf to end their plans, but Covici-Friede published it instead. Based on the counsel of attorney Morris Ernst, Donald Friede decided to take the offensive regarding the possible controversy. He called John Sumner, the head of the New York Society for the Suppression of Vice, told him that the book would be distributed and invited him to buy an advance copy from the publisher rather than to arrest a bookstore clerk later. Sumner did so, then returned a month later with his aides, confiscated the publisher's entire stock of the novel and arrested Friede. *The Well of Loneliness* promptly became the subject of a court case in *People v. Friede, 233 N.Y.S. 565 (1929)*, under which the defendants were charged with the possession and sale of an obscene book. The New York Society for the Suppression of Vice spearheaded the effort to ban publication of the book.

Magistrate Bushell declared in his decision that the novel portrayed the story of a "female invert" whose "sex experiences are set forth in some detail and also her visits to various resorts frequented by male and female inverts. . . . The unnatural and depraved relationships portrayed are sought to be idealized and extolled." He characterized the novel as "antisocial and offensive to public morals and decency" and noted that it sought to justify and idealize these ideas in a way that "is strongly calculated to corrupt and debase those members of the community who would be susceptible to its immoral influence."

Numerous well-known authors condemned the censorship and wrote or sent telegrams to the court. Sinclair Lewis wired that he viewed the novel as being "almost lugubriously moral," while Edna St. Vincent Millay's husband, Eugene Boissevain, wired the following: "Will not some Christian teach Mr. Sumner to abuse himself instead of us and thus get rid of all this public nuisance?" Calling upon the power of the Hicklin Statute, which allowed that if certain passages are judged obscene the work might also be judged obscene, Bushell determined that the novel "tends to debauch public morals" and "that it is calculated to deprave and corrupt minds open to its immoral influences and who might come into contact with it." He concluded that *The Well of Loneliness* was in violation of the statute.

## FURTHER READINGS

Brittain, Vera. *Radclyffe Hall: A Case of Obscenity?* New York: A.S. Barnes, 1969.

Dickson, Lovat. *Radclyffe Hall at the Well of Loneliness: A Sapphic Chronicle.* New York: Charles Scribner's Sons, 1975.

Faderman, Lillian. *Surpassing the Love of Men.* New York: William Morrow and Company, 1981.

Foster, Jeannette H. *Sex Variant Women in Literature.* Tallahassee, Fla.: The Naiad Press, 1985.

Hyde, H. Montgomery. *Lord Justice: The Life and Times of Lord Birkett of Ulverston.* New York: Random House, 1964.

Katz, Jonathan Ned. *Gay American History: Lesbians and Gay Men in the U.S.A.* Rev. ed. New York: Penguin Books, 1992.

Kendrick, Walter. *The Secret Museum.* New York: Viking Press, 1987.

# WORKING: PEOPLE TALK ABOUT WHAT THEY DO ALL DAY AND HOW THEY FEEL ABOUT WHAT THEY DO

**Author:**  Studs Terkel
**Original date and place of publication:**  1974, United States
**Original publisher:**  Pantheon Books
**Type:**  Collection of interviews

## SUMMARY

*Working* is a collection of interviews with people in a wide variety of occupations who reveal not only what they do but how they feel about their jobs and their lives. Terkel draws his subjects out and leads them to tell him what they hate and what they like about their jobs, their bosses and their coworkers. He interviewed such disparate individuals as a hooker, a priest, a farmer, a corporate executive, a writer, a producer, a baseball player, a hockey player, a waitress, a dentist, a supermarket box boy, a steelworker, a nun and 120 others.

In their sometimes blunt language, the workers reveal their daily humiliations and the violence of their work "to the spirit as well as to the body. In the introduction, Terkel speaks of the ulcers, accidents, nervous breakdowns and physical fights detailed by many of the people interviewed. He found that "to survive the day is triumph enough for the walking wounded among the great many of us." Although some are content with their jobs, a great number question the "work ethic" that rewards "the careless worker who turns out more that is bad rather than the careful craftsman who turns out less that is good." They complain of feeling indistinguishable from their fellow workers and unappreciated.

There are also those who find value in their work, such as Tom Patrick, the fireman who knows that he has the right job for him:

> The fuckin' world's so fucked up, the country's fucked up. But the firemen, you actually see them produce. You see them put out a fire. You see them

come out with babies in their hands. You see them give mouth-to-mouth when a guy's dying. You can't get around that shit. That's real. To me, that's what I want to be.

Terkel allows the interviews to reveal the feelings of the workers, without modifying them to serve his own purposes.

## CENSORSHIP HISTORY

*Working* has been challenged for reasons ranging from "obscene language" to the perception that it is too depressing for students, despite the fact that the book contains interviews with real workers. In a 1977 survey of a nationwide sample of English department chairpersons, Lee Burress recorded one challenge to the work by a California parent who wanted the book removed from the school library because it was "too negative" and contained "objectionable language." The request was denied. In 1978, 200 parents of students in Kettle Moraine High School in Wales, Wisconsin, signed a petition that called for the banning of *Working* because of the "obscene language" used by many of the workers and because an interview with a prostitute appeared in the book. The challenge was carefully orchestrated by a local group, but, as with many efforts to ban books, the group took great pains to disguise their organization. Teachers were aware that the parents shared an affiliation, although members of the group sat in different parts of the meeting room at board meetings called to deal with the issue. Claiming that "it takes only one paragraph to make a book obscene," parents blamed the "filth of the book" for the "drug problem" and for the words written on students' desks. A review committee appointed by the school board recommended use of the book as a supplemental reading, but alternatives were made available to students whose parents objected to the book.

In a 1982 survey of a national sample of librarians, Burress recorded one challenge by a Michigan parent who asked that the book be removed from the classroom because it contained "obscenities," but no action occurred because the parent did not follow through. That same year, parents challenged the assignment of the work in the senior vocational-technical English class in Girard, Pennsylvania. They complained that the book was "obscene" and "crude," but the school retained the book in the curriculum. In 1983, *Working* was removed from the optional reading list at South Kitsap (Washington) High School after parents complained that the interview with a prostitute demeaned marriage and "degraded the sex act." That same year, parents of seventh- and eighth-grade students in Washington (Arizona) School District demanded removal of the book from the curriculum due to its "profane language." They claimed that the book required "idealistic and sensitive youth to be burdened with despair, ugliness and hopelessness." The school board removed *Working* from the curriculum.

## FURTHER READINGS

Burress, Lee. *Battle of the Books: Literary Censorship in the Public Schools, 1950–1985.* Metuchen, N.J.: Scarecrow Press, 1989.

*Newsletter on Intellectual Freedom.* (July 1978): 89; (September 1978): 123; (July 1982): 143; (November 1983): 187; (January 1984): 10–11.

# A WORLD I NEVER MADE

**Author**   James T. Farrell
**Original date and place of publication:**   1936, United States
**Original publisher:**   Vanguard Press
**Type:**   Novel

## SUMMARY

*A World I Never Made* is the first entry and the only financially successful book in the O'Neill-O'Flaherty pentalogy, which followed Farrell's highly successful Studs Lonigan trilogy. The series is centered around a minor character from the earlier trilogy, Danny O'Neill, an intelligent, thoughtful and sensitive Irish-American youth who serves as Farrell's autobiographical persona. Set in Chicago in 1911, the novel relates the trauma suffered by the very young Danny when his working-class parents experience financial difficulty and send him to live with his widowed grandmother, Mary O'Flaherty. The move creates a conflict in the young boy, whose thoughts, values, attitudes and outlook are shaped by the differing perspectives of his working-class parents and his middle-class grandmother. For Danny, these class differences are personified by his shoe salesman uncle, Al O'Flaherty, and his teamster father, Jim O'Neill. Uncle Al places great stock in the acquisition of education and culture, but Danny's father is afraid that Al's ideas of education and culture will turn Danny into a soft "dude."

The novel deals realistically with Danny's Chicago milieu, citing Chicago landmarks and portraying Danny and a friend discussing whether the Chicago White Sox will win the pennant in 1911. Farrell also allows his characters, both the children and the adults, to freely use such terms as "shit," "fuck," "piss," "balls," "prick," "pecker" and "hard on." Unlike the earlier Studs Lonigan trilogy, this novel also contains substantial reference to emetic matter. Danny's brother Bill, described as "farting," states "I got to go and crap." Danny is aware of "the noise from the movement of Bill's bowels." In another scene, Danny's father listens to his wife "urinating into a pot."

The book also includes frankly sexual discussions between six-year-old Danny and his older brother, 11-year-old Bill. Such passages as the one that follows have been cited as "obscene":

> When Pa and Ma want a baby, they go to bed. And there is a hole in all women where they pee, and Pa puts his dick into Ma's hole.
>
> And does he pee into her, and does that make a baby? That's funny, I don't believe it. You're teasing me. God makes babies.

The family works hard and, as the novel ends, the O'Neills and the O'Flahertys enjoy temporary prosperity. Danny's uncle talks optimistically about sending him to military school after graduation from Catholic elementary school.

## CENSORSHIP HISTORY

*A World I Never Made* contains expressions and situations that Farrell's earlier novels had avoided, a difference noted by critics and readers alike. In 1936, *The New York Times* refused to sell Vanguard Press advertising space for *A World I Never Made*. The newspaper made its position clear to readers by stating that it did not object to the advertising copy that would appear. Rather, the paper refused the advertising because the publisher believed that the novel was itself "too frank."

In 1937, John Sumner and the Society for the Suppression of Vice took Vanguard Press to court, claiming that the novel was "obscene" and "pornographic," after sending a confederate named Bamberger to purchase a copy. The tone of the trial was more lighthearted than those occurring in other parts of the nation and those that had occurred in New York City in earlier decades. Before the trial began, a reporter passed a copy of the book around the courtroom to be autographed. Sumner wrote, "I thoroughly disapprove of this book" after his name. Literary scholar Carl Van Doren wrote his name beneath Sumner's and the following: "I thoroughly disapprove of John S. Sumner and his works." Van Doren joined writer Heywood Broun and literary critic Bernard DeVoto as witnesses for Farrell.

The court seemed to join in the lightheartedness. Ruling in *Bamberger v. The Vanguard Press, Inc.*, docket no. 329, as to whether or not the novel was pornography, Magistrate Henry Curran related the judgment to comparing contemporary swim apparel with what had been acceptable in an earlier age:

> I don't think this book is pornographic. I think it is photographic . . . consider the young ladies in their bathing suits nowadays, how they toil not neither do they spin, but the Gibson girl in all her glory was not arrayed like one of these. If one of those lovely creatures of the far away nineties had really appeared in one of the little forget-me-not suits of today, I fancy there would have been a commotion on the beach—and the rockers on the summer hotel piazzas would have rocked hard and long.

The case was dismissed.

In 1948, the novel was one of nine novels identified as obscene in criminal proceedings in the Court of Quarter Sessions in Philadelphia County, Pennsylvania. Indictments were brought by the state district attorney, John H. Maurer, against five booksellers who were charged with possessing and intending to sell them. The other allegedly obscene novels were James Farrell's Studs Lonigan trilogy (*Young Lonigan*, *The Young Manhood of Studs Lonigan* and *Judgment Day*), William Faulkner's *Sanctuary* and *Wild Palms*, Erskine Caldwell's *God's Little Acre*, Harold Robbins's NEVER LOVE A STRANGER and Calder Willingham's END AS A MAN. In his determination that the novels were not obscene, Judge Curtis Bok said of *A World I Never Made*:

> . . . this book is plastered with the short Saxon words of common vulgarity; they are consistent with the characters who use them and with the quality of their lives and actions that are the subject of the author's scrutiny.
>
> I am not of a mind, nor do I have the authority, to require an author to write about one kind of people and not about another, nor do I object to his effort to paint a complete picture of those whom he has chosen.

Although the book once again had been declared "not obscene" by a court, the Select Committee on Current Pornographic Materials, usually called the Gathings Committee, condemned the novel in 1953 as pornographic. Authorized by the House of Representatives to hold hearings, the committee established special commissions or licensing bureaus in some communities that informally pressured dealers to withdraw books on their blacklist. *A World I Never Made* was banned in Milwaukee, Wisconsin, and St. Cloud, Minnesota, as a result of the committee's efforts. In 1957, the U.S. Information Agency banned all of Farrell's novels from overseas libraries under its control.

## FURTHER READINGS

Blanshard, Paul. *The Right to Read*. Boston: Beacon Press, 1955.

Ernst, Morris, and Ernest Lindley. *The Censor Marches On*. New York: Doubleday, Doran, 1940.

Frohock, William M. *The Novel of Violence in America, 1920–1950*. Dallas, Tex.: Southern Methodist University Press, 1958.

Rideout, Walter. *The Radical Novel in the U.S.* New York: Hill & Wang, 1966.

# APPENDIX I

# BIOGRAPHICAL PROFILES

## ANGELOU, MAYA (1928– )

Born in St. Louis, Missouri, the author is an African-American writer, stage performer, and composer best known for her widely acclaimed authobiography, *I Know Why the Caged Bird Sings* (1970), an account of her childhood in segregated Arkansas. She has written several sequels and produced plays, screenplays, songs, musical scores and books of poetry, including *And Still I Rise* (1978), as well as a collection of meditative essays, *Wouldn't Take Nothing for My Journey Now* (1993). Critics have challenged use in the classroom of *I Know Why the Caged Bird Sings* because it describes Angelou's rape as a child, and the imagery of poems in *And Still I Rise* has led to calls for its removal from school libraries.

## BALDWIN, JAMES (1924–1987)

Born in Harlem in New York City, the author was a highly acclaimed African-American writer who made his home primarily in France, although he returned to the United States to teach and lecture. Baldwin's writing, which conveys the attitudes of blacks living in a white-dominated society, made him a vital literary voice in the 1950s and 1960s. His first novel, *Go Tell It on the Mountain* (1953), is a partially autobiographical account of his youth. This work, with *Giovanni's Room* (1956) and *Another Country* (1962), has been most frequently challenged as being "obscene" and "vulgar," although other works, including essay collections, a play and other novels that provide bitter, incisive views of American racism, have also come under attack.

## BANNERMAN, HELEN (1862–1946)

Born in Edinburgh, Scotland, Bannerman was a children's book author and illustrator who is best known for her first book, *Little Black Sambo* (1898), one of the most beloved as well as one of the most controversial books in children's literature. She wrote and illustrated 12 other books based on her experiences living in India, but the bright, unrefined illustrations, suspenseful narrative and rhythmic, repetitive sentences of the first book made it the most popular. The growth of racial consciousness in the 20th century made the book an object of harsh criticism, and critics have charged that it presents a patronizing and stereotypical view of blacks.

## BENCHLEY, PETER (1940– )

Born in New York City, Benchley became the most successful first novelist in literary history when *Jaws* stayed on the *New York Times* best-seller list for over 40 weeks. None of the author's succeeding novels achieved the same success or notoriety as *Jaws*. The sexual situations and language have made the novel a target of school censors.

## BLUME, JUDY (1938–   )

Born in Elizabeth, New Jersey, the author writes romantic books for young people and has earned a reputation for dealing candidly with problems of early adolescence that traditional children's literature ignores. Most of her 22 books have ignited challenges as to their appropriateness for school libraries and classrooms due to their language, religious references and sexual content. *Then Again, Maybe I Won't* (1971), *Blubber* (1974) and *Forever* (1975) have been the most frequent objects of challenges.

## BRADBURY, RAY (1920–   )

Born in Waukegan, Illinois, the author writes science fiction and fantasy and began his career by submitting stories to pulp magazines in the 1940s. Bradbury's works, several of which have been adapted for motion pictures, often comment on the dehumanizing influence of a machine-dominated society, and he is recognized as an innovator in that genre. He has also written stage and screen plays, verse and children's literature. His principal theme is the disruptive nature of imagination, and his most frequently challenged book, *Fahrenheit 451* (1953), is ironically a condemnation of censorship.

## BROWN, CLAUDE (1937–   )

Born in New York City, the African-American writer and lecturer presents a realistic portrayal of ghetto life and searing social criticism in his work. The autobiographical *Manchild in the Promised Land* (1965) is candid in its descriptions of the physical and psychological brutalities suffered by Brown in his Harlem boyhood, characteristics that have led many parents to demand removal of the novel from school libraries and classrooms. *The Children of Ham* (1976) is even grimmer, but it has received less attention.

## BURGESS, ANTHONY (1917–93)

Born John Anthony Burgess Wilson in Manchester, England, the versatile English author, who also published under his birth name and the name Joseph Kell, was an essayist, linguist, translator, musician and comic novelist who wrote contemporary fiction as well as critical studies and several important works in the field of linguistics. He is perhaps best known for his futuristic novel *A Clockwork Orange* (1962), a terrifying view of a violence-ridden world that has motivated parent and school board challenges.

## BURROUGHS, WILLIAM SEWARD (1914–1997)

Born in St. Louis, Missouri, into affluence as the grandson of the founder of the Burroughs Adding Machine Company, the novelist achieved distinction for his irreverent themes, related in a multiple-perspective, prismatic, stream-of-consciousness style. Both his first novel, *Junky* (1953), published under the pseudonym William Lee, and his second novel, *The Naked Lunch* (1959), are based on his experiences as a drug addict, and they alone among his works have received sufficient popular attention to motivate legal challenges for their content.

## CARROLL, LEWIS (1832–1898)

Born Charles Lutwidge Dodgson in Daresbury, Cheshire, England, the mathematician, logician and author is best known for his creation of the fantasy *Alice's Adventures in Wonderland*. He also published several mathematical treatises under his real name, in addition to works for children written under his pseudonym. Although widely accepted as a classic, *Alice* has had detractors who object to Alice's freedom and to the fantasy of the work.

## CHAPMAN, ROBERT L. (1920– )

Born in Huntington, West Virginia, the author has been a college English professor and served as the supervising editor on *Funk & Wagnall's Standard College Dictionary* (1963) and *The Hold Intermediate Dictionary of American English* (1966). He has also been the editor of *The New Dictionary of Slang* (1986) and the *New Dictionary of American Slang* (1987), which has been challenged in numerous schools due to the "obscene" nature of many of its entries.

## CHAUCER, GEOFFREY (1363?–1400)

Born the son of a prosperous wine merchant in London, England, the author is believed to have been a courtier and civil servant to the courts of Edward III and Richard II, as well as to have studied law at the Inns of Court. Best known for *The Canterbury Tales*, Chaucer is also credited with translations and adaptations of religious, political and philosophical works and poetry. The *Tales* contain bawdy language and imagery, and "The Miller's

Tale" has been declared "obscene" by contemporary standards and has been the subject of challenges.

## CHILDRESS, ALICE (1920–1994)

Born in South Carolina and raised in Harlem, Childress was first a playwright whose plays are saturated with alienated poor people. Her first novel, *A Hero Ain't Nothin' but a Sandwich*, also portrays African Americans who struggle to survive in a basically insensitive and unfriendly world. Unlike her later novels, which include *A Short Walk* (1979), *Rainbow Jordan* (1981) and *These Other People* (1990), *A Hero* . . . warned that black youth were threatened by drugs. The discussion of drugs and the street language have made this novel a target of censors.

## CLARK, WALTER VAN TILBURG (1909–1971)

Born in East Orlando, Maine, but raised in Nevada cattle country, the author was a college English professor and writer of prose fiction. His best-known work, *The Ox-Bow Incident* (1940), is set in 1885 in Nevada and presents a perceptive analysis of mob violence. The psychological realism of the novel and the brutality of the men's language and actions have led to removal of the novel from school curricula.

## CLEAVER, ELDRIDGE (1935– )

Born Leroy Eldridge Cleaver near Little Rock, Arkansas, the author is an African-American activist who presented a vivid, personal view of black experience in a white society in *Soul on Ice* (1968), a collection of essays and letters written in California's Folsom Prison. His later work, *Soul on Fire* (1978), describes is disillusionment with radical politics and governments, and his spiritual rebirth as a Christian, a topic upon which he now lectures. *Soul on Ice* has been challenged because of its raw language and graphic descriptions of violence, including rape.

## CORMIER, ROBERT (1925– )

Born in Leominster, Massachusetts, the author wrote three novels for adults before turning his talents to fiction for adolescents. Focusing in his novels on the relationship between good and evil and the abuse of authority, Cormier writes novels such as *The Chocolate War* (1974) that are disturbing in their realism. Reviewers, educators and parents have challenged the suitability of the novel for adolescents and have made numerous attempts to ban it from high school and public libraries.

## DAHL, ROALD (1916–1990)

Born in Llandaff, Wales, the author was widely known for both his children's books and his short stories for adults, which he wrote almost exclusively during the 1940s and 1950s, winning three Edgar Allan Poe Awards (1954, 1959, 1980). Dahl's success in children's literature began in 1961 with *James and the Giant Peach*, followed, most notably, by *Charlie and the Chocolate Factory* (1964). Dahl's fiction for children is fast-paced and usually contains a theme of harsh punishment, often death, for adult characters who meddle in the lives of his young protagonists, a factor that has led to challenges.

## DICKEY, JAMES LAFAYETTE (1923–1997)

Born in Atlanta, Georgia, the author was a major American poet who is probably best known for his novel *Deliverance* (1970), the story of four city-bred men who take a raft trip down a wild Southern river only to encounter savagery and death. Dickey used his experiences in World War II and Korea as a bomber pilot to inform some of his best poems and the themes that are prominent in his poetry—the war, family, nature—appear in his novels. From 1966 to 1968, Dickey was consultant in poetry to the Library of Congress.

## DOYLE, SIR ARTHUR CONAN (1859–1930)

Born in Edinburgh, Scotland, the British novelist and physician introduced the world's most famous fictional detective, Sherlock Holmes, in *A Study in Scarlet* (1887), later followed by four novels and 56 stories. Doyle had an inquiring mind that took an interest in history, science and technology; one of his tales foresaw the use of the submarine in World War I. He later became deeply involved in the study of spiritualism. Doyle did not want to be remembered for his detective stories but for what he viewed as his more notable work, the historical novels. He also wrote other tales of mystery and adventure, including science fiction novels and *History of Spiritualism*.

## DREISER, THEODORE (1871–1945)

Born in Terre Haute, Indiana, the American journalist, magazine editor, playwright and prolific novelist pioneered the literary movement known as naturalism. Dreiser depicted the lives of common people in such novels as *Sister Carrie* (1900) and *An American Tragedy* (1925). *Sister Carrie* was attacked and heavily censored as an immoral treatment of a scandalous woman's rise to success. He also endured failure due to censorship of *The Genius* (1915), an autobiographical novel about power and sex that was labeled "pornography" and attacked by moralists. In 1925, Dreiser published *An American Tragedy*, widely regarded as his finest achievement. Critics labeled it "immoral," and the novel became the subject of a notorious trial.

## DUMAS, ALEXANDRE JR. (1824–1895)

Born in Paris, France, and known as Dumas *fils*, the author wrote numerous novels and plays, and refined a genre known as the problem, or thesis, play. His most famous work is *La Dame aux Camelias*, known in English as *Camille* (1848), the story of a Parisian courtesan who becomes morally regenerated by the power of true love. The 1852 theatrical version inspired Verdi's opera *La Traviata*. Dumas attempted to analyze the social ills of his times, but this subject for study in *Camille* made the work a target of censors. He was admitted to the Académie française in 1875.

## ELLISON, RALPH (1914–1994)

Born in Oklahoma City, Oklahoma, the African-American essayist and novelist received international literary recognition with his first and most important novel, *The Invisible Man* (1952), which won the National Book Award in 1953. Its theme is a black man's search for identity in a society where black individuality is "invisible," and blacks are recognized only in the roles they have been assigned by whites. Challenges to oust the novel from schools have arisen because of the "vulgar" language and "inappropriate situations" in the novel. Because Ellison did not take militant public positions on the condition of black Americans, his influence upon the younger generation of black writers has not been widespread.

## FARRELL, JAMES THOMAS (1904–1979)

Born in Chicago, the poet, critic, journalist and novelist often depicts in his fiction the lives of Irish-Americans in Chicago from 1900 through the Depression of the 1930s. His best-known novels make up the *Studs Lonigan* trilogy, which, with *A World I Never Made* (1936), were repeatedly subjected to attempts to ban them for their language and sexual situations. Farrell's fiction is a part of the tradition of naturalistic writing.

## FAULKNER, WILLIAM (1897–1962)

Born in Oxford, Mississippi, this major figure of contemporary American literature wrote 19 novels, 80 short stories, two books of poems and numerous essays. One of America's most innovative novelists, he depicted ordinary society in terms of ageless human dramas. In 1949, Faulkner won the Nobel Prize for literature. He repeatedly explored the question of human freedom and the obstacles to it—racism, regimentation, shame, fear, pride and overly abstract principles—infusing his novels with this honesty. Such works as *I Lay Dying* (1930), *Sanctuary* (1931) and *The Wild Palms* (1939) have been attacked as being "vulgar" and "immoral" precisely because they depict realistically how people think, speak and feel.

## FOSSEY, DIAN (1932–1985)

Born in San Francisco, the author was a zoologist known for her field studies of rare mountain gorillas in their natural habitat in east central Africa. *Gorillas in the Mist* (1983) chronicles her observations of three generations of mountain gorillas and includes detailed information of the gorillas' sexual habits, a factor that has resulted in challenges to the book in classrooms and school libraries. Fossey was murdered on December 27, 1985 at the Karisoke Research Center in Rwanda, which she established in 1967.

## FRANK, ANNE (1929–1945)

Born in Amsterdam, The Netherlands, the young Jewish diarist hid with her family from the Nazi persecution in Amsterdam during World War II. She wrote *The Diary of Anne Frank*, producing the major testament of the Holocaust. She and her family lived in a secret apartment in Amsterdam for two years before being discovered. Anne died in a German concentration camp. An abridgment of her poignant diary was published in 1947; a complete English edition appeared in 1995. The work has been challenged in schools because Anne writes frankly of her adolescent longings and because parents view the book as a "downer."

## FRANKLIN, BENJAMIN (1706–1790)

Born in Boston, Massachusetts, the scientist, inventor, statesman, printer and writer figured prominently in the governmental organization of the emerging American nation. Franklin helped to start the first public lending library, the first fire department, a college (later the University of Pennsylvania), an insurance company and a hospital. Franklin's writings include numerous treatises and essays, and *Poor Richard's Almanack* (1732), a collection of aphorisms.

His *Autobiography* is among the most frequently expurgated books published in the United States and has been censored from its first publication.

## GAINES, ERNEST JAMES (1933–   )

Born in Oscar, Louisiana, the African-American author is best known for his 1971 novel *The Autobiography of Miss Jane Pittman*, a realistic account of the life of southern blacks from the time of slavery to the civil rights movement, as told by its centenarian heroine, Jane Pittman. Objections have been raised against the "obscene" language of the book, as well as the stereotyping of both African-American and white characters. Gaines wrote four other novels, none of which garnered significant attention.

## GARDEN, NANCY (1938–   )

Born in Boston, Massachusetts, the author has published more than 20 books for young people, including the highly acclaimed *Annie on My Mind*, which was selected for the 1982 *Booklist* Reviewer's Choice, the 1982 American Library Association (ALA) Best Books and the 1970–83 ALA Best of the Best lists. The novel has also been the target of numerous censors, who object to the theme of two romantically involved high school girls.

## GARDNER, JOHN (1933–1982)

Born in Batavia, New York, the author, critic and educator was a professor of medieval literature as well as a novelist. His fiction ranges from fairy tales for children to his imaginative fantasies and contemporary stories for adults, books in which he characteristically poses metaphysical problems. Of his four novels and one short story collection, only the novel *Grendel* (1971), which retells the Beowulf legend from the monster's point of view, gained notoriety. Challenges to its use in the classroom and in school libraries charge that the novel contains "obscene" language and "sexist" passages.

## GINSBERG, ALLEN (1926–1997)

Born in Newark, New Jersey, the poet and cultural rebel became a prophet of the Beat generation with his first published work, *Howl and Other Poems* (1956), which sparked the San Francisco Renaissance and defined the generation of the 1950s. In the 1960s, while vigorously participating in the anti–Vietnam War movement, he published several poetic works, including *Reality Sandwiches* (1963) and *Planet News* (1969), then won the National Book Award in 1974 for *The Fall of America*. Ginsberg's works have quietly been omitted from school anthologies and libraries, but *Howl and Other Poems* became the subject of a major trial as well as the object of a decision rendered by the Federal Communications Commission.

## GIOVANNI, NIKKI (1943– )

Born Yolande Cornelia Giovanni in Knoxville, Tennessee, the poet has infused her work with the unifying themes of the black struggle and her political activism. As one of the most noted poets of the new black renaissance that began in the 1960s, Giovanni has combined the raw language of the streets with sensitive imagery in her 15 poetry collections, including *My House* (1972), leading to challenges to their use in classrooms.

## GOLDING, WILLIAM GERALD (1911–1993)

Born in Cornwall, England, the prominent novelist, essayist and poet was one of the most original post–World War II British writers. Winner of the 1983 Nobel Prize for literature and knighted in 1988, he is best known for *Lord of the Flies* (1954), a bleak examination of human nature that is among the 10 most frequently banned books in the United States. The book has been challenged in numerous instances for "obscene" language, violence and racism. Golding's later novels did not win the critical praise his earlier works achieved.

## GRIFFIN, JOHN HOWARD (1920–1980)

Born in Dallas, Texas, the author worked as a photographer, lecturer and journalist before publishing nine books, including *The Devil Rides Outside* (1952), banned for its frank sexuality, and *Black Like Me* (1961), for which Griffin is best known. The Caucasian author used chemicals and ultraviolet light to darken his skin, then traveled throughout the South as a black man. The resulting realism was disturbing to society.

## GUEST, JUDITH ANN (1936– )

Born in Detroit, Michigan, the author is a former grade school teacher and housewife who achieved success with her first novel, *Ordinary People* (1976). The work reflects the story of a teenage boy who returns to his suburban home from a stay in a mental hospital after attempting suicide. Challenges to the book in the classroom or in school libraries criticize the "vulgar" language of the novel and the theme of suicide as being "unsuitable." Guest's later novels were *Second Heaven* (1982) and *Killing Time in St. Cloud* (1989).

## HALL, RADCLYFFE (1880–1943)

Born Marguerite Radclyffe-Hall in Lancashire, England, the author preferred to be known in her private life as "John." Openly lesbian, Hall identified herself with "the third sex" and was instantly recognizable by her close-cropped hair, tailored jackets, wide-brimmed hats and ties. The author of five volumes of poetry, one short story collection and six novels, she is best known as the author of *The Well of Loneliness*, a novel that dealt explicitly with a lesbian theme and was considered by critics to be the most important lesbian novel of the 20th century.

## HAWTHORNE, NATHANIEL (1804–1864)

Born in Salem, Massachusetts, Hawthorne was the first American writer to apply artistic judgment to Puritan society. He exhibited profound moral and psychological insight into human motivation in *The Scarlet Letter* (1850), written while he worked in the Boston Custom House and for which he was roundly criticized for the theme of adultery. *Twice-Told Tales* (1837) was a model for Edgar Allan Poe in his critical analysis of the art of the short story. In 1841 Hawthorne joined the utopian community at Brooke Farm for a time, and later became friendly with Ralph Waldo Emerson, Henry David Thoreau and their circle of transcendentalists. Following quickly upon the success of *The Scarlet Letter* came *The House of the Seven Gables* (1851) and *The Blithedale Romance* (1852).

## HEINLEIN, ROBERT (1907–1988)

Born in Butler, Missouri, Heinlein did much to popularize science fiction, beginning with a series of stories, first published in *The Saturday Evening Post* and later collected in *The Green Hills of Earth* (1951). Heinlein won science fiction's Hugo Award four times—for *Double Star* (1956), *Starship Troopers* (1959), *Stranger in a Strange Land* (1961) and *The Moon Is a Harsh Mistress* (1966). The last two novels became cult favorites in the late 1960s and the early 1970s among college students in the United States, and substantial criticism was heaped upon *Stranger in a Strange Land* for its views of marriage and family life that ran counter to those of traditional society.

## HELLER, JOSEPH (1923–    )

Born in Brooklyn, New York, the novelist and dramatist's works are satiric and often criticize the propensity of the military-industrial complex and similar forces to manipulate individuals in the name of reason or morality. His best-known novel, *Catch-22* (1961), uses protest and a sense of the absurd to explore the human condition and underscore the horrors of war and the power of modern society to destroy the human spirit. It has been the object of numerous challenges because of its language and pessimistic view of society. Its sequel, *Closing Time* (1994), takes the now-aged characters through the absurdities of the century's end and, with other of Heller's novels, continues the author's attack on society's values and conventions.

## HEMINGWAY, ERNEST (1899–1961)

Born in Oak Park, Illinois, the novelist, journalist, short story writer and novelist is considered one of the most influential authors of the first half of the 20th century. He was awarded the Nobel Prize for Literature in 1954 and created a large and distinguished body of literature, much of it based on his adventurous life. His most memorable novel, *The Sun Also Rises* (1926), became an immediate success and made him a leader of the so-called "lost generation" but its references to impotence and perceived undertones of homosexuality motivated efforts to censor the novel. *A Farewell to Arms* (1929) is his most successful novel but the sexual relationship between the unmarried main characters and hints at abortion made it the target of censors. *To Have and Have Not* (1937) was challenged and barred from sale for its language. *Across the River and Into the Trees* (1950) a novel that used a Venetian locale, was widely attacked for its sexual content.

## HESSE, HERMANN (1877–1962)

Born in Calw, Germany, the novelist and poet explored the conflicts of human nature through the application of Eastern and Western philosophy in his writings, which emphasized the human quest for spiritual enlightenment. *Demian* (1919), *Siddhartha* (1922) and *Steppenwolf* (1927) incorporate Jungian psychology and Buddhist mysticism with the influence of Nietzsche, Spengler and Dostoyevsky. He received the 1946 Nobel Prize for Literature. Although Hesse wrote no novels after 1943, his works gained immense popularity during the 1950s and 1960s in the English-speaking world, echoing the growing rebellion of the younger generation in their criticism of middle-class values and their interest in Eastern religious philosophy. The themes of Hesse's most popular novels, such as *Steppenwolf*, are often at odds with the aims of authority, thus making them targets of challenges in schools.

## HUGHES, LANGSTON (1902–1967)

Born James Mercer Langston Hughes in Joplin, Missouri, the African-American poet, dramatist and prose writer was prominent in the Harlem Renaissance movement. From his first published poem, "The Negro Speaks of Rivers" (1921), through his later critical essay "The Negro Artist and the Racial Movement" (1925), and his autobiography, *The Big Sea* (1940), Hughes conveys his belief in the commonality of all cultures and the universality of human suffering, which he dramatically projected in *Lament for Dark People and Other Suffering* (1944). Despite his body of work, he experienced censorship for his work as an editor for *The Best Short Stories by Negro Writers*, rather than as a writer.

## KESEY, KEN (1935–   )

Born in La Junta, Colorado, the novelist and screenwriter was a member of the Beat generation who is best known for his first novel, *One Flew Over the Cuckoo's Nest* (1962). The novel, based on his experiences as a ward attendant at a mental institution, has been the target of censors for its raw language and violent action. Kesey also achieved notoriety as an LSD advocate and a member of the Merry Pranksters, an LSD-fueled group that toured the country in a school bus, a trip that Kesey later condemned in *The Further Inquiry* (1990).

## KING, STEPHEN (1947–   )

Born in Portland, Maine, the writer of suspense and horror novels and stories is one of America's best-selling authors, under his own name and the pseudonym Richard Bachman, whose works have gained both critical acclaim and popular success. At the same time, many of his better-known works, among them *Carrie* (1974), *The Shining* (1977), *Cujo* (1981), *Christine* (1983), *Pet Sematary* (1983) and *The Stand* (1990), have been singled out by censors who have sought to remove these novels and, in some cases, all of King's works from their school and public libraries.

## KNOWLES, JOHN H. (1926–   )

Born in rural West Virginia, the author is best known for *A Separate Peace* (1960) and its sequel, *Peace Breaks Out* (1981), among his seven novels, a collection of short stories and a travel book. Challenges to *A Separate Peace* have cited "obscene" and "vulgar" language, as well as concerns that the novel contains an underlying theme of homosexuality.

## KOSINSKI, JERZY NIKODEM (1933–1991)

Born in Lodz, Poland, the novelist wrote in English and used sardonic humor in grimly pessimistic novels published under his own name, as well as two nonfiction works under the pseudonym Joseph Novak. His bitter first novel, *The Painted Bird* (1965), relates the dehumanizing childhood years he spent hiding from the Nazis in Poland during World War II. The pessimistic view of this novel is also evident in six later novels, among them *Being There* (1970), which was banned from high school reading lists for its masturbation scene and homosexual near-experience.

## LEE, HARPER (1926–   )

Born in Monroeville, Alabama, the novelist is known solely for her Pulitzer Prize–winning novel, *To Kill a Mockingbird* (1960), which relates the impact of a rape trial on a small southern town. The novel remains among the most frequently banned in the United States, and challengers cite the "vulgar" language, discussion of the rape and racial relationships among their complaints.

## LEWIS, SINCLAIR (1885–1951)

Born in Sauk Centre, Minnesota, the novelist is the first American writer to win the Nobel Prize for Literature as well as the first American to be awarded both the Nobel and Pulitzer prizes. He created satirical portraits of middle-class life in the United States during the 1920s in a succession of best-selling novels, including *Main Street* (1920), *Babbitt* (1922) and *Arrowsmith* (1925), which won the Pulitzer Prize in 1926. In 1930, he was awarded the Nobel Prize in Literature, after publishing *Elmer Gantry* (1927) and *Dodsworth* (1929). *Elmer Gantry* and *Kingsblood Royal* (1947), a savage attack on racial discrimination in both the South and North, have been targets of censors who have labeled both books "immoral" because of their language and "suggested" sexual scenes

## LOFTING, HUGH (1886–1947)

Born in Maidenhead, Berkshire, England, the author entered the United States in 1912 and became a naturalized citizen. He became a surveyor and civil engineer, traveling to Canada, Africa and the West Indies. He served with the British army in World War I, during which he conceived of the Dolittle story, which he wrote in letters home to his children. The first of the 13 books that eventually made up the Dolittle series was published in 1920 and maintained strong popularity until the 1960s, when growing racial awareness caused the books to be labeled racist and demeaning to African Americans

## LOUŸS, PIERRE (1875–1925)

Born Pierre Louis in Paris, the author lived his entire life in that city, leaving it only to travel around the Mediterranean coast, where so many of his works of art were set. He had many close friends among the writers of his day but preferred to remain apart from literary cliques. Louÿs's evocations of Hellenistic society brought him fame as a writer in both France and England, as much for his skill in recreating the ancient world as for the risqué subjects of such works as *Aphrodite* (1886) and *Les Chansons de Bilitis* (1894).

## MALAMUD, BERNARD (1914–1986)

Born in Brooklyn, New York, the novelist and short story writer is best known for his stories of ordinary people whose survival makes of them universal symbols of the triumph of the human spirit. *The Assistant* (1957), the author's most highly praised novel, is characteristic in both style and theme, as are *The Tenants* (1971) and *Dubin's Lives* (1979). *The Fixer* (1966), for which Malamud received both a National Book Award and a Pulitzer Prize, is his only work to be challenged by censors, who have labeled the novel anti-Semitic and complained of its language.

## MALCOLM X (1925–1965)

Born Malcolm Little in Omaha, Nebraska, he was for a time the leading spokesperson for the Black Muslims in the outside world. After a split developed between Malcolm and the more conservative Elijah Muhammad in 1963, Malcolm founded the rival Organization for Afro-American Unity, and he no longer preached racial separation but rather a socialist revolution. He was assassinated in 1965. *The Autobiography of Malcolm X*, which relates his life, has been attacked by censors who claim that the language and situations depicted are "obscene" and do not belong on high school reading lists.

## MANN, PATRICK (1923–   )

Born in Chicago, Illinois, as Leslie Waller, the author wrote 28 books for adults under his real name and two pseudonyms, Patrick Mann and C. S. Cody, as well as 16 books for juveniles. *Dog Day Afternoon* (1974), the most notorious of his works and the most successful, has motivated challenges in both school and public libraries for its language, transsexual character and sexual references.

## MITCHELL, MARGARET (1900–1949)

Born in Atlanta, Georgia, the novelist and journalist produced one of the most successful novels ever written in *Gone with the Wind*, which also won the Pulitzer Prize and the National Book Award. The novel, which made publishing history by setting a sales record of 50,000 copies in one day and 1.5 million copies in its first year of release, has been the target of censors who object to its language, the prominence of a female brothel owner and the marital rape of the protagonist.

## MOORE, GEORGE (1852–1933)

Born in County Mayo, Ireland, the novelist and playwright was active in the Irish Literary Renaissance of the early 1900s. His best-known novel, *Esther Waters* (1894), relates the story of a religious young woman with an illegitimate son. The novel was attacked for its subject matter and banned from Mudie's Circulating Library, as were the author's earlier novels, *A Modern Lover* (1883) and *A Mummer's Wife* (1885). A collection of short stories, *A Story Teller's Holiday* (1918), was banned by Customs for its perceived sexual content.

## MORRIS, DESMOND J. (1928– )

Born in Purton, Wiltshire, England, the author is a zoologist whose writings have detailed both animal and human behavior. Of his 26 books for adults, including the highly popular *Catwatching* (1986) and *Dogwatching* (1987), and four books for children, only *The Naked Ape* (1967) has generated significant controversy. Critics charge that Morris devotes one-fourth of the book to human sexual habits and ignores language and learning, but the omission did not prevent the book from selling over 8 million copies in 23 countries.

## MOWAT, FARLEY (1921– )

Born in Belleville, Ontario, the author is best known for his books about northern Canada. He has published works on other topics, including *My Discovery of America* (1985), which tells of his experience being barred from the United States as an "undesirable," and *Woman in the Mists* (1987), an account of zoologist Dian Fossey's dedication to saving mountain gorillas, which was banned because of its "profanity" and discussion of Fossey's abortion.

## NEWMAN, LESLEA (1955– )

Born in Brooklyn, New York, the author published a novel, *Good Enough to Eat* (1986), a poetry collection, *Love Me Like You Mean It* (1987), and a short story collection, *A Letter to Harvey Milk and Other Stories* (1988) before the taboo-shattering *Heather Has Two Mommies* in 1989. The latter children's book has been the source of vehement community outcry and efforts to ban it from both school and public libraries.

## O'HARA, JOHN (1905–1970)

Born in Pottsville, Pennsylvania, the novelist and short story writer is one of the most popular writers of the 20th century. His ear for irony and acute powers of observation made his first novel, *Appointment in Samarra* (1934) a great success, and many later novels, including *Butterfield 8* (1935), *A Rage to Live* (1955), *Ten North Frederick* (1955) and *From the Terrace* (1958) became popular films. He set most of his novels in the fictitious community of Gibbsville, Pennsylvania, and infused the works with realistic portrayals of the American upper middle class, including its sex and drinking patterns. *Appointment in Samarra* and *Ten North Frederick* both shocked reviewers and motivated censors, who complained of the "vulgarity" in the novels and their sexual suggestiveness.

## PATERSON, KATHERINE (1932– )

Born in Qing Jiang, China, to missionary parents, the author has earned numerous children's book awards for her 11 novels written for juveniles. *Bridge to Terabithia* (1977), winner of four awards, is her most frequently challenged novel because of its language and depressing subject, death.

## PECK, ROBERT NEWTON (1928– )

Born in rural Vermont, the author has set many of his more than 30 novels in the 1930s of his boyhood and focuses on the honest simplicity of the time. *A Day No Pigs Would Die* is his first novel, ranked by critics as among the most notable of his works. It is also the most severely criticized and challenged of Peck's works for its honest depiction of the brutality of farm life and the realistic portrayal of the life cycle.

## PERRAULT, CHARLES (1628–1703)

Born in Paris, France, the poet and literary critic is better known today for his *Tales of Past Times* (1697) than for his role during the 17th century as the leading champion of contemporary French writers in the "quarrel between the ancients and the moderns." The fairy tales collected by Perrault are frequently violent, and his version of "Little Red Riding Hood" has experienced several challenges in school districts.

## PLATH, SYLVIA (1932–1963)

Born in Boston, Massachusetts, the poet and novelist is best known for her semiautobiographical novel, *The Bell Jar* (1963), the account of a young woman's mental breakdown, which was published soon after her death. The novel has generated challenges in schools for containing "filthy" material. She published one collection of poetry, *Colossus* (1960), before committing suicide in 1963, but her fame rests on works that appeared after her death. The posthumous publication of *Ariel* (1965) made her a cult hero. Her status was reinforced by two other posthumous collections, *Crossing the Water* (1971) and *Winter Trees* (1971)

## RABELAIS, FRANÇOIS (1532–1564)

Born in Chinon, Touraine, France, the scholar and cleric remains best known for *Gargantua and Pantagruel* (1533–1564), his satiric portrait of 16th-century French society. Rabelais began his clerical career at a Franciscan monastery and later transferred to a Benedictine order, where he qualified as a physician. He practiced medicine in Lyon and was credited with performing the first public dissection in France. The first two books of the five-volume *Gargantua and Pantagruel* were condemned by the Sorbonne as "obscene," and the grotesque adventures of his giants and his comic and often obscene anecdotes made the work the target of censors in the United States.

## ROBBINS, HAROLD (1916–1997)

Born in New York City, the novelist has produced a large number of financially successful novels that have been derided by critics for being sensationalist and poorly constructed. His autobiographical first novel, *Never Love a Stranger* (1948), was the target of censors for its frank language and references to sexuality. *The Carpetbaggers* (1961) suffered attempts at suppression for its blatant portrayal of sexual activity. Changing mores have prevented further censorship of Robbins's increasingly explicit novels.

## SALINGER, JEROME DAVID (1919–   )

Born in New York City, the reputation of the reclusive novelist and short story writer is based largely on *The Catcher in the Rye* (1951), a novel that is frequently banned by schools on the request of parents who are made uncomfortable by the main character's "vulgar" language and sexuality oriented thoughts. The novel gained a large readership among high school and college students who could relate fully to the principal character, Holden Caulfield. The resulting public attention that came with the success of the book led Salinger to move from New York to the remote hills of Cornish, New Hampshire, to avoid admirers.

## SELBY, HUBERT JR. (1928–   )

Born in Brooklyn, New York, the author spent two years as a deckhand in the United States Merchant Marine and 14 years as an insurance analyst before publication of his first and best-known work, *Last Exit to Brooklyn*. An amoral exploration of the world of prostitutes, drug abusers and criminals, the work became the subject of an obscenity trial and other attempts to ban it.

## SENDAK, MAURICE BERNARD (1928–   )

Born in Brooklyn, New York, the illustrator and writer has been a major influence in children's literature for over three decades, beginning with the publication of *Where the Wild Things Are* (1963), which won the 1964 Caldecott Medal. Sendak has also written and illustrated *Higglety Pigglety Pop!* (1967), *In the Night Kitchen* (1970) and *Outside over There* (1981), in addition to illustrating many books for others. His drawings, described by critics as bizarre, display a nightmarish quality, but only *In the Night Kitchen* has generated controversy, in this case for its illustration of a naked boy which challengers labeled "pornography" and "obscene."

## SHULMAN, IRVING (1913–1995)

Born in Brooklyn, New York, the author was a college English professor, novelist, biographer and screenwriter who adapted his own novel *Children of the Dark* into the 1955 screenplay for *Rebel Without a Cause*. Of his 10 novels, *The Amboy Dukes (1947)* achieved notoriety as a result of efforts to ban it. Its popularity among high school students caused educators and parents to fear that its scenes of criminal activity and sexuality would promote "delinquency."

## SMITH, LILLIAN (1897–1966)

Born near Atlanta, Georgia, the author was referred to by contemporary critics as "the Negro's White Joan of Arc" for her founding of *Pseudopodia* (later *North Georgia Review* and *South Today*), the only southern literary journal to showcase African-American writers in the 1930s and 1940s. As with her nonfiction, Smith protested stereotyped gender and racial roles in *Strange Fruit*, the novel that was branded "obscene" and banned by the United States Department of the Post Office.

## STEINBECK, JOHN (1902–1968)

Born in Salinas, California, the novelist and short story writer was awarded the Nobel Prize for Literature in 1962. Much of his work focuses on the

American poor and the social injustices that the poor and dispossessed face. His first popular success was *Tortilla Flat* (1935), a semihumorous work that was quickly followed by grim, tragic novels and stories, such as *In Dubious Battle* (1936), *Of Mice and Men* (1937), *The Red Pony* (1938) and *The Grapes of Wrath* (1939), which won both the Pulitzer Prize and the National Book Award. In the 1940s and later, Steinbeck wrote numerous screenplays, some from his novels and stories, and moved his focus to the dispossessed in other areas of society. Among his successes are *The Wayward Bus* (1947) and *East of Eden* (1952), which with *The Red Pony* and *Of Mice and Men*, have been challenged for what critics view as "filthy" language, "vulgarity" and "bad grammar."

## STOKER, BRAM (1847–1912)

Born Abraham Stoker in Dublin, the civil servant, novelist and drama critic is best known for creating *Dracula* (1897), one of the most powerful Gothic figures in literary history. Other stories of horror written by Stoker have faded from existence, but his Transylvanian Count Dracula has become the subject of numerous films and books, as well as the prototype for most later vampire creations. The sexual overtones of the novel have been recognized from its first publication and underlie attempts to suppress it.

## STOPES, MARIE (1880–1958)

Born in Edinburgh, Scotland, Marie Stopes won international acclaim for her work in promoting birth control and opened the first free birth control clinic in the British Empire. Admired by George Bernard Shaw and the Duke of Windsor, she also gained detractors through her crusades that brought violent opposition from the Roman Catholic church. *Married Love*, which she characterized as "a book about the plain facts of marriage," sold over a million copies and was translated into 13 languages, but it was strongly attacked for being immoral.

## SWARTHOUT, GLENDON (1918–1992)

Born in Pinckney, Michigan, the author wrote short stories, mysteries, film scripts, plays and children's books, many of them set in the American West. Although Swarthout's novels *Where the Boys Are* (1961) and *The Shootist* (1975) achieved success in print and on the movie screen, *Bless the Beasts and the Children* (1970) brought him greater acclaim and it was also the source of numerous challenges and attempts at censorship.

## TERKEL, STUDS (1912–   )

Born Louis Terkel in New York City, the oral historian, radio broadcaster, journalist, sports columnist, lecturer and playwright has conducted interviews all over the world with people from all walks of life. He won the Pulitzer Prize in 1985 for *The Good War: An Oral History of World War II* (1984), and he has also dealt with urban unrest in *Division Street, America* (1966), the Depression in *Hard Times: An Oral History of the Great Depression* (1970), the dwindling American dream in *The Great Divide* (1988) and the 20th century in *Coming of Age* (1995). Only *Working* (1974) has motivated challenges for its "vulgar" and "offensive" language.

## THOMAS, PIRI (1928–   )

Born in Spanish Harlem in New York City, the author is a former drug addict and street gang member who served six years of a 15-year prison sentence for an attempted armed robbery in 1950. His memoir, *Down These Mean Streets* (1972), portrays the brutal life of his past in candid language and with vivid descriptions that have led critics to label the book "obscene" and to condemn it.

## TROCCHI, ALEXANDER (1925–1984)

Born in Glasgow, Scotland, the author was cofounder of *Merlin*, the first publisher of Romanian dramatist Eugene Ionesco and among the first to publish the work of French dramatist Jean Genet in English. He also wrote erotic novels on a work-for-hire basis for Olympia Press (Paris) while exploring his talents as a serious novelist. *Cain's Book* (1960) features a drug-addicted narrator who is neither remorseful for his addiction nor condemnatory of drugs, factors that led to seizures of the book and a lengthy trial in England.

## TWAIN, MARK (1835–1910)

Born Samuel Langhorne Clemens in Florida, Missouri, the humorist, novelist, journalist, lecturer and travel writer took his pseudonym from a phrase meaning "two fathoms deep" used by Mississippi river boatmen. Although largely associated with life on the Mississippi River because of the literary successes of *The Adventures of Tom Sawyer* (1876), *Life on the Mississippi* (1883) and *The Adventures of Huckleberry Finn* (1884–1885), Twain also chronicled his journeys to the West and experiences in California, as well as adventures abroad in *Innocents Abroad* (1869), *Roughing It* (1872) and others. Two of Twain's most popular works are also among the most frequently banned or censored in the United States: *The Adventures of Tom Sawyer* and *The Adventures of Huckleberry Finn*. Both books have been criticized as being "racist" and for containing "vulgar" and "profane" language.

## VONNEGUT, KURT JR. (1922–   )

Born in Indianapolis, Indiana, the novelist and short story writer combines science fiction, social satire and black comedy to expose the dehumanizing effects of 20th-century society and the technology and powerful institutions that perpetuate the dehumanization. Vonnegut's colloquial style and rebellious tone made him a campus favorite in the 1960s and the early 1970s, through such works as *Player Piano* (1952), *Cat's Cradle* (1963), *Welcome to the Monkey House* (1968) and *Slaughterhouse-Five* (1969). While several of Vonnegut's works have been challenged for their political or religious references, challenges to *Welcome to the Monkey House* have included complaints of "sexuality explicit language" and "vulgarities."

## WALKER, ALICE (1944–   )

Born in Eatonton, Georgia, the poet, novelist and short story writer grew up in a sharecropper family and participated in the 1960s civil rights movement, later using those events in *The Third Life of George Copeland* (1970) and *Meridian* (1976). In 1982, Walker won both the Pulitzer Prize and the American Book Award for *The Color Purple* (1982), followed by other successful novels, *The Temple of My Familiar* (1989) and *Possessing the Secret of Joy* (1992). Her most popular novel, *The Color Purple*, has also been frequently challenged for "explicit sexual language," "insulting" portraits of African-American males and "vulgarities."

## WENTWORTH, HAROLD (1904–   )

Born in Homer, New York, Wentworth is a college English professor who has edited or served as consulting editor for various dictionaries, including *Webster's New International Dictionary*, second edition, and others, in addition to the *Dictionary of American Slang*, which has been banned by school districts for its inclusion of "unacceptable" and "vulgar" words.

## WHITMAN, WALT (1819–1892)

Born in West Hill, Long Island, New York, the poet, journalist, newspaper editor and printer vowed to create a distinctly new form of poetry that would reflect the democratic nature and vastness of the United States. His first book of poetry, *Leaves of Grass* (1855) offended many of his contemporaries with its anatomical references. Whitman served as a hospital volunteer in the Civil War, then published *Drum-Taps* (1865). Two of his most famous works, "When Lilacs Last in the Dooryard Bloom'd" and "O Captain! My Captain!" that commemorated the death of Lincoln, appeared in *Sequel to Drum-Taps* (1865–1866).

## WILDER, LAURA INGALLS (1867–1857)

Born in Pepin, Wisconsin, the novelist's *Little House* series of autobiographical novels, recounting her childhood growing up on the American frontier, have become classics of childhood literature. The series began with *Little House in the Big Woods* (1932) and includes *Little House on the Prairie* (1935), the inspiration for a successful television series in the 1970s. The novels have been challenged for being "derogatory to Native Americans."

## WILLHOITE, MICHAEL A. (1946–   )

Born in Hobart, Oklahoma, the writer and illustrator began his career by publishing cartoons and caricatures in a weekly gay newspaper, the *Washington Blade*. In *Daddy's Roommate* (1990), Willhoite depicts a divorce in which the father begins cohabitation with another man while the mother explains to their child that his father is gay. Numerous challenges have emerged to the book because it "legitimizes" gay relationships. Willhoite's most recent book, *Daddy's Wedding* (1996), is a sequel that shows the father marrying his male roommate.

## WILLINGHAM, CALDER (1922–1995)

Born in Atlanta, Georgia, novelist and screenwriter Willingham became an instant literary star at 24 with the publication of *End as a Man*, the best known of his 10 novels and the one that generated both critical praise and controversy. The publicity surrounding the obscenity trial involving that novel cast a shadow on the author that he was never able to escape. From 1955 onward, Willingham also wrote screenplays for films, including those for *The Graduate* (1967), *Little Big Man* (1970) and *Rambling Rose* (1991).

## WOLFE, THOMAS (1900–1938)

Born Thomas Clayton Wolfe in Asheville, North Carolina, the novelist and playwright has been acclaimed as one of the great American novelists of the

20th century. After completing a master's degree in English in 1924 at Harvard University, where he wrote plays, Wolfe began the autobiographical novel *Look Homeward, Angel* (1929) when he found that he could not get his plays produced. His two major autobiographical novels, *Look Homeward, Angel* and *You Can't Go Home Again* (1940), established Wolfe as a major figure in American literature, and *Of Time and the River* (1935), a fictional account of his experience at Harvard, affirmed that reputation. The latter novel has been accused of being "racist," "anti-Semitic" and "pornographic."

## ZOLA, ÉMILE (1840–1902)

Born in Aix-en-Provence, France, the journalist and novelist used his fiction to campaign for social reform and justice. He became the major proponent of literary naturalism. Zola created a cycle of 20 novels called, collectively, *Les Rougon Macquart*, which were published between 1871 and 1893 and criticized for their gratuitous brutality and obscenity. Today they are valued as fictionalized sociology. Of particular interest are *Nana* (1880) and *La Terre*, translated variously as *The Earth* and *The Soil* (1887). In later years, Zola gained further notoriety for his celebrated campaign and notorious "J'accuse" letter in defense of Captain Alfred Dreyfus.

# BIBLIOGRAPHY

## BOOKS

Aggeler, Geoffrey. *Anthony Burgess: The Artist as Novelist*. Birmingham: University of Alabama Press, 1979.

Aldiss, Brian W. *Billion Year Spree: The True History of Science Fiction*. Garden City, N.Y.: Doubleday & Company, 1973.

Alexander, Paul. *Rough Magic: A Biography of Sylvia Plath*. New York: Viking Press, 1991.

Allen, William Rodney. *Understanding Kurt Vonnegut*. Columbia, S.C.: University of South Carolina Press, 1990.

* American Library Association. *Censorship and Selection: Issues and Answers for Schools*. Chicago: American Library Association, 1993.

Arnstein, Walter L. *The Bradlaugh Case*. Oxford: Clarendon Press, 1965.

Avery, Evelyn Gross. *Rebels and Victims: The Fiction of Richard Wright and Bernard Malamud*. Port Washington, N.Y.: Kennikat Press, 1979.

Babb, Valerie Melissa. *Ernest Gaines*. Boston: Twayne Publishers, 1991.

Baker, Carlos. *Hemingway: A Life Story*. New York: Charles Scribner's Sons, 1969.

Baldwin, James. *Conversations with James Baldwin*. Ed. by Fred L. Standley and Louis H. Pratt. Jackson, Miss.: University Press of Mississippi, 1989.

Baughman, Ronald. *Understanding James Dickey*. Columbia, S.C.: University of South Carolina Press, 1985.

Beckett, Samuel. "Censorship in the Saorstat." In *Disjecta: Miscellaneous Writings and a Dramatic Fragment by Samuel Beckett*. Ed. by Ruby Cohn, 84–88. London: John Calder, 1983.

Bedford, Sybille. *Aldous Huxley: A Biography*. London: Chatto and Windus Collins, 1973–1974. 2 vols.

Belford, Barbara. *Bram Stoker: A Biography of the Author of "Dracula"*. New York: Alfred A. Knopf, 1996.

Benson, Jackson J. *Hemingway: The Writer's Art of Self-Defense*. Minneapolis: University of Minnesota Press, 1969.

Bettelheim, Bruno. *The Uses of Enchantment: The Meaning and Importance of Fairy Tales*. New York: Random House, 1977.

Bjork, Christina. *The Other Alice: The Story of Alice Liddell and Alice in Wonderland*. New York: R&S Books, 1993.

* Blanshard, Paul. *The Right to Read*. Boston: Beacon Press, 1955.

Blodgett, Harold. *Walt Whitman in England*. Ithaca, N.Y.: Cornell University Press, 1934.

Brittain, Vera. *Radclyffe Hall: A Case of Obscenity?* New York: A.S. Barnes, 1969.

---

* Key sources

Broderick, Dorothy M. *Image of the Black in Children's Fiction*. New York: R.R. Bowker Company, 1973.

Broun, Heywood, and Margaret Leech. *Anthony Comstock: Roundsman of the Lord*. New York: The Literary Guild of America, 1927.

Bruccoli, Matthew Joseph. *The O'Hara Concern: A Biography of John O'Hara*. New York: Random House, 1975.

Burke, Redmond A., CSV, Ph.D. *What Is the Index?* Milwaukee, Wis.: Bruce Publishing Company, 1952.

* Burress, Lee. *Battle of the Books: Literary Censorship in the Public Schools, 1950–1985*. Metuchen, N.J.: Scarecrow Press, 1989.

Burroughs, William S. *Letters to Allen Ginsberg, 1953–1957*. Introd. by Allen Ginsberg. New York: Full Court Press, 1982.

Butscher, Edward. *Sylvia Plath: Method and Madness*. New York: Seabury Press, 1975.

Campbell, James. *Talking at the Gates: A Life of James Baldwin*. New York: Penguin Books USA, 1991.

Carson, Clayborne. *Malcolm X: The FBI File*. New York: Carroll & Graf Publishers, 1991.

Cavitch, David. *My Soul and I: The Inner Life of Walt Whitman*. Boston: Beacon Press, 1985.

Cech, John. *Angels and Wild Things*. University Park, Pa.: Pennsylvania State University Press, 1993.

Christian, Barbara. *Black Feminist Criticism*. New York: Pergamon Press, 1985.

Coale, Samuel. *Anthony Burgess*. New York: Frederick Ungar Publishing, 1981.

Cohen, Morton N. *Lewis Carroll: A Biography*. New York: A.A. Knopf, 1995.

Cowley, Malcolm, ed. *Walt Whitman's Leaves of Grass: The First (1855) Edition*. New York: Viking Press, 1959.

Cox, Don Richard. *Arthur Conan Doyle*. New York: Frederick Ungar Publishing, 1985.

Crowley, J. Donald, ed. *Hawthorne: The Critical Heritage*. New York: Barnes & Noble, 1970.

Cummins, Eric. *The Rise and Fall of California's Radical Prison Movement*. New York: Oxford University Press, 1995.

Dave, R. A. "*To Kill a Mockingbird*: Harper Lee's Tragic Vision." In *Indian Studies in American Literature*. Ed. by M. K. Naik, S. K. Desai and S. Mokashi, 311–323. Dharwar, India: Karnatak University, 1974.

* Davis, James E., ed. *Dealing with Censorship*. Urbana, Ill.: National Council of Teachers of English, 1983.

* De Grazia, Edward. *Censorship Landmarks*. New York: R.R. Bowker Company, 1969.

*Key sources

*De Grazia, Edward. *Girls Lean Back Everywhere: The Law of Obscenity and the Assault on Genius.* New York: Random House, 1992.

D'Emilio, John, and Estelle B. Freedman. *Intimate Matters: A History of Sexuality in America.* New York: Harper & Row, 1988.

Dickson, Lovat. *Radclyffe Hall at the Well of Loneliness: A Sapphic Chronicle.* New York: Charles Scribner's Sons, 1975.

Donald, David Herbert. *Look Homeward: A Life of Thomas Wolfe.* Boston: Little, Brown & Company, 1987.

Donelson, Kenneth, ed. *The Student's Right to Read.* Urbana, Ill.: National Council of Teachers of English, 1972.

Donelson, Kenneth L., and Alleen Pace Nilsen. *Literature for Today's Young Adults.* Glenview, Ill.: Scott Foresman, 1989.

Dreiser, Theodore. "The Early Adventures of Sister Carrie." Foreword to *Sister Carrie.* New York: The Modern Library, 1927.

Dyson, Michael Eric. *Making Malcolm: The Myth and Meaning of Malcolm X.* New York: Oxford University Press, 1994.

Elliot, Jeffrey, ed. *Conversations with Maya Angelou.* Jackson, Miss.: University of Mississippi Press, 1989.

*Ernst, Morris, and Ernest Lindley. *The Censor Marches On.* New York: Doubleday, Doran, 1940.

Everson, William. *American Bard: The Original Preface to 'Leaves of Grass.'* New York: Viking Press, 1982.

Faderman, Lillian. *Surpassing the Love of Men.* New York: William Morrow & Company, 1981.

Farrell, Walter C., Jr. "*Black Like Me*: In Defense of a Racial Reality." In *Censored Books: Critical Viewpoints.* Ed. by Nicholas Karolides, Lee Burress and John M. Kean: 117–124. Metuchen, N.J.: Scarecrow Press, 1993.

Ferrell, Keith. *John Steinbeck: The Voice of the Land.* New York: M. Evans, 1986.

Foster, Jeannette H. *Sex Variant Women in Literature.* Tallahassee, Fla.: The Naiad Press, 1985.

*Fowell, Frank, and Frank Palmer. *Censorship in England.* New York: Burt Franklin, 1913. Reprinted in 1970.

Frank, Otto. "Introduction." In *Anne Frank, The Diary of a Young Girl: The Definitive Edition.* Ed. by Otto Frank and Mirjam Pressler. New York: Doubleday & Company, 1995.

Franklin, Howard Bruce. *Robert A. Heinlein: America as Science Fiction.* New York: Oxford University Press, 1980.

Freedman, Ralph. *Hermann Hesse: Pilgrim of Crisis.* New York: Pantheon Books, 1978.

---

*Key sources

Frohock, William M. *The Novel of Violence in America, 1920–1950*. Dallas, Tex.: Southern Methodist University Press, 1958.

Fryer, Peter. *The Birth Controllers*. London: Corgi Books, 1967.

Gaines, Ernest. *Porch Talk with Ernest Gaines: Conversations on the Writer's Craft*. Baton Rouge: Louisiana State University Press, 1990.

Gardner, John. *On Moral Fiction*. New York: Basic Books, 1978.

* Geller, Evelyn. *Forbidden Books in American Public Libraries, 1876–1939: A Study in Cultural Change*. Westport, Conn.: Greenwood Press, 1984.

Gentry, Tony. *Alice Walker*. New York: Chelsea House Publishers, 1993.

Ginsberg, Allen. "Introduction." In *Junky*, v–ix. Written by William S. Burroughs. New York: Penguin Books, 1977.

Giovanni, Nikki. *Conversations with Nikki Giovanni*. Jackson, Miss.: University Press of Mississippi, 1992.

Goodman, Michael B. *Contemporary Literary Censorship: The Case History of Burroughs' Naked Lunch*. Metuchen, N.J.: Scarecrow Press, 1981.

Greenblatt, Stephen Jay. *Three Modern Satirists: Waugh, Orwell, and Huxley*. New Haven, Conn.: Yale University Press, 1965.

Griffin, John Howard. *Racial Equality: The Myth and the Reality*. ERIC Education Document Reprint Series, No. 26 (March 1971).

Gutman, Stanley T. *Mankind in Barbary: The Individual and Society in the Novels of Norman Mailer*. Hanover, N.H.: University Press of New England, 1975.

* Haney, Robert W. *Comstockery in America: Patterns of Censorship and Control*. Boston: Beacon Press, 1960.

Harris, Trudier. *Black Women in the Fiction of James Baldwin*. Knoxville, Tenn.: University of Tennessee Press, 1985.

Harwell, Richard, ed. *Margaret Mitchell's 'Gone with the Wind' Letters, 1936–1949*. New York: Macmillan Company, 1976.

Haskins, James. *Profiles in Black Power*. Garden City, N.Y.: Doubleday & Company, 1972.

Hawthorn, Jeremy. *Multiple Personality and the Disintegration of Literary Character: From Oliver Goldsmith to Sylvia Plath*. New York: Ballantine Books, 1983.

Helterman, Jeffrey. *Understanding Bernard Malamud*. Columbia, S.C.: University of South Caroline Press, 1985.

Hemingway, Ernest. *Selected Letters: 1917–1961*. Ed. by Carlos Baker. New York: Charles Scribner's Sons, 1981.

Hemmings, F. W. J. *The Life and Times of Emile Zola*. New York: Charles Scribner's Sons, 1977.

Henderson, Jeff. *Thor's Hammer: Essays on John Gardner*. Conway, Ark.: University of Central Arkansas Press, 1985.

---

*Key sources

Hipkiss, Robert A. *The American Absurd: Pynchon, Vonnegut, and Barth.* Port Washington, N.Y.: Associated Faculty Press, 1984.

Holman, C. Hugh. *The Letters of Thomas Wolfe to His Mother.* Chapel Hill, N.C.: University of North Carolina Press, 1968.

Howell, John Michael. *Understanding John Gardner.* Columbia, S.C.: University of South Carolina Press, 1993.

Huck, Charlotte S., Susan Hepler and Janet Hickman. *Children's Literature in Elementary School.* New York: Holt, Rinehart & Winston, 1987.

* Hurwitz, Leon. *Historical Dictionary of Censorship in the United States.* Westport, Conn.: Greenwood Press, 1985.

Hyde, H. Montgomery. *Lord Justice: The Life and Times of Lord Birkett of Ulverston.* New York: Random House, 1964.

*Index of Prohibited Books.* Revised and published by the order of His Holiness Pope Pius XII. Vatican: Polyglot Press, 1948.

* Jenkinson, Edward B. *Censors in the Classroom: The Mind Benders.* Carbondale: Southern Illinois University Press, 1979.

Johnson, Claudia. *Stifled Laughter: A Woman's Story About Fighting Censorship.* Golden, Colo.: Fulcrum Publishing, 1994.

Johnson, Wayne L. *Ray Bradbury.* New York: Frederick Ungar Publishing Company, 1980.

Josephson, Matthew. *Zola and His Time.* Garden City, N.Y.: Garden City Publishing Company, 1928.

Kallen, Stuart A. *Maya Angelou: Woman of Words, Deeds, and Dreams.* Minneapolis, Minn.: Abdo and Daughters, 1993.

Karolides, Nicholas J., Lee Burress and John M. Kean, eds. *Censored Books: Critical Viewpoints.* Metuchen, N.J.: Scarecrow Press, 1993.

Katz, Jonathan Ned. *Gay American History: Lesbians and Gay Men in the U.S.A.* Rev. ed. New York: Penguin Books, 1992.

Kendrick, Walter. *The Secret Museum.* New York: Viking Press, 1987.

King, Stephen. "Banned Books and Other Concerns: The Virginia Beach Lecture." In *The Stephen King Companion.* Ed. by George Beahm, 51–61. Kansas City, Mo.: Andrews and McMeel, 1989.

Kirk, Ersye. *The Black Experience in Books for Children and Young Adults.* Ardmore, Okla.: Positive Impact, 1993.

Knowles, Sebastian. *British and Irish—A Purgatorial Flame: Seven British Writers in the Second World War.* London: Routledge Paul, 1991.

Kostelanetz, Richard. *Politics in the African-American Novel: James Weldon Johnson, W.E.B. DuBois, Richard Wright, and Ralph Ellison.* New York: Greenwood Press, 1991.

Kramer, Barbara. *Alice Walker: Author of 'The Color Purple.'* Springfield, N.J.: Enslow Publishers, 1995.

---

* Key sources

Kronhausen, Eberhard, and Phyllis Kronhausen. *Pornography and the Law.* New York: Ballantine Books, 1959.

Lamond, John. *Arthur Conan Doyle: A Memoir.* Port Washington, N.Y.: Kennikat Press, 1972.

Larabee, Leonard W., ed. *The Autobiography of Benjamin Franklin.* New Haven, Conn.: Yale University Press, 1964.

Leatherdale, Clive. *Dracula: The Novel and the Legend.* Northamptonshire, England: Aquarian Press, 1985.

Lennon, Florence Becker. *The Life of Lewis Carroll.* New York: Dover Publications, 1972.

Lennon, J. Michael, ed. *Conversations with Norman Mailer.* Jackson, Miss.: University Press of Mississippi, 1988.

* Lewis, Felice Flanery. *Literature, Obscenity, and Law.* Carbondale, Ill.: Southern Illinois University Press, 1976.

Light, Martin. *The Quixotic Vision of Sinclair Lewis.* West Lafayette, Ind.: Purdue University Press, 1975.

Lingeman, Richard. *Theodore Dreiser: At the Gates of the City, 1871–1907.* Vol. 1. New York: G.P. Putnam's Sons, 1986.

Lockwood, Lee. *Conversation with Eldridge Cleaver: Algiers.* New York: McGraw-Hill, 1970.

Loth, David. *The Erotic in Literature.* New York: Dorset Press, 1961.

Louÿs, Pierre. "Preface." *Aphrodite.* Trans. by Lewis Galantiere. New York: Modern Library, 1933.

MacPherson, Pat. *Reflecting in the Bell Jar.* New York: Routledge Kegan Paul, 1991.

Manso, Peter. *Mailer: His Life and Times.* New York: Simon & Schuster, 1985.

Manvell, Roger. *The Trial of Annie Besant and Charles Bradlaugh.* New York: Horizon Press, 1976.

May, Jill. "In Defense of *To Kill a Mockingbird.*" In *Censored Books: Critical Viewpoints.* Ed. by Nicholas J. Karolides, Lee Burress and John M. Kean, 476–484. Metuchen, N.J.: Scarecrow Press, 1993.

* McCoy, Ralph E. *Banned in Boston: The Development of Literary Censorship in Massachusetts.* Urbana, Ill.: University of Illinois, 1956.

Meeks, Christopher. *Roald Dahl: Kids Love His Stories.* Vero Beach, Fla.: Rourke Publishing, 1993.

Mellow, James R. *Hemingway: A Life Without Consequences.* New York: Houghton Mifflin Company, 1992.

Meyers, Jeffrey. *Hemingway: A Biography.* New York: Harper & Row, 1985.

Mileck, Joseph. *Hermann Hesse: Life and Art.* Berkeley: University of California Press, 1978.

---

* Key sources

Miles, Barry. *William Burroughs: El Hombre Invisible*. New York: Hyperion Publishing, 1983.

Miller, Edwin Haviland. *Salem Is My Dwelling Place: A Life of Nathaniel Hawthorne*. Iowa City: University of Iowa Press, 1991.

Montgomery, Sy. *Walking with the Great Apes*. Boston: Houghton Mifflin, 1991.

Mordell, Albert. *Notorious Literary Attacks*. New York: Boni & Liveright, 1926.

Morgan, Charles. *Epitaph on George Moore*. New York: Macmillan Company, 1935.

Morgan, Ted. *Literary Outlaw: The Life and Times of William S. Burroughs*. New York: Henry Holt & Company, 1988.

Nethercot, Arthur H. *The Last Four Lives of Annie Besant*. Chicago: University of Chicago Press, 1963.

Noble, Donald R. *The Steinbeck Question*. Troy, N.Y.: Whitston Publishing, 1993.

* Noble, William. *Bookbanning in America: Who Bans Books?—And Why*. Middlebury, Vt.: Paul S. Eriksson, Publisher, 1990.

* O'Higgins, Paul. *Censorship in England*. London: Nelson, 1972.

Olander, Joseph D., and Martin Harry Greenberg. *Robert A. Heinlein*. New York: Taplinger Publishing, 1978.

Oldsey, Bernard. *Hemingway's Hidden Craft: The Writing of "A Farewell to Arms"*. University Park: Pennsylvania State University Press, 1979.

* O'Neil, Robert M. *Classrooms in the Crossfire: The Rights and Interests of Students, Parents, Teachers, Administrators, Librarians, and the Community*. Bloomington, Ind.: Indiana University Press, 1981.

Orel, Harold, ed. *Critical Essays on Sir Arthur Conan Doyle*. New York: G. K. Hall, 1992.

Padover, Saul Kussiel. *The Complete Jefferson*. New York: Duell, Sloan & Pearce, 1943.

Padover, Saul Kussiel. *The Complete Madison*. New York: Harper & Brothers, 1953.

* Paul, James C. N., and Murray L. Schwartz. *Federal Censorship: Obscenity in the Mail*. New York: Free Press of Glencoe, 1961.

* People for the American Way. *Attacks on the Freedom to Learn, 1990–91 Report*. Washington, D.C.: People for the American Way, 1991.

* Perrin, Noel. *Dr. Bowdler's Legacy: A History of Expurgated Books in England and America*. Boston: David R. Godine, 1992.

Petersen, William. *The Politics of Population*. Garden City, N.Y.: Doubleday & Company, 1964.

Pettit, Jayne. *Maya Angelou: Journey of the Heart*. New York: Lodester Books, 1996.

---

* Key sources

Pinsker, Sanford. *Understanding Joseph Heller*. Columbia, S.C.: University of South Carolina Press, 1991.
Popkin, Michael. *Modern Black Writers*. New York: Frederick R. Ungar, 1978.
Porter, Horace A. *Stealing the Fire: The Art and Protest of James Baldwin*. Middletown, Conn.: Wesleyan University Press, 1989.
Potts, Stephen. *Catch-22: Antiheroic Antinovel*. Boston: Twayne Publishing, 1989.
Potts, Stephen. *From Here to Absurdity: The Moral Battlefields of Joseph Heller*. San Bernardino, Calif.: Borgo Press, 1982.
Powling, Chris. *Roald Dahl*. London: Evans Bros., 1993.
Reed, James. *From Private Vice to Public Virtue: The Birth Control Movement and American Society*. New York: Basic Books, 1978.
* Reichman, Henry. *Censorship and Selection: Issues and Answers for Schools*. Chicago: American Library Association; Arlington, Va.: American Association of School Administrators, 1993. A joint publication.
Reynolds, Michael. *Hemingway: The American Homecoming*. Cambridge, Mass.: Blackwell Publishers, 1992.
Reynolds, Michael S. *Hemingway's First War: The Making of "A Farewell to Arms"*. Princeton, N.J.: Princeton University Press, 1976.
Rideout, Walter. *The Radical Novel in the U.S.* New York: Hill & Wang, 1966.
Robertson, Geoffrey. *Obscenity: An Account of the Censorship Laws and Their Enforcement in England and Wales*. London: Weidenfeld & Nicolson, 1979.
Robins, Natalie. *Alien Ink: The FBI's War on Freedom of Expression*. New York: William Morrow & Company, 1992.
Rollyson, Carl. *The Lives of Norman Mailer*. New York: Paragon House, 1991.
Rose, June. *Marie Stopes and the Sexual Revolution*. Boston: Faber & Faber, 1992.
Samuelson, David W. "Stranger in the Mirror: Model or Mirror?" In *Critical Encounters: Writers and Themes in Science Fiction*. Ed. by Dick Riley, 144–175. New York: Frederick Ungar, 1978.
Sanders, Ed. *The Family: The Story of Charles Manson's Dune Buggy Attack Battalion*. New York: Berkeley Books, 1971.
Saunders, Edith. *The Prodigal Father*. New York: Longmans, Green & Company, 1951.
Schom, Alan. *Emile Zola: A Biography*. New York: Henry Holt & Company, 1987.
Select Committee on Pornographic Materials, House of Representatives, 82nd Congress. *Report of the Committee on Pornographic Materials*. House Report No. 2510. 1952. (Known as the Gathings Committee Report because E. C. Gathings headed the committee.)
Shaw, George Bernard. "The Censorship." *Irish Statesman* 11 (1928): 206–208. Reprinted in *Banned in Ireland: Censorship and the Irish Writer*.

* Key sources

Ed. by Julia Carlson, 133–141. Athens, Ga.: The University of Georgia Press, 1990.

Shuker, Nancy. *Maya Angelou.* Englewood Cliffs, N.J.: Silver Burdett Press, 1990.

Skaggs, Merrill. *The Folk of Southern Fiction.* Athens, Ga.: University of Georgia Press, 1972.

Slayton, Paul. "Teaching Rationale for William Golding's *Lord of the Flies.*" In *Censored Books: Critical Viewpoints.* Ed. by Nicholas J. Karolides, Lee Burress and John M. Kean, 351–357. Metuchen, N.J.: Scarecrow Press, 1993.

Sloan, James Park. *Jerzy Kosinski: A Biography.* New York: E.P. Dutton & Company, 1996.

Slusser, George Edgar. *Robert A. Heinlein: Stranger in His Own Land.* San Bernardino, Calif.: Borgo Press, 1976.

Smith, Grover, ed. *Letters of Aldous Huxley.* London: Chatto & Windus, 1969.

Spain, Valerie. *Meet Maya Angelou.* New York: Random House, 1995.

Steinbeck, Elaine, and Robert Wallsten, eds. *Steinbeck: A Life in Letters.* New York: Viking Press, 1975.

Stutman, Suzanne, ed. *My Other Loneliness: Letters of Thomas Wolfe and Aline Bernstein.* Chapel Hill, N.C.: University of North Caroline Press, 1983.

Sullivan, Charles, ed. *Children of Promise: African-American Literature and Art for Young People.* New York: Harry N. Abrams, 1991.

* Sutherland, John. *Offensive Literature: Decensorship in Britain, 1960–1982.* London: Junction Books, 1982.

Symons, Ann K. *Protecting the Right to Read: A How-to-Do Manual for School and Public Librarians.* New York: Neal-Schuman Publishers, 1996.

Tatar, Maria. *The Hard Facts of the Grimm's Fairy Tales.* Princeton, N.J.: Princeton University Press, 1987.

Taylor, Helen. *Scarlett's Women: "Gone with the Wind" and Its Female Fans.* New Brunswick, N.J.: Rutgers University Press, 1989.

* Tebbel, John. *A History of Book Publishing in the United States, 1630–1865.* Vol. 1. New York: R.R. Bowker Company, 1972.

* Tebbel, John. *A History of Book Publishing in the United States.* Vol. 4. New York: R.R. Bowker & Company, 1981.

Timmerman, John. *John Steinbeck's Fiction: The Aesthetics of the Road Taken.* Norman, Okla.: University of Oklahoma Press, 1986.

Treglown, Jeremy. *Roald Dahl: A Biography.* New York: Farrar, Straus & Giroux, 1994.

Van Doren, Carl. *Ben Franklin.* New York: Bramhall House, 1987.

Weathersby, Dorothy T. *Censorship of Literature Textbooks in Tennessee: A Study of the Commission, Publishers, Teachers, and Textbooks.* Ed.D. diss., University of Tennessee, 1975.

---

*Key sources

Weil-Norden, P. *Sir Arthur Conan Doyle.* Centenary edition. Garden City, N.Y.: Doubleday & Company, 1959.

Wenke, Joseph. *Mailer's America.* Hanover, N.H.: University Press of New England, 1987.

Williams, John A. "Blackballing." In *Censored Books: Critical Viewpoints.* Ed. by Nicholas J. Karolides, Lee Burress and Jon M. Kean: 11–18. Metuchen, N.J.: Scarecrow Press, 1992.

Wood, James Playsted. *The Unpardonable Sin.* New York: Pantheon Books, 1970.

Wullschlager, Jackie. *Inventing Wonderland: The Lives and Fantasies of Lewis Carroll, Edward Lear, J. M. Barrie, Kenneth Grahame and A. A. Milne.* New York: Free Press, 1995.

Wylder, Delbert E. *Hemingway's Heroes.* Albuquerque, N.M.: University of New Mexico Press, 1969.

* Young Adult Services Division, Intellectual Freedom Committee. *Hit List: Frequently Challenged Young Adult Titles: References to Defend Them.* Chicago: YASD, American Library Association, 1989.

Zipes, Jack. *Fairy Tales and the Art of Subversion: The Classical Genre for Children and the Process of Civilization.* New York: Wildman Press, 1983.


## PERIODICALS

Alvino, James. "Is It Book Burning Time Again?" *The New York Times* (December 28, 1980): 11:18.

"Annie Goes Back to School." *School Library Journal* 42 (January 1996): 13.

"Another Furor over Books." *Ohio State University Monthly* 55 (December 1963): 8–12.

"*Aphrodite* Brings Fine." *New York Times* (June 24, 1930): 8.

Baker, Augusta. "The Black Experience in Children's Literature—An Introductory Essay." *New York Public Library Bulletin* 75 (March 1971): 143–145.

Baldwin, Deborah. "John Gardner: The Serious Optimist." *Common Cause* 15 (September 1989): 34–38.

Barr, Donald. "Should Holden Caulfield Read These Books?" *New York Times Book Review* 91 (May 4, 1986): 1, 50–51.

Blaine, Diana York. "The Abjection of Addie and Other Myths of the Maternal in *As I Lay Dying.*" *Mississippi Quarterly* 47 (Summer 1994): 418–419.

Booth, Wayne C. "Censorship and the Values of Fiction." *English Journal* 53 (March 1964): 155–164.

"Book Burning in North Dakota." *Chicago Sun-Times* (November 14, 1973): 40.

"Book Scored, Seller Held." *New York Times* (March 5, 1930): 25.

---

* Key sources

"Boston Bans Sale of 'Elmer Gantry'." *New York Times* (April 13, 1927): 16.

Bradley, Julia T. "Censoring the School Library: Do Students Have the Right to Read?" *Connecticut Law Review* 10 (Spring 1978): 747–771.

Brooks, Peter. "Storied Bodies, or *Nana* at Last Unveil'd." *Critical Inquiry* 16 (Autumn 1989): 1–32.

Brown, Claude. "Manchild in Harlem." *New York Times Magazine* (April 14, 1996): 111.

Brown, Frederick. "Zola and the Making of *Nana*." *Hudson Review* 45 (Summer 1992): 191–217.

Bruell, Edwin. "Keen Scalpel on Racial Ills." *English Journal* 53 (December 1964): 658–661.

Budd, John M. "Law and Morality in *Billy Budd* and *The Ox-Bow Incident*." "CLA Journal 35 (December 1991): 185–197.

Burgess-Jackson, Keith. "Rape and Persuasive Definition." *Canadian Journal of Philosophy* 25 (September 1995): 415–454.

Buttenwieser, Susan. "A Child's Garden of . . . Diversity." *Ms.* 3 (January 1993): 61–62.

Carrington, Ildiko de Papp. "Talking Dirty: Alice Munro's 'Open Secrets' and John Steinbeck's 'Of Mice and Men'." *Studies in Short Fiction* 31 (Fall 1994): 595–606.

Cart, Michael. "Carte Blanche: Winning One for the First Amendment." *Booklist* 92 (April 15, 1996): 1,431.

Chase, Richard, Jr. "Little Red Riding Hood: Werewolf and Prostitute." *Journal of History* 57 (Summer 1995): 769–776.

Cirillo, Nancy R. "A Girl Need Never Go Wrong, or, the Female Servant as Ideological Image in Germinie Lacerteux and Esther Waters." *Comparative Literature Studies* 28 (1991): 68–88.

Clarke, Elyse. "A Slow, Subtle Exercise in Censorship." *School Library Journal* 32 (March 1986): 93–96.

"Class *Aphrodite* as Indicent Book." *New York Times* (June 14, 1930): 12.

Cloonan, Michele. "The Censorship of the Adventures of Huckleberry Finn." *Top of the News* (Winter 1984): 191–194.

Cohen, David. "Selection and Racism." *Library Journal* (October 15, 1969): 3,585.

Cohen, Peter F. "'I Won't Kiss You . . . I'll Send Your English Girl': Homoerotic Desire in 'A Farewell to Arms'." *Hemingway Review* 15 (Fall 1995): 42–53.

Conroy, Stephen S. "Sinclair Lewis's Sociological Imagination." *American Literature* 42 (November 1970): 348–362.

Corbett, Edward P. J. "Raise High the Barriers, Censors." *America* 54 (January 7, 1961): 441–444.

Croley, Laura Sagolla. "The Rhetoric of Reform in Stoker's *Dracula*: Depravity, Decline, and the Fin-de-siecle 'Residium'." *Criticism* 37 (Winter 1995): 85–108.

"Daddy Is Out of the Closet: *Daddy's Roommate* by Michael Willhoite / *Heather Has Two Mommies* by Leslea Newman." *Newsweek* 117 (January 7, 1991): 60.

Davis, Mavis Wormley. "Black Images in Children's Literature: Revised Editions Needed." *Library Journal* (January 15, 1972): 261–263.

Djos, Matt. "Alcoholism in Ernest Hemingway's *The Sun Also Rises*: A Wine and Roses Perspective on the Lost Generation." *Hemingway Review* 14 (Spring 1995): 64–78.

Donaldson, Scott. "Censorship and 'A Farewell to Arms'." *Studies in American Fiction* 19 (Spring 1991): 85–93.

Early, Gerald. "Their Malcolm, My Problem." *Harper's* 285 (December 1992): 62–74.

Ebersole, Peter. "Dickey's *Deliverance*." *Explicator* 49 (Summer 1991): 249–251.

Egan, John M. "Golding's View of Man." *America* 108 (January 26, 1963): 140–141.

Egan, James. "Sacral Parody in the Fiction of Stephen King." *Journal of Popular Culture* 23 (Winter 1989): 125–141.

Elliott, Ira. "Performance Art: Jake Barnes and 'Masculine' Signification in *The Sun Also Rises*." *American Literature* 67 (March 1995): 77–94.

"'Elmer Gantry' Banned in Boston." *Publishers' Weekly* (April 16, 1927): 1,569.

Fox-Genovese, Elizabeth. "Myth and History: Discourse of Origins in Zora Neale Hurston and Maya Angelou." *Black American Literature Forum* 42 (Summer 1990): 221–235.

Gebhard, Ann O. "The Emerging Self: Young Adult and Classic Novels of the Black Experience." *English Journal* 82 (September 1993): 50–54.

Grant, S. S., and S. E. Angoff. "Massachusetts Censorship." *Boston University Law Review* 10 (1946): 147.

Green Daniel. "A World Worth Laughing At: *Catch-22* and the Humor of Black Humor." *Studies in the Novel* 27 (Summer 1995): 186–196.

Hale, Dorothy J. "*As I Lay Dying*'s Heterogeneous Discourse." *Novel: A Forum on Fiction* 23 (Fall 1989): 5–23.

Hardigg, Viva. "Censors at Work." *U.S. News & World Report* 117 (September 26, 1994): 29.

Hartshorne, Thomas L. "Horatio Alger in Harlem: Manchild in the Promised Land." *Journal of American Studies* 24 (August 1990): 243–248.

Hartvigsen, M. Kip. "Haven Peck's Legacy in *A Day No Pigs Would Die*." *English Journal* 74 (April 1985): 41–45.

Hayes, Elizabeth. "Tension Between Darl and Jewel." *Southern Literary Journal* 24 (Spring 1992): 49–61.

Hendershot, Cyndy. "Vampire and Replicant: The One-Sex Body in a Two-Sex World." *Science-Fiction Studies* 22 (November 1995): 373–398.

Herrick, Robert. "What Is Dirt?" *Bookman* 70 (November 1929): 258–262.

Hildebrand, Joan M. "Books for Children: *Daddy's Roommate*." *Childhood Education* 70 (1994): 306.

Hildebrand, Joan M. "Books for Children: *Heather Has Two Mommies*." *Childhood Education* 70 (1994): 305.

Hitchens, Christopher. "The Grimmest Tales." *Vanity Fair* (January 1994): 26–30.

Hohne, Karen A. "The Spoken Word in the Works of Stephen King." *Journal of Popular Culture* 28 (Fall 1994): 93–103.

Kermode, Frank. "'Obscenity' and the 'Public Interest'." *New American Review* 3 (April 1968): 229–244.

Kincaid, Nanci. "As Me and Addie Lay Dying." *Southern Review* 30 (Summer 1994): 582–595.

Klein, Norma. "Some Thoughts on Censorship: An Author Symposium." *Top of the News* 39 (Winter 1983): 137–153.

Lane, James B. "Violence and Sex in the Post-War Popular Urban Novel: With a Consideration of Harold Robbins's *A Stone for Danny Fisher* and Hubert Selby, Jr.'s, *Last Exit to Brooklyn*." *Journal of Popular Culture* 8 (Fall 1974): 295–308.

Lanes, Selma G. "Doctor Dolittle, Innocent Again." *The New York Times Book Review* (August 28, 1988): 20.

Leary, Timothy, and Ralph Metzner. "Hermann Hesse: Poet of the Interior Journey." *Psychedelic Review* 1 (1963): 167–182.

Lewis-House, Nancy. "Books Worth Teaching Even Though They Have Proven Controversial: *The Chocolate War* by Robert Cormier." *English Journal* 82 (April 1993): 88.

Lisack, Thomas. "Books Worth Teaching Even Though They Have Proven Controversial: *Invisible Man* by Ralph Ellison." *English Journal* 82 (April 1993): 88.

Mallet, Isabelle. "Unruly Local Color." *New York Times Book Review* (March 7, 1948): 26.

Mandel, Miriam. "Ferguson and Lesbian Love: Unspoken Subplots in 'A Farewell to Arms'." *Hemingway Review* 14 (Fall 1994): 18–24.

Manfred, Frederick. "Sinclair Lewis: A Portrait." *American Scholar* 23 (Spring 1954): 162–184.

Massie, Dorothy C. "Censorship in the Schools: Something Old and Something New." *Today's Education* 69 (November/December 1980): 56–62.

Matter, William W. "The Utopian Tradition and Aldous Huxley." *Science Fiction Studies* 2 (1975): 146–151.

McClure, Robert C. "Literature, the Law of Obscenity, and the Constitution." *Minnesota Law Review* 38 (March 1954): 325.

McCullough, Debbie. "Idealism and Reality in the Works of Laura Ingalls Wilder." *English in Education* 26 (Spring 1992): 33–37.

McGee, Tim. "The Adolescent Novel in AP English." *English Journal* (April 1992): 57–58.

Meriwether, James B. "The Dashes in Hemingway's *A Farewell to Arms*." *The Papers of the Bibliographical Society of America* 58 (Fourth Quarter, 1964): 449–457.

Messiano, Lindalee. "Even When It Offends." *Library Journal* (May 15, 1969): 2,031.

Meyer, Howard N. "Neutralism Isn't Neutral." *CIBC Bulletin* 11 (1980): 13.

Miller, Warren. "One Score in Harlem—Review of *Manchild in the Promised Land*, by Claude Brown." *Saturday Review* (August 28, 1965): 49.

Mills, Claudia. "From Obedience to Autonomy: Moral Growth in the 'Little House' Books." *Children's Literature: An International Journal* 24 (1996): 127–140.

"'Miss Jane Pittman' Is Removed from a Class at Blacks' Behest." *New York Times* (January 22, 1995): Sec. 1, 19.

*Modern Fiction Studies* (special Burgess issue) 27 (Autumn 1981).

Moore, Everett T. "A Rationale for Bookburners: A Further Word from Ray Bradbury." *ALA Bulletin* 55 (May 1961): 403–404.

Moore, Michael. "Pathological Communication Patterns in Heller's *Catch-22*." *Et Cetera* 52 (Winter 1995): 431–459.

Moore, Robert B. "From Rags to Witches: Stereotypes, Distortions and Anti-Humanism in Fairy Tales." *CIBC Bulletin* 8 (1975): 1.

Moorhead, Michael. "Dickey's *Deliverance*." *Explicator* 51 (Summer 1993): 247–248.

Morrell, Virginia. "Called 'Trimates,' Three Bold Women Shaped Their Field." *Science* 260 (April 16, 1993): 420–425.

Nahmod, Sheldon H. "Controversy in the Classroom: The High School Teacher and Freedom of Expression." *George Washington University Law Review* 39 (July 1974): 1,031.

Nelms, Elizabeth D. "Books, Films, and Culture: Reading in the Classroom: *The Chocolate War*/'The Chocolate War'." *English Journal* (January 1991): 85.

Nelson, Emmanuel. "Critical Deviance: Homophobia and the Reception of James Baldwin's Fiction." *Journal of American Culture* 14 (Fall 1991): 91–96.

Nelson, Randy F. "Banned in Boston and Elsewhere." *The Almanac of American Letters*. Los Altos, Calif.: William Kaufman, 1981.

* *Newsletter on Intellectual Freedom*. Judith F. Krug, ed. Chicago: American Library Association, Intellectual Freedom Committee. Numerous issues from April 1956 through May 1995.

Oboler, Eli M. "Idaho School Librarians and Salinger's *Catcher in the Rye*: A Candid Report." *Idaho Librarian* 15 (October 1963): 137–139.

Olson, Renee. "Battles over Books Usher in New School Year." *School Library Journal* 41 (October 1995): 10–11.

---

*Key sources

O'Neil, Robert M. "Libraries, Liberty and the First Amendment." *University of Cincinnati Law Review* 42:2 (1973): 209–252.

Overmyer, Janet. "The Invisible Man and White Women." *Notes on Contemporary Literature* 6 (May 1976): 13–15.

Pace, Eric. "Fears of Local Censorship Haunt the Book Trade." *New York Times* (January 8, 1974): 26.

Parker, Ian. "Making Advances." *The New Yorker* (April 1, 1996): 72–80.

Parr, J. L. "Calder Willingham: The Forgotten Novelist." *Critique* 11 (1969): 57–65.

Pinsker, Sanford. "Individual Authors: A Rotten Way to Be Wounded." *Journal of Modern Literature* 18 (Spring 1993): 277–278.

Podhoretz, Norman. "Gibbsville and New Leeds: The America of John O'Hara and Mary McCarthy." *Commentary* 1 (March 1956): 493–499.

Rice, Anne M. "Still Good Reading: Adolescent Novels Written Before 1967—*A Separate Peace* by John Knowles." *English Journal* (April 1992): 88.

Rigolet, François. "Rabelais, Misogyny, and Christian Charity: Biblical Intertextuality and the Renaissance Crisis of Exemplarity." *PMLA* 109 (March 1994): 225–237.

Roberts, Terry. "Irreconcilable Talents: Thomas Wolfe's Struggle to Compose *Of Time and the River*." *Mississippi Quarterly* 43 (Winter 1989): 22–32.

Rothman, Nathan L. "A Slick Toughie." *Saturday Review of Literature* (May 22, 1948): 27.

Rowden, Terry. "A Play of Abstractions: Race, Sexuality, and Community in James Baldwin's *Another Country*." *Southern Review* 29 (Winter 1993): 41–50.

Rudat, Wolfgang. "Sexual Dilemma in *The Sun Also Rises*: Hemingway's Count and the Education of Jacob Barnes." *Hemingway Review* 8 (Spring 1989): 2–13.

"Sambo Banned by Montgomery County Schools." *Library Journal* (September 15, 1971): 2,813–2,814.

"Sambo Removal Sought by National Black Coalition." *Library Journal* (January 15, 1972): 237–238.

Scala, Elizabeth. "Canace and the Chaucer Canon." *Chaucer Review* 30 (1995): 15–39.

Schaffer, Talia. "A Wilde Desire Took Me: The Homoerotic History of 'Dracula'." *ELH* 61 (Summer 1994): 381–425.

Schwab, A. T. "Irish Author and American Critic." *Nineteenth Century Fiction* 8 (March 1954): 256–277.

Seed, David. "The Flight from the Good Life: 'Fahrenheit 451' in the Context of Postwar American Dystopias." *Journal of American Studies* 28—pt. 2 (August 1994): 225–240.

Segel, Elizabeth. "Laura Ingalls Wilder's America: An Unflinching Assessment." *Children's Literature in Education* 8 (February 1978): 63–70.

Senf, Carol A. "Dracula and the Victorian Male Sexual Imagination." *International Journal of Women's Studies* 3 (1980): 455.

Sharpe, Ernest, Jr. "The Man Who Changed His Skin." *American Heritage* 40 (February 1989): 44–55.

Sloan, James Park. "Kosinski's War." *New Yorker* (October 10, 1994): 46–53.

Solotaroff, Robert. "Sexual Identity in 'A Farewell to Arms'." *Hemingway Review* 9 (Fall 1989): 2–17.

"Steinbeck's *East of Eden*." *The Asterisk: An Occasional Journal of English Traditions* (October 1978): 2.

"Steinbeck Novel Creates Controversy." *The Los Angeles Times* (June 3, 1978): 1.

St. Lifer, Evan. "*Daddy's Roommate* Challenged in VT." *Library Journal* 120 (July 1995): 14–16.

Straus, Dorothea. "Remembering Jerzy Kosinski." *Partisan Review* 60 (Winter 1993): 138–142.

Strychacz, Thomas. "Dramatizations of Manhood in Hemingway's *In Our Time* and *The Sun Also Rises*." *American Literature* 61 (May 1989): 245–260.

Trilling, Lionel. "John O'Hara Observes Our Mores." *New York Times Book Review* (March 18, 1945): 1, 9. Reprinted as the introduction to *Selected Short Stories of John O'Hara*. New York: Random House, 1956.

Twitchell, James B. "Women and Vampires: *Dracula* as a Victorian Novel." *Midwest Quarterly* 18 (1977): 392–405.

"Using Adolescent Novels as Transitions to Literary Classics: *Bless the Beasts and the Children*." *English Journal* 78 (March 1989): 83–84.

Vincent, Ted. "The Garveyite Parents of Malcolm X." *Black Scholar* 20 (March 1989): 10–13.

Waldrep, Shelton. "Being Bridges: Cleaver, Baldwin and Lorde and African-American Sexism and Sexuality." *Journal of Homosexuality* 26 (1993): 167–180.

Webb, C. Anne. "The Battle Continues." *English Journal* 84 (September 1995): 123–124.

Webb, C. Anne. "Censorship in the Pennsylvania Schools." *English Journal* 84 (April 1995): 84.

Wertime, Richard A. "Psychic Vengeance in *Last Exit to Brooklyn*." *Literature and Psychology* 24 (November 1974): 153–166.

Wisse, Ruth. "A Romance of the Secret Annex." *New York Times Book Review* (July 2, 1989): 2.

Wolf, Virginia L. "The Symbolic Center: *Little House in the Big Woods*." *Children's Literature in Education* 13 (Fall 1982): 107–114.

Yarrow, Andrew L. "Allen Ginsberg's 'Howl' in a New Controversy." *The New York Times* (January 6, 1988): C2.

# Works Discussed in the Other Volumes of This Series

WORKS DISCUSSED IN *BANNED BOOKS: LITERATURE SUPPRESSED ON POLITICAL GROUNDS* BY NICHOLAS J. KAROLIDES

*ABOUT DAVID*
Susan Beth Pfeiffer

*THE AFFLUENT SOCIETY*
John Kenneth Galbraith

*THE AGE OF KEYNES*
Robert Lekachman

*ALL QUIET ON THE WESTERN FRONT*
Erich Maria Remarque

*AMERICA IN LEGEND*
Richard M. Dorson

*AMERICAN CIVICS*
William H. Hartley and William S. Vincent

*THE AMERICAN PAGEANT: A HISTORY OF THE REPUBLIC*
Thomas A. Bailey

*ANDERSONVILLE*
MacKinlay Kantor

*ANIMAL FARM*
George Orwell

*AREOPAGITICA*
John Milton

*BLACK BOY*
Richard Wright

*BLOODS: AN ORAL HISTORY OF THE VIETNAM WAR
BY BLACK VETERANS*
Wallace Terry

*BORN ON THE FOURTH OF JULY*
Ron Kovic

*BOSS: RICHARD J. DALEY OF CHICAGO*
Mike Royko

*BURGHER'S DAUGHTER*
Nadine Gordimer

*BURY MY HEART AT WOUNDED KNEE*
Dee Brown

*BY WAY OF DECEPTION: THE MAKING AND UNMAKING
OF A MOSSAD OFFICER*
Victor Ostrovsky and Claire Hoy

*CANCER WARD*
Aleksandr Solzhenitsyn

*THE CASE FOR INDIA*
Will Durant

*CAT'S CRADLE*
Kurt Vonnegut Jr.

*CHILD OF ALL NATIONS*
Pramoedya Ananta Toer

*THE CHINA LOBBY IN AMERICAN POLITICS*
Ross Y. Koen

*THE CIA AND THE CULT OF INTELLIGENCE*
Victor Marchetti and John D. Marks

*CITIZEN TOM PAINE*
Howard Fast

*THE COMMERCIAL RESTRAINTS OF IRELAND CONSIDERED*
John Hely Hutchinson

*COMPARATIVE POLITICS TODAY: A WORLD VIEW*
Gabriel A. Almond, general ed.

*CRY AMANDLA!*
June Goodwin

*DAS KAPITAL*
Karl Marx

*DAUGHTER OF EARTH*
Agnes Smedley

*THE DAY THEY CAME TO ARREST THE BOOK*
Nat Hentoff

*DECENT INTERVAL: AN INSIDER'S ACCOUNT
OF SAIGON'S INDECENT END*
Frank Snepp

*DOCTOR ZHIVAGO*
Boris Pasternak

*THE DRAPIER'S LETTERS*
Jonathan Swift

*A DRY WHITE SEASON*
André Brink

*DU PONT: BEHIND THE NYLON CURTAIN*
Gerald Colby Zilg

*EL SEÑOR PRESIDENTE*
Miguel Angel Asturias

*FAIL-SAFE*
Eugene Burdick and Harvey Wheeler

*FIELDS OF FIRE*
James Webb

*A FLEET IN BEING: NOTES OF TWO TRIPS WITH
THE CHANNEL SQUADRON*
Rudyard Kipling

*THE FRAGILE FLAG*
Jane Langton

*THE FUGITIVE*
Pramoedya Ananta Toer

*A GLOBAL HISTORY OF MAN*
Leften S. Stavrianos

*THE GRAPES OF WRATH*
John Steinbeck

*THE GREEN POPE*
Miguel Angel Asturias

*THE GULAG ARCHIPELAGO 1918–1956*
Aleksandr Solzhenitsyn

*GULLIVER'S TRAVELS*
Jonathan Swift

*HANDBOOK FOR CONSCIENTIOUS OBJECTORS*
Robert A. Seeley, ed.

*A HERO ON A DONKEY*
Miodrag Bulatovic

*THE HOAX OF THE TWENTIETH CENTURY*
Arthur R. Butz

*I AM THE CHEESE*
Robert Cormier

*INSIDE RUSSIA TODAY*
John Gunther

*INSIDE THE COMPANY: A CIA DIARY*
Philip Agee

*IN THE SPIRIT OF CRAZY HORSE*
Peter Matthiessen

*AN INTRODUCTION TO PROBLEMS OF AMERICAN CULTURE*
Harold O. Rugg

*THE INVISIBLE GOVERNMENT*
David Wise and Thomas B. Ross

*IT CAN'T HAPPEN HERE*
Sinclair Lewis

*JOHNNY GOT HIS GUN*
Dalton Trumbo

*A JOURNEY FROM ST. PETERSBURG TO MOSCOW*
Aleksandr Nikolaevich Radishchev

*JULIE OF THE WOLVES*
Jean Craighead George

*THE JUNGLE*
Upton Sinclair

*KEEPING FAITH: MEMOIRS OF A PRESIDENT*
Jimmy Carter

*THE LAND AND PEOPLE OF CUBA*
Victoria Ortiz

*LAND OF THE FREE: A HISTORY OF THE UNITED STATES*
John W. Caughey, John Hope Franklin and Ernest R. May

*LAUGHING BOY*
Oliver LaFarge

*LES MISÉRABLES*
Victor Hugo

*MANIFESTO OF THE COMMUNIST PARTY*
Karl Marx and Friedrich Engels

*MARXISM VERSUS SOCIALISM*
Vladimir G. Simkhovitch

*MEIN KAMPF*
Adolf Hitler

*MEN AND NATIONS*
Anatole G. Mazour and John M. Peoples

*MY BROTHER SAM IS DEAD*
James Lincoln Collier and Christopher Collier

*MY NAME IS ASHER LEV*
Chaim Potok

*MY PEOPLE: THE STORY OF THE JEWS*
Abba Eban

*NELSON AND WINNIE MANDELA*
Dorothy Hoobler and Thomas Hoobler

*NINETEEN EIGHTY-FOUR*
George Orwell

*NOVEL WITHOUT A NAME*
Duong Thu Huong

*OIL!*
Upton Sinclair

*ONE DAY IN THE LIFE OF IVAN DENISOVICH*
Aleksandr Solzhenitsyn

*ONE PEOPLE, ONE DESTINY: THE CARIBBEAN AND CENTRAL AMERICA TODAY*
Don Rojas

*OUR LAND, OUR TIME*
Joseph Robert Conlin

*PARADISE OF THE BLIND*
Duong Thu Huong

*THE PRINCE*
Niccolò Machiavelli

*PRINCIPLES OF NATURE*
Elihu Palmer

*PROMISE OF AMERICA*
Larry Cuban and Philip Roden

*RED STAR OVER CUBA*
Nathaniel Weyl

*REPORT OF THE SIBERIAN DELEGATION*
Leon Trotsky

*THE RIGHTS OF MAN*
Thomas Paine

*RUSSIA*
Vernon Ives

*SECRECY AND DEMOCRACY: THE CIA IN TRANSITION*
Stansfield Turner

*SLAUGHTERHOUSE-FIVE OR THE CHILDREN'S CRUSADE*
Kurt Vonnegut Jr.

*SPYCATCHER*
Peter Wright

*THE STATE AND REVOLUTION*
Vladimir I. Lenin

*STRONG WIND*
Miguel Angel Asturias

*THE STRUGGLE IS MY LIFE*
Nelson Mandela

*A SUMMARY VIEW OF THE RIGHTS OF BRITISH AMERICA*
Thomas Jefferson

*SYLVESTER AND THE MAGIC PEBBLE*
William Steig

*TEN DAYS THAT SHOOK THE WORLD*
John Reed

*THE THINGS THEY CARRIED*
Tim O'Brien

*THIS EARTH OF MANKIND*
Pramoedya Ananta Toer

*365 DAYS*
Ronald J. Glasser

*TODAY'S ISMS: COMMUNISM, FASCISM, CAPITALISM, SOCIALISM*
William Ebenstein

*THE UGLY AMERICAN*
William J. Lederer and Eugene Burdick

*UNCLE TOM'S CABIN*
Harriet Beecher Stowe

*UNITED STATES VIETNAM RELATIONS, 1945–67 ("THE PENTAGON PAPERS")*
U.S. Department of Defense

*WHY ARE WE IN VIETNAM?*
Norman Mailer

*WORDS OF CONSCIENCE: RELIGIOUS STATEMENTS OF CONSCIENTIOUS OBJECTORS*
Shawn Perry, ed.

WORKS DISCUSSED IN *BANNED BOOKS: LITERATURE SUPPRESSED ON RELIGIOUS GROUNDS* BY MARGARET BALD

*ADDRESS TO THE CHRISTIAN NOBILITY OF THE GERMAN NATION*
Martin Luther

*THE ADVANCEMENT OF LEARNING*
Francis Bacon

*THE AGE OF REASON*
Thomas Paine

*ALCIPHRON, OR THE MINUTE PHILOSOPHER*
George Berkeley

*THE ANALECTS*
Confucius

*ARCANA COELESTIA*
Emanuel Swedenborg

*THE BABYLONIAN CAPTIVITY OF THE CHURCH*
Martin Luther

*THE BIBLE*

*THE BLOUDY TENENT OF PERSECUTION*
Roger Williams

*THE BOOK OF COMMON PRAYER*
Thomas Cranmer and others

*CHILDREN OF THE ALLEY*
Naguib Mahfouz

*THE CHRISTIAN COMMONWEALTH*
John Eliot

*CHRISTIANITY NOT MYSTERIOUS*
John Toland

*CHRISTIANITY RESTORED*
Michael Servetus

*CHURCH: CHARISM AND POWER: LIBERATION THEOLOGY AND THE INSTITUTIONAL CHURCH*
Leonardo Boff

*COLLOQUIES*
Desiderius Erasmus

*COMMENTARIES*
Averroës (Ibn Rushd)

*COMPENDIUM REVELATIONUM*
Girolamo Savonarola

*CONCERNING HERETICS*
Sebastian Castellio

*THE COURSE OF POSITIVE PHILOSOPHY*
Auguste Comte

*CREATIVE EVOLUTION*
Henri Bergson

*THE CRITIQUE OF PURE REASON*
Immanuel Kant

*DE ECCLESIA*
John Hus

*DE INVENTORIBUS RERUM*
Polydore Vergil

*DE L'ESPRIT*
Claude Adrien Helvétius

*DIALOGUE CONCERNING THE TWO CHIEF WORLD SYSTEMS*
Galileo Galilei

*DIALOGUES CONCERNING NATURAL RELIGION*
David Hume

*DISCOURSE ON METHOD*
René Descartes

*DON QUIXOTE*
Miguel de Cervantes Saavedra

*DRAGONWINGS*
Laurence Yep

*ÉMILE*
Jean-Jacques Rousseau

*ENCYCLOPÉDIE*
Denis Diderot and Jean d'Alembert, eds.

*AN ESSAY CONCERNING HUMAN UNDERSTANDING*
John Locke

*ESSAYS*
Michel de Montaigne

*ETHICS*
Baruch (Benedict) Spinoza

*THE FABLE OF THE BEES*
Bernard Mandeville

*THE GUIDE OF THE PERPLEXED*
Moses Maimonides

*THE HIDDEN FACE OF EVE: WOMEN IN THE ARAB WORLD*
Nawal El Saadawi

*HISTORICAL AND CRITICAL DICTIONARY*
Pierre Bayle

*HISTORY OF THE CONFLICT BETWEEN RELIGION AND SCIENCE*
John William Draper

*THE HISTORY OF THE DECLINE AND FALL OF THE ROMAN EMPIRE*
Edward Gibbon

*INFALLIBLE? AN INQUIRY*
Hans Küng

*AN INQUIRY CONCERNING HUMAN UNDERSTANDING*
David Hume

*INSTITUTES OF THE CHRISTIAN RELIGION*
John Calvin

*INTRODUCTION TO THEOLOGY*
Peter Abelard

*AN INTRODUCTION TO THE PRINCIPLES OF MORALS
AND LEGISLATION*
Jeremy Bentham

*INTRODUCTORY LECTURES ON PSYCHOANALYSIS*
Sigmund Freud

*THE KORAN*

*LAJJA* (SHAME)
Taslima Nasrin

*THE LAST TEMPTATION OF CHRIST*
Nikos Kazantzakis

*LETTER ON THE BLIND*
Denis Diderot

*LETTERS CONCERNING THE ENGLISH NATION*
Voltaire (François Marie Arouet)

*LEVIATHAN*
Thomas Hobbes

*THE LIFE OF JESUS*
Ernest Renan

*MEDITATIONS ON FIRST PHILOSOPHY*
René Descartes

*THE MERITORIOUS PRICE OF OUR REDEMPTION*
William Pynchon

*THE METAPHYSICS*
Aristotle

*THE NEW ASTRONOMY*
Johannes Kepler

*THE NEW TESTAMENT*
William Tyndale, trans.

*NINETY-FIVE THESES*
Martin Luther

*OF THE VANITIE AND UNCERTAINTIE OF ARTES AND SCIENCES*
Henricus Cornelius Agrippa

*OLIVER TWIST*
Charles Dickens

*ON CIVIL LORDSHIP*
John Wycliff

*ON JUSTICE IN THE REVOLUTION AND IN THE CHURCH*
Pierre-Joseph Proudhon

*ON MONARCHY*
Dante Alighieri

*ON THE INFINITE UNIVERSE AND WORLDS*
Giordano Bruno

*ON THE LAW OF WAR AND PEACE*
Hugo Grotius

*ON THE ORIGIN OF SPECIES*
Charles Darwin

*ON THE REVOLUTION OF HEAVENLY SPHERES*
Nicholas Copernicus

*OPUS MAIUS*
Roger Bacon

*PENGUIN ISLAND*
Anatole France (Jacques Anatole Thibault)

*THE PERSIAN LETTERS (1721)*
Charles-Louis de Secondat de Montesquieu

*PHILOSOPHICAL DICTIONARY*
Voltaire (François Marie Arouet)

*THE POLITICAL HISTORY OF THE DEVIL*
Daniel Defoe

*POPOL VUH*

*THE POWER AND THE GLORY*
Graham Greene

*THE PRAISE OF FOLLY*
Desiderius Erasmus

*PRINCIPLES OF POLITICAL ECONOMY*
John Stuart Mill

*THE PROVINCIAL LETTERS*
Blaise Pascal

*THE RAPE OF SITA*
Lindsey Collen

*THE RED AND THE BLACK*
Stendhal (Marie Henri Beyle)

*RELIGIO MEDICI*
Sir Thomas Browne

*RELIGION WITHIN THE LIMITS OF REASON ALONE*
Immanuel Kant

*THE RIGHTS OF THE CHRISTIAN CHURCH ASSERTED*
Matthew Tindal

*THE SANDY FOUNDATION SHAKEN*
William Penn

*THE SATANIC VERSES*
Salman Rushdie

*A SHORT DECLARATION OF THE MISTERY OF INIQUITY*
Thomas Helwys

*THE SHORTEST WAY WITH THE DISSENTERS*
Daniel Defoe

*THE SOCIAL CONTRACT*
Jean-Jacques Rousseau

*THE SORROWS OF YOUNG WERTHER*
Johann Wolfgang von Goethe

*THE SPIRIT OF LAWS*
Charles-Louis de Secondat de Montesquieu

*SPIRITS REBELLIOUS*
Khalil Gibran

*THE STORY OF ZAHRA*
Hanan al-Shaykh

*A TALE OF A TUB*
Jonathan Swift

*THE TALMUD*

*THEOLOGICAL-POLITICAL TREATISE*
Baruch (Benedict) Spinoza

*THREE-PART WORK*
Meister Eckhart

*THE VEIL AND THE MALE ELITE: A FEMINIST INTERPRETATION OF WOMEN'S RIGHTS IN ISLAM*
Fatima Mernissi

*VOYAGES TO THE MOON AND THE SUN*
Savinien Cyrano de Bergerac

*ZOONOMIA*
Erasmus Darwin


## WORKS DISCUSSED IN *BANNED BOOKS: LITERATURE SUPPRESSED ON SEXUAL GROUNDS* BY DAWN SOVA

*AN AMERICAN TRAGEDY*
Theodore Dreiser

*THE ARABIAN NIGHTS*
Sir Richard Burton, trans.

*THE ART OF LOVE*
Ovid (Publius Ovidius Naso)

*BESSIE COTTER*
Wallace Smith

*THE BLUEST EYE*
Toni Morrison

*BOY*
James Hanley

*CANDIDE*
Voltaire (François Marie Arouet)

*CANDY*
Maxwell Kenton

*THE CARPETBAGGERS*
Harold Robbins

*CASANOVA'S HOMECOMING*
Arthur Schnitzler

*THE CHINESE ROOM*
Vivian Connell

*CHRISTINE*
Stephen King

*THE CLAN OF THE CAVE BEAR*
Jean Auel

*CONFESSIONS*
Jean-Jacques Rousseau

*THE DECAMERON*
Giovanni Boccaccio

*THE DEER PARK*
Norman Mailer

*THE DEVIL RIDES OUTSIDE*
John Howard Griffin

*THE DIARY OF SAMUEL PEPYS*
Samuel Pepys

*DROLL STORIES*
Honoré de Balzac

*DUBLINERS*
James Joyce

*FANNY HILL, OR MEMOIRS OF A WOMAN OF PLEASURE*
John Cleland

*THE FIFTEEN PLAGUES OF A MAIDENHEAD*
Anonymous

*FLOWERS FOR ALGERNON*
Daniel Keyes

*THE FLOWERS OF EVIL*
Charles Baudelaire

*FOREVER*
Judy Blume

*FOREVER AMBER*
Kathleen Winsor

*FROM HERE TO ETERNITY*
James Jones

*THE GENIUS*
Theodore Dreiser

*THE GILDED HEARSE*
Charles Gorham

*THE GINGER MAN*
James Donleavy

*GOD'S LITTLE ACRE*
Erskine Caldwell

*THE GROUP*
Mary McCarthy

*HAGAR REVELLY*
Daniel Goodman

*THE HANDMAID'S TALE*
Margaret Atwood

*THE HEPTAMERON*
Queen Margaret of Navarre

*THE HISTORY OF TOM JONES, A FOUNDLING*
Henry Fielding

*HOMO SAPIENS*
Stanley Przybyskzewski

*IF IT DIE*
André Gide

*ISLE OF PINES*
Henry Neville

*JANET MARCH*
Floyd Dell

*JUDE THE OBSCURE*
Thomas Hardy

*JURGEN*
James Cabell

*JUSTINE, OR THE MISFORTUNES OF VIRTUE*
*JULIETTE, HER SISTER, OR THE PROSPERITIES OF VICE*
Marquis de Sade

*THE* KAMA SUTRA *OF VATSAYANA*
Sir Richard Burton, F. F. Arbuthnot, trans.

*THE KREUTZER SONATA*
Leo Tolstoy

*LADIES IN THE PARLOR*
Jim Tully

*LADY CHATTERLEY'S LOVER*
D. H. Lawrence

*LA TERRE* (THE EARTH)
Émile Zola

*LOLITA*
Vladimir Nabokov

*THE LUSTFUL TURK*
Anonymous

*MADAME BOVARY*
Gustave Flaubert

*MADELEINE*
Anonymous

*MADEMOISELLE DE MAUPIN*
Théophile Gautier

*MAID OF ORLEANS*
Voltaire (François Marie Arouet)

*MEMOIRES*
Giovanni Casanova

*MEMOIRS OF A YOUNG RAKEHELL*
Guillaume Apollinaire

*MEMOIRS OF HECATE COUNTY*
Edmund Wilson

*THE MERRY MUSES OF CALEDONIA*
Robert Burns

*MOLL FLANDERS*
Daniel Defoe

*MY LIFE AND LOVES*
Frank Harris

*A NIGHT IN A MOORISH HAREM*
Anonymous

*NOVEMBER*
Gustave Flaubert

*THE 120 DAYS OF SODOM*
Marquis de Sade

*OUR LADY OF THE FLOWERS*
Jean Genet

*PAMELA, OR VIRTUE REWARDED*
Samuel Richardson

*PANSIES*
D. H. Lawrence

*THE PERFUMED GARDEN*
Sir Richard Burton, trans.

*PEYTON PLACE*
Grace Metalious

*THE PHILANDERER*
Stanley Kauffmann

*POEMS AND BALLADS*
Algernon Charles Swinburne

*POINT COUNTER POINT*
Aldous Huxley

*RABBIT, RUN*
John Updike

*THE RAINBOW*
D. H. Lawrence

*REPLENISHING JESSICA*
Max Bodenheim

*SANCTUARY*
William Faulkner

*THE SATYRICON*
Gaius Petronius Arbiter

*SEPTEMBER IN QUINZE*
Vivian Connell

*SERENADE*
James M. Cain

*SEXUS*
Henry Miller

*SIMON CALLED PETER*
Robert Keable

*1601: A FIRESIDE CONVERSATION IN YE TIME
OF QUEEN ELIZABETH*
Mark Twain

*SLEEVELESS ERRAND*
Norah Jacobs

*A STORY TELLER'S HOLIDAY*
George Moore

*STUDS LONIGAN: A TRILOGY*
James T. Farrell

*SUSAN LENOX: HER FALL AND RISE*
David Graham Phillips

*SWEETER THAN LIFE*
Mark Tryon

*TEN NORTH FREDERICK*
John O'Hara

*TESS OF THE D'URBERVILLES*
Thomas Hardy

*THEN AGAIN, MAYBE I WON'T*
Judy Blume

*THE THIEF'S JOURNAL*
Jean Genet

*THREE WEEKS*
Elinor Glyn

*TOBACCO ROAD*
Erskine Caldwell

*TRAGIC GROUND*
Erskine Caldwell

*TRILBY*
George du Maurier

*TRIUMPH OF DEATH*
Gabriele D'Annunzio

*TROPIC OF CANCER*
*TROPIC OF CAPRICORN*
Henry Miller

*ULYSSES*
James Joyce

*VENUS AND TANNHAUSER (UNDER THE HILL)*
Aubrey Beardsley

*THE WILD PALMS*
William Faulkner

*WOMEN IN LOVE*
D. H. Lawrence

*A YOUNG GIRL'S DIARY*
Anonymous

# Index

**A**

*Adventures of Huckleberry Finn, The*
(Twain) 2–5, 9, 133, 171
early challenges to 3
Ellison on 3–4
National Association for the
Advancement of Colored People and 3
racist language complaints 4–5
*Adventures of Sherlock Holmes, The*
(Doyle) 6–7
ban in USSR 7
*Adventures of Tom Sawyer, The* 2, 3,
7–9
racism complaints and 9
African Americans, literature offensive to
Bannerman 168–72
Lofting 93–95
Twain 2–5
*Again, Dangerous Vision* (Ellison) 236
Ailey, Robert 77–78
alcohol use, in *Little Red Riding Hood*
174–76
*Alice's Adventures in Wonderland* (Carroll) 9–11
Chinese ban on 11
Allen, Donald 78
Allen, Hervey 131
*All God's Children Need Traveling Shoes*
(Angelou) 146

*Allinghams, The* (Sinclair) 107
*All the King's Men* (Warren) 119
*Amboy Dukes, The* (Shulman) 11–13
Gathings Committee Report and
13
National Organization for
Decent Literature and 13
obscenity charges and 12
American Civil Liberties Union
Dickey 91
Faulkner 30
Garden 21–22
Ginsberg 145
Hemingway 231
Plath 42
Whillhoite 86
*American Heritage Dictionary of the
English Language* (American
Heritage Publishing Company)
13–15
People for Better Education and
13–14
Daughters of the American Revolution and 15
Educational Research Analysts
and 14–15
obscenity complaints and 14–15
American Jewish Committee 122
American Library Association Intellectual Freedom Committee
115
Andrews, V. C. 209

*And Still I Rise* (Angelou) 16–17
  hatred toward whites and 17
  sexual content complaints and
    16
Angelou, Maya 16–17, 146–48, 200,
  246
*Anne Frank: The Diary of a Young Girl*
  (Frank) 17–19
  father's editing of 18
  German translation censorship
    and 19
  sexual content complaints and 19
*Annie on My Mind* (Garden) 20–22
  American Civil Liberties Union
    and 21, 22
  homosexuality depiction and
    21–22
  1995 judicial ruling on 22
*Another Country* (Baldwin) 22–24
  Federal Bureau of Investigation
    and 23–24
*Anthony Adverse* (Allen) 131
anti-Semitism
  Malamud 120–23
  O'Hara 27–29
  Wolfe 198–200
*Aphrodite* (Louÿs) 24–26
  homosexuality depiction in 26
  New York Society for the Sup-
    pression of Vice and 26
  National Organization for
    Decent Literature and 26
  United States Custom Bureau
    ban 26
*Appointment in Samarra* (O'Hara)
  27–29
  National Organization for
    Decent Literature and 28
  New York Society for the Sup-
    pression of Vice and 28
  obscene language complaints and
    28
  United States Post Office index
    of banned books and 28
*Arabian Nights, The* (Burton) 127

Aristophanes 64
*Art of Love* (Ovid) 127
*As I Lay Dying* (Faulkner) 29–31
  American Civil Liberties Union
    and 30
  Graves County Baptist Associa-
    tion and 30
  profanity and masturbation com-
    plaints and 30
  religious complaints and 30
Asquith, Henry, on Zola 192
*Attorney General v. A Book Named
  "Naked Lunch"* (Burroughs)
  188–89
autobiographies
  Angelou 146–48
  Brown 178–81
  Cleaver 216–19
  Franklin 31–33
  Malcolm X 33–35
  Thomas 98–100
*Autobiography of Benjamin Franklin,
  The* (Franklin) 31–33
  publisher's editing of 32
  *Roth v. United States* and 33
  sexual contents complaints and
    32–33
*Autobiography of Malcolm X , The*
  (Malcolm X with Haley) 33–35
  film version of 35
  racism complaints and 35
*Autobiography of Miss Jane Pittman,
  The* (Gaines) 36–38
  immoral behavior objections and
    37
  racial slurs in 37
  sexual content objections and 37


**B**

Baldwin, James 22–24, 43, 136–38,
  246
*Bamberger v. The Vanguard Press, Inc.*
  (Farrell) 243

Bannerman, Helen 168–72, 246
Baraka, Imamu Amiri 218
*Being There* (Kosinski) 38–40
  homosexuality depiction in 40
  sexual content objections and
    39–40
*Bell Jar, The* (Plath) 40–43
  American Civil Liberties Union
    and 42
  objectionable lifestyle complaints
    and 41
  *Zykan v. Warsaw Community
    School Corporation and Warsaw
    School Board of Trustees* 42
Benchley, Peter 155–57, 246
*Beowulf* 138–40
Bernstein, Aline 199
Besant, Annie, on Knowlton 124–25
*Best Short Stories by Negro Writers, The*
  (Hughes) 43–45, 65
  *Board of Education, Island Trees
    School District No. 26 v. Pico and*
    44–45
*Bicknell v. Vergennes Union High School
  Board* (Mann) 97–98
biographies (*See* autobiographies)
*Black Boy* (Wright) 44, 104
*Black Like Me* (Griffin) 45–48
  obsenity complaints and 47
  racism and 48
Blatty, William P. 78
*Bless the Beasts and Children*
  (Swarthout) 48–50
  violence complaints and 50
*Blubber* (Blume) 50–53
  language complaints and 53
  nastiness complaints and 52
Blume, Judy 50–53, 247
Board of Censors of Ireland 55, 183
*Board of Education, Island Trees Union
  Free School District No. 26 v. Pico*
  Anonymous (*Go Ask Alice*) 130
  Chaucer 65
  Cleaver 216–19
  Hughes 44–45

Malamud 122
Morris 186
*Bob Cary, et al. v. Board of Education of
  Adams-Arapahoe School District 28-J,
  Aurora, Colorado* 78
Boccaccio, Giovanni 127, 128
Boles, Robert 43
Boussevain, E., on Hall 239
bowdlerism (*See* expurgated and
  bowdlerized literature)
Bradbury, Ray 113–16, 247
Bradlaugh, Charles, on Knowlton
  124–25
*Brave New World* (Huxley) 53–55, 70
  Board of Censors of Ireland and
    55
  *Parker v. Board of Education* 55
  sexual behavior complaints and
    55
  language and moral content
    complaints and 55
*Bridge to Terabithia* (Paterson) 56–58
  profanity complaints and 57
Brown, Claude 178–81, 247
Burgess, Anthony 76–79, 247
Burroughs, William Seward (William
  Lee) 78, 144, 157–58, 187–89, 248
Burton, Sir Richard 127


C

*Cain's Book* (Trocchi) 58–60
  judgment of obscenity and 59
  legal appeal and 60
  public burnings of 60
  seizure of books in U.K. 59
Caldwell, Erskine 110, 194, 244
*Camille* (Dumas Jr.) 60–62
  British obscenity laws and 62
  *la Dame aux camélias* based on 62
  *La Traviata* based on 61
  Vatican's list of forbidden books
    and 62
Campbell, Lord, on Dumas 62

*Canterbury Tales, The* (Chaucer)
62–65
American Civil Liberties Union
and 65
expurgation of in U.S. 64
language complaints and 64
*Virgil v. School Board of Columbia
County* and 65
*Carrie* (King) 82
Carroll, Lewis (Charles Dodgson)
9–11, 248
Cassady, Neal 144
*Catch-22* (Heller) 66–68
language complaints and 68
Ohio legal actions and 67
U.S. Court of Appeals ruling and
67–68
*Catcher in the Rye, The* (Salinger)
68–72
Australian Customs seizure of
70
Communist plot complaints and
71
profanity complaints and 70–71
sexual content complaints and
71–72
*Cat's Cradle* 67
Chapman, Robert L. 92–93, 248
*Charles Bradlaugh and Annie Besant v.
The Queen* (Knowlton) 125
Chaucer, Geoffrey 62–65, 248
Chestnutt, Charles W. 43
child abuse, Sendak on 148–50
Childress, Alice 142–44, 249
*Chocolate War, The* (Cormier) 72–75
obscenity complaints and 73–75
sexual content complaints and
73–75
*Christine* (King) 82
Clark, Walter Van Tilburg 205–7,
249
Cleaver, Eldridge 216–19, 249
Clemens, Samuel Langhorne (Mark
Twain) 2–5, 7–9, 133, 265
*Clockwork Orange, A* (Burgess) 76–79

*Bob Cary, et al. v. Board of Educa-
tion of Adams-Aprapahoe School
District* 78
brutality and sexual violence
complaints and 77
language complaints and 78
local standards cases and 77–78
obscenity ordinances and 78
*Collected Works of Pierre Louys*
(Galantiere, translator) 26
*Color Purple, The* (Walker) 79–81
immoral behavior complaints
and 80
sexual explicitness complaints
and 80–81
*Commonwealth of Massachusetts v. Isen-
stadt* (Smith) 223
*Commonwealth v. Gordon* (Robbins)
194
*Complete Works of Doctor François
Rabelais, The* 127
*Coney Island of the Mind* (Ferlinghetti)
78
*Confessions* (Rousseau) 127
Conrad, Joseph 133
Conroy, Pat 205
*Contemporary Short Stories* 152
Cormier, Robert 72–75, 249
corruption, in Willingham 108–10
Council on Interracial Books for
Children 94–95, 117
Coxe, Rev. Arthur C. 211
*Cujo* (King) 82–84
language complaints and 83
sexual content complaints and 83
*Cupid's Yokes* 167

**D**

*Daddy's Roommate* (Willhoite) 84–87,
141
American Civil Liberties Union
and 86
Bladen Coalition of Christians
and 86

homosexuality depiction and 85–86
language complaints and 84–85
Oregon Citizens Alliance and 86
right-to-life group objections 85–86
Dahl, Roald 153–55, 250
*Dame aux Camélias, la* (Dumas Jr.) 60–62
*Dark Angel* (Andrews) 209
*Darkest Hour* (Andrews) 209
*Dark Half, The* (King) 82
Daughters of the American Revolution 15
*Dawn* (Andrews) 209
*Day No Pigs Would Die, A* (Peck) 87–89
  language complaints and 88–89
  violence towards animals and 89
  sexuality complaints and 89
*Dead Zone, The* (King) 82
*Death of Artemio Cruz, The* (Fuentes) 152
*Death of a Salesman* (Miller) 119
*Decameron, The* (Boccaccio) 127, 128
*Deenie* (Blume) 51
delinquency, contribution to, Shulman 11–13
*Deliverance* (Dickey) 89–91
  American Civil Liberties Union and 91
  book burnings and 91
  language complaints and 91
  sexuality complaints and 90–91
  sodomy scene and 90
Dickey, James Lafayette 89–91, 250
*Dictionary of American Slang, A* (Wentworth and Flexner) 92–93
  John Birch Society and 93
  obscenity charges and 93
  profanity complaints and 93
*Dictionary of Slang and Unconventional English* (Partridge) 92–93
  profanity complaints and 93
*Different Seasons* (King) 82

*Doctor Dolittle* (Lofting) 93–95
  Council on Interracial Books for Children and 94–95
  *New York Times* on 95
  radical censoring of (later editions) 95
Dodgson, Charles (*See* Carroll, Lewis)
*Dog Day Afternoon* (Mann) 95–98
  *Bicknell v. Vergennes Union High School Board* 97–98
  language complaints and 97
  *Presidents Council* decision and 98
  sexual content complaints and 97
*Doll's House, A* (Ibsen) 200
*Doubleday Dictionary, The* 14
*Down These Mean Streets* (Thomas) 44, 97, 98–100
  *Board of Education, Island Trees Union Free School District No.26 v. Pico* 100
  Court of Appeals ruling and 99–100
  *Presidents Council, District 25 v. Community School Board, No. 25 (New York City)* 99
  Supreme Court and 100
Doyle, Sir Arthur Conan 6–7, 250
*Dracula* (Stoker) 100–2
  sexual overtones of 101–2
  author advocating censorship 101
*Drawing of the Three, The* (King) 82
Dreiser, Theodore 215–16, 250
drug abuse
  Anonymous (*Go Ask Alice*) 128–31
  Brown 178–81
  Burgess 76–79
  Burroughs 187–89
  Childress 142–44
  Hesse 219–21
  Huxley 53–55
  Lee 157–58

drug abuse (*continued*)
   Selby 161–64
   Thomas 98–100
   Trocchi 58–60
Dumas, Alexandre, Jr. 60–62, 251
Dunbar, Paul Laurence 43
*Dutchman* (Baraka) 218


**E**


*East of Eden* (Steinbeck) 103–4
   obscenity challenges and 104
Ehrlich, Max 78
Eliot, George 133
Ellis, Havelock 182
Ellison, Harlan 236
Ellison, Ralph 43, 150–63, 251
   on Twain 3–4
*Elmer Gantry* (Lewis) 104–7
   Massachusetts banning of
      106–7
   United States Post Office ban
      107
   Watch and Ward Society and
      106
Emerson, Ralph Waldo, on Whitman
   167
*End as a Man* (Willingham) 108–10,
   194, 244
   legal proceedings and 109–10
   New York Society for the Sup-
      pression of Vice and 109
   *People v. Vanguard Press, Inc.* 109
*Ester Waters* (Moore) 110–13
   British libraries censoring of
      112–13
*Exorcist, The* (Blatty) 78
expurgated and bowdlerized literature
   Bradbury 115–16
   Chaucer 64
   Frank 19
   Franklin 32
   Hemingway 118–19
   Lofting 94–95
   Stopes 182

Twain 4
Whitman 167–68
*Eyes of the Dragon, The* (King) 82


**F**


*Fahrenheit 451* (Bradbury) 113–16
   American Library Association
      Intellectual Freedom Commit-
      tee and 115
   language complaints and 115
   special edition for high schools
      of 115
*Fanny Hill* 59, 163
*Farewell to Arms, A* (Hemingway)
   116–20, 208
   *Bookman* review of 119
   language complaints and 117
   Maxwell Perkins editing and
      118
   National Organization for
      Decent Literature and 119
   Nazi burnings of 119
   *Scribner's Magazine* and 119
   sexual innuendo complaints and
      117
Farrell, James Thomas 110, 194,
   242–44, 251
Farris, Michael 171
Faulkner, William 29–31, 110, 194,
   244, 252
Federal Bureau of Investigation
   Baldwin 23–24
   Lewis 160
*Feminine Plural: Stories by Women
   About Growing Up, The* 42
Ferlinghetti, Lawrence 78, 145
Fielding, Henry 127, 128
*Fifty Book* (Rabelais) 126–28
*Firestarter* (King) 82
*Fixer, The* (Malamud) 44, 120–23
   American Jewish Committee and
      122
   anti-Semitic complaints and
      121–22

*Board of Education, Island Trees Union Free School District No.26 v. Pico* 122
    Jewish organizations involvement and 122
    language complaints and 121–22
Flexner, Stuart Berg 92–93
*Flowers in the Attic* (Andrews) 209
*Forever* (Blume) 51
Fossey, Dian 134–36, 252
*Four Past Midnight* (King) 82
*Fourth Book* (Rabelais) 126–28
Frank, Anne 17–19, 252
Franklin, Benjamin 31–33, 252
Franklin, William Temple 32
*Fruits of Philosophy: The Private Companion of Married Couples* (Knowlton) 123–25
    *Charles Bradlaugh and Annie Besant v. The Queen* 124–25
    Free Thought Publishing Society and 124
    immorality charges 124
Fuentes, Carlos 152

**G**

Gaines, Ernest James 36–38, 253
Galantiere, Lewis 26
Garden, Nancy 20–22, 253
*Garden of Shadows* (Andrews) 209
Gardner, John 138–40, 253
*Gargantua and Pantagruel* (Rabelais) 126–28
    English translation of 127
    French Parliament suppression of 127
    New York Society for Suppression of Vice and 127–28
    obscenity charges and 126
    United States Customs Office ban on 128
*Gather Together in My Name* (Angelou) 146

Gathings Committee Report 13
Ginsberg, Allen 78, 144–46, 253
Giovanni, Nikki 183–85, 254
*Go Ask Alice* (Anonymous) 42, 44, 128–31
    *Board of Education, Island Trees Union Free School District No.26 vs. Pico* 130
    drug use depiction and 130, 131
    language complaints and 131
    sexual content complaints and 130
*God Bless You, Mr. Rosewater* (Vonnegut) 67
*God's Little Acre* (Caldwell) 110, 194, 244
Golding, William Gerald 119, 176–78, 254
*Gone with the Wind* (Mitchell) 131–33
    immorality concerns 133
    language complaints and 133
    New York Society for the Suppression of Vice and 133
    Watch and Ward Society and 133
Gordimer, Nadine 152
*Gorillas in the Mist* (Fossey) 134–36
    sexual behavior depictions and 135
*Go Tell It on the Mountain* (Baldwin) 136–38
    anti-white rhetoric and 137
    library "poison shelves" and 137
*Grapes of Wrath, The* (Steinbeck) 119, 208
*Great Santini, The* (Conroy) 205
*Grendel* (Gardner) 138–40
    obscenity challenges and 139–40
    sexual overtone complaints and 140
    violence complaints and 140
Griffin, John Howard 45–48, 254
Grimm, Jacob and Wilhelm 174–76
Griswold, R. W., on Whitman 166
*Growing Up Female in America* 42

Guest, Judith Ann 203–5, 254
Gunther, John 107

**H**

Haley, Alex 33–35
Hall, Radclyffe 237–40, 255
Hawthorne, Nathaniel 209–12, 255
*Hazelwood School District v. Kuhlmeier*
  65
*Heart of a Woman, The* (Angelou) 146
*Heather Has Two Mommies* (Newman)
  85, 86, 140–42
  acceptability for children 140
  homosexuality depiction 141–42
Hegner, William 78
Heinlein, Robert Anson 224–26, 255
Helbront, Maurice 158
Heller, Joseph 66–68, 55
Hemingway, Ernest 116–20, 208,
  227–29, 229–32, 256
*Heptameron, The* (Queen Margaret of
  Navarre) 127
*Hero Ain't Nothin' But a Sandwich, A*
  (Childress) 44, 142–44
  *Board of Education, Island Trees
    Union Free School District No 26
    vs. Pico* 143
  drug use in 143
  objectionable language com-
    plaints 143
Hesse, Hermann 219–21, 256
*Het Achterhuis (Anne Frank: The Diary
  of a Young Girl)* 18
Hicklin Statute 239
*Histoires ou Contes du temps passé, avec
  des Moralités* (Perrault) 174–76
*Histories or Tales of Past Times* (Sam-
  ber) 174
homosexuality
  Dickey 89–91
  Garden 20–22
  Hall 237–40
  Kosinski 38–40
  Mann 95–98

Newman 140–42
Walker 79–81
Willhoite 84–85
*Howl and Other Poems* (Ginsberg)
  144–46
  American Civil Liberties Union
    and 145
  broadcast ban on reading
    145–46
  *Roth v. the United States* and 145
  San Francisco Police seizure of
    145
  United States Customs seizure of
    145
Hughes, Langston 43–45, 256
*Humanities: Cultural Roots and Conti-
  nuities Volume I, The* 64, 65
Huston, Zora Neale 43
Huxley, Aldous 53–55

**I**

Ibsen, Henrik 200
*Idolators, The* (Hegner) 78
*If There Be Thorns* (Andrews) 209
*I Know Why the Caged Bird Sings*
  (Angelou) 146–48, 200
  child molestation in 147
  rape scene and 147
  sexual content complaints and
    147–48
*Index Librorum Prohibitorum* 62, 127,
  192
*I Never Promised You a Rose Garden*
  202
*In re Worthington Company* 128
*In the Night Kitchen* (Sendak) 148–50
  nudity in 149–50
  pornography complaints 149–50
*Invisible Man* (Ellison) 150–63
  language complaints and 152
  National Book Award for 152
  Newspaper Publisher's Award for
    152
  Russwurm Award for 152

violence and sexuality complaints and 152
*It* (King) 82
*It's Not the End of the World* (Blume) 51

**J**

*Jacob Have I Loved* (Paterson) 57
*James and the Giant Peach* (Dahl) 153–55
    suitablility for children and 154
    unsavory activity complaints and 154
*Jaws* (Benchley) 155–57
    language complaints 156
    sexual content complaints 156
John Birch Society 93
Johnson, Marguerite (*See* Angelou, Maya)
Joyce, James, Hemingway on 231
*Judgment Day* (Farrell) 110, 194, 244
*July's People* (Gordimer) 152
*Junky* (Lee) 157–58
    first unexpurgated edition of 158
    Ginsberg introduction to 158
    publisher nervousness and 158
    special preface and introduction for 158
    use of pseudonym for 158

**K**

*Kaddish and Other Poems, 1958–1960* (Ginsberg) 78
Kerouac, Jack 144
Kesey, Ken 200–3, 257
King, Stephen 82–84, 257
*Kingsblood Royal* (Lewis) 159–61
    *Ebony* magazine award for 160
    Federal Bureau of Investigation interest in 160
    racial prejudice and 160
    Society for the Suppression of Vice and 160
    Southern reaction toward 160
Knowles, John H. 212–14, 257
Knowlton, Charles 123–25
Kosinski, Jerzy Nikodem 38–40, 258

**L**

language, objections to
    Angelou 16–17
    Anonymous (*Go Ask Alice*) 128–31
    Benchley 155–57
    Blume 50–53
    Brown 178–81
    Burroughs 187–89
    Chaucer 62–65
    Childress 142–44
    Clark 205–7
    Cleaver 216–19
    Cormier 72–75
    dictionaries 13–15, 92–93
    Ellison 150–53
    Faulkner 29–31
    Gaines 36–38
    Gardner 138–40
    Ginsberg 144–46
    Giovanni 183–85
    Guest 203–5
    Heller 66–68
    Hemingway 116–20, 227–29, 229–32
    Kesey 200–3
    King 81–84
    Knowles 212–14
    Malamud 120–23
    Malcolm X 33–35
    Mann 95–98
    Paterson 56–58
    Rabelais 126–28
    Robbins 192–94
    Salinger 68–72
    Steinbeck 195–98, 207–9

language, objections to (*continued*)
    Swarthout 48–50
    Terkel 240–42
    Thomas 98–100
    Twain 4–5, 7–9
    Whitman 165–68
    Willingham 108–10
*Last Exit to Brooklyn* (Selby) 161–64
    censorship in England 163–64
    legal proceedings against
        163–64
    off-Broadway play of 163
    seizure of 163
*Last Tango in Paris* (Ailey) 77–78
*La Terre* (Zola) 192
*La Traviata* (opera) 61
*Laughing Boy* 44
Leary, Timothy, on Hesse 220
*Leaves of Grass* (Whitman) 165–68
    British censorship of 168
    Emerson praise for 167
    Haywood arrest for mailing 167
    *New Criterion* review of 166
    obscenity charges and 166
    *Saturday Review* on 166
    New York Society for the Sup-
        pression of Vice and 167
    U.S. censorship of 166–67
    Whitman's firing for 166–67
Lee, Harper 133, 232–34, 258
Lee, William (William Seward Bur-
    roughs) 78, 144, 157–58, 187–89,
    248
legal cases (*See specific cases*)
lesbianism
    Garden 20–22
    Hall 237–40
    Newman 140–42
    Walker 79–81
*Les Rougon-Macquart* (Zola) 189
Levin, Ira 78
Lewis, Sinclair 104–7, 159–61, 258
    on Hall 239
*Literature at Nurse, or Circulating*
    *Morals* (Moore) 113

*Little Black Sambo* (Bannerman)
    168–72
    Council on Interracial Books for
        Children and 171
    dehumanizing nature of 169–70
    British complaints and 171
    dictionary definitions based on
        170
    Moral Majority and 171
    racism complaints and 169–71
*Little House in the Big Woods* (Wilder)
    172
*Little House on the Prairie* (Wilder)
    172–73
    Laura Ingalls Wilder Award and
        173
    Native American complaints and
        173
*Little Red Riding Hood* (Perrault)
    174–76
    alcohol use in 175
    Caldecott Honor Book Award
        and 175
    court of Louis XIV and 174
    Grimm's rewriting of 174, 175
    violence complaints and 175
Lofting, Hugh John 93–95, 258
*Lord of the Flies* (Golding) 119,
    176–78
    brutality in 177
    indecency complaints and 178
    pessimistic views in 177
    racism complaints and 177
    social standards complaints 178
Louÿs, Pierre 24–26, 259
*Love Story* 202
Lucas, Victoria (Sylvia Plath) 40–43
*Lunch Poems* (O'Hara) 78
*Lysistrata* (Aristophanes) 64

**M**

Malamud, Bernard 120–23, 259
Malcolm X 33–35, 259

Mallet, Isabelle, on Robbins 194
*Manchild in the Promised Land*
(Brown) 178–81, 202
among most frequently chal-
lenged books 180
Concerned Citizens and Taxpay-
ers for Decent Books and 181
explicitness complaints and
180–81
language and content complaints
and 180
Mann, Patrick 95–98, 259
Manson, Charles 226
Margaret of Angoulême, queen of
Navarre 127
*Married Love* (Stopes) 181–83
forced editing of 182
Irish Censorship Board and 183
Sanger and 182
seizure of 182
United States Customs Bureau
and 182–83
*United States v. One Obscence Book
Entitled "Married Love"*
182–83
Melville, Herman 64
Miller, Arthur 119
*Miller v. California* (Burgess) 78
Milner, Ronald 43
miscegenation, Smith on 221–23
Mitchell, Margaret 131–33, 260
*Moby Dick* (Melville) 64
*Modern Love, A* (Moore) 113
Moore, George 110–13, 260
Moral Majority 171
Morris, Desmond J. 185–86, 260
Motley, Willard 43
Motteaux, Peter 127, 128
Mowat, Farley 135, 260
*Mummer's Wife, A* (Moore) 113
*My House* (Giovanni) 183–85
sexual content complaints and
184
racism complaints and 184
vulgarity complaints and 184

*My Sweet Audrina* (Andrews) 209

**N**

*Naked Ape, The* (Morris) 44, 185–86
*Board of Education, Island Trees
Union Free School District No.
26 v. Pico* 186
sexual content complaints and
186
*Naked Lunch* (Burroughs) 187–89
*Attorney General v. A Book Named
"Naked Lunch"* 188–89
Ciardi as witness for 100
Ginsberg as witness for 188
last literary work declared
obscene 188
legal proceedings and 188–89
Mailer as witness for 188
U.S. customs seizure of 188
*Nana* (Zola) 189–92
ban in England 191–92
Gambetta on 191
*Index Librorum Prohibitorum* and
192
legal actions against 192
National Vigilance Association
and 191
prepublication censorship of
191
publisher imprisonment in En-
gland 192
Roman Catholic *Tablet* on 192
serialization in *Le Voltaire* 191
U.S. Customs Department
seizure of 191
*Whitehall Review* on 192
*Narcotic Agent* (Helbront) 158
Nasier, Alcofribas (François Rabelais)
126–28
National Organization for Decent
Literature 28
Hemingway 119
Louÿs 26

National Organization for Decent
  Literature (*continued*)
    O'Hara 28
    Shulman 13
National Vigilance Association 191
Native Americans, literature offensive
  to, Wilder 172–73
*Native Son* (Wright) 152
Nazi Germany 119, 220
*Never Love a Stranger* (Robbins) 110,
  192–94, 244
    *Commonwealth v. Gordon* and
      194
    language complaints and 193
    legal proceedings against 194
    *New York Times* review of 194
    post–World War II trends and
      193
    *Saturday Review of Literature* and
      194
    sexual content and 193
*New American Poetry 1945–1960*
  (Allen) 78
*New Dictionary of American Slang*
  (Chapman) 92–93
    profanity complaints and 93
Newman, Leslea 140–42, 260
*New Women: A Motive Anthology of
  Women's Liberation, The* 42
*Nicodemus and Sally* 171
*Nigger of the "Narcissus," The* (Conrad)
  133
*Night Shift* (King) 82
*Nursery and Household Tales* (Grimm)
  174–76


O

Obscene Publications Act of 1959
  163–64, 238
*Of Mice and Men* (Steinbeck) 119,
  195–98, 208
    Ireland ban on 196
    language complaints and 196–98
    morbidness of theme and 196
    racial slurs and 197
    sexual overtones and 197
*Of Time and the River* (Wolfe)
  198–200
    Aline Bernstein depiction in 199
    anti-Semitism complaints and
      199–200
    obscenity charges and 200
    Perkins editing of 199
    racism complaints and 199
    Scribner's censorship of 199
O'Hara, Frank 78
O'Hara, John 27–29, 261
*One Flew Over the Cuckoo's Nest*
  (Kesey) 200–3
    *Fogarty v. Atchley* and 203
    language complaints and 202
    obscenity charges and 202
*Ordinary People* (Guest) 203–5
    anti-Christian complaints 205
    language complaints and 204–5
    masturbation depiction in 204
    sexual content complaints and
      204–5
    suicide depiction in 204
*Other, The* (Tryon) 204
Ovid 127
*Ox-Bow Incident, The* (Clark) 205–7
    language complaints and 206–7


P

*Pantagruel* (Rabelais) 126–28
*Parducci v. Rutland* (Vonnegut) 236
*Parker v. Board of Education*, Huxley
  55
Partridge, Eric 92–93
Paterson, Katherine 56–58, 261
Peck, Robert Newton 87–89, 261
*People v. Friede* 239
*People v. Vanguard Press, Inc.* (Willing-
  ham) 109
Perkins, Maxwell 118, 199
Perrault, Charles 174–76, 261
*Petals on the Wind* (Andrews) 209

*Pet Sematary* (King) 82
*Piping Hot* (Zola) 192
Piri, Thomas 265
Plath, Sylvia 40–43, 262
poetry
  Ginsberg 144–46
  Giovanni 183–85
  Whitman 165–68
Porter, Noah, on Whitman 167
*Pot-bouille* (Zola) 192
*Presidents Council, District 25 v. Com-
  munity School Board, No. 25 (New
  York City)* 97–98, 99
profanity (*See* language, objections to)

R

Rabelais, François 126–28, 262
racism
  Angelou 146–48
  Baldwin 136–38
  Bannerman 168–72
  Gaines 36–38
  Giovanni 183–85
  Griffin 45–48
  Kesey 200–3
  Lee 232–34
  Lewis 159–61
  Lofting 93–95
  Malcolm X 33–35
  Mitchell 131–34
  O'Hara 27–29
  Smith 221–23
  Twain 2–5, 7–9
  Wilder 172–73
  Wolfe 198–200
Radclyffe-Hall, Marguerite (*See* Hall,
  Radclyffe)
*Random House College Dictionary, The*
  14
*Reader for Writers, A* 44
rebellion against authority
  Cormier 72–75
  Kesey 200–3
  Salinger 68–72

*Red Pavilion, The* (Gunther) 107
*Red Pony, The* (Steinbeck) 119, 207–9
  birth process depiction in 209
  language complaints and 208–9
*Reincarnation of Peter Proud, The*
  (Ehrlich) 78
right-to-life groups 85–86
Robbins, Harold 110, 192–94, 244,
  262
Robinson, W. J. 182
*Rosemary's Baby* (Levin) 78
Rossetti, William Michael 168
Rothman, Nathan L., on Robbins
  194
*Roth v. United States*
  Franklin 33
  Ginsberg 145
Rousseau, Jean-Jacques 127
R.R. Bowker Company 107

S

sadism, in Willingham 108–10
*Salem's Lot* (King) 82
Salinger, Jerome David 68–72, 262
Samber, Robert 174
*Sanctuary* (Faulkner) 110, 194, 244
Sanger, Margaret 182
satire, Rabelais and 126–28
*Scarlet Letter, The* (Hawthorne)
  209–12
  adultery theme and 211, 212
  *Brownson's Quarterly* review of
    210
  *Church Review* of 211
  *Commonwealth of Massachusetts v.
    Gordon* and 211
  Hawthorne forced to move 211
  immorality complaints and 211
  religious objections to 210–11
*Seeds of Yesterday* (Andrews) 209
Selby, Hubert, Jr. 161–64, 263
Select Committee on Pornographic
  Materials (Gathings Committee)
  244

Sendak, Maurice Bernard  148–50, 263
*Separate Peace, A* (Knowles)  119, 208, 212–14
   homosexuality depiction in  213
   language complaints and 213–14
sexual subjects, objections to (*See also* homosexuality)
   Angelou  16–17, 146–48
   Baldwin  22–24, 136–38
   Burgess  76–79
   Chaucer  62–65
   Cormier  72–75
   Dreiser  215–16
   Dumas  60–62
   Farrell  242–44
   Fossey  134–36
   Frank  17–19
   Franklin  31–33
   Gaines  36–38
   Guest  203–5
   Hawthorne  209–12
   Heinlein  224–26
   Heller  66–68
   Hemingway  116–20, 229–32
   Hughes  43–45
   Huxley  53–55
   Knowlton  123–25
   Kosinski  38–40
   Lewis  104–7
   Louÿs  24–26
   Mann  95–98
   Mitchell  131–34
   Moore  110–13
   Morris  185–86
   Peck  87–89
   Plath  40–43
   Rabelais  126–28
   Robbins  192–94
   Salinger  68–72
   Selby  161–64
   Sendak  148–50
   Steinbeck  103–4
   Stoker  100–2
   Stopes  181–83
   Thomas  98–100
   Walker  79–81
   Whitman  165–68
   Zola  189–92
Shaw, George Bernard, on Stopes 183
*Shining, The* (King)  82
short story collections
   Doyle  6–7
   Hughes  43–45
   Vonnegut  234–36
Shulman, Irving  11–13, 263
*Silas Marner* (Eliot)  133
Sinclair, May  107
*Singin' and Swingin' and Gettin' Merry Like Christmas* (Angelou)  146
*Sister Carrie* (Dreiser)  215–16
   Doubleday Page and  216
   first uncut version of  216
   frankness of  216
   Harper & Brothers objection to 216
*Skeleton Crew, The* (King)  82
slang dictionaries  13–15
*Slaughterhouse-Five* (Vonnegut)  44, 91
Smith, Lillian  221–23, 263
social criticism literature
   Angelou  146–48
   Bradbury  113–16
   Burgess  76–79
   Cleaver  216–19
   Ellison  150–53
   Gardner  138–40
   Golding  176–78
   Huxley  53–55
   Lee  232–34
   Moore  110–13
   Salinger  68–72
   Selby  161–64
   Vonnegut  234–36
   Zola  189–92
Society for the Suppression of Vice
   Farrell  243

Hall 239
Lewis 160
Louÿs 26
Mitchell 133
O'Hara 28
Rabelais 127–28
Whitman 167
Willingham 109
*Soil, The* (Zola) 192
*Songs of Bilitis, The* (Louÿs) 26
*Soul on Ice* (Cleaver) 44, 216–19
　*Board of Education, Island Trees
　　Union Free School District No.
　　26 vs. Pico* 218
　obscenity charges and 218
　profanity complaints and 218
　Save Our Children and 217
spiritualism, and Doyle 6–7
*Stand, The* (King) 82
*Starring Sally Freedman as Herself*
　(Blume) 51
*Starting from San Francisco* (Fer-
　linghetti) 78
Steinbeck, John 103–4, 119, 195–98,
　207–9, 264
*Stepford Wives, The* 42
*Steppenwolf* (Hesse) 219–21
　Beat Generation and 220
　Boston Watch and Ward Society
　　and 220
　Leary on 220
　Nazi Germany ban on 220
　sexual content complaints and
　　220
Stoker, Bram 100–2, 264
Stopes, Marie Carmichael 181–83,
　264
*Story of Doctor Dolittle, The* (Lofting)
　94
Stowe, Harriet Beecher 133
*Strange Fruit* (Smith) 221–23
　*Commonwealth of Massachusetts v.
　　Isenstadt* 223
　language complaints and 222
　legal proceedings and 222–23

　sexual content complaints and
　　222–23
　United States Department of the
　　Post Office and 222–23
*Stranger in a Strange Land* (Heinlein)
　224–26
　Charles Manson association with
　　226
　G.P. Putnam's Sons editing and
　　publishing of 225
　Hugo award for 225
　original version publication 226
　sexual content complaints and
　　226
*Studs Lonigan* trilogy (Farrell) 110,
　194, 244
suicide, in Guest 203–5
*Summer Reading* (R.R. Bowker Com-
　pany) 107
*Sun Also Rises, The* (Hemingway) 118,
　227–29
　Hemingway's mother's com-
　　plaints on 228
　language complaints and 228–29
　Perkins and 228
　Watch and Ward Society of
　　Boston and 228
*Superfudge* (Blume) 51
Swarthout, Glendon 48–50, 264


**T**

*Talisman, The* (King) 82
Teller, Fanny and Ida 182
*Ten North Frederick* (O'Hara) 28
Terkel, Studs 240–42, 265
"The Fireman" (Bradbury) 114
*Then Again, Maybe I Won't* (Blume)
　51
*Thinner* (King) 82
*Third Book* (Rabelais) 126–28
Thomas, Piri 97, 98–100
*Through the Looking Glass and What
　Alice Found There* (Carroll) 9–11

*Tiger Eyes* (Blume) 51
*To Kill a Mockingbird* (Lee) 70, 119, 133, 208, 232–34
   Committee on Intellectual Freedom of the American Library Association and 233
   racial representation in 233
   language complaints and 233
*Tom Jones* (Fielding) 127, 128
*Tommyknockers, The* (King) 82
*To Have and Have Not* (Hemingway) 229–32
   American Civil Liberties Union and 231
   Catholic organizations complaints 231
   Charles Scribner's Sons change requests and 231
   language complaints and 231
   obscenity charges and 231
   sexual suggestiveness of 231
Toomer, Jean 43
Trocchi, Alexander 58–60, 265
*Tropic of Cancer* (Miller) 23
*Tropic of Capricorn* (Miller) 23
Tryon, Thomas 204
Twain, Mark 2–5, 7–9, 133, 265
*Twilight* (Andrews) 209
*Twilights of the Nymphs, The* (Louÿs) 26

United States Supreme Court (*See specific cases*)
*United States v. One Obscene Book Entitled "Married Love"* (Stopes) 183
Urquhat, Sir Thomas 127

**V**

Van Doren, Carl, on Sumner 243
violence
   Benchley 155–57
   Burgess 76–79
   Burroughs 187–89
   Childress 142–44
   Dickey 89–91
   Ellison 150–53
   Gardner 138–40
   Golding 176–78
   Kesey 200–3
   King 81–84
   Peck 87–89
   Perrault 174–76
   Selby 161–64
   Smith 221–23
   Swarthout 48–50
   Willingham 108–10
*Virgil v. School Board of Columbia County* 65
Vonnegut, Kurt, Jr. 67, 91, 234–36, 266

**U**

*Uncle Tom's Cabin* (Stowe) 133
United States Customs Office
   Burroughs 188
   Ginsberg 145
   Louÿs 26
   Rabelais 128
   Stopes 182–83
   Zola 191
United States Post Office
   Lewis 107
   O'Hara 28
   Smith 222–23

**W**

Walker, Alice 43, 79–81, 266
Waller, Leslie (Patrick Mann) 95–98
*Wanderers, The* 97
Warren, Robert Penn 119
Watch and Ward Society
   Hemingway 228
   Hesse 220
   Lewis 106
   Mitchell 133
*Webster's New World Dictionary of the American Language* 14

*Webster's New World Dictionary of the English Language* 14
*Webster's Seventh New Collegiate Dictionary* 14
*Welcome to the Monkey House* (Vonnegut) 234–36
    language complaints and 235–36
    legal proceedings and 235–36
    *Parducci v. Rutland* and 236
    teacher dismissal and 235
*Well of Loneliness, The* (Hall) 237–40
    Boissevain on 239
    British Customs seizure of 238
    expurgated version of 238
    Hicklin Statute and 239
    Knopf and 239
    legal proceedings and 238–39
    Lewis on 239
    *London Sunday Express* review 238
    New York Society for the Suppression of Vice 239
    *People v. Friede* and 239
    sexual content complaints and 238–39
Wentworth, Harold 92–93, 266
Whitman, Walt 165–68, 266
Wilder, Laura Ingalls 172–73, 267
*Wild Palms* (Faulkner) 110, 194, 244
Willhoite, Michael A. 84–87, 267
Williams, John A. 43
Williams, William Carlos 144
Willingham, Calder Bayard, Jr. 108–10, 194, 244, 267
Wilson, John Anthony Burgess (Anthony Burgess) 76–79, 247
Wolfe, Thomas 198–200, 268
*Woman in the Mists* (Mowat) 135

*Word Extra, The* 167
*Working: People Talk About What They Do All Day and How They Feel About What They Do* (Terkel) 240–42
    language complaints and 241
*World I Never Made, A* (Farrell) 110, 194, 242–44
    *Bamberger v. The Vanguard Press, Inc.* 243
    legal actions and 243–44
    *New York Times* and 243
    Select Committee on Current Pornographic Materials and 244
    Society for Suppression of Vice and 243
    U.S. Information Agency ban of 244
    Vanguard Press and 243
Wright, Richard 43, 104, 152


**Y**

*Yage Letters, The* (Burroughs and Ginsberg) 78
Yerby, Frank 43
*Young Lonigan* (Farrell) 110, 194, 244
*Young Manhood of Studs Lonigan, The* (Farrell) 110, 194, 244


**Z**

Zola, Émile 189–92, 268
*Zykan v. Warsaw (IN) Community School Corporation and Warsaw School Board of Trustees* (Plath) 42